POPULATION HEALTH

CREATING A CULTURE OF WELLNESS

David B. Nash, MD, MBA

Dean
Jefferson School of Population Health
Thomas Jefferson University

JoAnne Reifsnyder, PhD, ACHPN

Senior Vice President
Care Transitions CareKinesis, Inc.

Raymond J. Fabius, MD

Chief Medical Officer
Thomson Reuters, Healthcare and Science

Valerie P. Pracilio, MPH

Project Manager for Quality Improvement
Jefferson School of Population Health
Thomas Jefferson University

JONES & BARTLETT
L E A R N I N G

World Headquarters

Jones & Bartlett Learning
40 Tall Pine Drive
Sudbury, MA 01776
978-443-5000
info@jblearning.com
www.jblearning.com

Jones & Bartlett Learning
Canada
6339 Ormindale Way
Mississauga, Ontario L5V 1J2
Canada

Jones & Bartlett Learning
International
Barb House, Barb Mews
London W6 7PA
United Kingdom

Jones & Bartlett Learning books and products are available through most bookstores and online booksellers. To contact Jones & Bartlett Learning directly, call 800-832-0034, fax 978-443-8000, or visit our website, www.jblearning.com.

Substantial discounts on bulk quantities of Jones & Bartlett Learning publications are available to corporations, professional associations, and other qualified organizations. For details and specific discount information, contact the special sales department at Jones & Bartlett Learning via the above contact information or send an email to specialsales@jblearning.com.

This publication is designed to provide accurate and authoritative information in regard to the Subject Matter covered. It is sold with the understanding that the publisher is not engaged in rendering legal, accounting, or other professional service. If legal advice or other expert assistance is required, the service of a competent professional person should be sought.

Production Credits

Publisher: Michael Brown
Associate Editor: Catie Heverling
Editorial Assistant: Teresa Reilly
Associate Production Editor: Tiffany Sliter
Senior Marketing Manager: Sophie Fleck
Manufacturing and Inventory Control Supervisor:
  Amy Bacus

Composition: Glyph International
Cover Design: Scott Moden
Cover Image: © Vladislav Gajic/ShutterStock, Inc.
Printing and Binding: Malloy, Inc.
Cover Printing: Malloy, Inc.

Library of Congress Cataloging-in-Publication Data
Population health: creating a culture of wellness / David B. Nash . . . [et. al.].
    p. ; cm.
  Includes bibliographical references and index
  ISBN-13: 978-0-7637-8043-2 (pbk.)
  ISBN-10: 0-7637-8043-X (pbk.)
  1. Medical care—United States.   2. Health promotion—United States.
  3. Health education—United States.   I. Nash, David B.
  [DNLM: 1. Delivery of Health Care—organization & administration—United States.
    2. Delivery of Health Care—cconomics—United States 3. Disease Management—United States.
    4. Health Care Reform—United States. 5 Health Promotion—United States. W 84 AA1 P831 2011]
  RA395.A3P638 2011
  362.1—dc22
                              2010011845
6048
Printed in the United States of America
14 13 12 11 10   10 9 8 7 6 5 4 3 2 1

DEDICATION

To Es, Leah, Rachel, and Jake, we remember AJN with love.

— DBN

To Rachel, my inspiration.

— JR

To my mentors, my friends, and my family, especially my Sara, Mike, and Dan.

— RJF

To my family, friends, and mentors (DS and CB) who have supported me in my endeavors.

— VPP

and

To our current and future students who challenge us with their complex questions and whose quest for solutions will bring about much needed improvements in population health.

CONTENTS

Valerie P. Pracilio, MPH, JoAnne Reifsnyder, PhD, ACHPN,
David B. Nash, MD, MBA, and Raymond J. Fabius, MD

SECTION I. PROVIDING POPULATION HEALTH

Jaan Sidorov, MD, MHSA, and Martha Romney, MS, JD, MPH

CHAPTER 6   **Risk Management and Law 105**
Henry C. Fader, Esq.

SECTION II. THE BUSINESS OF HEALTH

CHAPTER 7   **Making the Case for Population Health Management:**
The Business Value of Better Health 121
Ronald R. Loeppke, MD, MPH, FACOEM, FACPM

SECTION III. MAKING POLICY TO ADVANCE POPULATION HEALTH

CHAPTER 14   Population Health in Action: Successful Models 241

Paul Wallace, MD

CHAPTER 15   Research and Development in Population Health 257

R. Dixon Thayer, Raymond J. Fabius, MD, and Sharon Frazee, PhD

ABOUT THE AUTHORS

DAVID B. NASH, MD, MBA

Dr. Nash, a board-certified internist, founded the original Office of Health Policy in 1990. Thirteen years later, the Office evolved into one of the first Departments of Health Policy in an American medical college. In 2008, the Board of Thomas Jefferson University approved the creation of the new school. The Jefferson School of Population Health represents the first time a health-sciences university has placed four Masters Programs under one roof, namely a Masters in Public Health, Health Policy, Healthcare Quality, and Safety and Chronic Care Management. The goal of this innovative school is to produce a new type of healthcare leader for the future.

Dr. Nash is internationally recognized for his work in outcomes management, medical staff development, and quality-of-care improvement; his publications have appeared in more than 100 articles in major journals. He has edited nineteen books, including *A Systems Approach to Disease Management* published by Jossey-Bass, *Connecting with the New Healthcare Consumer* published by Aspen, *The Quality Solution* published by Jones & Bartlett Learning, *Practicing Medicine in the 21st Century* published by the American College of Physician Executives (ACPE), and most recently, *Governance for Healthcare Providers* published by Productivity Press. In 1995, he was awarded the Latiolais ("Lay-shee-o-lay") Prize by the Academy of Managed Care Pharmacy for his leadership in disease management and pharmacoeconomics. He also received the *Philadelphia Business Journal* Healthcare Heroes Award in October 1997 and was named an honorary distinguished fellow of the American College of Physician Executives in 1998. In 2006, he received the Elliot M. Stone Award for leadership in public accountability for health data from NAHDO. Dr. Nash received the Wharton Healthcare Alumni Achievement Award in 2009.

Repeatedly named by *Modern Healthcare* as one of the top 100 most powerful persons in healthcare, his national activities include membership on the board of directors of DMAA:

The Care Continuum Alliance, Chair of an NQF Technical Advisory Panel, membership in the American College of Surgeons Health Policy Research Institute, three key national groups focusing on quality measurement and improvement. He continues as one of the principal faculty members for quality of care issues of the ACPE in Tampa, Florida, and is the developer of the ACPE Capstone Course on Quality. For the last decade, he was a member of the board of trustees of Catholic Healthcare Partners in Cincinnati, Ohio—one of the nation's largest integrated delivery systems—and he chaired the Board Committee on Quality and Safety. He was recently appointed to the board of Main Line Health—a four hospital system in suburban Philadelphia, Pennsylvania. He also serves on the board of directors of Humana, a Fortune 200 company headquartered in Louisville, Kentucky.

Dr. Nash is a consultant to organizations in both the public and private sectors including the Technical Advisory Group of the Pennsylvania Health Care Cost Containment Council (a group he has chaired for the last decade), and numerous corporations within the pharmaceutical industry. From 1984 to 1989, he was deputy editor of *Annals of Internal Medicine* at the American College of Physicians. Currently, he is editor-in-chief of four major national journals including *P&T*, *Population Health Management*, *Biotechnology Healthcare*, and the *American Journal of Medical Quality*. Through his writings, public appearances, and his digital presence, his message reaches more than 100,000 persons every month.

Dr. Nash received his BA in economics (Phi Beta Kappa) from Vassar College, Poughkeepsie, New York; his MD from the University of Rochester School of Medicine and Dentistry, where he was recently named to the Alumni Council, and his MBA in Health Administration (with honors) from the Wharton School at the University of Pennsylvania. While at the University of Pennsylvania, he was a Robert Wood Johnson Foundation Clinical Scholar and Medical Director of a nine-physician faculty group practice in general internal medicine.

Dr. Nash lives in Lafayette Hill, Pennsylvania, with his wife, Esther J. Nash, MD, fraternal twin twenty-three-year-old daughters, and nineteen-year-old son. He is an avid tennis player. Please visit: http://jefferson.edu/population_health/ and his new blog at: http://www.nashhealthpolicy.blogspot.com. Dr. Nash can be contacted at david.nash@jefferson.edu.

JOANNE REIFSNYDER, PHD, ACHPN

JoAnne Reifsnyder is an advanced practice nurse in palliative care with more than 25 years of experience in palliative and end-of-life care clinical practice, administration, consulting, education, and research. She completed a two-year postdoctoral fellowship in psychosocial oncology at University of Pennsylvania and holds a PhD in nursing from the University of Maryland, a Master's Degree in nursing from Thomas Jefferson University, and a BSN from Holy Family College. She led the development of the first Masters' program in Chronic Care Management at Jefferson School of Population Health (JSPH),

Thomas Jefferson University in Philadelphia, Pennsylvania, and formerly served as Program Director. She also served as chief quality outcomes officer for excelleRx, Inc., the parent company of Hospice Pharmacia, where she led a group of researchers and clinicians in an agenda that included health services research, development of clinical decision support and QAPI tools, and dissemination of findings through publication and presentation. Dr. Reifsnyder was co-founder and partner in Ethos Consulting Group, LLC, a company focused on program development, education/training, and research/evaluation to advance end-of-life care. She has been the director of the hospice program for the Visiting Nurse Association of Greater Philadelphia and was director of Patient Services for Samaritan Hospice, located in Marlton, New Jersey. Reifsnyder codeveloped and is the coordinator of a palliative care minor at the University of Pennsylvania School of Nursing, and taught both core courses in palliative care to nursing, social work, and medical students. Dr. Reifsnyder is the President of the Board of Directors for Pennsylvania Hospice Network, and a Board Member for both the Hospice Foundation of America and the Hospice and Palliative Nurses Association. She speaks frequently on topics related to palliative care program development, policy and regulatory issues, and ethics. Dr. Reifsnyder can be contacted at joanne.reifsnyder@yahoo.com.

RAYMOND J. FABIUS, MD

Dr. Fabius currently serves as Chief Medical Officer of Thomson Reuters Healthcare and Science—the world's leading source of intelligent information for businesses and professionals. Thomson Reuters combines industry expertise with innovative technology to deliver critical information to leading decision makers in the financial, legal, tax and accounting, healthcare and science, and media markets, powered by the world's most trusted news organization. As CMO, Dr. Fabius spearheads thought leadership efforts, develops and deepens relationships with customers, advises on product development, and provides counsel to Thomson Reuters on medical issues.

Previously Dr. Fabius served as strategic advisor to the president of Walgreens' Health and Wellness division. In this role, he provided guidance to integrate an array of services through their extensive national network of pharmacies, many with retail clinics, workplace health and fitness centers, and infusion therapy sites, into a seamless population health network.

Dr. Fabius is the principal of Ab3Health, LLC, and a founder of HealthNEXT, two organizations focused on population health, health and productivity, and building organizational "cultures of health". To accomplish this, both entities utilize the five-stage road-map advocated by the American College of Occupational and Environmental Medicine as well as Six Sigma methodology. During the assessment process, organizations are compared to benchmarks to determine gaps, which are then prioritized in an implementation plan to achieve best practice.

Dr. Fabius was I-trax (AMEX:DMX)/CHD Meridian's President and Chief Medical Officer for the three years prior to its sale to Walgreens. During this tenure, he served on

the board of directors and was principally responsible for converting this financially struggling organization into a workplace health leader while quadrupling the DMX market
capitalization. CHD Meridian operated over 300 workplace health centers providing
fitness centers, wellness programming, occupational health, acute episodic illness treatment, and comprehensive primary care and pharmacy services. Leveraging the *trusted
clinician at the workplace*™, I-trax integrated wellness, disease, and disability management
programs within the proven advantaged on-site model. In his role Dr. Fabius provided
visionary guidance, new product development, clinical leadership, as well as setting the
research and development agenda.

Dr. Fabius also served previously as global medical leader of General Electric, responsible for the health and safety of over 330,000 employees worldwide. He spent his first
decade in medical management within the health plan space, serving as a regional medical
director and then corporate medical director for Cigna, U.S. Healthcare, and Aetna. This
included leadership roles in utilization, disease and quality management, national accounts,
e-health, and health informatics.

Dr. Fabius is boarded in pediatrics and medical management and has written two
other books. The most recent one, *Total Care Management*, was published by the American
College of Physician Executives and received the ACPE Robert A. Henry Literary Book
Award in 2001. Dr. Fabius can be contacted at raymond.fabius@thomsonreuters.com.

VALERIE P. PRACILIO, MPH

Valerie P. Pracilio is a Project Manager for quality improvement in the Jefferson School
of Population Health at Thomas Jefferson University, where she is responsible for organizing efforts on various research projects that are primarily related to healthcare quality and
patient safety improvement.

At Thomas Jefferson University, she is currently facilitating performance improvement initiatives in each of the Jefferson University Physician ambulatory practices and
serves as a member of the Jefferson Clinical Care Subcommittee. Ms. Pracilio is working
to implement a smoking cessation initiative across all Jefferson University Physician (JUP)
practices through funding from Pfizer Inc. and has been involved in evaluating provider
participation in pay-for-performance programs.

Ms. Pracilio is a graduate of the American Hospital Association (AHA) Patient Safety
Leadership Fellowship. Through this experience, she worked on an initiative for post-
discharge medication reconciliation at Jefferson, with the goal of advancing patient safety
and improving health outcomes. Ms. Pracilio currently serves as a medication safety expert
on development of the Center for Medicare and Medicaid Services Physician Quality
Reporting Initiative Measures.

Ms. Pracilio's research interests include quality and patient safety, organizational
culture, teamwork and communication as well as oncology, and public health. Her
research efforts have included a project focused on the capacity for colorectal cancer

screening in Pennsylvania, which was submitted to the Legislative Budget and Finance Committee, and an initiative to improve quality at two rural hospitals in Pennsylvania through funding from State Representative Todd Eachus.

Ms. Pracilio also served as managing editor and author of *Governance for Health Care Providers: The Call to Leadership*, which was published in 2008 by Productivity Press, New York, New York.

Ms. Pracilio has a bachelor's degree in Healthcare Administration from the University of Scranton and a Masters of Public Health degree from Thomas Jefferson University. Ms. Pracilio can be contacted at valerie.pracilio@jefferson.edu.

FOREWORD

In the past five years, I have had the opportunity to visit a number of medical practices and health plans transitioning from paper medical records to electronic health records. In one of my favorite examples, Dr. Brent James of Intermountain Healthcare (IHC) in Utah brought me to meet a "late adopter" of the IHC electronic system. This physician ruefully reported on his longstanding reluctance to convert to electronic records, and then delightedly showed me what the change had done for him. He pulled up charts and graphs for the patients in his panel to demonstrate the good results and continuous improvement he had achieved for Hemoglobin A1C levels, an important indicator of diabetes control. I was watching someone who had shifted his focus from his individual patients to the overall population he serves. With digitization of records and registries supported by good analytic tools, healthcare providers can move up from the assembly line to a more strategic view of their work. This is an example of the power of population health on the front lines—at the provider level.

The National Committee for Quality Assurance (NCQA) has had an agenda rooted in population health since its inception. As we wrote standards for health plans and developed the Healthcare Effectiveness Data and Information Set (HEDIS), there were many heated arguments about the role of health maintenance organizations (HMOs) in holding the plan's entire population accountable, rather than limiting accountability to those who visited their physicians. The beauty of the population view is that it offers a systematic approach to improving well-being and a framework for keeping track of our nation's health status, indicating where we are improving and where we need to adopt new strategies.

Ten years ago, I had the opportunity to visit Bhutan, a country that is working on a project called the Gross National Happiness (GNH). Health status and healthcare were considered foundational elements of the GNH, along with indicators including average income, educational attainment, and forestation rate. The work being done in Bhutan is a great example of population health at the national level: the King and Parliament developed a set of goals and have successfully worked with their public health system to achieve them.

Accountability for population health is a more complex concept in the United States. The fragmented nature of healthcare and health insurance systems contributes to the complexity. In almost all the developed nations of the world, it is well understood that the health of the citizens is a national responsibility. This goes beyond the rhetorical because the nation is either the insurer or the assembler of insurers in a scheme that covers all the citizens and because it is usually (and more obviously) the tax revenues of the country that are paying for or arranging for services. In the United States, insurance may be obtained from the federal government, a state government, an employer, directly from an insurance company, or through some combination of these. Because we do not have a national consensus that health care is a good to which all of our citizens are entitled, notions of accountability vary and often citizens are grateful that they have coverage and access to a source of care *at all.* Sorting out who is responsible for what is essential to achieving national goals.

Another key issue is our emerging understanding of the important role of citizens or patients in their own health. We have come to understand, in a much more definitive way, that the healthcare system has limits to what it can achieve and that the best health care can only be achieved with the cooperation and engagement of patients. Recent reports on the social determinants of health also highlight the importance of this issue. We have begun to understand how to motivate patients and engagement strategies will remain an important part of the agenda for the next decade. The challenge is to help patients achieve a level of understanding, motivate them to positively affect their own health, and, ultimately, to realize or build their own self-efficacy. With new technology, the patient record can become a tool shared by patients and their providers. This has the potential to make the engagement of patients around their care a reality on a broad scale.

Although there are important practical, ethical, and legal issues to be sorted out, much progress has been made by those who are already managing the health of populations. This book offers a primer on how the United States can better manage population health, from wellness and health promotion to chronic disease management, to care of the frail elderly, and palliative care for those at the end of life. While the issues are different, the underlying techniques of population management are consistent: measuring the current state, determining what needs to be done, reaching out to those in need of intervention, and establishing a new steady state. Although best individual results are achieved when each patient is supported according to his or her level of need, population health approaches address the broader landscape of healthcare consumers to preserve wellness and minimize the impact of illness.

There are unparalleled opportunities today to move a vigorous population health agenda. Many health plans and systems have established a track record and expertise in population health management, and they have good results to show for it. A growing number of medical practices have embraced the medical home model, which is based on accountability for a panel of patients and care coordination across settings. Larger entities, like medical groups, hospitals, and integrated delivery systems, seek to become accountable care organizations committed to maintaining the health status of a population.

These developments will be facilitated by another revolution: the widespread adoption of health information technology (HIT), thanks to the commitment of the federal government to reward adoption and meaningful use of HIT. HIT opens a number of other new vistas: widespread implementation of decision support systems, real-time research using the data made available by electronic health records, and personal health records that can make patient engagement much more real and meaningful.

The road ahead, while exciting, is also fraught with challenges; however, the time to improve the health of Americans is now. Often, we are tempted to turn back or hunker down when the road ahead looks difficult. As with most challenges, going back or staying put may sound like the easy or safe option, but that is an illusion. It is increasingly clear that both the health and the health care of Americans are on a worrisome downward trajectory. A population health strategy, enabled by the new tools offered by technology and coupled with learning collaboratives, offers our best hope for a healthy future for individual Americans and for the nation as a whole.

Margaret O'Kane
President
National Committee for Quality Assurance

PREFACE

In July of 2008, the Board of Trustees of Thomas Jefferson University in Philadelphia, Pennsylvania, voted unanimously to approve the creation of the first School of Population Health in the United States, aptly named the Jefferson School of Population Health (JSPH). As part of a strategy to become a recognized national leader in health sciences education, the university has made an important public commitment to improving the health of its citizenry. As the first school of population health in the nation, we have a particular responsibility and burden. Our challenge is to train leaders for the future from across the healthcare spectrum who will go forward and improve the health of the population. This book provides a strong foundation for helping us meet that challenge.

A number of important questions must be answered as we develop a population health agenda. What exactly is population health, and how does it differ from public health? Why create a multi-authored textbook at this juncture? How did we organize such a book and who is the intended audience? We will tackle these issues in turn.

Population health is a term that is gaining greater traction in our everyday lexicon. Most thought leaders agree that population health refers to "the distribution of health outcomes within a population, the health determinants that influence distribution and the policies and interventions that impact the determinants."[1,2] Population health may also be looked at as "the aggregate health outcome of health adjusted life expectancy of a group of individuals, in an economic framework that balances the relative marginal returns from the multiple determinates of health. This definition proposes a specific unit of measure of population health and also includes consideration of the relative cost-effectiveness of resource allocation to multiple determinates."[1] Finally, other observers have noted that the term "public health has increasingly seemed too confining, whereas, the term population health has been increasingly used because it suggests a broad set of concerns, a particular perspective, rather than a specific set of activities, actors or approaches."[2]

For the authors, population health is an idea whose time has come. It is embodied in the creation of the JSPH. Population health sends an undeniably strong signal that we must take a broader perspective if we are truly to improve the health of the public. We must explicitly recognize the systems nature of care. We must strive for a better understanding of the evidentiary basis of what we do every day at the bedside and across every setting where care is provided—in assuring wellness, preventing and treating illness, and supporting populations across the life span. Finally, we must be accountable as stewards of the vast public resources for which we are accountable to our citizens.

Why a new textbook? As we launched the JSPH, it became clear that there was no single unifying treatise that captured the philosophy and mission of our school. While there have been many contributors to the science of population health, no one had brought forth a single volume as a survey of the field. No one had previously articulated the scope of the field and the need for innovative approaches, new strategies, and new practices. This text breaks new ground, and in so doing, it both suggests solutions and raises many new questions.

We hope our readers would also agree that our nation faces a population health challenge of unprecedented scope. The failure of health reform to actually tackle the issues of health and instead focus nearly exclusively on insurance reform is another reflection of how difficult this cultural challenge of improving the health of the population will be in our nation. The launch of a new school, contiguous with one of the nation's oldest and largest private medical colleges, gives us a platform and a voice that population health so desperately needs.

In his eloquent and inspiring address, "Healing and Heeling," at the Association of American Medical Colleges (AAMC'S) 2007 annual meeting, Daniel D. Federman, MD, Senior Dean for Alumni Relations and Clinical Teaching at Harvard Medical School noted that "I believe we should enlist some medical students as agents of change committed to designing a system of care that is equitable, cost-effective, prevention oriented, universal and thus, moral."[3] Now, simply change the words *medical students* to *all health science students* and one recognizes the mission of the Jefferson School of Population Health and the need for a unifying textbook to provide a platform and the tools necessary for creating such a moral system.

How is this book organized? We present three sections, including an introductory chapter (The Population Health Mandate), where we carefully define the field and describe its current state and evidentiary foundation. Section I, Providing Population Health, describes current activities, the navigation of the system, continuity of care, and the critical concepts of quality, patient safety and risk management. Section II, The Business of Health, recognizes the business case for population health and describes the financial tools, information technology, decision support and marketing necessary to bring those tools to fruition. Section III, Making Policy to Advance Population Health, is a description of the national policy discussion as it relates to improving the full spectrum of care and the educational challenges and political landscape that we will face. The concluding section, The Future of Population Health, provides a glimpse into the next decade.

Who should read this book? The editors are grateful for the participation of a large number of nationally recognized experts from across the spectrum of population health practitioners. The book is principally organized for graduate work in population health and it could serve as the foundation for courses in schools of public health, health administration, medical care, nursing care, and pharmaceutical sciences. Every section contains content of importance to anyone else who cares about how we might more effectively improve the health of our population. Practitioners in the field will be interested in this book; perhaps even undergraduates in colleges and universities across the country who will answer the call laid out by the Institute of Medicine to improve the public's understanding of these themes. We also hope that many schools of medicine facing the challenge of educating the physicians of tomorrow will adopt this book.

Many persons played a role in the genesis of this book. As the senior editor, I would particularly like to thank our university president, Robert L. Barchi, MD, PhD, for his visionary leadership and support in the creation of the JSPH. I also want to recognize other current campus leaders including Michael Vergare, MD, Senior Vice President for Academic Affairs, and Thomas J. Lewis, Chief Executive Officer of our university hospital. This triumvirate of Drs. Barchi, Vergare, and Mr. Lewis represent a senior leadership team practically unrivaled in any other health sciences university in the country. I am also grateful to the faculty and staff of the JSPH who have traveled this unmarked path with us together in the successful launch of our new school. As authors, we would like to thank others who have built the foundation that has led to the development of this new discipline and school. Without the pioneers in utilization management, case management, disease management, health informatics, public health, and health and productivity we would not be able to realize, measure, or improve the health status of communities. We would also like to mention our gratitude to friends and family who have supported us as we pursue our passion for improving the health of populations.

Finally, we are grateful to our current and future students who challenge us with their complex questions and whose quest for solutions will bring about much-needed improvements in population health.

As authors, we take responsibility for any errors of omission or commission. Most importantly, we greatly value your feedback as readers and would appreciate hearing from you as fellow travelers on the unmarked path of population health. We are particularly interested in the value of the text as a pedagogic tool as well.

One of the hallmarks of good leadership is to help prepare the leaders of tomorrow. We hope that *Population Health: Creating a Culture of Wellness* will go a long way in pursuit of training the future leaders in our discipline.

REFERENCES

1. Kindig D, Stoddart G. What is population health? *Am J Public Health*. 2003;93(3):380–383.
2. Kindig DA. Understanding population health terminology. *Milbank Q*. 2007;85(1):139–161.
3. Mseshiro, R. Responding to the challenge: population health education for physicians. *Acad Med*. 2008;83(4):319–320.

CONTRIBUTORS

Francis Barchi, MS, MBE
School of Social Policy and Practice
University of Pennsylvania
Philadelphia, PA
fbarchi@mail.med.upenn.edu

John K. Cuddeback, MD, PhD
Chief Medical Informatics Officer
Anceta, LLC
Alexandria, VA
jcuddeback@anceta.com

Susan DesHarnais, PhD, MPH
Program Director, Healthcare Quality
and Safety
Jefferson School of Population Health
Thomas Jefferson University
Philadelphia, PA
susan.desharnais@jefferson.edu

Dee W. Edington, PhD
Director
Health Management Research Center
University of Michigan
Ann Arbor, MI
dwe@umich.edu

Henry C. Fader, Esq.
Partner and Chair, Health Care
Practice Group
Pepper Hamilton, LLC
Philadelphia, PA
faderh@pepperlaw.com

Donald W. Fisher, PhD
President and Chief Executive Officer
American Medical Group Association
Chairman
Anceta, LLC
Alexandria, VA
dfisher@amga.org

Sharon Frazee, PhD
Vice President, Corporate Innovation
Walgreens
Deerfield, IL
sharon.frazee@walgreens.com

William Haggett, EdD
Independent Health Insurance Consultant
Philadelphia, PA
billhaggett@comcast.net

Abbie Leibowitz, MD, FAAP
Chief Medical Officer, EVP and
Cofounder
Health Advocate Inc.
Plymouth Meeting, PA
aleibowitz@healthadvocate.com

**Ronald R. Loeppke, MD, MPH,
FACOEM, FACPM**
Vice Chairman
U.S. Preventive Medicine
Jacksonville, FL
RLoeppke.MD@USPreventiveMedicine.com

Alan Lyles, ScD, MPH, RPh
Henry A. Rosenberg Professor of Public,
Private and Nonprofit Partnerships and
Professor, School of Public Affairs,
University of Baltimore
Docent, University of Helsinki
Baltimore, MD
alanlyles@comcast.net

Kip MacArthur
Director, Government Affairs
DMAA: The Care Continuum Alliance
Washington, DC
kmacarthur@dmaa.org

Jeanette C. May, PhD, MPH
Vice President, Research & Quality
DMAA: The Care Continuum Alliance
Washington, DC
jmay@dmaa.org

Tracey Moorhead
President and Chief Executive Officer
DMAA: The Care Continuum Alliance
Washington, DC
tmoorhead@dmaa.org

Mario Moussa, PhD, MBA
Academic Director
Aresty Institute of Executive Education
The Wharton School of Business
University of Pennsylvania
Philadelphia, PA
mmoussa@wharton.upenn.edu

Margaret E. O'Kane, MHS
President
National Committee for Quality Assurance
(NCQA)
Washington, DC
okane@ncqa.org

James Plumb MD, MPH
Professor
Department of Family and Community
Medicine
Director
Center for Urban Health
Thomas Jefferson University and Hospital
Philadelphia, PA
james.plumb@jefferson.edu

James O. Prochaska, PhD
Director, Cancer Prevention Research
Center
Professor of Clinical and Health Psychology
University of Rhode Island
Kingston, RI
jop@uri.edu

Janice M. Prochaska, PhD
President and Chief Executive Officer
Pro-Change Behavior Systems, Inc.
Kingston, RI
jprochaska@prochange.com

Martha C. Romney, MS, JD, MPH
Project Director
Jefferson School of Population Health
Thomas Jefferson University
Philadelphia, PA
martha.romney@jefferson.edu

Brooke Salzman, MD
Assistant Professor & Medical Director
Jefferson Family Medicine Associates at the
Philadelphia Senior Center Department
Family and Community Medicine, Division
of Geriatric Medicine
Thomas Jefferson University
Philadelphia, PA
Brooke.Salzman@jefferson.edu

Alyssa B. Schultz, PhD
Health Science Analyst
Health Management Research Center
University of Michigan
Ann Arbor, MI
abelaire@umich.edu

Jaan Sidorov, MD, MHSA
Medical Director
Medical Informatics Center of Excellence
HP Enterprise Services
Camp Hill, PA
jaan.sidorov@hp.com

Matthew C. Stiefel, MPA
Senior Director
Care and Service Quality
Kaiser Permanente
Oakland, CA
matt.stiefel@kp.org

R. Dixon Thayer
Chairman and Chief Executive Officer
HealthNEXT
Unionville, PA
rdthayer@ab3resources.com

Jennifer Tomasik, MS
Principal
Center For Applied Research, Inc. (CFAR)
Philadelphia, PA
jtomasik@cfar.com

Paul Wallace, MD
Medical Director for Health and
Productivity Programs
Kaiser Permanente
Oakland, CA
paul.wallace@kp.org

Richard Wender, MD
Alumni Professor and Chair
Deptartment of Family & Community
Medicine
Thomas Jefferson University
Philadelphia, PA
richard.wender@jefferson.edu

Theresa P. Yeo, PhD, MPH, MSN, CRNP
Associate Professor
Jefferson School of Nursing
Thomas Jefferson University
Philadelphia, PA
theresa.yeo@jefferson.edu

THE POPULATION HEALTH MANDATE

Valerie P. Pracilio, MPH
JoAnne Reifsnyder, PhD, ACHPN
David B. Nash, MD, MBA
Raymond J. Fabius, MD

Executive Summary

The population health mandate is to promote health and prevent disease; the strategy is to create an epidemic of health and wellness.

The need for population health management has never been more urgent. More than 43.8 million[1] Americans are uninsured and almost half (45%) of the United States (U.S.) population suffers from at least one chronic condition.[2] Healthcare quality is suboptimal and patient safety is lagging.[3] The public health system is egregiously underfunded, and while healthcare reform is a national priority, it will take at least 10 years before any benefits are realized.[4]

Population health refers broadly to the distribution of health outcomes within a population, the health determinants that influence distribution, and the policies and interventions that impact the determinants.[5,6] Accordingly, population health is holistic in that it seeks to reveal *patterns and connections* within and among multiple systems and to develop approaches that respond to the needs of populations. Population health tactics include rigorous analysis of outcomes. Understanding population-based patterns of outcomes distribution is a critical antecedent to addressing population needs in communities. That is, patterns inform the selection of effective population health management strategies to diminish problems and develop strategies to prevent reoccurrence in the future.

In 2008, the National Priorities Partnership convened by the National Quality Forum set out to address four major healthcare challenges that affect all Americans: eliminating harm, eradicating disparities, reducing disease burden, and removing waste.[7] One of the six priorities identified to address these challenges is *improving the health of the population*. This goal is ambitious, but also fundamental to healthcare reform. Improving the health of the population will require improved efforts to promote healthy behaviors and to prevent illness. The so-called "silos" in healthcare delivery must be dismantled—providers must cooperate to advance seamless, coordinated care that traverses settings, health conditions, and reimbursement mechanisms. Interdisciplinary teams of healthcare providers committed to diligent management of chronic conditions and providing safe, high quality care will play a central role. Policy makers will be called upon to craft policies that support illness prevention, health promotion, and public health, and healthcare professionals must continue their efforts to enforce recommendations in communities. All of these efforts must align to promote health and wellness and to advance a new population health agenda. Population health is no longer a strategy, it is a mandate that has the potential to trigger *an epidemic of health and wellness.*

Learning Objectives

1. Explain the concept of population health.
2. Recognize the need for a population health approach to healthcare education, delivery, and policy.
3. Discuss the integration of the four pillars of population health.
4. Utilize this text as a resource for further population health study and practice.

Key Words

chronic care management	population health management
health policy	public health
National Priorities Partnership (NPP)	quality
population health	safety

INTRODUCTION

The term **population health** is not new, yet there is no clear consensus on a single definition. In the evolving healthcare environment where the need for positive change is evident, population health is viewed across constituencies as a solution to key gaps in healthcare delivery. In this text, population health is defined as the distribution of health outcomes within a population, the health determinants that influence distribution and the policies and interventions that impact the determinants.[5,6] Population health represents the confluence of the healthy and the unhealthy, the acute and the chronic, the clinical and the nonclinical and the public and the private. There are many determinants that affect the health of populations, but the ultimate goal that healthcare providers, public health professionals, employers, payers, and policy makers set out to achieve is the same: healthy people comprising healthy populations that create productive workforces and thriving communities.

Population health is both a concept of health and a field of study.[5] Populations can be defined by geography or grouped according to some common element, such as employees, ethnicity, or condition. As the name implies, population health involves everyone; it does not exclude any one person or group and each individual and group comprising a population may wear many labels. For example, a man of Mexican descent who works for a carpenters union may be part of the Mexican community, as well as employee and union populations. To address needs at the population level, all of these associations must be considered. As a field of study, attention must be given to multiple determinants of health outcomes including medical care, public health interventions, and the social environment, as well as the physical environment, individual behavior, and the patterns among each of these domains.[6] This book provides the foundational knowledge and tools to consider population needs at all levels and develop strategies to meet those needs. As authors, our purpose is to promote an understanding of population health and encourage discussions and engagement of key stakeholders (healthcare providers, public health professionals, payers/health plans, employers, and policy makers) in population health.

THE CURRENT STATE OF POPULATION HEALTH

Health care in the United States (U.S.) is complex. Many argue that while we refer to health care as a "system", health care is neither structured nor does it function as a true system. Consider the characteristics of systems, such as interactivity of independent elements to form a complex whole, harmonious or orderly interaction, and coordinated methods or procedures. Health care may well represent the antithesis to a true system. Despite the devotion of more than 17% of its GDP to health care (projected to top 20% by 2018[8]), the United States performs low on five dimensions of performance: quality, access, efficiency, equity, and healthy lives compared to similar developed countries such as Australia, Canada, Germany, New Zealand, and the United Kingdom. The common element among these five nations is a universal healthcare delivery system, and some argue that the absence of universal health care in the United States explains the access disparities, inequity, and poor outcomes in addition to the exorbitant and uncontrolled costs.[9] Despite spending considerably more than any other nation on health care, the United States has a long way to go to improve the health of the nation. For example, 8% of adults (18–64 years of age) reported that they did not receive needed medical care in 2006, 10% received delayed care, and 9% indicated they did not get needed prescription drugs in the last 12 months as a result of cost.[10] Major disparities exist based on socioeconomic status. More than 43.8 million[1] Americans are uninsured and almost half (45%) of the U.S. population suffers from at least one chronic condition.[2] Healthcare **quality** is suboptimal and patient **safety** is lagging.[3] The public health system is egregiously underfunded,[11] and while healthcare reform is a national priority, it will take at least 10 years before the benefits are realized.[4] The need for **population health management** has never been more urgent.

Advances in science and technology have contributed to increases in life expectancy of more than 30 years in the past century,[12] but growth in the older population has introduced new pressures on healthcare providers to support this burgeoning population of older adults, many of whom have one or more chronic diseases. For example, 65% of men and 80% of women aged 75 years and older had a diagnosis of high blood pressure or were taking antihypertensive medication in 2003–2006 and nearly a quarter of adults aged 60 years and older had diabetes.[10] Chronic conditions require frequent monitoring and evaluation, placing a strain on the healthcare system and making the need for care coordination even more apparent. In essence, health care in the United States is a sick care system, fueled by payment policies that reward both consumers and providers for health care that is sought primarily when illness strikes or in an emergency. While caring for the sick will always be part of health care's mission, we must finally move away from the historically disproportionate emphasis on sick care to more fully embrace health promotion and disease prevention.

POPULATION HEALTH DEFINED

Population health is the distribution of health outcomes within a population, the determinants that influence distribution, and the policies and interventions that impact the determinants.[5,6] These three key components—health outcomes, health determinants, and policies—serve as the foundation for this book. Health determinants are the varied factors that affect the health of individuals, ranging from aspects of the social and economic environment to the physical environment and individual characteristics or behaviors.[13] While some of these factors can be controlled by individuals, some are external to an individual's locus of control. For example, individuals may be coached to adopt healthier lifestyles, thereby reducing their risk for lifestyle-related diseases such as hypertension, diabetes, and smoking-related illnesses. Those same people may be genetically predisposed to cardiovascular disease or may reside in geographic locations where exercise outdoors is unsafe or air quality is extremely poor—that is, a subset of health determinants are outside of their control.

Health determinants are a core component of the ecological model used in **public health** to describe the interaction between behavior and health.[14] The model assumes that overall health and well-being are influenced by interaction among the determinants of health.[15] At the intrapersonal level, knowledge, attitude, and beliefs of individuals affect their behavior. Relationships with peers, family, and friends influence behavior at the interpersonal level and at the community level there are institutional factors such as rules, regulations, and other community factors that influence social networks. At the public level, policies and laws regulate certain behaviors.[14] These variables have a cumulative effect on health and the ability of individuals and populations to stay well in the communities where they live, work, and play.

Interaction among the determinants of health leads to outcomes, which comprise the second component of the population health definition. Population-level and individual disparities and risk factors exert significant influence on health-related outcomes. Health outcomes could be improved through access to and the provision of quality health care to all populations, regardless of insurance status, with a primary focus on health maintenance and prevention to decrease health risks. Policy development is a mechanism that supports population health management and improvement. Support and guidance for these efforts is provided by policies at local, state, and federal levels.

Public health is a core element of population health that focuses on determinants of health in communities, preventive care, interventions and education, and individual and collective health advocacy and policies. However, population health is not synonymous with public health. The principal characteristic that differentiates population health from public health is its focus on a *broad set of concerns*, rather than specific activities.[5] Population health efforts generate information to inform public health strategies that can be deployed in communities. The combination of information gathered to define problems and build awareness coupled with strategies to address needs comprises **population health management**.

As an example, consider a hypothetical community member—Wendy McDonald— whose situation illustrates the importance of considering multiple factors when using a population health approach. Wendy is obese and lives in a community where healthy food is unavailable and she does not have the resources to travel to access more nutritious options. Safe neighborhood parks and recreation centers are lacking, making physical activity a challenge for Wendy in her neighborhood. Inadequate insurance restricts her ability to receive primary medical care or guidance from a healthcare provider on how to address her obesity, and she is unaware of the disease risk factors that it presents. The population health approach provides the conceptual model underlying approaches to care delivery. Primary care practice in communities such as Wendy's could be reengineered as a patient-centered medical home, providing a comprehensive, integrated approach to disease and **chronic care management** that would support health promotion and disease prevention, leading to better short- and long-term health outcomes. In the community, a population health approach to address the challenges that Wendy faces could include adding green space for recreation and supporting healthy food options through tax credits to food stores that offer them. Underlying both of these approaches are policies that support community improvements and make health a priority, leading to better health outcomes.

The population health mandate requires that we focus on both health promotion and disease prevention. While we cannot abandon our current focus on caring for the ill, we will only advance health if we proportionately focus our efforts on promoting healthy habits and preventive care. During his 2009 plenary presentation at the Institute for Healthcare Improvement (IHI) National Forum on Quality Improvement in Health Care, Don Berwick, President and CEO of IHI, remarked, "health care has no inherent value, health does." We value our health and that of our families, communities, cities, states, and our country. Under the current healthcare model, we seek care to restore health when it is compromised and seek prevention primarily when we are sufficiently fearful about potential loss of health. Under an aspirational model of health and wellness promotion, we would seek preventive care because we value optimum health, not just because we fear health will become compromised. To that end, population health must promote health and prevent disease and create a new epidemic of health and wellness.

FOUNDATIONS OF POPULATION HEALTH

The Science

Health is a state of well-being; population health provides a conceptual framework for the study of well-being and variability between populations.[5,16] The healthcare enterprise is one small contributor to a population's overall health, yet it receives the greatest volume of resources and attention. Interactions between the healthcare, business, and political communities are rarely considered in the current illness-focused model for healthcare delivery, yet they are the drivers of population health outcomes. There is significant and as yet unrealized opportunity to advance the population health agenda and to improve health through efforts focusing on personal behavior and health promotion within each of these interactions.[17]

For healthcare providers, the expectation that they must care for *their* patients in *their* practice setting is rapidly changing as new models for affecting outcomes at the population level are being introduced. Treatment of populations aims to increase recommended prevention and screening practices and improve adherence to recommended treatment according to evidence-based, nationally recognized guidelines. These aims require teams of healthcare providers cooperating within and across settings. While individualized treatment has been the traditional approach to patient care, population level interventions that integrate a set of common aims and standards are needed to support significant and sustainable health improvements in the United States.

A key priority area in population health is management of chronic disease. Nearly half of all Americans have one or more chronic diseases, and the current and projected prevalence are only partly explained by population growth. Importantly, the emergent burden of chronic disease is the strongest signal that our current strategies are not effectively helping people get well and stay well.[2] This burgeoning population drives both cost and utilization of healthcare services.

Although we have a great deal of evidence to inform strategies to improve population health, processes remain poorly defined and implementation success is variable. While numerous national goals for population health have been proposed and targeted outcomes have been defined, the challenges of translating best practices into action remains. The Chronic Care Model provides an example of a conceptual model that could guide development of effective programs to provide better chronic care to patents. The devil is, of course, in the details. Each of the six system components that comprise the Chronic Care Model is covered in some detail in subsequent chapters of this book (Figure FM-1).

The greatest contributor to premature death from preventable chronic illness is patient behavior. Of the six model components, the degree to which patients are informed and active is critical to improved patient outcomes. Informed, active patients are more likely to learn self-management strategies and to adopt healthy behaviors. To effectively help patients manage their chronic conditions, providers need an array of tools. Because they typically have neither the time nor resources to consult the evidence base to support

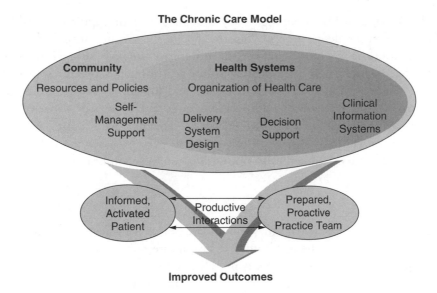

Figure FM-1   The Chronic Care Model

their clinical decisions, they need robust clinical decision support tools at the point of care. Further, they need a reimbursement model that rewards appropriate interdisciplinary communication, collaboration, and follow-up, as well as access to interoperable technologies that permit data sharing in real-time. All of these components must be supported by clinical information systems that track progress in management of chronic conditions. These practice-based components combined with community efforts (such as community-wide screenings, in-home support for elderly persons, or nutritious school lunch programs) and active participation of patients who productively interact with healthcare providers will support effective, quality chronic care management while reducing health risks and costs.[18]

One of the greatest challenges to improving the population's health is translating evidence into practice. A few state initiatives provide examples of successful population health strategies in action. In Vermont, state legislation has supported efforts to provide high quality care and control costs. The Vermont Department of Health implemented a Blueprint for Health, which focuses on improving health and the healthcare system through prevention. Vermont's statewide approach to wellness and disease prevention includes the establishment of medical homes and community health teams of nurses, social workers, dieticians, community health workers, care coordinators, and public health prevention specialists. The major commercial insurers and plans are participating, assuring that financial incentives are aligned with the state's goals. Future plans seek to include Medicare and Medicaid in such financial reform efforts within the state.[19]

In Wisconsin, David Kindig, a key thought leader in population health, is driving efforts to earn the designation of "healthiest state." The state earmarked 35% of monies realized from the sale of insurance stock to improve public health. Through a collaboration between public health and **health policy** practitioners across the state of Wisconsin, efforts to assess the state's population health and develop a plan to achieve health with less disparity are underway.[20,21] Both the Vermont and Wisconsin initiatives demonstrate that population health extends beyond health care. Achieving health and well-being at the individual, population, state, and national levels requires the collective efforts of healthcare providers, public health professionals, payers and health plans, employers, and policy makers.

The Business

As illustrated by the initiatives in Vermont and Wisconsin, there is a shared responsibility for population health. The cost burden of health care is shared between these constituents, although the distribution of costs is not always proportionate. Because more than 60% of Americans obtain health insurance coverage through their employers, businesses have a significant stake in their employees' health.[22] As healthcare costs continue to escalate, businesses are searching for strategies to decrease the cost of health benefits to employees without compromising quality. In no small way, the health of its employees determines the health of a business—a healthy employee is more productive while in the workplace and misses fewer days of work. The bottom line is that prevention generates a positive return on investment for employers. In 2009, an average of $3.27 in healthcare costs were saved for every dollar spent on employee wellness programs.[22] In this scenario everyone benefits—employees are healthier, businesses can operate more cost-effectively through improved employee performance and reduced health benefits costs, and health plans reduce outlays for preventable morbidity.

Worksites provide an ideal venue for promoting health and wellness, because consumers spend the majority of their time at work. While the business case for promoting wellness is clear, competing priorities present a challenge in many organizations. Corporate cultures, incentives for participation in the initiative, and employee health behaviors are potential barriers to implementing a workplace wellness program. However, workplace programs may be effective in two major domains of health: promoting behavior change to prevent illness, and supporting employees to self-manage chronic conditions. In the first instance, we know that 40% of premature deaths can be attributed to behavior and that behavior is a key contributor to both main causes of preventable death: obesity and smoking.[22] Workplace smoking cessation programs, for example, have been shown to be effective in mitigating risk for health effects of smoking, which cost employers $3,391 per smoker per year.[23] Unmanaged or mismanaged chronic conditions place undue burden on the healthcare system and draw on scarce resources. Employer involvement in health plan-supported disease management efforts provides employees with access to education and tools necessary to properly manage chronic diseases. In the case of employer sponsorship of health and wellness programs, the best available evidence supports common sense—that employees who are well provide the greatest benefit to their organization.[24,25]

The Politics

Prevention, health, and wellness efforts must be supported by policy and regulation to advance the population health agenda. Just as in any improvement effort, building awareness is the first step toward making lasting change. Throughout this book you will learn more about the key roles of population members in identifying population health needs and the importance of data and measurement on which to base causal inferences and actions. For example, the current rates of obesity and smoking in the United States, the top two causes of preventable death, represent needs that must be addressed through population-based initiatives.[22] Policies that drive population health efforts must be created at the local, state, and national levels. Policy making serves as the foundation of the population health infrastructure. Implementation of policies to improve the health of the population often requires significant resources, causing stakeholders to face difficult decisions about priorities. In both Vermont and Wisconsin, federal monies made initiatives possible to improve health in their state.[19–21]

The workforce that will provide high-quality, population-based health care in the future must be trained now. Education reform is needed to ensure the competency of future leaders and practitioners in health care, public health, business, and health policy. Finally, research is needed to inform strategies to address population health needs. Similar to the benefits of disease management and wellness initiatives realized by employers, policies that support health and wellness will also contribute to the wealth of the nation.

FRAMEWORKS FOR INNOVATION

Healthy People 2020

A few key initiatives provide a framework for innovation that aspires to make population health efforts the norm rather than the exception. As in all industries, common goals and objectives, guidelines and standards in healthcare provide an understanding of expectations and drive efforts to provide safe, quality care. Since 1979, the U.S. Department of Health and Human Services (DHHS) has been leading efforts to promote health and prevent disease through identification of threats and implementation of mechanisms to reduce threats. *Healthy People* sets national health objectives for a 10-year period based on broad consensus and founded on scientific evidence.[26] The current version, *Healthy People 2010*, focuses on two key overarching goals: to increase quality and years of healthy life and eliminate health disparities. To provide a blueprint for health promotion efforts, *Healthy People 2010* delineates 28 focus areas ranging from access to care to communication. In addition, clinical conditions were defined as priorities to achieve the two broad goals.[27] The next iteration, *Healthy People 2020*, contains 38 focus areas. The four overarching goals outlined in the 2020 version include: attaining high quality, longer lives free of preventable disease, disability, injury, and premature death; achieving health equity, elimi-nate disparities, and improve the health of all groups; creating social and physical environ-ments that promote good health for all; and promoting quality of life, healthy development, and healthy behaviors across all life stages.[28] The *Healthy People* objectives are primarily used by public health professionals to drive community efforts based on defined needs. Containing both clinical and non-clinical measures, *Healthy People* can also serve as a guide for population health efforts and a roadmap for interdisciplinary collaboration, creating a shared responsibility for health and wellness.

Triple Aim

In 2007, the Institute for Healthcare Improvement launched the Triple Aim, an example of population health in action. The Triple Aim provides an agenda for optimizing perfor-mance on three dimensions of care: (1) the health of a defined population, (2) the experi-ence of care for individuals in the population, and (3) the cost per capita for providing care for this population.[29] "Population" is defined by enrollment or inclusion in a registry. Groups of individuals defined by geography, condition, or other attributes can be consid-ered a population if data are available to track them over time. At the core of this initiative are efforts to optimize value. A number of integrators across the United States are working to implement strategies to achieve the Triple Aim. At the macro-level, integrators pool resources and make sure the system structure supports the needs of the population. At the micro-level, integrators ensure that the most appropriate care is provided to patients.[29] Healthcare institutions that are successful at meeting the Triple Aim would reduce hospi-talizations, apply resources to patient care that are commensurate with their needs, and build sustained relationships that are mindful of patient needs.[30] While there is still a great deal of work to be done to optimize performance on the three objectives and achieve this ideal situation, the Triple Aim has built awareness and offers a framework for population health management. (See Chapter 10 for more information on the Triple Aim.)

National Priorities and Goals

Many groundbreaking reports have grabbed the public's attention and set priorities for improvement, but few have enacted an action plan to reach the goals. The **National Priorities Partnership (NPP)** is unique. The Partnership represents the confluence of key thought leaders with a variety of backgrounds who joined together to achieve a common goal: to create a plan for transformational change in the way we deliver care. This collaboration of representatives from 28 multi-stakeholder organizations was con-vened by the National Quality Forum to develop a set of National Priorities and Goals. The Partners recognized that "we must fundamentally change the ways in which we deliver care" to improve access to safe, effective, and affordable health care and envisioned a plan to achieve transformational change. The priorities were set with four key challenges in mind: eliminating harm, eradicating disparities, reducing disease burden, and removing waste.[31] To address these challenges, six priority areas were identified based on opportunity for the greatest impact; these include patient and family engagement, population health, safety, care coordination, palliative and end-of-life care, and overuse. Workgroups were established for each priority area to identify high-leverage areas where there is greatest opportunity for substantial improvement and to develop strategies to address those areas.[31] The collaboration within the workgroups represents the establishment of a population health action plan that the NPP will be integral in carrying out.

The second priority area identified by the Partners was to improve the health of the population. To achieve this priority, health and wellness must be fostered at the community level through a partnership between public health and healthcare systems. The goal is to promote preventive services, healthy lifestyle behaviors, and measurement based on a national index to assess health status.[31] The strategies developed by the workgroup endeavoring to achieve this goal will form the future of population health. These priorities and goals will continue to spur action and innovation and serve as a model for population health improvement.

WORKING IN POPULATION HEALTH

In order to achieve the ambitious goal of improving the healthcare system in the United States, we must be prepared to broaden our current focus, the results of which will allow managed withdrawal from our addiction to acute, episodic health care. This will mean making a commitment to incorporate population health primary prevention strategies in our lives, as well as better coordinating care for those suffering from chronic illnesses. Key thought leaders and policy analysts are in agreement that focusing on primary prevention strategies, i.e., health promotion and wellness activities, will ultimately improve the overall health of our citizens and decrease the costs associated with over-medicalization. Three lifestyle modifications—eliminating and reducing tobacco use, weight reduction, and increasing regular physical activity—have been consistently identified in population-based epidemiologic research as most likely to reduce the prevalence of chronic conditions. In addition to lifestyle changes, utilizing preventive services such as cancer screenings, blood pressure and cholesterol monitoring, and health counseling promotes early detection of disease. Secondary prevention healthcare strategies are important for early detection of disease. These prevention efforts will reduce barriers to early treatment or completion of therapy, leading to improved treatment outcomes and reduced disease chronicity. Detecting an early stage breast cancer during mammography followed by initiation of treatment is an example of secondary prevention. The third population health preventive strategy, tertiary prevention, focuses on minimizing disease complications and co-morbidities through appropriate, evidence-based treatment and—critical to reducing healthcare costs—by coordinating and providing continuity of care for chronic conditions. This is best accomplished by incorporating the Chronic Care Model into healthcare systems and monitoring disease-specific indicators to ensure quality care and maximize quality of life for patients and their families.[32] Prevention and disease management are integral to maintaining population health and encouraging wellness. All healthcare professionals have a role to play.

Population health rests on four pillars: chronic care management, quality and safety, public health, and health policy (Figure FM-2). The interaction between each of these pillars in education and practice lays the foundation for achieving population health goals and strategies (Figure FM-3). Only 55% of U.S. adults receive recommended preventive care, acute care, and care for chronic conditions such as hypertension (high blood pressure) and diabetes.[33] This daunting figure illustrates the need for collective patient, provider, public health, employer, health plan, and policymaker efforts to improve health and wellness. Given the large proportion of the population suffering from chronic conditions, we must consider how we can improve coordination of care across the many settings where care is delivered, and promote evidence-based clinical management and effective self-management. Both behavior and prevention play an important role in chronic care management. Access to screening and counseling for chronic conditions is integral to effective treatment. For the diabetic patient, regular HbA1c blood tests are needed to assess whether the disease is under control. Education is another key component in chronic care management because treatment decisions need to be made jointly by the patient and the provider. Patients' understanding of their disease and treatment options is integral to well-informed healthcare decisions. Taken together, these approaches will support quality of life and function, contribute to the health of populations, and reduce the use of costly acute care for preventable problems arising from poorly managed chronic illness.

Similar to chronic care management, the second pillar, quality and safety requires collective efforts of patients and interprofessional teams of healthcare providers. Quality and safety improvement relies on activated patients as well as provider teams that are motivated to examine and modify the structure of healthcare delivery and the processes or workflows that lead to errors. Since the 1999 Institute of Medicine Report, *To Err Is Human*, a number of organizations have identified best practices and made recommendations on how to design systems and processes to make health care safer.[34] Synergy between these groups will be integral to achieving gains in quality and safety. Local, state, and national public health efforts must support and complement the work being done in local healthcare institutions. The resulting public attention and awareness of quality and safety goals can serve to activate consumers.

Through interaction with communities and healthcare institutions, public health professionals serve as educators and advocates. The third pillar, public health, provides a framework for identifying health determinants, health disparities, and disease burden and for implementing strategies to address community-wide health concerns. As the fourth pillar, policy efforts support population-focused chronic care management, quality and safety, and public health. For example, current pay-for-performance initiatives represent policy support that will drive adoption of community-wide quality and safety standards. Taken a step further, making the data available for other healthcare constituents and consumers to review and compare their performance (i.e., transparency) creates a sense of accountability for performance, which the evidence supports creates an impetus for improvement. Future policy changes supporting transparency and public accountability

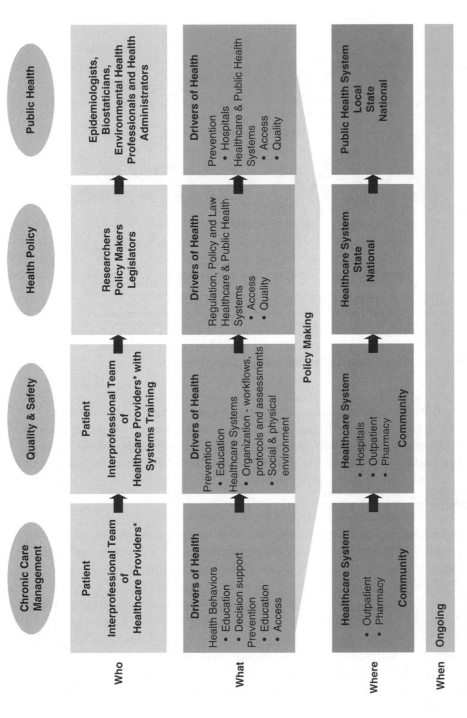

Figure FM-2   The Four Pillars of Population Health

* An interprofessional team of healthcare providers includes both clinical (physicians, nurses, pharmacists, allied health professionals, dentists, radiologists) and nonclinical (healthcare administrators, quality, safety, and public health professionals) professionals.

Data from Booske BC, Kindig DA, Nelson H, Remington PL. *What Works? Policies and Programs for a Healthier Wisconsin–Draft.* University of Wisconsin Population Health Institute, January 2009.

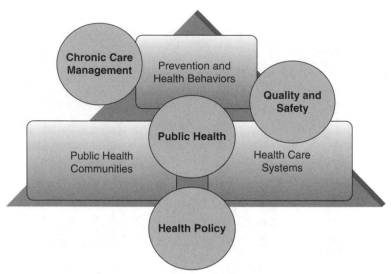

Public health communities and healthcare systems serve as the foundation on which the population health infrastructure rests. Healthcare providers, researchers, policy makers, legislators and public health professionals who work in the public health communities and healthcare systems partner with patients to focus on prevention and healthy behaviors. Professionals in chronic care management, quality and safety, public health, and health policy must work together to develop a framework to prevent conditions that burden the population both physically and economically. Interdisciplinary collaboration will strengthen the foundation of the population health infrastructure and lead to improved population health management.

Figure FM-3   An Interdisciplinary Model for Population Health

for health and wellness will be necessary to meet the population health mandate. Taken together, the population health goals, strategies, and implementation tactics associated with the four pillars of chronic care management, quality and safety, public health, and health policy will drive population health efforts to achieve health and wellness.

ORGANIZATION OF THIS BOOK

Population Health: Creating a Culture of Wellness aims to integrate evidence, practice innovations, and business perspectives that have neither been well defined nor articulated in the past. Because population health is a rapidly evolving discipline and science, there is disagreement, and even controversy, about the inherent value of many of the key concepts and their conceptual and operational definitions. We hope that the diverse perspectives of the authors, each an expert in her or his field, will trigger rich dialogue among students and professionals, thoughtful consideration of the premises, and ultimately—*change*.

The book is organized into three sections representing the perspectives of healthcare providers and public health professionals, businesses such as payers and employers, and policy makers. This book has been designed to serve as a primer on population health for students and professionals alike. Each of the chapter topics has been carefully selected to provide an overview of current thinking and strategies that must be initiated to create a healthcare system that emphasizes health and wellness to the same degree—and eventually a greater extent—as treatment of acute illness. The first section, *Providing Population Health*, covers the need to change our approach to healthcare delivery by providing an overview of the current efforts and recommendations for improvement. The second section, *The Business of Health*, provides a discussion of the value proposition for health and tools that can be utilized in practice to promote wellness. The third section, *Making Policy to Advance Population Health*, provides an overview of policy and ethical considerations and offers support for education as well as research and development to learn more about how to make population health efforts successful. Each of the chapters can be used independently to broaden knowledge on a specific topic or combined with other chapters in a section to provide a comprehensive overview of each of the perspectives. Each author has included study and discussion questions at the conclusion of the chapter to assess accomplishment of the learning objectives. These questions can also serve as a tool to generate conversation with peers. "Suggested Readings and Web Sites" are also included in each chapter to provide additional resources related to the chapter contents.

This text has been designed to serve as an educational foundation for both professionals and students on the genesis and growth of this important topic. It describes a population-based approach to education applicable to professionals in disease management, chronic care management, quality and patient safety in addition to students studying those topics in addition to public health, health policy, healthcare administration, medicine, nursing, and other related health professions. The contributing authors are key thought leaders in their fields with broad experience across the domains of population health management. We invite you to adapt and rigorously apply the tools and strategies described in this text to address population health needs in your practice, business, or policy realm and to advance the nation's population health mandate—indeed, to spark a new *epidemic of health and wellness*.

CONCLUSIONS

We are faced with many challenges in health care and the strategies we use to address both existing and emerging challenges will determine the future health of our nation. Traditionally, our focus has been on health care that is reactive, but we realize to improve the health of our nation, we must be proactive in promoting health and wellness.[25] Currently available evidence has identified population needs, but there has not yet been a population health action plan defined to address those needs. In the words of Goethe, "Knowing is not enough; we must apply. Willing is not enough; we must do."[15] The National Priorities Partnership represents the best example of an action plan, but it will require the collective efforts of many to truly create transformational change. After reading this text you will be primed to participate in population health efforts to promote health and wellness. As a student or a population health professional, we hope that you will consider this text a call to action.

STUDY AND DISCUSSION QUESTIONS

1. What is population health?
2. Why is a population health approach needed to promote health and wellness?
3. How do the four pillars of population health work together to improve population health?
4. What is your role in population health?

SUGGESTED READINGS AND WEB SITES

READINGS

Institute of Medicine. *Crossing the Quality Chasm: A New Health System for the 21st Century.* Washington, DC: National Academy Press; 2001.

Institute of Medicine. *To Err Is Human: Building a Safer Health System.* Washington, DC: National Academy Press; 2000.

Kindig DA. Understanding population health terminology. *Milbank* Q. 2007;85: 139–161.

Kindig D, Stoddart G. What is population health? *Am J Public Health.* 2003;93: 380–383.

National Priorities Partnership. *National priorities and goals: Aligning our efforts to transform America's healthcare.* Washington, DC: National Quality Forum; 2008. Available from: http://www.nationalprioritiespartnership.org/.

Population Health Theme Issue. *Academic Medicine.* 2008;83.

WEB SITES

Dartmouth Atlas of Health Care: http://www.dartmouthatlas.org/

DMAA: The Care Continuum Alliance: http://www.dmaa.org/

Institute for Healthcare Improvement (IHI) http://www.ihi.org/ihi
    Triple Aim http://www.ihi.org/IHI/Programs/StrategicInitiatives/TripleAim.htm

National Priorities Partnership: http://www.nationalprioritiespartnership.org/

Partnership to Fight Chronic Disease: http://fightchronicdisease.org/index.cfm

Trust for America's Health: http://healthyamericans.org/report/61/shortchanging09

Understanding the U.S. Public Health System: http://www.cahpf.org/GoDocUserFiles/207.CHI%20Brief%20United%20States.pdf

U.S. Preventive Services Task Force (USPSTF): http://www.ahrq.gov/clinic/uspstfab.htm

REFERENCES

1. Cohen RA, Makuc DM, Bernstein AB, Bilheimer LT, Powell-Griner E. *National health statistics reports: Health insurance coverage trends, 1959–2007: Estimates from the national health interview survey.* Hyattsville, MD: U.S. Department of Health and Human Services, Centers for Disease Control and Prevention, National Center for Health Statistics; 2009;17. Available from: http://www.cdc.gov/nchs/data/nhsr/nhsr017.pdf. Accessed July 7, 2009.

2. Partnership to Fight Chronic Disease. *Almanac of chronic disease 2009. Partnership to Fight Chronic Disease; 2009.* Available from: http://fightchronicdisease.org/index.cfm. Accessed July 2, 2009.

3. Agency for Healthcare Research and Quality. *National healthcare quality report, 2008.* Rockville, MD: Agency for Healthcare Research and Quality; 2009;09-0001:1–153. Available from: www.ahrq.gov/qual/qrdr08.htm. Accessed July 10, 2009.

4. Davis K, Stremikis K, Schoen C, et al. *Front and center: Ensuring that health reform puts people first.* New York, New York: The Commonwealth Fund; 2009. Available from: http://www.commonwealthfund.org/Content/Publications/Fund-Reports/2009/Jun/Front-and-Center.aspx. Accessed July 8, 2009.

5. Kindig DA. Understanding population health terminology. *Milbank* Q. 2007;85:139–161.

6. Kindig D, Stoddart G. What is population health? *Am J Public Health.* 2003;93:380–383.

7. Kindig DA, Asada Y, Booske B. A population health framework for setting national and state health goals. *JAMA.* 2008;299:2081–2083.

8. Sisko A, Truffer C, Smith S, et al. Health spending projections through 2018: Recession effects add uncertainty to the outlook. *Health Aff.* 2009;28:w346–357.

9. Davis K, Schoen C, Schoenbaum SC, et al. Mirror, Mirror on the Wall: An International Update on the Comparative Performance of American Health Care. Available at: http://www.commonwealthfund.org/Content/Publications/Fund-Reports/2007/May/Mirror--Mirror-on-the-Wall--An-International-Update-on-the-Comparative-Performance-of-American-Health.aspx. Accessed January 15, 2010.

10. Health, United States 2008. U.S. Department of Health and Human Services, Centers for Disease Control and Prevention, National Center for Health Statistics; 2009;2009–1232:374–603. Available from: http://www.cdc.gov/nchs/data/hus/hus08.pdf#094. Accessed September 14, 2009.

11. Trust for America's Health—Robert Wood Johnson Foundation. *Shortchanging America's health: A state-by-state look at how federal public health dollars are spent and key state health facts.* Washington, DC: Robert Wood Johnson Foundation; 2009. Available from: http://healthy-americans.org/report/61/shortchanging09. Accessed March 19, 2009.

12. Centers for Disease Control. A framework for assessing the effectiveness of disease and injury prevention. *MMWR* [serial online]. 1992;41: 2/4/2010. Available from: http://www.cdc.gov/mmwr/preview/mmwrhtml/00016403.htm. Accessed February 9, 2010.

13. World Health Organization. The determinants of health. Available from: http://www.who.int/hia/evidence/doh/en/. Accessed January 20, 2010.

14. U.S. Department of Health and Human Services, National Cancer Institute. *Theory at a glance: A guide for health promotion practice.* U.S. Department of Health & Human Services National Institutes of Health; 2005.

15. Gebbie K, Rosenstock L, Hernandez LM, eds. *Who Will Keep the Public Healthy? Educating Public Health Professionals for the 21st Century.* Washington, DC: Institute of Medicine of the National Academies; 2003.

16. Young T. *Population Health Concepts and Methods.* 1st ed. New York: Oxford University Press; 1998.

17. Schroeder SA. We can do better—improving the health of the American people. *N Engl J Med.* 2007;357:1221–1228.

18. Institute for Healthcare Improvement: Changes. Available from: http://www.ihi.org/IHI/Topics/ChronicConditions/AllConditions/Changes/. Accessed February 9, 2010.

19. Vermont blueprint for health: 2009 annual report. Burlington, VT: Department of Health; 2010. Available from: http://healthvermont.gov/prevent/blueprint/documents/Blueprint_2009 AnnualRpt_0110.pdf. Accessed January 26, 2010.

20. UW Population Health Institute Available from: http://uwphi.pophealth.wisc.edu/. Accessed February 9, 2010.

21. The Wisconsin partnership fund for a healthy future. University of Wisconsin Medical School and the Oversight and Advisory Committee; 2010. Available from: http://www.wisconsin.edu/news/2003/04_apr2003/WI_Partnership_Fund.pdf. Accessed January 26, 2010.

22. Baicker K, Cutler D, Song Z. Workplace wellness programs can generate savings. *Health Aff.* 2010.

23. Centers for Disease Control. Annual smoking-attributable mortality, years of potential life lost, and economic costs—United States, 1995–1999. *MMWR.* 2002;51:300–303.

24. Neftzger A, Walker S. *Why Employee Well-Being Matters to Your Bottom Line.* Available at: http://www.shrm.org/hrdisciplines/benefits/Articles/Pages/EmployeeWellBeing.aspx. Accessed February 10, 2010.

25. White M. The cost-benefit of well employees. *HBR.* 2005.

26. Healthy People: What Is Its History? Available from: http://www.healthypeople.gov/About/history.htm. Accessed April 19, 2009.

27. U.S. Department of Health and Human Services. *About Healthy People.* Available from: http://www.healthypeople.gov/About/. Accessed February 9, 2010.

28. U.S. Department of Health and Human Services. *Healthy People 2020 Framework.* Available at: http://healthypeople.gov/HP2020/objectives/framework.aspx. Accessed Februaury 9, 2010.

29. Institute for Healthcare Improvement. *The Triple Aim.* Available from: http://www.ihi.org/IHI/Programs/StrategicInitiatives/TripleAim.htm. Accessed January 28, 2010.

30. Berwick DM, Nolan TW, Whittington J. The triple aim: Care, health, and cost. *Health Aff.* 2008;27:759–769.

31. National Priorities Partnership. *National priorities and goals: Aligning our efforts to transform america's healthcare.* Washington, DC: National Quality Forum; 2008. Available from: http://www.nationalprioritiespartnership.org/.

32. Centers for Disease Control. Updated guidelines for evaluating public health surveillance systems. *MMWR.* 2001;50:1–35.

33. McGlynn EA, Asch SM, Adams J, et al. The quality of healthcare delivered to adults in the United States. *N Engl J Med.* 2003;348:2635–2645.

34. Institute of Medicine. *To Err Is Human: Building a Safer Health System.* Washington, DC: National Academy Press; 2000.

SECTION I

PROVIDING
POPULATION HEALTH

THE SPECTRUM OF CARE

JAAN SIDOROV, MD, MHSA, AND
MARTHA ROMNEY, MS, JD, MPH

Executive Summary

Population health—a strategy to address national health needs

Population health provides unique opportunities in applying overlapping and synergistic interventions to care for populations that can be defined by need, condition, or geography. While this approach to care continues to undergo rapid evolution, there is a growing consensus that it will be a key component in addressing the twin healthcare challenges of quality and cost. An important feature of population health is the application of modern and culturally competent patient engagement and communication strategies that promote self care. This includes mutually agreed-to goal setting and collaborative decision making that allow patients to identify and manage potential health risks or disease exacerbations early. When combined with ready access to a medical home supported by a healthcare team enabled with disease management approaches and health information technology and integrated in the local community, the literature suggests that clinically and statistically significant increases in healthcare quality and decreases in unnecessary utilization are likely to result. This "packaged" care approach cannot only be applied to populations defined by the presence of a chronic illness (such as diabetes mellitus or coronary heart disease), but also for groups of persons who would benefit from health promotion and disease prevention activities. Examples include employer- or insurer-based wellness, immunization, screening, and medication compliance programs. Population health also has significant potential to reduce health disparities and serve as a building block in U.S. initiatives to address national health needs through many state-based programs and the National Priorities Partnership, as well as the Healthy People programs.

Learning Objectives

1. Define the concept and components of "population health."
2. Identify determinants of health and their impact on health care.
3. Discuss the social and economic imperative of "health promotion."
4. Define the concept "disease management" and understand the business case.
5. Identify the need for and value of integrating healthcare services in the community, including worksites and healthcare institutions.

Key Words

chronic care management	National Priorities Partnership
disease management	Patient-Centered Medical Home
health determinants	patient self-management
health disparities	population health
health promotion	prevention
Healthy People 2020	screening

INTRODUCTION

Population health is a framework that seeks to realign the healthcare delivery system, which is widely recognized as fragmented, ineffective, poorly managed, wasteful, and economically inequitable.[1] This chapter will describe the population health paradigm and its promise of refocusing the system on achieving improved clinical and economic outcomes, reducing disparities of care, diminishing the prevalence of chronic illness, and realigning public and private healthcare financing. Ultimately, population health initiatives seek to slow the upward trajectory of healthcare spending and "bend the curve."

WHAT IS "POPULATION HEALTH" AND WHY IS THIS APPROACH NECESSARY?

Population health can be defined as a "cohesive, integrated, and comprehensive approach to health care that considers the distribution of health outcomes within a population, the **health determinants** that influence distribution of care, and the policies and interventions that impact and are impacted by the determinants."[2] This approach calls for coordination of a variety of care interventions, including **health promotion**, **prevention**, **screening**, behavioral change, consumer education with a special emphasis on self-management, **disease management**, and **chronic care management**. Simultaneously, population health also seeks to eliminate healthcare disparities, increase safety, and promote effective, equitable, ethical, and accessible care.

Supporters of population health believe that increasing the quality of care will eventually lead to decreasing costs.[1] When possible, quality is founded on evidence-based medicine that not only includes clinical data, but also economic and patient-centered outcomes. Other outcomes may include measures such as quality of life, quality-adjusted life years, patient satisfaction, caregiver satisfaction, and provider assessments.

From a clinical perspective, the population health paradigm requires that integrated care be focused on health promotion, illness prevention, and chronic condition management and be addressed in tandem with the active and engaged collaboration of the patient-consumers, along with public health resources and services. In fact, attention to **patient self-management** of chronic illness is based on an increasingly sophisticated approach to behavior change and patient education. Given the spectrum of cultural, language, education, and economic barriers to achieving equitable health care, behavior change management requires a tailored, multifaceted approach. Accordingly, population health seeks integration of its culturally appropriate clinical care interventions with community health resources. Accomplishment of such integration will create local synergies that lead to alliances with local public health efforts to promote well-being of populations in their communities.

The prevalence and incidence rates, as well as the predicted trends of chronic illness and associated projected economics are dire and underlie the need for better prevention and chronic care management. Data from 2006, reported by the federal government in collaboration with healthcare associations, reflect that heart disease was the leading cause of death among Americans, followed by cancers, cerebrovascular disease, chronic lower respiratory disease, and diabetes.[3,4] The projected incidence for new and recurrent coronary attacks is 785,000 and 470,000, respectively.[5] Annual rates of stroke, new and recurrent, are reported to be 795,000.[5] The prevalence of hypertension in U.S. adults is estimated to be 74,500,000, and more than 35 million adults are reported to have total serum cholesterol levels ≥240 mg/dL.[5] Overweight and obesity contribute to cardiac and metabolic conditions, as well as cancer, and these rates in adults and children continue to rise. According to the Centers for Disease Control and Prevention (CDC), in 2008, more then26% of U.S. adults were obese and approximately 24 million had diabetes, with 5.7 million cases undiagnosed.[6]

The associated costs of chronic care and chronic care management are equally astronomical. In 2009, $2.5 trillion was spent on health care, yet with more than 45 million consumers uninsured, expenditures are expected to increase to $4.3 or $4.4 trillion over the next decade.[7,8] Additionally, in 2008 an estimated 90 million consumers with chronic disease spent $1.8 billion for care and an increase to $2.8 billion is projected for 2010.[9] The costs of health care continue to consume a large percentage of the national gross domestic product (GDP), increasing from 16.2% in 2007 to 17.6% in 2009, and costs are projected to grow to 20.3% by 2018 without significant changes to our national approach to health and health care.[8] The expected average annual national health expenditure growth is projected to rise faster than the GDP (6.2% per year compared to 4.1% per year, respectively), corresponding to $4.3–4.4 trillion in healthcare spending by 2018.[1,8] With 80% of healthcare spending dedicated to the treatment of chronic care and an increasing older population experiencing one or more chronic diseases, significant changes are critically needed to bend the spending curve. A population health approach promises to realign the health focus, priorities, education, training, and incentives from treatment to wellness for all U.S. healthcare consumers.

ATTRIBUTES OF THE POPULATION HEALTH PARADIGM

Time and experience have demonstrated that a healthcare delivery approach focused on individual care is limited by both the underuse and overuse of healthcare resources, resulting in diminished clinical quality and increased expense. Supporters of population-based care suggest their approach is a more effective and viable alternative. The population health paradigm integrates existing clinical delivery systems with public health–based models of care as the foundations for each of the components. Combining this focus with patient self-management represents a drastically different approach to care than that offered by traditional healthcare education, training, servicing, and resourcing. Individual states and private healthcare entities are adopting population health models that differ only in the details of care delivery. Endorsement of this overall framework requires national support for requisite legislative, policy, and economic changes that will be necessary for its widespread adoption.

Investments will be required to build infrastructure to support this paradigm, address the bases for health inequities, integrate healthcare services, educate providers and consumers, and realign the financing of care in the United States. As population-based care expands, many observers believe a growing body of evidence will emerge that demonstrates that this approach addresses the twin challenges of improving quality of care and reducing costs. How the attributes of population health combine will form the basis of local efforts aimed at eliminating disparities, improving quality, and bending the cost curve.

BOX 1-1   BASIC ATTRIBUTES OF A POPULATION HEALTH PARADIGM

- Patient-centered care
- An identified primary care provider ("medical home")
- An interdisciplinary healthcare team to provide supportive services
- Knowledge and recognition about determinants of health and impact on population health and individual health
- Integration of clinical, public health, and community systems
- Utilization of evidence-based guidelines to provide quality, cost-effective care
- Provision of culturally and linguistically appropriate care and health education
- Implementation of interoperable cross-sector health information technology[10,11]

COMPONENTS OF THE POPULATION HEALTH PARADIGM

The primary components of the population health paradigm are integrated health promotion and chronic illness disease management in the context of determinants of health. Health promotion can be defined as the provision of clinical and public health services to collaboratively address the impact of health determinants on consumers for the purpose of improving and sustaining the highest quality of well-being attainable. Disease management also relies on these integrated healthcare systems to apply evidence-based clinical guidelines to provide timely, quality, and cost-effective treatment, both in healthcare and worksite settings to minimize the severity, length, and costs of care associated with chronic illness.[12]

Both strategies seek to leverage those determinants of health that impact an individual's well-being. These determinants include not only individual factors such as gender, age, ethnicity, socioeconomic, and educational status, but also population-based factors.[13] This latter group includes geographic locale, environment and occupation exposures, availability of secure and habitable housing, physical safety, degree of psychological and physical stress in communities, availability and quality of employment, economic stability and business opportunities, accessible and affordable quality preventive and disease management services, accessible nutritious foods, clean water, and areas for adequate physical activity.[13] These determinants of health are ultimately key factors in causing inequities in prevention, screening, treatment, morbidity, and mortality.[13] As a result, disadvantaged populations bear a greater burden of disease and experience higher rates of infant mortality, cardiovascular disease, diabetes, cancer, and HIV/AIDS.[13]

HEALTH PROMOTION

The World Health Organization defines health promotion as "the process of enabling people to increase control over their health and its determinants, and thereby improve their health."[14] Health promotion encompasses "activities … to maximize the development of resilience to … threats to health."[12] Health promotion involves an integrated, collaborative patient-centric approach to assessing, promoting, and managing health through prevention, screening, education, behavior change, and patient self-care.[10] The contributions of each strategy will be briefly described.

PREVENTION

Prevention consists of the interlocking and mutually supportive strategies and interventions aimed at the deterrence, early detection, and minimization or cessation of disease and injury at a population level.[12] With more than 50% of adult deaths associated with preventable disease and 80% of the U.S. healthcare expenditures attributed to treatment for chronic illness and associated complications, most policy makers, regulators, and politicians have recognized that the need for preventive care is paramount.[15] An estimated

95% of U.S. healthcare spending covers interventions to treat chronic illness, including many preventable diseases, compared to 5% budgeted for health promotion and prevention.[16]

Prevention activities are generally categorized as primary, secondary, and tertiary. Primary prevention involves interventions directed at preemptively preventing disease onset.[17] Immunizations, seat belt use, safe sex, stress management, and cigarette and illicit drug avoidance are examples of evidence-based primary prevention interventions.[18,19] Secondary prevention is the "early detection and swift treatment of disease ... to cure disease, slow its progression, or reduce its impact on individuals or communities."[17] Screening is a form of secondary prevention and includes interventions for detecting diseases such as colon, breast, and cervical cancers, as well as smoking cessation, weight loss programs, and the monitoring of body weight, blood pressure, and blood cholesterol levels.[17,20] Tertiary prevention is aimed at slowing the progression of confirmed disease.[12] Examples of tertiary prevention include routine foot and eye examinations for diabetic patients and screening for abdominal aortic aneurysms among high-risk tobacco users.[21,22] Numerous studies have demonstrated the efficacy of preventive measures in reducing the risks of chronic disease and mortality.[23] One telling example of this approach is the U.S. childhood immunization initiative, which has demonstrated the value of health promotion using a population health paradigm. While legislation, mandatory tracking, and incentives are not always necessary to ensure a cost-effective program, the collaboration and integration of health services, culturally and linguistically appropriate communication, education, care, tracking, reporting, and evaluation are all critical components of successful population health efforts.

Employers and health insurers have long recognized the value of wellness programs. While individual program components, resources, and funding vary, common population-based objectives are to maintain optimum employee health and to minimize disease and injury.[18] The benefits to employers are direct (measured as expenses related to interventions such as medical treatment, medications, and hospitalizations) and indirect (manifested as increased employee productivity by decreasing presenteeism and absenteeism) cost savings.[18] General interventions in these employer- and insurer-sponsored wellness programs include health risk assessments, health screenings, education and wellness coaching, and healthy behavior challenges.[18]

While the benefits are substantial, the short-term costs of preventive care are high.[24] In addition to cost, gaps in participation are common as a result of the traditional focus of health care on treating sickness, diminished access to and availability of preventive services, lack of insurance coverage, health illiteracy, and minimal integration between public and clinical health.[24] Telling examples of these shortcomings include smoking cessation programs and increasing the appropriate use of aspirin among persons at high risk for blood clotting. Both initiatives are comparatively inexpensive and can reduce cardiovascular risks, yet concerns about the value and cost-efficacy of prevention programs have been raised.[24]

SCREENING

Screening is defined as the "presumptive identification of unrecognized disease or health risks by the application of tests or other procedures that can be applied rapidly."[20] The efficacy of screening is based upon two measures of validity: sensitivity and specificity. The four potential outcomes associated with screening are: "true positive," which reflects a positive test result in the presence of actual disease; "true negative," which is a negative test result in the absence of disease; "false positive," which means the test is positive in the absence of disease; and "false negative," which indicates the test result is negative in presence of disease."[20] When assessing the appropriateness of screening, healthcare providers should consider the distribution of disease, the evidence supporting screening and validity of available tests, the benefits and risks associated with the screening, the availability and costs of treatment, and the determination of whether evidence-based and eligibility criteria exist.[20]

The benefits of screening include early detection of disease with potential opportunities to institute early treatment that, in turn, results in better health outcomes and lower morbidity, mortality, and costs.[20] For example, health risk assessments and measures of blood pressure, as well as weight/BMI, vision, hearing, blood cholesterol/lipid profile, bone density, environment exposure (e.g., lead, asbestos, and toxic) measurement, and diagnostic examinations to rule out cancers have demonstrated benefits and lowered costs.[20]

There are also limitations and potential harms associated with screening—including costs; unnecessary tests, unneeded care, and associated risks based upon false positive results; as well as patient inconvenience and discomfort—to warrant evidence-based assessment of the appropriateness of screening for individual patients.[20] In addition, significant individual patient stress, harm, and death may result from test-associated complications or injuries, unnecessary interventions, and the failure to pursue further tests following a false negative result.[20]

Screening programs are commonly included in employer-sponsored and health insurance plans. Measurements used for screening purposes may be offered to employees through their insurance benefit, as part of a worksite clinic, or through a special employee-based program that is combined with other wellness and prevention initiatives.[24] Employers promote, and most employees welcome, sharing the employees' results with the employees' primary care providers. The role of the primary care provider is to consider the needs of each consumer-patient and utilize additional age/gender-appropriate and evidence-based testing to prevent and minimize the impact of any newly detected illness.

BEHAVIOR CHANGE (HEALTH MANAGEMENT)

An estimated 30–60% of patients are not compliant with their physician-directed treatment or medication regimens.[25] Sixty-four percent of hospital admissions for congestive heart failure are associated with failure to take prescribed medications and only 7% of diabetic patients perform all self-care activities.[25] Urgent needs to reduce avoidable complications and costs associated with chronic disease suggest that modifying behavior is imperative and is an integral part of the population health paradigm.[25] Behavior change encompasses significant physical, emotional, habitual, and cultural factors that, in turn, influence health status. Population-based care seeks an interdisciplinary approach in which primary care providers collaborate with allied health staff to educate, support, follow up, and evaluate the efficacy of their treatment plans.[25] When paired with usual clinical care, behavior change interventions have demonstrated positive patient outcomes in cancer prevention; weight control; treatment of diabetes, hypertension, and lipid disorders; stress management; tobacco cessation; and alcohol moderation programs.[25]

PATIENT SELF-CARE

Population-based care acknowledges that consumers are critically necessary partners in achieving good outcomes. Unlike traditional care models, in which patients are passive recipients of treatment, a growing body of research has repeatedly demonstrated that health status is improved through behavior change and patient self-care. Through culturally and linguistically appropriate education, skill training, and integrated public and private healthcare delivery systems, healthcare consumers can readily learn to care for themselves, and participate in goal setting and collaborative decision making.[25] Patient self-care also lowers the demand for follow-up care as a result of greater compliance with health-promoting behaviors, such as adherence to dietary restrictions and participation in wellness activities. Actively engaged patients also have an enhanced ability to identify potential health risks early, enabling them to address the risk themselves or through timely communication with their primary provider.[25]

PATIENT-CENTERED MEDICAL HOME

The **Patient-Centered Medical Home (PCMH)** concept is a professionally endorsed, integrated, and collaborative healthcare delivery model centered on primary care to manage chronic illness, improve patient outcomes, and lower healthcare costs.[11] The PCMH model has been or is being implemented by government and private providers, including the Veterans Affairs Administration, UnitedHealthcare, Aetna, Humana, and CIGNA.[26] A growing body of evidence indicates that the PCMH is associated with the reduction of medical errors, improved quality of care, and increased consumer satisfaction.[26]

The PCMH is rapidly emerging as a key component of population health management. In this model, the primary care physician is the consumer's primary point of contact and is charged with responsibility for coordinating health and disease management while ensuring that integrated clinical and community medical and psychosocial care is provided.[11] The primary care services of the PCMH are based upon evidence-based guidelines enhanced through decision support with emphasis on patient self-care and behavior change.[11] Interoperable information technology systems are necessary to integrate care across practices, sites, and healthcare systems enabling appropriate access to medical records, e-prescribing capabilities, and disease registries.[11] Economic incentives and savings are realized through the monitoring, evaluation, reporting, and improvement of the quality of care and patient outcomes.[27]

CHRONIC CARE MANAGEMENT AND DISEASE MANAGEMENT

Chronic care management is the integrated primary care health paradigm focused on improving the quality of care and management of illness through "self-management, clinical information systems, evidence-based clinical decision support, redesigned integrated healthcare delivery clinical and community systems, and policies."[28,29] Disease management is a "system of targeted coordinated population-based healthcare interventions and communications for specific conditions in which patient self-care efforts are significant."[10,30] Disease management seeks to reverse the skyrocketing incidence and prevalence of serious, costly, chronic illness through improving patient outcomes with quality and cost-effective care that includes the PCMH.[10,31,32]

Chronic illnesses are taking a significant toll on the American population's health and economy, affecting more than 133 million Americans and anticipated to increase to 157 million in 10 years.[33] At least half of the population experiences more than one chronic illness, consuming more than 75% of national healthcare expenditures.[33] With the exception of accidents, preventable diseases accounted for the greatest number of deaths in 2006: these include heart disease, cancer, cerebrovascular disease, chronic lower respiratory disease, and diabetes.[4] More than half of the U.S. population is overweight and obese.[5] Centers for Disease Control and Prevention (CDC) data reflect that the direct costs (treatment, diagnosis, prevention) and indirect costs (e.g., absenteeism, reduced productivity, lowered quality of life, limited activity) associated with overweight and obesity were $92.6 billion, 50% of which was covered by the federal government.[34] The 2007 direct medical costs for asthma treatment were an estimated $37.2 billion.[35] The prevalence of cancers exceeds one million, with associated mortality rates ranging from more than 40,000 to more than 160,000, respectively, for breast and lung cancers.[4] Cardiac disease continues to be the leading cause of death in the United States. Americans experience an estimated 758,000 primary and 470,000 subsequent heart attacks annually.[36] Costs for treating cardiovascular disease and stroke exceed $475 billion.[36] Annual deaths from diabetes exceed 73,000 with an associated economic burden greater than $174 billion, including $58 billion as "decreased national productivity costs."[37]

In response to the escalating prevalence of chronic illness and its associated economic burdens, many independent companies and health plans have implemented disease management programs. Such programs utilize evidence-based, patient-focused strategies across populations to change behavior through collaborative health care, education, coaching, and financial incentives and to increase self-care and compliance.[10,18,38] In addition, the measurement and evaluation with improvement initiatives and the reporting of processes and outcomes must be defined and implemented to create and sustain disease management interventions.[10,18] Implementation of user-friendly, interoperable information technology is an integral component to support this health paradigm.[10,18] Employers and insurance health plans have demonstrated that these strategies increase productivity and decrease direct and indirect costs associated with chronic illness.[26] Many chronic care management strategies have been developed to combat obesity, coronary heart disease and heart failure, diabetes, chronic obstructive pulmonary disease, asthma, and cancer.[10,30,31] In 2005, an estimated $1.2 billion was directed by employers and health plans to disease management plans.[30,39] As of 2009, more than 80% of large U.S. employers offer chronic care management programs to lower healthcare costs.[34,39]

Evaluation of disease management programs produces mixed results. Some studies report improvements in congestive and coronary heart disease, diabetes, and depression.[30] In addition, programs are reported to increase productivity while decreasing absenteeism, presenteeism, and hospitalizations.[27] However, in many instances, the costs associated with implementing disease management programs can be considerable and may not always be immediately associated with reduced healthcare costs. As a result, the cost-effectiveness of chronic management programs remains an open question.[30–32] Proponents of chronic care programs posit that increasing participation and measuring outcomes will improve cost-effectiveness. To address the need for demonstrating and validating the cost-effectiveness of chronic management programs, public and private health and quality organizations, including the Agency for Healthcare Research and Quality (AHRQ), National Committee for Quality Assurance (NCQA), Joint Commission, and DMAA: The Care Continuum Alliance, are developing clinical and financial outcome measurements to determine if there is a financial return on investment.[19] Suggested outcome measures include healthcare utilization, clinical outcomes, healthcare including new comorbidity and pharmaceutical costs, and productivity measures.[40]

ELIMINATING HEALTH DISPARITIES

Health disparities are defined as "differences in the incidence, prevalence, mortality, and burden of diseases, as well as other adverse health conditions or outcomes that exist among specific population groups, and have been well-documented in subpopulations based on socioeconomic status, education, age, race and ethnicity, geography, disability, sexual orientation, or special needs."[41,42] These subpopulations experience disproportionate burdens of illness as a result of the barriers imposed by discrimination as well as differences in culture, language, beliefs, and values leading to considerable social and economic burdens associated with poor quality of care and lack of access to affordable, quality primary care.[41–43]

Disparities in health care, particularly for minority populations, are manifested in access to quality care, burdens of illness reflected in morbidity and mortality rates, life expectancy, and quality of life.[41–43] Minority and ethnic populations, including African

Americans, Latinos or Hispanics, Asian Americans, Native Hawaiians, Pacific Islanders, Alaskan Natives, and Native Americans, residents of rural communities, children, the elderly, individuals with physical or psychological disabilities, and other disenfranchised populations, tend to live in lower socioeconomic communities with higher rates of violence and environmental exposures, work in jobs with greater occupational hazards, have less access to affordable nutritious foods, and have higher rates of uninsurance.[41–43] These populations have less access to preventive and diagnostic care and treatment, resulting in higher rates of morbidities, emergency department utilization, hospitalizations, and mortalities.[33,41,42] The Institute of Medicine's report, *Unequal Treatment: Confronting Racial/ Ethnic Disparities in Health Care*, cited more than 175 studies documenting diagnostic and treatment disparities of various conditions among racial/ethnic populations, even when confounding factors (e.g., insurance and socioeconomic status, comorbidities, age, healthcare venue, stage of diseases) were controlled for in analyses.[41,42] Specific examples include higher rates of hypertension, diabetes, breast cancer, cervical cancer, colon cancer, and cardiovascular diseases in African Americans; diabetes in Native Americans, Alaskan Natives, and Latino populations; and heart disease mortality in certain Asian American, Latino or Hispanic, and Native American groups.[44] Lower rates of immunization and higher rates of infant mortality have been reported in African American, Hispanic, and Native American populations.[44]

Barriers to health care have been conceptualized as organizational, structural, and clinical, including lack of diversity in the healthcare workforce, lack of cultural and linguistic competency, health illiteracy, and inadequate access to and coordination of care.[41] In practical terms, health disparities include a spectrum of factors that impact access, diagnostics, treatment, follow-up, and continuity of care. These barriers result in day-to-day inability to obtain prescription medications, prevent illness, and avoid hospitalizations or emergency room use, all of which lead to poorer clinical outcomes and higher costs.[41] The population health approach integrates clinical and public healthcare approaches to explicitly address these cultural determinants of health through the targeted provision of appropriate services that seek to reduce the myriad barriers to care.

CULTURAL COMPETENCY

Cultural competency involves "acknowledg[ing] and incorporat[ing] [and] ... understanding the importance of social and cross-cultural influences of different populations' values, health beliefs and behaviors, disease prevalence and incidence and treatment outcome; considering how these factors interact with and impact multiple levels of health care delivery systems; and implementing interventions to assure quality care to diverse patient populations."[41] This requires the assessment of cross-cultural relations and barriers, expansion of cultural knowledge, and awareness of integration of health beliefs and behaviors.[41]

Sociocultural barriers to health care have been described as organizational, structural, and clinical, all of which contribute to disparities in health and care.[41] Organizational barriers include inadequate diversity in institutional leadership and healthcare providers, workforce, limited clinic hours, and extended waiting for appointments and care.[41] Studies have demonstrated correlations between consumer satisfaction and racial concordance with providers.[41] Clinical barriers exist where healthcare providers lack knowledge and appreciation for differences in ethnic, religious or health beliefs, values, and culturally endorsed treatments.[41] In clinical settings, even language differences without availability of interpreters (i.e., "monolingual" or "unilingual" education and patient information resources) create important structural barriers that significantly impede consumer understanding of assessments, diagnosis, care recommendations, the necessity of specialty referrals, and mutually agreed-upon compliance with treatments.[41]

In 2001, the U.S. Department of Health and Human Services' Office of Minority Health published National Standards on Culturally and Linguistically Appropriate Services (CLAS).[45] The 14 CLAS standards were developed to assist healthcare organizations in developing a framework to respond to diverse patient populations, to support the elimination of ethnic and racial disparities, and to improve the health of all consumers.[45] The 14 CLAS standards address respectful treatment of consumers; implementation of culturally appropriate policies, goals, and programs; recruitment of diverse leadership and staff; ongoing training of employees; ensuring the availability of interpreters and patient materials; performing self-assessments; collaborating with patient and community organizations to implement CLAS-related activities; instituting grievance procedures; and compiling data on progress and innovations utilizing CLAS standards.[45]

NATIONAL INITIATIVES ADDRESSING POPULATION HEALTH NEEDS

The federal government and prominent public–private collaborations have been active proponents and participants in establishing priorities, strategies, and funding for programs to address the most critical, pressing healthcare issues. Two of the most significant initiatives are the **National Priorities Partnership** and the Healthy People programs.

THE NATIONAL PRIORITIES PARTNERSHIP

The National Priorities Partnership (NPP) is a collaboration of 28 nationally influential public and private organizations, convened by the National Quality Forum (NQF) in 2008. Collectively, the NPP partners identified priorities and goals that addressed four major challenges facing the U.S. healthcare system: "eliminating harm, eradicating disparities, reducing disease burden and removing waste."[46] The priority areas and designated goals are engaging patients and families to make decisions about and manage their care; improving the population's health; improving the safety and reliability of the U.S. healthcare system; ensuring well-coordinated care throughout and among all healthcare entities; guaranteeing appropriate and compassionate care for those with terminal illness; ensuring the delivery of appropriate care; and eliminating unscientific and excessive care.[46]

This partnership marks the first national effort that identified population health as an explicit priority.

HEALTHY PEOPLE INITIATIVES

The U.S. Department of Health and Human Services (HHS), through the Centers for Disease Control and Prevention (CDC), formally established national health priorities in 1979.[47] The Healthy People programs set national public health priorities for implementation over a 10-year period by national, state, and local entities. Periodic reviews are conducted to measure and report progress toward the goals.

The two overarching goals for Healthy People 2010 were (1) increasing quality as well as years of healthy life and (2) eliminating health disparities. To guide achievement of these goals, 10 Leading Health Indicators representing the major health concerns were identified. Twenty-eight focus areas with 467 objectives were established to serve as guides for public and private sector participants who were implementing initiatives aimed at improving the population's health.[47]

The **Healthy People 2020** overarching goals are: "attaining high quality, longer lives free of preventable disease, disability, injury, and premature death; achieving health equity, eliminating disparities, and improving the health of all groups; creating social and physical environments that promote good health for all; and promoting quality of life, healthy development, and healthy behaviors across all life stages."[47] Deliberation and consensus among experts and stakeholders will determine the current Leading Health Indicators, focus areas, and objectives, which will undoubtedly include the unmet needs identified in Healthy People 2010.

STATE-BASED INITIATIVES

All 50 states and the District of Columbia have been active participants in national initiatives, including the NPP and the Healthy People programs. In addition, individual states have implemented their own reforms to eliminate self-identified healthcare disparities, increase access to quality and cost-effective care, and improve healthcare delivery at manageable costs. Almost every state has developed Healthy People health plans.[48] Of note is Massachusetts, which was the first state to provide universal coverage for all residents in 2006.[49,50] Approximately 97% of Massachusetts residents are insured, reflecting the lowest rate of uninsured residents in the United States.[49,50] Insurance coverage is subsidized for residents earning less than 300% of the Federal Poverty Level, and low-cost insurance is offered to those ineligible for employer-sponsored coverage.[49,50] Preventive services and prescription drugs are covered, and deductibles and out-of-pocket spending are capped.[49,50]

Vermont has implemented the Blueprint for Health, which is a legislated chronic care management program incorporating policies and support for accessible, appropriate, and timely coordinated clinical and community care, self-management tools, and information technology.[51] Vermont's plan has already yielded positive outcomes in each of these interventions.[51] Wisconsin's 10-year state health plan, Healthiest Wisconsin 2010, focuses on increasing the percentage of insured citizens to 92%, reducing barriers to access, and building capacity for culturally sensitive prevention, screening, and referral.[52]

CHALLENGES IN IMPLEMENTING A POPULATION HEALTH APPROACH

Most stakeholders in healthcare reform agree that the status quo cannot remain and that the time for implementing systematic change is now. The most pressing challenges related to implementing a population health paradigm fall into three broad arenas: clinical, policy, and business.

CLINICAL

Healthcare students and providers need to learn about incorporating healthcare promotion and prevention into the day-to-day flow of patient management. In addition, health behavior counseling that emphasizes self-care needs to be incorporated into primary and treatment care. Evidence-based models of care need to be expanded and used in the creation of clinical care guidelines that are readily accessible at the point of care and also inform health insurance coverage.

POLICY

A broad array of legislative, regulatory, and policy changes that economically and structurally support a health promotion or disease prevention delivery system needs to be enacted. In addition, legislative and regulatory changes will be needed to enable economically sound changes in versions of health insurance that improve access to chronic care, wellness, and prevention activities. Furthermore, legislative, regulatory, and policy changes are critically needed to increase the systemic quality of care and eliminate waste. Last but not least, the integration of community/public health and clinical care systems, as envisioned in the Patient-Centered Medical Home, need to be broadly promoted across the entire spectrum of care.

BUSINESS

As the use of health information technology continues to expand in the health sector, purchasers need to be critically aware of the business case for defining and implementing meaningful interoperable systems and data warehouses that support population health interventions across multiple healthcare settings. This is critically important to establishing the links between outcome measures, evaluation of competing healthcare interventions, and reimbursement for various services. This will enable the incorporation of mandatory reporting and improvement procedures that lead to continuous quality improvement and reducing the rate of healthcare cost inflation.

CONCLUSIONS

Population health is a dynamic approach to health care that consists of a variety of inter-related approaches; it ultimately seeks to simultaneously improve healthcare quality and optimize healthcare spending. At its core, population health advances patient self-care so that recipients are better able to work with the healthcare system to improve their health status, intervene early in any exacerbations of chronic illness, reduce the incidence complications, and rely on efficient and effective healthcare options. While there are other health reform efforts underway, population health promises to be a key component of the United State's—and possibly the rest of the world's—efforts to reduce chronic illness. Tying self-care to other ingredients, such as increasing the use of health information technology, promoting interdisciplinary healthcare teamwork, supporting community health organizations, adopting disease management approaches, and instituting primary care reform with the Patient-Centered Medical Home, has yet to be systematically developed as a strategy and remains a dynamic and exciting area of healthcare reform. Given the twin challenges of quality and cost, population health so far remains an important option in reducing the burden of chronic illness, promoting wellness, increasing prevention, reducing health disparities, and meeting our national healthcare goals.

STUDY AND DISCUSSION QUESTIONS

1. What is the definition of population health and what are its key attributes?
2. What are the determinants of a population's health status and what are the roles of health promotion and disease management?
3. What are the roles of behavior change and self-care in achieving population health outcomes?
4. How can population health address healthcare disparities?
5. How can population health assist in achieving goals of the national and state initiatives addressing population health needs?

SUGGESTED READINGS AND WEB SITES

READINGS

Adler NE, Rehkopf DH. U.S. disparities in health: descriptions, causes, and mechanisms. *Annu Rev Public Health.* 2008;29:235–252.

Barr VJ, Robinson S, Marin-Link B, et al. The expanded Chronic Care Model: an integration of concepts and strategies from population health promotion and the Chronic Care Model. *Hosp Q.* 2003;7(1):73–82.

Betancourt JR, Green AR, Carillo JE, et al. Defining cultural competence: a practical framework for addressing racial/ethnic disparities in health and health care. *Public Health Rep.* 2003:118:293–302.

Bodenheimer T. Helping patients improve their health-related behaviors: what system changes do we need? *Dis Manag.* 2005;8(5):319–330.

Bodenheimer T, Chen E, Bennett HD. Confronting the growing burden of chronic disease: can the U.S. health care workforce do the job? *Health Aff.* 2009;28(1):64–74.

Braveman P, Gruskin S. Defining equity in health. *J Epidemiol Community Health.* 2003;57(4):254–258.

Carney PA, Eiff MP, Saultz JW, et al. Aspects of the Patient-Centered Medical Home currently in place: initial findings from preparing the personal physician for practice. *Fam Med.* 2009;41(9):632–639.

Frazee SG, Sherman B, Fabius R, et al. Leveraging the trusted clinician: increasing retention in disease management through integrated program delivery. *Popul Health Manag.* 2008;11(5):247–254.

Goetzel RZ, Ozminkowski RJ, Villagra VG, et al. Return on investment in disease management: a review. *Health Care Financing Rev.* 2005;26(4):1–19.

Grandes G, Sanchez A, Cortada JM, et al. Is integration of healthy lifestyle promotion into primary care feasible? Discussion and consensus sessions between clinicians and researchers. *BMC Health Serv Res.* 2008;8:213.

Musich SA, Schultz AB, Burton WN, Edington DW. Overview of disease management approaches: implications for corporate-sponsored programs. *Dis Manage Health Outcomes.* 2004;12(5):299–326.

Rosenthal TC. The medical home: growing evidence to support a new approach to primary care. *J Am Board Fam Med.* 2008;21(5):427–440.

Sisko A, Truffer C, Smith S, et al. Health spending projections through 2018: recession effects add uncertainty to the outlook. *Health Aff.* 2009;28(2):w346–w357.

WEB SITES

The Centers for Disease Control and Prevention: http://www.cdc.gov/

DMAA: The Care Continuum Alliance: http://www.dmaa.org/phi_definition.asp

The DMAA Outcomes Guidelines Report Volume 4—User Agreement: http://www.dmaa.org/OGR_user_agreement.asp

Health Reform Center of the New England Journal of Medicine: http://healthcarereform.nejm.org/?query=rthome

Healthy People 2010: http://www.healthypeople.gov/

The Kaiser Family Foundation: http://www.kff.org/

National Business Coalition on Health: http://www.nbch.org/

The National Coalition on Health Care: http://nchc.org/

National Priorities Partnership: http://www.nationalprioritiespartnership.org/

The National Quality Forum: http://www.qualityforum.org/
The Patient-Centered Primary Care Collaborative: www.pcpcc.net
The US Preventive Services Task Force: http://www.ahrq.gov/CLINIC/uspstfix.htm
World Health Organization: http://www.who.int/en/

REFERENCES

1. National Coalition on Health Care. NCHC white paper identifies more than $1 trillion in cost-savings. Now it's time to put fiscal responsibility and patient well-being before profits. http://nchc.org/issue-areas/cost. Published 2009. Accessed October 15, 2009.

2. Kindig D, Stoddart G. What is population health? *Am J Public Health*. 2003;93(3):380–383.

3. Lloyd-Jones D, Adams RJ, Brown TM, et al. Heart disease and stroke statistics—2010 update: a report from the American Heart Association. *Circulation*. 2010;121:e46-e215. http://circ.ahajournals.org/cgi/content/full/121/7/e46. Accessed December 10, 2009.

4. Heron MP, Hoyert DL, Murphy SL, Xu JQ, Kochanek KD, Tejada-Vera B. Deaths: final data for 2006. *National Vital Statistics Report*. 2009; 57(14):1-135. http://www.cdc.gov/nchs/data/nvsr/nvsr57/nvsr57_14.pdf. Accessed December 1, 2009.

5. Centers for Disease Control and Prevention. Heart disease facts: America's heart disease burden. CDC Web site. http://www.cdc.gov/heartdisease/facts.htm. Accessed December 18, 2009.

6. Highest rates of obesity, diabetes in the South, Appalachia, and some tribal lands: estimates of obesity now available for all U.S. counties [news release]. Atlanta, GA: Centers for Disease Control and Prevention; November 19, 2009. http://www.cdc.gov/media/pressrel/2009//r091119c.htm. Accessed December 18, 2009.

7. Kaiser Family Foundation. Kaiser Daily Health Policy Report. More large employers offer chronic disease management programs to reduce health care costs. Kaiser Family Foundation Web site. http://www.kaiserhealthnews.org/daily-reports/2009/april/03/dr00057858.aspx?referrer=search. Published 2009. Accessed October 15, 2009.

8. Sisko A, Truffer C, Smith S, et al. Health spending projections through 2018: recession effects add uncertainty to the outlook. *Health Aff*. 2009;28(2):w346–w357.

9. Frazee SG, Sherman B, Fabius R, et al. Leveraging the trusted clinician: increasing retention in disease management through integrated program delivery. *Popul Health Manag*. 2008;11(5): 247–254.

10. DMAA: The Care Continuum Alliance. DMAA definition of disease management. DMAA Web site. http://www.dmaa.org/dm_definition.asp. Accessed December 18, 2010.

11. Carney PA, Eiff MP, Saultz JW, et al. Aspects of the Patient-Centered Medical Home currently in place: initial findings from preparing the personal physician for practice. *Fam Med*. 2009; 41(9):632–639.

12. Starfield B. Basic concepts in population health and health care. *J Epidemiol Community Health*. 2001;55(7):452–454.

13. Gehlert S, Sohmer D, Sacks T, Mininger C, McClintock M, Olufunmilayo O. Targeting health disparities: a model linking upstream determinants to downstream interventions. *Health Aff*. 2008;27(2):339–349.

14. World Health Organization. 6th Global Conference on Health Promotion. The Bangkok Charter for health promotion in a globalized world. World Health Organization Web site. http://www.who.int/healthpromotion/conferences/6gchp/bangkok_charter/en/. Published August 11, 2005. Accessed October 2009.

15. Shenson D. Putting prevention in its place: the shift from clinic to community. *Health Aff*. 2006; 25(4):1012–1015.

16. Kelley E, Moy E, Kosiak B, et al. Prevention health care quality in America: findings from the first National Healthcare Quality and Disparities

Reports. *Prev Chronic Dis.* 2004;1(3):1–5. http://www.ncbi.nlm.nih.gov/pmc/articles/PMC1253468/htm. Accessed October 5, 2009.

17. Oleckno WA. Selected disease concepts in epidemiology. In: Oleckno WA. *Essential Epidemiology: Principles and Applications.* Long Grove, Ill: Waveland Press, Inc., 2002:30–31.

18. Goetzel RZ, Ozminkowski RJ. The health and cost benefits of work site health-promotion programs. *Ann Rev Public Health.* 2008;29:303–323.

19. Chapman LS, Pelletier KR. Population health management as a strategy for creation of optimal healing environments in worksite and corporate settings. *J Altern Complement Med.* 2004;10(Suppl 1):S-127–S-140.

20. Durojaiye OC. Health screening: is it always worth doing? *Internet J Epidemiol.* 2009;7(1). http://www.ispub.com/journal/the_internet_journal_of_epidemiology/volume_7_number_1_24/article/health-screening-is-it-always-worth-doing.html. Accessed October 1, 2009.

21. 2007 National diabetes fact sheet: general information and national estimates on diabetes in the United States [fact sheet]. Atlanta, GA: U.S. Department of Health and Human Services, Centers for Disease Control and Prevention; 2007. http://www.cdc.gov/diabetes/pubs/factsheet07.htm. Accessed December 18, 2009.

22. U.S. Prevention Task Force. Screening for Abdominal Aortic Aneurysm. Agency for Healthcare Research and Quality Web site. http://www.ahrq.gov/CLINIC/uspstf/uspsaneu.htm. Published February 2005. Accessed December 18, 2009.

23. Cohen JT, Neumann PJ, Weinstein MC. Does preventive care save money? Health economics and the presidential candidates. *New Engl J Med.* 2008;358(7):661–663.

24. Kahn R, Robertson RM, Smith R, Smith R, Eddy D. The impact of prevention on reducing the burden of cardiovascular disease. *Diabetes Care.* 2008;31(8):1686–1696.

25. Bodenheimer T. Helping patients improve their health-related behaviors: what system changes do we need? *Dis Manage.* 2005;8(5):319–330.

26. Rosenthal TC. The medical home: growing evidence to support a new approach to primary care. *J Am Board Fam Med.* 2008;21(5):427–440.

27. Musich SA, Schultz AB, Burton WN, Edington DW. Overview of disease management approaches: implications for corporate-sponsored programs. *Dis Manage Health Outcomes.* 2004;12(5):299–326.

28. Bodenheimer T, Wagner EH, Grumbach K. Improving primary care for patients with chronic illness. *JAMA.* 2002;288(14):1775–1779.

29. Wagner EH, Austin BT, Davis C, Hindmarsh M, Schaefer J, Bonomi A. Improving chronic illness care: translating evidence into action. *Health Aff.* 2001;20(6):64–78.

30. Mattke S, Seid M, Ma S. Evidence for the effect of disease management: is $1 billion a year a good investment? *Am J Managed Care.* 2007;12(12):670-676. http://www.rand.org/health/abstracts/2007/071210_mattke.html. Accessed October 15, 2009.

31. Lewis A. How to measure the outcomes of chronic disease management. *Popul Health Manag.* 2009;12(1):47–54.

32. Congressional Budget Office. An analysis of the literature on disease management programs. Congressional Budget Office Web site. http://www.cbo.gov/ftpdocs/59xx/doc5909/10-13-DiseaseMngmnt.pdf. Published October 13, 2004. Accessed October 15, 2009.

33. Bodenheimer T, Chen E, Bennett HD. Confronting the growing burden of chronic disease: can the U.S. health care workforce do the job? *Health Aff.* 2009;28(1):64–74.

34. National Center for Health Statistics. U.S. Mortality Data 2006. Centers for Disease Control and Prevention Web site. http://www.cdc.gov/nchs/deaths. htm. Accessed December 17, 2009.

35. American Lung Association. Lung cancer fact sheet. American Lung Association Web site. http://www.lungusa.org/lung-disease/lung-cancer/resources/facts-figures/lung-cancer-fact-sheet.html. Accessed October 2009.

36. American Heart Association. Cardiovascular disease statistics. American Heart Association Web site. http://www.americanheart.org/presenter.jhtml?identified=4478. Accessed December 18, 2009.

37. American Diabetes Association. American Diabetes Association Web site. http://www.diabetes.org/. Accessed October 15, 2009.

38. Barr VJ, Robinson S, Marin-Link B, et al. The expanded Chronic Care Model: an integration of concepts and strategies from population health promotion and the Chronic Care Model. *Hosp Q.* 2003;7(1):73–82.

39. Medical News Today. More large employers offer chronic disease management programs to reduce health care costs. http://www.medicalnewstoday.com/articles/145136.php. Published April 6, 2009. Accessed October 15, 2009.

40. Goetzel R, Ozminkowski RJ, Villagra VG, et al. Return on investment in disease management: a review. *Health Care Financing Rev.* 2005;26(4): 1–19.

41. Betancourt JR, Green AR, Carrillo JE, et al. Defining cultural competence: a practical framework for addressing racial/ethnic disparities in health and health care. *Public Health Rep.* 2003; 118: 293–302.

42. Adler NE, Rehkopf DH. U.S. disparities in health: descriptions, causes, and mechanisms. *Annu Rev Public Health.* 2008;29:235–252.

43. National Association of Chronic Disease Directors. National Association of Chronic Disease Directors Web site. http://www.chronicdisease.org/i4a/pages/index.cfm?pageid=1. Accessed December 18, 2009.

44. Office of Minority Health. Disease burden and risk factors. http://minorityhealth.hhs.gov/. Accessed November 20, 2009.

45. Office of Minority Health. *National Standards for Culturally and Linguistically Appropriate Services in Health Care: Final Report.* Washington, DC: U.S. Department of Health and Human Service; 2001. http://minorityhealth.hhs.gov/assets/pdf/checked/finalreport.pdf. Accessed November 20, 2009.

46. National Priorities Partnership. *Aligning Our Efforts to Transform America's Healthcare: National Priorities & Goals.* Washington, DC: National Quality Forum; 2008. http://www.nationalprioritiespartnership.org/uploadedFiles/NPP/08-253-NQF%20ReportLo%5B6%5D.pdf. Accessed December 1, 2009.

47. U.S. Department of Health & Human Services. Healthy People 2020 Public Meetings: Proposed Healthy People 2020 Objectives. http://www.healthypeople.gov/hp2020/Objectives/TopicAreas.aspx. Accessed November 28, 2009.

48. Healthy People 2010. Websites for state Healthy People 2000 plans. Health.gov Web site. http://www.health.gov/hpcomments/state/hpstate.htm. Accessed December 19, 2009.

49. Office of Health and Human Services. Healthcare Reform. Office of Health and Human Services Web site. http://www.mass.gov/?pageID=eohhs2subtopic&L=4&L0=Home&L1=Government&L2=Special+Commissions+and+Initiatives&L3=Healthcare+Reform&sid=Eeohhs2. Accessed December 18, 2009.

50. Massachusetts Trial Court Law Libraries. Massachusetts laws about health insurance. Commonwealth of Massachusetts. Trial Court Law Libraries Web site. http://www.lawlib.state.ma.us.subject/about/healthinsurance.htm. Accessed December 18, 2009.

51. Vermont Department of Health. Healthy Vermonters 2010. Vermont Department of Health Web site. http://healthvermont.gov/pubs/hv2010/hv2010.aspx. Accessed December 18. 2009.

52. Wisconsin Department of Health Services. Tracking the state health plan 2010: state-level data. Wisconsin Department of Health Services Web site. http://dhfs.wisconsin.gov/statehealthplan/track2010. Accessed December 18, 2009.

BEHAVIOR CHANGE

Chapter 2

JAMES O. PROCHASKA, PhD, AND
JANICE M. PROCHASKA, PhD

Executive Summary

Behavior change—an essential component of a well-care system

Health risk behaviors like smoking, inactivity, unhealthy diets, nonadherence to prescribed therapies, and ineffectively managed stress significantly contribute to a population's morbidity, disability, mortality, reduced productivity, and escalating healthcare costs. To have a significant and sustainable impact on these behaviors, a model of behavior change is needed to address the needs of entire populations, not just the minority who are motivated to take immediate action. The Transtheoretical Model of Behavior Change (TTM) is founded on stages of change, which categorize segments of populations based on where they are in the process of change. Principles and processes are applied to initiate movement through the stages of change. Interventions tailored to specific needs allow programs to be interactive and broadly applicable for treatment of entire populations. Computer Tailored Interventions (CTIs) delivered through various modalities, such as clinical guidance, telephonic counseling, and the Internet produce high impact on both single and multiple behaviors for disease prevention and management. These interventions involve new paradigms that complement existing ones, such as proactive stage-matched interventions for multiple behaviors delivered to homes via computers with evidence based on population trials using impact metrics. These integrated paradigms have the potential to provide the foundation for a well-care system, which will complement the existing sick-care system.

Learning Objectives

1. Learn the major constructs of the Transtheoretical Model of Behavior Change (TTM).
2. Select and apply TTM principles at each stage of change when working with patients and populations.
3. Understand the critical assumptions of the TTM.
4. Realize the importance of multiple behavior changes.
5. Describe the provider's role in understanding and managing the behaviors of patient populations.

Key Words

multiple behavior changes

processes of change

stages of change

Transtheoretical Model of Behavior Change

INTRODUCTION

Healthcare providers and patients have a shared responsibility for population health. As the ultimate authority on their personal health, patients have responsibility for sharing health-related information with their providers. Healthcare providers are responsible for listening to patients' concerns and providing advice accordingly. This shared responsibility is essential for all patient populations and is especially important for those dealing with chronic conditions. Behaviors affect morbidity, and extremely unhealthy behaviors may lead to mortality. Understanding what causes patients to exhibit certain behaviors and what motivates them to change provides information that can be broadly applicable to populations with similar characteristics.

In this chapter, we focus on the provider's role in understanding and managing the behaviors of patient populations. Behavior change is important in several domains of chronic care management: (1) in personal health care, when providers work with a patient to change the behaviors that are contributing to or exacerbating the patient's disease; (2) in quality and safety, as it relates to advising patients on the risks of smoking, for example; and (3) in public health activities, in advising populations to receive the H1N1 vaccination for protection from the pandemic. Behavior affects three of the four pillars of population health, demonstrating that it is a key driver in population health management. (See Box 2-1) It is the healthcare provider's role to advise patients on the risks of their behaviors and the benefits of changing unhealthy ones. Providers can follow the **Transtheoretical Model of Behavior Change (TTM)** in advising patients, but it is the patient's responsibility for accepting the provider's advice and taking action. While this model has traditionally been applied to individuals, it can also be used to describe the health of populations because communities can influence the behavior of its members.

BOX 2-1   FOUR PILLARS OF POPULATION HEALTH

Population Health

Chronic Care Management   Health Policy

Quality and Safety   Public Health

THE TRANSTHEORETICAL MODEL OF BEHAVIOR CHANGE

The Transtheoretical Model of Behavior Change (TTM) uses stages to integrate processes and principles of change across major theories of intervention—hence, the name Transtheoretical. This model emerged from a comparative analysis of leading theories grounded in psychotherapy and behavior change. Because more than 300 psychotherapy theories were found, the authors determined that there was a need for systematic integration.[1] Ten **processes of change** emerged, including consciousness raising from the Freudian tradition, contingency management from the Skinnerian tradition, and helping relationships from the Rogerian tradition.

In an empirical analysis of self-changers compared to smokers in professional treatments, researchers assessed how frequently each group used each of the ten processes.[2] Research participants indicated that they used different processes at different times in their struggles with smoking. These naive subjects were teaching us about a phenomenon that was not included in any of the multitude of therapy theories. They were revealing that behavior change unfolds through a series of stages.[3] This early discovery is the reason that TTM is often applied to smoking-cessation interventions.

From the initial studies of smoking, the stage model rapidly expanded in scope to include investigations and applications to a broad range of health and mental health behaviors. Examples include alcohol and substance abuse, stress, bullying, delinquency, depression, eating disorders and obesity, high-fat diets, HIV/AIDS prevention, mammography screening, medication compliance, unplanned pregnancy prevention, pregnancy and smoking, radon testing, sedentary lifestyles, and sun exposure. Over time, behavior studies have expanded, validated, applied, and challenged the core constructs of the Transtheoretical Model.

CORE CONSTRUCTS

The TTM has concentrated on six *stages* of change, 10 *processes* of change, decisional balance (the pros and cons of changing), self-efficacy, and temptation. Stages of change lie at the heart of the TTM. Studies of change have found that people move through a series of stages when modifying behavior. While the time a person can stay in each stage is variable, the tasks required to move to the next stage are not. Certain principles and processes of change work best at each stage to reduce resistance, facilitate progress, and prevent relapse. These include decisional balance, self-efficacy, and processes of change. Only a minority (usually less than 20%) of a population at risk is prepared to take action at any given time. Thus, action-oriented advice disserves individuals in the early stages. Advice based on the TTM results in increased participation in the change process because it appeals to the whole population rather than the minority ready to take action.

STAGES OF CHANGE

The stage construct represents a temporal dimension. Change implies phenomena occurring over time. Surprisingly, none of the leading theories of therapy contained a core construct representing time. Traditionally, behavior change was often construed as an event, such as quitting smoking, drinking, or overeating, but the TTM recognizes change as a process that unfolds over time, involving progress through a series of stages.

Precontemplation   People in the precontemplation stage do not intend to take action in the foreseeable future, usually measured as the next six months. Being uninformed or underinformed about the consequences of one's behavior may cause a person to be in the precontemplation stage. Multiple unsuccessful attempts at change can lead to demoralization about the ability to change. Both the uninformed and underinformed tend to avoid reading, talking, or thinking about their high-risk behaviors. They are often characterized in other theories as resistant, unmotivated, or unready for health promotion programs. The fact is, traditional population health promotion programs were not ready for such individuals and were not motivated to meet their needs.

Contemplation   Contemplation is the stage in which people intend to change in the next six months. They are more aware of the pros of changing, but are also acutely aware of the cons. In a meta-analysis across 48 health risk behaviors, the pros and cons of changing were equal. This weighting between the costs and benefits of changing can produce profound ambivalence that can cause people to remain in this stage for long periods of time. This phenomenon is often characterized as chronic contemplation or behavioral procrastination. Individuals in the contemplation stage are not ready for traditional action-oriented programs that expect participants to act immediately.

Preparation   Preparation is the stage in which people intend to take action in the immediate future, usually measured as the next month. Typically, they have already taken some significant action in the past year. These individuals have a plan of action, such as joining a health education class, consulting a counselor, talking to their physician, buying a self-help book, or relying on a self-change approach. These are the people who should be recruited for action-oriented programs.

Action   Action is the stage in which people have made specific overt modifications in their lifestyles within the past six months. Because action is observable, the overall process of behavior change often has been equated with action. But in the TTM, action is only one of six stages. Typically, not all modifications of behavior count as action in this model. In most applications, people have to attain a criterion that scientists and professionals agree is sufficient to reduce risk of disease. For example, reduction in the number of cigarettes or switching to low-tar and low-nicotine cigarettes were formerly considered acceptable actions toward smoking cessation. Now the consensus is clear—only total abstinence counts.

Maintenance   Maintenance is the stage in which people have made specific overt modifications in their lifestyles and are working to prevent relapse; however, they do not apply change processes as frequently as do people in action. While in the maintenance stage, people are less tempted to relapse and grow increasingly more confident that they can continue their changes. Based on temptation and self-efficacy data, researchers have estimated that maintenance lasts from six months to about five years. While this estimate may seem somewhat pessimistic, longitudinal data in the 1990 Surgeon General's report support this temporal estimate.[4] After 12 months of continuous abstinence, 43% of individuals returned to regular smoking. It was not until 5 years of continuous abstinence that the risk for relapse dropped to 7%.[4]

Termination   Termination is the stage in which individuals are not tempted; they have 100% self-efficacy. Whether depressed, anxious, bored, lonely, angry, or stressed, individuals in this stage are sure they will not return to unhealthy habits as a way of coping. It is as if the habit was never acquired in the first place or their new behavior has become an automatic habit. Examples include adults who have developed automatic seatbelt use or who automatically take their anti-hypertensive medication at the same time and place each day. In a study of former smokers and alcoholics, researchers found that less than 20% of each group had reached the criteria of zero temptation and total self-efficacy.[5] The criterion of 100% self-efficacy may be too strict or it may be that this stage is an ideal goal for population health efforts. In other areas, like exercise, consistent condom use, and weight control, the realistic goal may be a lifetime of maintenance. Termination has not been given as much emphasis in TTM research because it may not be a practical reality for populations and it occurs long after interventions have ended.

PROCESSES OF CHANGE

Processes of change are the experiential and behavioral activities that people use to progress through the stages. It is important for all practitioners of population health to understand these progressions. They provide important guides for intervention programs, serving as independent variables that are applied to move from stage to stage. Ten processes have received the most empirical support in our research to date.

Consciousness Raising   Consciousness raising involves increased awareness about the causes, consequences, and cures for a particular problem behavior. Healthcare provider interventions that can increase awareness include feedback, confrontations, interpretations, and bibliotherapy. Sedentary patients, for example, may not be aware that their inactivity can have the same risk as smoking a pack of cigarettes a day.

Dramatic Relief   Dramatic relief initially produces increased emotional experiences followed by reduced affect or anticipated relief if appropriate action is taken. Healthcare providers can provide health risk feedback and success stories to move people emotionally.

Environmental Reevaluation   Environmental reevaluation combines both affective and cognitive assessments of how the presence or absence of a personal habit affects one's social environment, such as the effect of smoking on others. It can also include the awareness that one can serve as a positive or negative role model for others. Providers can have patients ask others about their behavior and have family interventions that lead to such reassessments.

Self-Reevaluation   Self-reevaluation combines both cognitive and affective assessments of one's self-image with and without a particular unhealthy habit, such as one's image as a couch potato versus an active person. Values clarification, identifying healthy role models, and imagery are techniques that healthcare providers can use to move patients toward self-reevaluation. During interaction with a patient, the provider might ask, "Imagine you were free from smoking. How would you feel about yourself?"

Self-Liberation   Self-liberation is both the belief that one can change and the commitment, as well as the recommitment, to act on that belief. Encouraging patients to make New Year's resolutions, public testimonies, or a contract are ways of enhancing willpower. The provider might say, "Telling others about your commitment to take action can strengthen your willpower. Who are you going to tell?"

Social Liberation   Social liberation requires an increase in social opportunities or alternatives, especially for patients who are relatively deprived or oppressed. For example, advocacy, empowerment procedures, and appropriate policies can produce increased opportunities for minority health promotion, gay health promotion, and health promotion for impoverished segments of the population. These same procedures can also be used to help populations change; examples include smoke-free zones, salad bars in school cafeterias, and easy access to condoms and other contraceptives. Healthcare providers can promote changes in society, encouraging a healthy lifestyle and making it easier to achieve.

Counterconditioning   Counterconditioning requires learning healthy behaviors as substitutes for problem behaviors. Examples of counterconditioning include healthcare provider recommendations for use of nicotine replacement as a safe substitute for smoking or walking as a healthier alternative than "comfort" foods as a way to cope with stress.

Helping Relationships   Helping relationships combine caring, trust, openness, and acceptance, as well as support for healthy behavior change. Rapport building, a therapeutic alliance, supportive calls, and buddy systems can be sources of social support that healthcare providers could offer. SilverSneakers, an exercise program often covered by Medicare, is an example of a program that providers could offer to their patients.

Reinforcement Management   Reinforcement management provides consequences for taking steps in a positive direction. While contingency management can include the use of punishment, we found that self-changers rely on reward much more than punishment. So, we recommend that healthcare providers emphasize reinforcement because a philosophy of the stage model is to work in harmony with how people change naturally. Patients expect to be reinforced by others more frequently than occurs, so they should be encouraged to reinforce themselves through self-statements like "Nice going—you handled that temptation." They also need to treat themselves at milestones as a way to provide reinforcement and to increase the probability that healthy responses will be repeated.

Stimulus Control   Stimulus control removes cues for unhealthy habits and adds prompts for healthier alternatives. In this process, healthcare providers can recommend removing all the ashtrays from the house and car or removing high-fat foods that are tempting cues for unhealthy eating.

DECISIONAL BALANCE

The process of reflecting and weighing the pros and cons of changing is decisional balance. Originally, TTM relied on Janis and Mann's[6] model of decision making that included four categories of pros: instrumental gains for self, instrumental gains for others, approval from self, and approval from others. The four categories of cons were instrumental costs to self, instrumental cost to others, disapproval from self, and disapproval from others. In a long series of studies attempting to produce this structure of eight factors, a much simpler structure was almost always found—the pros and cons of changing. Sound decision making requires the consideration of the potential gains (pros) and losses (cons) associated with a behavior's consequences. Providers can tell patients, for example, that there are more than 50 scientific benefits of regular physical activity and encourage patients to make a list to see how many they can identify. They can also list the cons. The more the list of pros outweighs the cons, the better prepared patients will be to take effective action.

SELF-EFFICACY

Self-efficacy is the situation-specific confidence that people have while coping with high-risk situations without relapsing to their unhealthy habit. This construct was integrated from Bandura's[7] self-efficacy theory.

TEMPTATION

Temptation reflects the intensity of urges to engage in a specific habit while in the midst of difficult situations. Typically, three factors reflect the most common types of tempting situations: negative affect or emotional distress, positive social situations, and craving. Asking patients how they will cope with emotional distress without relying on a cigarette or comfort foods can help them cope more effectively and thereby build their confidence or self-esteem.

CRITICAL ASSUMPTIONS

The Transtheoretical Model is also based on critical assumptions about the nature of behavior change and population health interventions that can best facilitate such change. The following set of assumptions drives Transtheoretical theory, research, and practice:

1. Behavior change is a process that unfolds over time through a sequence of stages and providers and health population programs will need to assist patients as they progress over time.
2. Stages are both stable and open to change, just as chronic behavioral risk factors are both stable and open to change. Population health initiatives can motivate change by enhancing the understanding of the pros and diminishing the value of the cons.
3. The majority of at-risk populations is not prepared for action and will not be served by traditional action-oriented prevention programs. Helping patients set realistic goals, like progressing to the next stage, will facilitate the change process.
4. Specific processes and principles of change need to be emphasized at specific stages for progress through the stages to occur. Table 2-1 outlines which processes to apply at each stage.

Table 2-1   Processes of Change That Mediate Progression Between the Stages of Change

Precontemplation	Contemplation	Preparation	Action	Maintenance
Consciousness Raising				
Dramatic Relief				
Environmental Reevaluation				
	Self-Reevaluation			
		Self-Liberation		
			Counterconditioning	
			Helping Relationships	
			Reinforcement Management	
			Stimulus Control	

Note: Social Liberation was omitted due to its unclear relationship to the stages.

These critical assumptions need to be taken into consideration when developing a population-based approach to behavior change and facilitating progress through the stages.

EMPIRICAL SUPPORT AND CHALLENGES

Each of the core constructs has been the subject of a number of studies across a broad range of behaviors and populations. Applying the TTM to new behaviors involves formative research and measurement,[8] followed by intervention development and refinement, eventually leading to formalized efficacy and effectiveness trials. We have selected a sample of these studies for discussion.

STAGE DISTRIBUTION

If interventions are to match the needs of entire populations, there is a need to know the stage distributions of specific high-risk behaviors. A series of studies on smoking in the United States clearly demonstrated that less than 20% of smokers are in the preparation stage in most populations.[9,10] Approximately 40% of smokers are in the precontemplation stage and another 40% are in the contemplation stage. In countries that have not had a long history of tobacco control campaigns, the stage distributions are even more challenging. In Germany, about 70% of smokers are in precontemplation and about 10% of smokers are in preparation,[11] while in China, more than 70% are in precontemplation and about 5% are in preparation.[12] With a sample of 20,000 members of an HMO across 15 health risk behaviors, only a small portion were ready for action.[13]

PROS AND CONS STRUCTURE ACROSS 12 BEHAVIORS

Across studies of 12 different behaviors (smoking cessation, quitting cocaine, weight control, dietary fat reduction, safer sex, condom use, exercise acquisition, sunscreen use, radon testing, delinquency reduction, mammography screening, and physicians practicing preventive medicine), the two-factor structure was remarkably stable. This means that helping patients to make better decisions involves focus on just the pros and cons of changing.

INTEGRATION OF PROS AND CONS AND STAGES OF CHANGE ACROSS 12 HEALTH BEHAVIORS

Stage is not a theory; it is a construct. A theory requires systematic relationships between a set of constructs, ideally culminating in mathematical relationships. Systematic relationships have been found between stages and the pros and cons of changing for 12 health behaviors.

In all 12 studies, the pros of changing were higher than the cons for people in precontemplation.[14] In all 12 studies, the pros increased between precontemplation and contemplation. From contemplation to action for all 12 behaviors, the cons of changing were lower in action than in contemplation. In 11 of the 12 studies, the pros of changing were higher than the cons for people in action. These relationships suggest that to progress from precontemplation, the pros of changing need to increase; to progress from contemplation, the cons need to decrease; and to progress to action, the pros need to be higher than the cons.

STRONG AND WEAK PRINCIPLES OF PROGRESS

Across these same 12 studies and 48 behaviors, mathematic relationships were found between the pros and cons of changing and progress across the stages.[15]

The Strong Principle is: $PC \rightarrow A \cong 1\ SD \uparrow PROS$

Progress from precontemplation (PC) to action (A) involves an approximate one standard deviation (SD) increase in the pros of changing. On intelligence tests, a one SD increase would be 15 points, which is a substantial increase. In a recent meta-analysis of 48 health behaviors and 120 data sets from 10 countries, it was predicted that the pros of changing would increase 1 SD. The remarkable result was that the Strong Principle was confirmed to the second decimal, with the increase being 1.00 SD.[16]

The Weak Principle is: $PC \rightarrow A \cong 0.5\ SD \downarrow CONS$

Progress from precontemplation to action involves approximately 0.5 SD decrease in the cons of changing. The evidence from the recent meta-analysis for the Weak Principle was not as exact, with the result being 0.56 SD. Nevertheless, the multitude of data on 48 behaviors from 120 data sets could be integrated in a single graph that supports the two mathematic principles.

Practical implications of these principles to population health programs are that for change to occur, the pros of changing must increase about twice as much as the cons must decrease. Perhaps twice as much emphasis should be placed on raising the benefits as on reducing the costs or barriers. For example, if couch potatoes in precontemplation can list only 5 pros of exercise, then being too busy will be a big barrier to change. But if program participants come to appreciate that there can be more than 65 benefits for 150 minutes of exercise a week, being too busy becomes a relatively smaller barrier.[17]

PROCESSES OF CHANGE ACROSS BEHAVIORS

One of the assumptions of the TTM is that there is a common set of change processes that people can apply across a broad range of behaviors. Across problem behaviors, the higher order structure of the processes (experiential and behavioral) replicates better than the specific processes.[18] Typically, support has been found for the standard set of 10 processes across behaviors such as smoking, diet, cocaine use, exercise, condom use, and sun exposure. However, the structure of the processes across studies has not been as consistent as the structure of the stages and the pros and cons of changing. The processes used to initiate change vary by behavior. An infrequent behavior, such as conforming to an annual screening test (e.g., mammogram), may require fewer processes to progress to long-term maintenance.[19]

RELATIONSHIP BETWEEN STAGES AND PROCESSES OF CHANGE

One of the earliest empirical integrations was the discovery of systematic relationships between the stages people were in and the processes they were applying. This discovery allowed an integration of processes from theories that were typically seen as incompatible and in conflict. For example, the Freudian theory relied almost entirely on consciousness-raising for producing change. This theory was viewed as incompatible with Skinnerian theory that relied entirely on reinforcement management for modifying behavior. But self-changers did not know that these processes were theoretically incompatible and their behavior revealed that processes from very different theories needed to be emphasized at different stages of change. This integration suggests that, in early stages of population health management, efforts should support the application of cognitive, affective, and evaluative processes to progress through the stages. In later stages, these programs should rely more on commitments, conditioning, rewards, environmental controls, and support to progress toward maintenance or termination.

Table 2-1 has important practical implications to population health projects. To help people progress from precontemplation to contemplation, processes such as consciousness raising and dramatic relief need to be applied. Applying reinforcement management, counterconditioning, and stimulus control processes in precontemplation would represent a theoretical, empirical, and practical mistake. Conversely, such strategies would be optimally matched for people in the action stage.

Integration of the processes and stages has not been as consistent as the integration of the stages with the pros and cons of changing. Part of the problem may be the greater complexity of integrating 10 processes across six stages, but the processes of change require more basic research.

APPLIED STUDIES

A large, diverse body of evidence on the application of TTM has revealed several trends. The most common application involves TTM computerized, tailored communications, which match intervention messages to an individual's particular needs[20,21] across all TTM constructs. Tailored interventions are population-based. They combine the best of population health with clinical health to provide individualized help. Providers could prescribe them to their patients. For example, individuals in precontemplation could receive feedback designed to increase their pros of changing to help them progress to contemplation. These interventions have most commonly been either printed on-site or mailed to participants at home.[22] However, a growing range of applications are developing, and developers are evaluating more immediate multimedia computerized, tailored interventions[23] that can be delivered in clinic settings, at worksites, in schools, or online at home.

The growing range of settings where TTM is being applied also includes primary care offices,[24,25,26] churches,[27] campuses,[28] and communities.[29] Increasingly, employers and health plans are making such TTM-tailored programs available to entire employee or subscriber populations. Providers can assess whether patients have access to such programs and recommend the patients apply the programs as part of the change process that has been initiated through the clinical relationship. A recent meta-analysis of tailored print communications found that TTM was the most commonly used theory across a broad range of behaviors.[30] TTM or Stage of Change Models were used in 35 of the 53 studies. In terms of effectiveness, significantly greater effect sizes were produced when tailored communications included each of the following TTM constructs: stages of change, pros and cons of changing, self-efficacy, and processes of change.[30] In contrast, interventions that included the non-TTM construct of perceived susceptibility had significantly worse outcomes. Tailoring non-TTM constructs, like social norms and behavioral intentions, did not produce significant differences.[30]

These unprecedented impacts require scientific and professional shifts in our approach to population health:

- from an action paradigm to a stage paradigm;
- from reactive to proactive recruitment of participants;
- from expecting participants to match the needs of our programs to having our programs match their needs;
- from clinic-based to community-based behavioral health programs that still apply the field's most powerful individualized and interactive intervention strategies; and
- from assuming some groups do not have the ability to change to making sure that all groups have easy accessibility to evidence-based programs that provide stage-matched tailored interventions. Without such access, behavior change programs cannot serve entire populations.

MULTIPLE BEHAVIOR CHANGE PROGRAMS: INCREASING IMPACTS

One of the greatest challenges for the application of any theory is to keep raising the bar, that is, to be able to increase the theory's impact on enhancing health. Our original impact equation was Impact = Reach × Efficacy. With TTM clinical trials having recruited 80% or more of eligible smokers in a population, any increase in impact would have to come from increased efficacy, such as the abstinence rate among smokers. After more than a decade of attempts, this promise has not been fulfilled. The reason for a decline in outcomes probably was due to a mismatch of an action-oriented intervention to smokers who were not prepared to quit.[31] For example, doubling the number of computer interactions failed to improve efficacy because there were no dose–response relationships.[32] Adding a handheld computer designed to bring smoking under stimulus control, followed by nicotine fading, actually produced worse outcomes. Similarly, providing patches for nicotine replacement therapy (NRT) also showed no evidence of increasing efficacy.[33] Adding telecounseling, with computers calling smokers on a set schedule and interacting with them on the telephone or smokers calling into the computers, also failed to increase efficacy.[33]

Recruitment limitations create a ceiling on recruitment and efficacy, which have not improved since our first population-based clinical trial in 2001. This is a problem for many interventions in the realms of behavioral health and mental health. The efficacy of antidepressant medication has not improved in more than 25 years, even though the pharmaceutical industry has invested many resources to produce breakthroughs that could generate huge profits.

One potential alternative for TTM is to treat multiple behaviors in a population because populations with multiple behavior risks are at greatest risk for both chronic disease and premature death. These multiply comorbid populations also account for a disproportionate percentage of healthcare costs. The best estimates are that about 60% of healthcare costs are generated by about 15% of populations, who have multiple behavior risks and medical conditions.[34] The research literature indicates that changing multiple behaviors on a population basis would be a particularly risky test. A thorough review of the literature funded by the Robert Wood Johnson Foundation failed to find any evidence for the efficacy of treating multiple behaviors. The established wisdom has been that it is not possible to successfully treat multiple behaviors simultaneously, because it places too many demands on a population.[35] An example might be a patient in his late 40s, who was diagnosed with type 2 diabetes; his physician told him he needed to test his glucose four times a day, take his medications twice a day, change his diet, start to exercise, quit smoking, and lower his stress. Such prescriptions for so much action would be overwhelming, and this patient was only prepared to take action on one behavior. With the help of a healthcare provider, this patient would likely make progress toward changing multiple behaviors.

The studies conducted to date on **multiple behavior changes** have been limited by reliance on the action paradigm, the frequent use of quasi-experimental designs, and the lack of applying the most promising interventions, such as interactive and individualized TTM-tailored communications.[36] From a TTM perspective, applying an action paradigm to multiple behaviors would indeed risk overwhelming populations, because action is the most demanding stage and taking action on two or more behaviors at once could be overwhelming. Furthermore, in individuals with four health behavior risks, like smoking, diet, sun exposure, and sedentary lifestyles, less than 10% of the population was ready to take action on two or more behaviors.[37] The same thing was true for populations with diabetes who needed to change four behaviors.[38]

Applying our best practices through the use of a stage-based multiple behavior manual and computerized tailored feedback reports over 12 months, we proactively intervened on a population of parents of teens who were participating in parallel projects at school.[39] We were able to engage 83.6% of the available parents. The treatment group received up to three expert system reports at 0, 6, and 12 months. At 24 months, the treatment group was outperforming the control on all three cancer prevention behaviors: smoking cessation, healthier diets, and safer sun exposure practices.

With a population of 5,545 patients from primary care practices, we were able to proactively recruit 65% for a second multiple behavior change project.[40] In this project, mammography screening was targeted in addition to the three aforementioned cancer prevention behaviors. Significant treatment effects were found for all four target behaviors at 24 months.

Comparisons across three multiple-risk behavior studies demonstrated that the efficacy rates for smoking cessation were no better than the 22% and 25% abstinence effect that we consistently found when targeting only the single behavior of smoking.[41] Further, it was found that smokers with a single risk were no more successful in quitting than smokers who were treated for two or three risk behaviors. The same was found for participants with a single risk of diet or sun exposure compared to those with two or three risk behaviors. Overall, these results indicate that TTM-tailored interventions may be producing unprecedented impacts on multiple behaviors for disease prevention and health promotion.

FUTURE RESEARCH

While research results to date are encouraging, much still needs to be done to advance practical behavior change through evidence-based efforts such as the Transtheoretical Model. Basic research needs to be done with other theoretical variables, such as processes of resistance, framing, and problem severity, to determine if such variables relate systematically to the stages and if they predict progress across particular stages. More research is needed on the structure or integration of the processes and stages of change across a broad range of behaviors, including acquisition behaviors such as exercise and extinction behaviors like what has been accomplished for smoking cessation.[42] What modifications are needed for specific types of behaviors, such as fewer processes, perhaps, for infrequent behaviors like mammography screening?

Because tailored communications represent the most promising interventions for applying TTM to entire populations, more research is needed comparing the effectiveness, efficiency, and impacts of alternative technologies. The Internet is excellent for individualized interactions at low cost, but it has not produced the high participation rates generated by person-to-person outreach via telephone or visits to primary care practitioners. Increasingly, employers are incentivizing employee populations to participate in more integrated

Internet, telephone, and provider programs. Interventions that were once seen as applicable only on an individual basis are being applied as high-impact programs for population health.

How do diverse populations respond to stage-matched interventions and to high-tech systems? How could programs best be tailored to meet the needs of diverse populations? Could menus of alternative intervention modalities (e.g., telephone, Internet, neighborhood or church leaders, person-to-person, or community programs) empower diverse populations to best match health-enhancing programs to their particular needs?

Changing multiple behaviors represents special challenges, such as the number of demands placed on participants and providers. Alternative strategies need to be tried beyond the sequential (one at a time) and simultaneous (all treated intensely at the same time). Integrative approaches are promising. For example, with bullying prevention, there are multiple behaviors (e.g., hitting, stealing, ostracizing, mean gossiping, labeling, damaging personal belongings) and multiple roles (bully, victim, and passive bystander) that need to be treated. An integrated approach is needed to address these needs in the given time constraints. If behavior change is construct-driven (e.g., by stage or self-efficacy), what is a higher order construct that could integrate all of these more concrete behaviors and roles? In a study where relating with mutual respect was used as a higher order construct, significant and important improvements across roles and behaviors were found for elementary, middle, and high school students.[43] As with any theory, effective applications may be limited more by our creativity than by the ability of the theory to drive significant research and effective interventions.

FUTURE PRACTICE

Applying TTM on a population basis to change multiple health risks has required the use of innovative paradigms that complement established paradigms. Table 2-2 illustrates how a population paradigm using proactive outreach to homes complements the individual patient paradigm that passively reacts when patients seek clinical services. The use of the stage paradigm complements the action paradigm which assumes that because patients are seeking services, they are prepared to take action. The use of CTIs complements the traditional reliance on clinicians, and the treatment of multiple behaviors complements the established clinical wisdom of treating one behavior at a time. The population-theme paradigm based on impacts (reach × efficacy × Σ # of behaviors changed) complements individualized clinical trials with select samples that rely on efficacy. Integrating these new paradigms can produce the foundation for a well-care system to complement the established sick-care system. Combining the two systems would enhance the health and well-being of many more people by healing the sick, while maximizing wellness for all.

Table 2-2 Inclusive Care from Two Clusters of Paradigms for Individual Patients and Entire Populations

Patient Health	complemented by	Population Health
1. Individual patients		Entire populations
2. Passive reactance		Proactive
3. Acute conditions		Chronic conditions
4. Efficacy trials		Effectiveness trials
5. Action-oriented		Stage-based
6. Clinic-based		Home-based
7. Clinician-delivered		Technology-delivered
8. Standardized		Tailored
9. Single target behavior		Multiple target behaviors
10. Fragmented		Integrated

CONCLUSIONS

The Transtheoretical Model is a dynamic theory of change and it must remain open to modifications and enhancements as more students, scientists, and practitioners apply the stage paradigm to a growing number of diverse theoretical issues, public health problems, and at-risk populations.

STUDY AND DISCUSSION QUESTIONS

1. What is the Transtheoretical Model of Behavior Change?
2. What are the stages of change included in the Transtheoretical Model?
3. What is your role, as a healthcare provider, in helping a patient who is in precontemplation realize the benefits of changing?
4. If you are encountered by a smoker with multiple health behavior risks, how would you help manage this patient's need for multiple behavior changes?

SUGGESTED READINGS AND WEB SITES

READINGS

Hall KL, Rossi JS. Meta-analytic examination of the strong and weak principles across 48 health behaviors. *Prev Med*, 2008;46(3):266–274.

Prochaska JO, DiClemente CC, Norcross JC. In search of how people change: applications to addictive behaviors. *Am Psychol.* 1992;47(9):1102–1114.

Prochaska JO, Norcross JC, DiClemente CC. *Changing for Good.* New York, NY: Morrow; 1994.

Prochaska JO, Velicer WF, Redding C, et al. Stage-based expert systems to guide a population of primary care patients to quit smoking, eat healthier, prevent skin cancer, and receive regular mammograms. *Prev Med.* 2005;41(2):406–416.

WEB SITES

Basic Transtheoretical Model Training: contact elearning@prochange.com

Cancer Prevention Research Center: www.uri.edu/research/cprc

Coaches' Guide for Using the TTM with Clients: contact info@prochange.com

Pro-Change Behavior Systems, Inc.: www.prochange.com

REFERENCES

1. Prochaska JO, Norcross JC. *Systems of Psychotherapy: A Transtheoretical Analysis.* 7th ed. Belmont, CA: Brooks/Cole, Cengage Learning; 2009.

2. DiClemente CC, Prochaska JO. Self-change and therapy change of smoking behavior: a comparison of processes of change in cessation and maintenance. *Addict Behav.* 1982;7(2):133–142.

3. Prochaska JO, DiClemente CC. Stages and processes of self-change of smoking: toward an integrative model of change. *J Consult Clin Psychol.* 1983;51(3):390–395.

4. US Department of Health and Human Services. *The Health Benefits of Smoking Cessation: A Report of the Surgeon General.* Washington, DC: US Department of Health and Human Services; 1990. DHHS Publication No. (CDC) 90–8416.

5. Snow MG, Prochaska JO, Rossi JS. Stages of change for smoking cessation among former problem drinkers: a cross-sectional analysis. *J Subst Abuse.* 1992;4(2):107–116.

6. Janis IL, Mann L. *Decision Making: A Psychological Analysis of Conflict, Choice, and Commitment.* London: Cassel & Collier Macmillan; 1977.

7. Bandura A. Self-efficacy mechanism in human agency. *Am Psychol.* 1982;37(2):122–147.

8. Redding CA, Maddock JE, Rossi JS. The sequential approach to measurement of health behavior constructs: issues in selecting and developing measures. *Californian J Health Promotion.* 2006; 4(1):83–101.

9. Velicer WF, Fava JL, Prochaska JO, Abrams DB, Emmons KM, Pierce JP. Distribution of smokers by stage in three representative samples. *Prev Med.* 1995;24(4):401–411.

10. Wewers ME, Stillman FA, Hartman AM, Shopland DR. Distribution of daily smokers by stage of change: Current Population Survey results. *Prev Med.* 2003;36(6):710–720.

11. Etter JF, Perneger TV, Ronchi A. Distributions of smokers by stage: international comparison and association with smoking prevalence. *Prev Med.* 1997;26(4):580–585.

12. Yang G, Ma J, Chen A, et al. Smoking cessation in China: findings from the 1996 national prevalence survey. *Tob Control.* 2001;10(2):170–174.

13. Rossi JS. Stages of change for 15 health risk behaviors in an HMO population. Paper presented at 13th meeting of the Society for Behavioral Medicine; 1992; New York, NY.

14. Prochaska JO, Velicer WF, Rossi JS, et al. Stages of change and decisional balance for 12 problem behaviors. *Health Psychol.* 1994;13(1):39–46.

15. Prochaska JO. Strong and weak principles for progressing from precontemplation to action on the basis of twelve problem behaviors. *Health Psychol.* 1994;13(1):47–51.

16. Hall KL, Rossi JS. Meta-analytic examination of the strong and weak principles across 48 health behaviors. *Prev Med*, 2008;46(3):266–274.

17. Johnson SS, Paiva AL, Cummins CO, et al. Transtheoretical model-based multiple behavior intervention for weight management: effectiveness on a population basis. *Prev Med*. 2008;46(3): 238–246.

18. Rossi JS. Common processes of change across nine problem behaviors. Paper presented at: 100th meeting of the American Psychological Association; 1992; Washington, D.C.

19. Rakowski WR, Ehrich B, Goldstein MG, et al. Increasing mammography among women aged 40–74 by use of a stage-matched, tailored intervention. *Prev Med*. 1998;27(5 Pt 1P):748–756.

20. Kreuter MW, Strecher VJ, Glassman B. One size does not fit all: the case for tailoring print materials. *Ann Behav Med*. 1999;21(4):276–283.

21. Skinner CS, Campbell MD, Rimer BK, Curry S, Prochaska JO. How effective is tailored print communication? *Ann Behav Med*. 1999;21(4): 290–298.

22. Velicer WF, Prochaska JO, Bellis JM, et al. An expert system intervention for smoking cessation. *Addict Behav*. 1993;18(3):269–290.

23. Mauriello LM, Sherman KJ, Driskell MM, Prochaska JM. Using interactive behavior change technology to intervene on physical activity and nutrition with adolescents. *Adolesc Med*. 2007; 18(2):383–399.

24. Goldstein MG, Pinto BM, Marcus BH, et al. Physician-based physical activity counseling for middle-aged and older adults: a randomized trial. *Ann Behav Med*. 1999;21(1):40–47.

25. Hoffman A, Redding CA, Goldberg DN, et al. Computer expert systems for African-American smokers in physicians' offices: a feasibility study. *Prev Med*. 2006;43(3):204–211.

26. Hollis JF, Polen MR, Whitlock EP, et al. Teen REACH: outcomes from a randomized, controlled trial of a tobacco reduction program for teens seen in primary medical care. *Pediatr*. 2005;115(4):981–989.

27. Voorhees CC, Stillman FA, Swank RT, Heagerty PJ, Levine DM, Becker DM. Heart, body, and soul: impact of church-based smoking cessation interventions on readiness to quit. *Prev Med*. 1996;25(3):277–285.

28. Prochaska JM, Prochaska JO, Cohen FC, Gomes SO, Laforge RG, Eastwood AL. The Transtheoretical Model of Change for multi-level interventions for alcohol abuse on campus. *J Alcohol Drug Educ*. 2004;47(3):34–50.

29. The CDC AIDS Community Demonstration Projects Research Group. Community-level HIV intervention in 5 cities: final outcome data from the CDC AIDS Community Demonstration Projects. *Am J Public Health*. 1999;89(3):336–345.

30. Noar SM, Benac CN, Harris MS. Does tailoring matter? Meta-analytic review of tailored print health behavior change interventions. *Psychol Bull*. 2007;133(4):673–693.

31. Prochaska JO, Velicer WF, Fava JL, Rossi JS, Tsoh JY. Evaluating a population-based recruitment approach and a stage-based expert system intervention for smoking cessation. *Addic Behav*. 2001;26(4):583–602.

32. Velicer WF, Prochaska JO, Fava JL, Laforge RG, Rossi JS. Interactive versus noninteractive interventions and dose–response relationships for stage-matched smoking cessation programs in a managed care setting. *Health Psychol*. 1999;18(1): 21–28.

33. Velicer WF, Friedman RH, Fava JL, et al. Evaluating nicotine replacement therapy and stage-based therapies in a population-based effectiveness trial. *J Consult Clin Psychol*. 2006;74(6):1162–1172.

34. Edington DW. Emerging research: a view from one research center. *Am J Health Promot*. 2001; 15(5):341–349.

35. Patterson R, ed. *Changing Patient Behavior: Improving Outcomes in Health and Disease Management*. San Francisco, CA: Jossey-Bass; 2001.

36. Prochaska JO, Velicer WF, Fava JL, et al. Counselor and stimulus control enhancements of a stage-matched expert system intervention for smokers in a managed care setting. *Prev Med*. 2001;32(1):23–32.

37. Prochaska JO, Velicer WF. The transtheoretical model of health behavior change. *Am J Health Promot*. 1997;12(1):38–48.

38. Ruggiero L, Glasgow R, Dryfoos JM, et al. Diabetes self-management: self-reported recommendations and patterns in a large population. *Diabetes Care.* 1997;20(4):568–576.

39. Prochaska JO, Velicer WF, Rossi JS, et al. Multiple risk expert systems: impact of simultaneous stage-matched expert system interventions for smoking, high-fat diet, and sun exposure in a population of parents. *Health Psychol.* 2004;3(5):503–516.

40. Prochaska JO, Velicer WF, Redding C, et al. Stage-based expert systems to guide a population of primary care patients to quit smoking, eat healthier, prevent skin cancer, and receive regular mammograms. *Prev Med.* 2005;41(2):406–416.

41. Prochaska JJ, Velicer WF, Prochaska JO, Delucchi K, Hall SM. Comparing intervention outcomes in smokers treated for single versus multiple behavioral risks. *Health Psychol.* 2006;25(3):380–388.

42. Rosen CS. Is the sequencing of change processes by stage consistent across health problems? A meta-analysis. *Health Psychol.* 2000;19(6):593–604.

43. Evers KE, Prochaska JO, Mauriello LM, Padula JA, Prochaska JM. A randomized clinical trial of a population- and transtheoretical model-based stress-management intervention. *Health Psychol.* 2006;25(4):521–529.

Chapter 3

HEALTH SYSTEM NAVIGATION: THE ROLE OF HEALTH ADVOCACY AND ASSISTANCE PROGRAMS

ABBIE LEIBOWITZ, MD, FAAP

Executive Summary

Health advocate—a guiding light through a disintegrated system

Health care is confusing and difficult to navigate for the average consumer. Add the stress placed on an individual and a family dealing with a chronic, serious, or life-threatening illness, and even those with a reasonable understanding of how health benefits and care delivery systems work are likely to be overwhelmed. As health insurance costs have risen, individuals buying coverage on their own and companies offering health benefits to their employees have found that they can no longer afford to buy or offer the same level of coverage. The result has been a combination of higher premiums, plan designs that provide less coverage and require greater individual participation in the care decision process, and greater cost shifts from employers to employees. These conditions have caused people to "get lost" in the healthcare system. While these disenfranchised individuals are considered a population in their own right, it is more useful to think of them as a subset of the larger population of people with healthcare issues, diseases, and chronic needs. They need help dealing with health benefits and medical services, and without this assistance they are unlikely to reach the best possible medical outcomes. Population health must address the needs of the entire population.

The idea of a health advocate as a guide to help individuals more efficiently and effectively use the healthcare system is not a new concept. To a certain extent, even the managed care models going back to the 1980s envisioned primary care physicians becoming health advocates, guiding their patients through the disjointed healthcare system and serving as a coordinator of all of their healthcare needs. However, over the last 10 years, health advocacy and assistance programs have developed as a new benefit service category targeted at employers. These programs support individuals and help them navigate through the healthcare system. Employers have embraced these programs as a means of accomplishing their goal of promoting the employees' responsibility for lifestyle and medical decisions. Employers' support for health advocacy and assistance is based on their belief that engaging the employee in his or her care to a greater degree will help the company constrain the increasing cost of health benefits.

There are several models of advocacy and assistance programs to accomplish employee engagement. Opt-in, open-ended programs invite members to contact an advocate when they have an issue of any sort related to their health care. Other programs use claims and other administrative data to identify various clinical populations, targeting interventions specific to the group, much like disease management programs. While intervention-specific efforts are likely to identify consumers who need assistance and are willing to participate, the more inclusive scope of opt-in, open-ended models increases the likelihood of engaging more people and identifying those who are earlier in the course of dealing with their medical conditions.[1]

Health insurers have taken steps to make their systems more transparent and have improved the clinical and administrative support they offer their members under the umbrella of becoming the member's "advocate."[2] The uptake of advocacy and assistance programs in the individual consumer market has been slower, although a Google search reveals no shortage of companies and individuals offering these services. Some programs feature nurses and other health professionals who will help people through a clinical situation. Others focus on negotiating medical bills to lower a consumer's out-of-pocket costs and are paid by receiving a percentage of the savings they achieve.[3–6]

Advocacy programs integrate services across multiple vendors and coordinate care between multiple providers, improving the efficiency and effectiveness of the medical system and resolving disputes that may arise between those who insure or administer health benefits programs and the consumers or members who use them. Large employers find these integration opportunities to be especially useful as a means of making their multivendor health benefits programs more usable and effective.

Helping users navigate the confusing healthcare environment is both a clinically effective and a cost-effective strategy. These programs relieve stress, increase job productivity, and save money by helping patients more readily access qualified providers to receive appropriate care in a timely manner. Their value may not be adequately captured by traditional measures of monetary return. By providing vital navigation assistance and support to individuals at their time of need, advocacy and assistance programs increase consumer engagement in the healthcare system and in their own and their family's health management, resulting in a greater likelihood of improved medical outcomes and, typically, lower medical costs.

Learning Objectives

1. Examine the forces driving employers and health plans to find new strategies for controlling health costs.
2. Review the different types and varying challenges of health benefits programs offered in different employer market segments.
3. Appreciate consumers' needs for help navigating the healthcare system.
4. Assess the total value that advocacy and assistance programs provide.

Key Words

carve-outs

consumer-driven health care

fully insured

health advocate

pharmacy benefit manager (PBM)

preferred provider organization (PPO)

self-insured

step-edit

third-party administrator (TPA)

INTRODUCTION

The U.S. healthcare system is technologically sophisticated and systematically disorganized. We spend more per capita on health care than any other developed country, but the quality of our medical care is not better than many countries that spend considerably less.[7,8] Our healthcare system offers seemingly limitless options to those who can understand its access points, have the means to pay for its services, and possess the wherewithal to make reasonable decisions regarding the many treatment options it offers. Unfortunately, the number of individuals possessing these skills is relatively small. Add the stress of dealing with a serious medical condition, the need to find one's way through the boundless online environment of legitimate and bogus health information, and the confusion of dealing with the provisions of a health insurance program, and the challenges to navigation appear almost insurmountable.

We often look at healthcare issues in terms of populations and refer to population health because, ultimately, it is possible to categorize every individual into a referent group based on his or her characteristics and personal medical circumstances. Diabetics, patients with glaucoma, asthmatics, and individuals with heart disease are viewed by healthcare providers and payers as members of a subgroup of the population who have a common condition. One can view this patient-centered approach at a macro- or a micro-level to understand a population's health needs, further stratifying individuals by clinical severity, medications they take, companies they work for, insurance plans they belong to, and doctors they see. Substituting order for chaos somehow reassures us that we can, in some way, manage to meet the needs of all those who make up these disparate groups. However, health care is ultimately delivered to individuals and only two groups really exist: those with a health-associated problem and those at risk for developing a health problem. Regardless of the group in which individuals find themselves, help navigating the healthcare system could prove tremendously useful in gaining access to the appropriate care at the appropriate time.

Health advocates, who help patients navigate the healthcare system, recognize two groups of consumers: those who are able to find their way through the healthcare maze and those who cannot. Health advocacy and assistance programs focus on assisting those "lost" somewhere in the healthcare system. While we can consider these individuals to be a population in their own right, it is more useful to consider them to be merely a subset of the larger population of people with healthcare issues, diseases, and chronic needs. They need help dealing with health benefits and medical services, and without this assistance they are unlikely to reach the best possible medical outcomes. Because they use the medical care system inefficiently, they also incur unnecessary costs. They are individuals, family members, employees, and health plan members, and, unfortunately, their numbers are growing as our system of health benefits and medical delivery becomes increasingly more fragmented and disorganized. They are people who are inevitably being forced to participate in a self-service healthcare environment without being provided the skills or guidance to succeed, and the consequences of their predicament affect us all.

THE EMERGENCE OF HEALTH ADVOCACY AND ASSISTANCE PROGRAMS

Over the last 10 years, a new category of "health advocates" has emerged. These individuals and companies offer assistance to consumers for a fee, paid either directly or as a benefit incorporated into an employer's or group's health benefits program.[6,9] For the purposes of this discussion, we will focus on the independent advocacy companies providing health assistance and navigational support as an employer benefit because this model has gained impressive traction. This rapidly growing service sector has established its value as a means of helping people deal with a myriad of health, benefits, and access issues, providing support to individuals facing the healthcare system on their own.[10]

This focus is not meant to diminish in any way our recognition of the vitally important role played by thousands of advocacy groups across the country that work in support of changes in social and health systems to make the systems more responsive to the needs of individuals with chronic conditions and provide invaluable services to the community and those in need. In many ways, the goals of such organizations become confluent with those of commercial advocacy and assistance organizations, and to the extent that individual consumers are helped in their quest for better health, this is a good outcome. The best of these programs work in concert with the patient's physicians, reinforcing the concept of a holistic medical home and enhancing the opportunity for the individual to receive the best possible health result.

GOALS OF ADVOCACY AND ASSISTANCE PROGRAMS

What measures can we use to assess whether health advocacy programs are effective? Is their goal consumer engagement? Empowerment? Education? Behavior change? Change in the underlying health system? Transparency? Cost reduction? Or is the goal simply to help the individual with a problem find a way to a solution? Whether or not we formally set out to change consumer behavior, most people will learn from an experience. Certainly, it would be useful if those who design health benefits would learn from the travails of their employees and members, and modify the structure of their programs to make them easier to use. It would be helpful if health insurers and plan administrators recognized the value of making information on provider performance more accessible and easier to understand. It would be easier to explain the concept of a medical home if doctors were paid to spend more time with patients and took a more active role in coordinating access to medical services for them. And it would go a long way to reduce consumer frustration if hospitals would adopt billing practices that an average person could easily understand. However, in the meantime, those in the advocacy and assistance role are simply trying to help people navigate the health system and cope. (See Box 3-1)

BOX 3-1 FACTORS DRIVING HEALTH ADVOCACY

- Healthcare cost increases
- The complexity of health benefits programs
- Consumers being asked to assume greater responsibility for managing their own health
- Medical care system disorganization and inefficiencies
- Access to care problems
- Increasing medical technology and super specialization
- Information overload
- Increasing focus on quality of care and patient safety
- The difficulty of managing a parent's health issues
- Privacy concerns
- Nowhere else to turn for help

THE CONSTITUENTS

THE EMPLOYERS' PERSPECTIVE

While the many constituencies in the healthcare continuum are fundamentally interconnected, we will start by examining the employers' perspective because, at this time, the majority of Americans obtain health benefits through their employer. Sixty percent of employers offer health benefits to their employees. Of the employers who have 50 or more employees, 95% offer benefits.[11]

Regardless of their size, companies are focused on the cost of health benefits. They seek to buy health benefits within some budgeted allocation and, to the degree that it can be measured, they want the best value for the price. Employers understand that good health benefits encourage good employee health, reduce absenteeism, increase productivity, and provide an effective tool for attracting new employees and retaining existing ones. However, in a competitive global business environment, businesses are forced to take a hard look at the health benefits they offer and to take steps to constrain the seemingly relentless increase in their costs.[12] The result of these well-intentioned efforts is often a confusing, multilayered array of programs that become difficult, if not impossible, for the average employee to understand and use effectively.

According to the Kaiser Family Foundation, the average health insurance premium for a family of four in 2009 reached $13,375.[11] Since 1999, the average cost of family health insurance has increased 131%, while wages over this period have increased only 29%.[11,13] Where possible, employers use adjustments in the design of their health benefit offerings to encourage certain employee behaviors that they believe will help control the company's healthcare costs.[14]

It is convenient to consider employers on the basis of size, because so many of the benefit decisions they make are affected by the number of employees for whom they provide health coverage. Although we must be flexible in classification, for the purposes of this discussion we will define small employers as those with fewer than 100 employees, the middle market as those employers with 100 to 1,500 employees, and large employers as those with more than 1,500 employees.

In the small-employer market, health benefits programs tend to be relatively straightforward. The company is usually "insured," meaning it pays a premium to the insurance company for coverage and the benefits programs it offers follow one of several "standard" options offered by the health insurer they choose. While the benefits are relatively clear-cut, there are typically few supports within the employer's environment to answer complicated benefit questions or deal with coverage or access problems. Small companies rarely have a dedicated human resources or benefits administration staff. The small companies and the health plans that do business in this market depend on health benefits brokers to help them shop for the best available (and typically least expensive) coverage and to support their needs after the sale.

The middle market is a bit more complicated. Depending on the cost of health insurance on an insured or premium basis, companies with as few as 200 employees may decide to be "**self-insured**." They contract with an administrator, which may be a health insurer or a **third-party administrator (TPA)**, to administer their health benefits program and pay bills using the plan's underlying contracts. While largely broker driven, health benefits consultants also compete for the business of servicing these accounts.

With self-insurance comes the ability to craft a benefits program unique to the perceived needs of the company or organization, which may not align with the needs or desires of the employees. In this space, we start to see the introduction of "**carve-outs**," or health benefits services that are not offered by the company's basic health coverage provider. Pharmacy benefits are commonly provided using this carve-out approach. Employers that carve out their pharmacy benefits typically contract with a **pharmacy benefit manager (PBM)** to administer the prescription drug coverage program. These programs promote the use of mail-order pharmacies and are structured around a "cost-advantaged" formulary that encourages the use of less expensive generic drugs. They feature multiple tiers of copays and several layers of **step-edits** and precertification requirements. It is easy to see how this commonplace approach complicates the simple consumer task of getting a prescription filled.[15]

Large employers are nearly universally self-insured. Their benefits programs typically include an array of programs purchased from multiple unrelated benefits vendors, a so-called "Best of Breed" approach. In addition to the plan administrator (more likely to be a health plan than a TPA in the largest end of this market segment), we may see carve-out PBMs, mental health managers, disease management programs, general case managers, cancer case managers, transplant case managers, an employee assistance program (EAP), a telephonic nurse triage service, and a "wellness" program, as well as the expected dental coverage, workers' compensation, and short-term and long-term disability management programs. Sometimes, these different vendor relationships are managed by the health plan and are presented as though they were the plan's services, but in many large employer benefits programs there could be more than 20 different vendors providing some aspect of coverage or services in some way related to the health benefits an employee receives.[16,17]

Looking at the situation objectively, there are both good motives and bad effects that coexist in many employer benefit strategies. Pharmacy formularies encourage the use of generic drugs, which offer lower cost and equivalent efficacy to branded products, but introduce a complexity to the simple process of getting a prescription filled. Mail-order drug programs reduce costs but require physicians to write a prescription for a 90-day supply and place the responsibility on the consumer to reorder the medication with enough time so that therapy is not interrupted. Mental health provider networks may channel individuals into care from less highly trained and less expensive professionals, but may also make access to traditional psychiatric care more difficult for those who need it. Disease management and case management programs help individuals with chronic conditions focus on strategies to improve their health, but often exist in isolation, disconnected from the patient's relationship with their treating physician. In their quest to get the injured worker back to work as soon as possible, disability management and workers' compensation programs may paradoxically increase the likelihood that injured workers receive surgery and other aggressive therapies rather than giving time for conservative treatment to work.[18–21] For the patient receiving conflicting advice, independent advocates can help explain the rationales of the different approaches and support the individual through the decision process.

It is little wonder that advocacy and assistance programs have gained popularity among employers as a means of helping employees navigate the healthcare system.

THE CONSUMER'S PERSPECTIVE—CONSUMER-DRIVEN HEALTH CARE

While many employers offer a choice of plans, **preferred provider organization (PPO)** plans that include "in-network" and "out-of-network" options dominate the benefits landscape.[11] These benefit designs also introduce an increased level of complexity because individuals deal with balance billing from out-of-network providers and "reasonable and customary" (R&C) reimbursement rates.

Today's health benefits programs shift costs to the consumer in the form of higher payroll contributions, larger deductibles, and greater coinsurance responsibilities and by introducing benefit limitations and exclusions.[11] Such programs have been dubbed "**consumer-driven health care**" because they encourage the individual to take a greater role in making healthcare decisions and managing their own health. The obvious driver is the out-of-pocket costs the consumer has to pay. The belief is that if people have to spend more of their own money on health care, they will spend it more wisely.[14,22] Many emphasize the ability of these programs to motivate individuals to be more conscious of their health and the impact of lifestyle choices, believing that such programs will lead people to take better care of themselves to avoid preventable health expenses in the future.[23]

There is no question that consumers who are asked to pay more money out of pocket get less care. There is good documentation of this effect from the RAND studies of the 1970s. However, there is also no doubt that consumers do not discriminate well between care they need and care that is unnecessary when making these decisions.[24]

One can fairly say that the long-term health status effects of these programs on populations and communities are uncertain.[24] However, regardless of whether these programs are or will be effective, shifting costs to employees and requiring them to be more engaged in managing their own health is an approach not likely to disappear anytime soon. However, as a strategy in isolation, simply asking people to pay more of their own money for health care does not make anyone any smarter about using the healthcare system. Neither does it make the system more transparent or easier to navigate.

Additionally, the tools available to consumers to help them function as informed users of the healthcare system are few. Finding quality provider information applicable to one's needs, discussing billing issues with a hospital, appealing a denial of coverage, finding qualified physicians, getting appointments with specialists, understanding what is said at a doctor's visit, and evaluating the validity of information from the Internet are daunting tasks, and the difficulty of dealing with them creates great consumer frustration. Advocacy and assistance programs are a good fit in such situations, providing support to help individuals navigate the healthcare world they must face.

THE PHYSICIAN'S PERSPECTIVE

Physicians often try to insulate themselves from their patients' health benefit issues. Years of frustration with administrative hassles and payment problems have driven many doctors to drop out of provider networks and Medicare altogether.[25] Ironically, the popularity of PPO plans with their out-of-network benefits (however limited they may be), may encourage this trend.

Though most doctors are willing to help their patients deal with administrative issues up to a point, the truth is that they do not have the time, may not have the expertise, and are not paid to spend hours out of each day talking with health plan administrators on their patients' behalf. While a physician may be willing to make a reasonable effort to deal with a formulary exception or make a call to get a piece of equipment covered, when the problem becomes too time-intensive they drop out of the process, leaving it to the patients to deal with it on their own.[26]

Facing the realities of a changing benefit environment, doctors have been supporters of health advocacy and assistance programs. They recognize that these programs support the concept of a medical home and reinforce the patient–physician relationship. Not surprisingly, doctors understand the value of helping the patient navigate the healthcare system, because much of the help and support offered by advocacy and assistance companies is similar to what a physician would want to do for a patient if time permitted.

THE PERSPECTIVE OF HEALTH PLANS AND ADMINISTRATORS

Several health plans have their own advocacy programs. These programs primarily focus on issues involving the plan's network, benefits, and programs. Many of these programs are enhancements to the member assistance and clinical management services the plan offers.

Although their concerns may be overstated, consumers as a whole don't trust health plans. In the Kaiser Family Foundation's April 2004 health poll, two-thirds of consumers said that they were "very worried" or "somewhat worried" that their health plan was more concerned about saving money than providing the right treatment for its members.[27] In an earlier study, researchers found that just less than half of the adult health plan members surveyed reported that they had experienced a problem with their health plan in the previous year.[28] In the face of this mistrust, it is hard for the health plan to be the solution to the members' issues when the health plans are also part of the problem.

Health advocacy programs commonly interface with health plans and administrators on their members' behalf. These interactions are typically free of the acrimony that might exist if the member contacted the plan directly. Additionally, dealing with an experienced advocate can be more efficient for the health plan. The advocate better understands the member's myriad of benefits, services, and the specific employer plan's policies, enabling the advocate to quickly get to the root of the problem, reducing the time the health plan's staff would have spent dealing with the issue had the member called. The advocate may, and frequently does, give the member the same answer they received from the health plan, but coming from a trusted, independent source with no agenda, the response is more likely to be well received, trusted, and acted upon.

HEALTH ADVOCACY AS AN INDEPENDENT SERVICE

There is no shortage of individuals and organizations offering services related to health advocacy. Type "health advocate" into Google and you'll get more than 25 million "hits" in English (in 0.58 seconds).[29] However, the marketplace is dominated by a handful of companies that sell their services to employers and help employees and family members navigate the healthcare system.

Advocacy programs attempt to engage individuals in their time of need, regardless of the circumstances. Data-driven programs attempt to anticipate those needs based on claims and administrative data. They are largely the design of disease management companies and health plans that have access to large stores of information about members, and they suffer from many of the same problems of engaging the targeted population that diminish the effectiveness of disease management programs. Because the identifying information is derived from claims, it targets people late in the course of their problems. These programs must then attempt to convince the individual to participate in the effort.[1]

Opt-in advocacy and assistance programs encourage those eligible to reach out to the advocate for help any time they face a health issue. Naturally, there is limited ability to predict when such needs will arise, so the message must be repeatedly communicated throughout the year with the hope that the employee, plan member, or consumer will remember to contact the advocate when they have an issue. The holistic nature of this "We'll help with anything" approach encourages consumer participation.

A MATTER OF TRUST

Trust is an important component of any population health strategy. With trust, healthcare consumers are more likely to engage and change suboptimal behaviors. A key advantage of health advocacy and assistance programs that are not associated with health plans is their independence. They can be viewed as a trusted party by patients and family members. The information they gain is strictly protected in accordance with the Health Insurance Portability and Accountability Act (HIPAA) requirements.[30] Users typically sign a release allowing the advocate to represent them in dealing with physicians, hospitals, and health plans. Importantly, none of the individual's private health information is ever shared with the health plan or the employer without the individual's explicit permission.

Advocacy programs create a personal relationship between the user and the advocate. This bond is founded on trust and provides confidence for the consumer that the advocate's only motive is to get the "right" answer. It should be obvious that in many cases there is a difference between the correct answer and what the consumer may have wanted to hear.

Not surprisingly, people often want coverage for services that are not covered by their health plan or want to pay less of their own money for care than their benefits program requires. The advocate is often called upon to explain that the issue is not one of medical necessity, but one of medical coverage, or that the problem is not that the plan did not pay the claim properly, but that the member is required to pay a deductible. Health advocates will often try to help the member find the most appropriate provider for a required service, or access community resources or compassionate care programs for services or medications that are needed but not covered under the consumer's health benefits. Taking these extra steps is an important part of being the individual's true advocate.

WHAT HELP DO CONSUMERS NEED?

Measured over the course of a year, most people do not use these assistance programs. In a given year, 18% of adults do not see a physician.[31] For the vast majority of those who do, the health system works fine. When they have a problem, they can get an appointment to see their doctor. The care they receive appears to meet their needs, and if they have questions, they talk to their physician and get an answer that satisfies them. Bills are submitted and processed for payment appropriately, or if they aren't, an easy call to the insurance company solves the problem. If they need health information, there are friends, neighbors, books, and the Internet. It all just seems to work.

So, who needs the help of an advocate, and what type of help do they need? While utilization varies across employers, advocacy programs will serve about 8–10% of the families in large companies and 15–20% in small companies.[32] Overall, the reasons consumers use advocacy programs mirror changes in an employer's benefit design, as well as circumstances in the local medical delivery system. When companies change health insurers, requests for help finding new in-network providers increase. When plan designs are altered, benefit questions spike. When there is worry about an influenza pandemic, advocates see more requests for medical information. When specialized care cannot be provided in the local area, people ask for help finding qualified experts elsewhere.

We can gain meaningful insights into what is wrong with the healthcare system from a population health standpoint by looking at the reasons consumers contact an advocate for assistance with a health-related issue. Recognizing that circumstances across employer groups from which these data are derived differ, as Figure 3-1 shows, more than half of all initial reasons consumers contact advocacy programs for help are related to an administrative issue. These are questions or problems with a bill, a benefit, a denial of coverage, an appeal, a grievance, or a referral. They are the administrative issues that get in the way of people dealing with a health issue, typically after they have received care.

The remaining first calls are driven directly by health needs: the need for health information, problems accessing care, finding a new doctor, identifying a qualified specialist for a rare or specific problem, and arranging a second opinion. Questions about physician

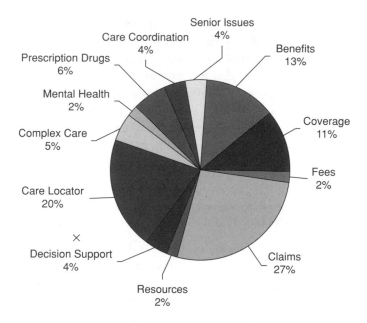

Figure 3-1   Situations That Prompt a First Call to a Health Advocate
Health Advocate, Inc. internal data. Cases completed January 2008–June 2009.

interactions and the need to locate community-based resources are also included in this group. Help dealing with senior care issues is a common need. Interestingly, considering the emphasis placed on the cost of medical care, requests for information about the price of care are not common today. One can only expect that this will change in the near future.

However, focusing only on the reason for the patient's initial call may miss the bigger picture and the greater opportunity to influence consumer behavior. For example, employees may call after receiving a bill for a service that they believe was processed incorrectly. The advocate will examine the bill, the service that was provided, how it was billed, how the bill was adjudicated, and how that adjudication was applied to the provisions of the individual's benefits policy. If an error was made, the advocate will attempt to facilitate correction of the problem where the mistake was made along the chain of activities.

It is self-evident that the people who receive bills required care; most people asking about a benefit are asking either because they used the benefit and have an issue or because they anticipate using the benefit and hope to avoid any problems. Health advocates can use their contacts as triggers to anticipate other services and needs the insured may have. Unlike the data-driven approach, these encounters and interventions happen in real time. For example, a woman calling about the company's maternity benefit is probably pregnant, contemplating getting pregnant, or has recently delivered a child. During the

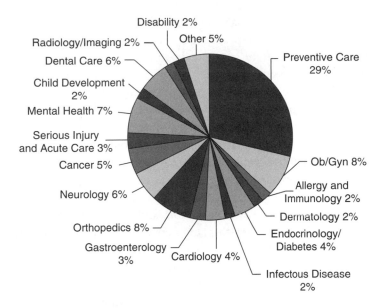

Figure 3-2   Distribution of Clinical Cases
Health Advocate, Inc. internal data. Cases completed January 2008–June 2009.

discussion, there is an opportunity, a "teachable moment," to not only discuss the benefit, but also talk about selecting an in-network obstetrician or pediatrician, address any outstanding questions about pregnancy and child care, and channel the woman into a prenatal care program.

In many cases, the issues people call about are relatively simple problems involving acute care services that will likely have no further consequences. However, as demonstrated in Figure 3-2, many are related to chronic conditions or recurrent needs, and the opportunity to intervene can have a dramatic effect on the future care the individual is likely to incur.

ACCESS TO CARE

One of the most common requests for assistance is help finding a doctor. This is surprising when one considers the expense health plans go through to provide members with network directories, in both online and paper formats. Regardless, these compendia are outdated the moment they are made available.[33] Of course, no one who asks for help finding a new doctor wants to go to a "bad," or in most cases, even an "average" doctor, although most consumers have difficulty communicating the attributes of a good or "the best" doctor.[34] People tend to be satisfied with the care they receive and, likewise, define good care as the care they received.

Many health plans now make provider quality and cost information available to members. While this would appear to be a move toward greater consumer engagement and transparency, in its present state the data provided are not very good.[35] The personal interaction found in advocacy programs helps consumers understand why considering better doctors or facilities is important when locating a physician or selecting a hospital.

It is simple logic that the most common requests for help finding a physician involve finding "common" physicians. These may not necessarily be primary care doctors. The member may need an orthopedist for an injured shoulder or an allergist for hay fever. It is actually more difficult to explain how to apply quality criteria to discriminate among the many providers of common care than it is to locate highly specialized providers. Of course, one can check the doctor's credentials, training, society memberships, and years of experience. Public databases are available and can be searched for sanctions, but a physician's acceptance into a health plan's network can be taken as a sign that he or she has passed the plan's credentialing review.

How, beyond checking these measures, does one identify a "good" family doctor, general internist, or pediatrician? It is most helpful for the advocate to identify what members want and what characteristics they are looking for in a doctor. Do they want a man or a woman? Do they prefer a group practice or a solo practice? Are evening hours important? If so, what nights can they get to the doctor's office? While many plans identify whether languages other than English are spoken in the office, members might also want to know if a Spanish-speaking staff member is available if they need an appointment on a Tuesday evening. If members need to be admitted to the hospital, do they have a hospital preference? These objective criteria can be used to define the member's view of a "good" doctor. Establishing relationships between health consumers and primary care practices is foundational to improving population health.

From this member-reported information, the advocate can then begin to reduce the available options to a manageable few. Finally, the advocate will contact offices to determine first, that they are still in business, and second, that they are still in the plan's network. Does the office have appointments available? Which hospital do they use for admissions? A match is made against the member's criteria, and choices are developed and presented to the member. Then, depending on the member's preference, appointments can be scheduled, records transferred, and referrals and authorizations facilitated.

The process is similar, albeit somewhat easier, when trying to identify specialists who deal with more unusual conditions. While the conditions presented may be of greater urgency, putting added pressure on the advocate to complete the search quickly, there is often a greater amount of objective information available about the proficiency of specific physicians and hospitals in the context of a particular medical condition. Some of this information is in the public domain.[36,37] Some health plans make their proprietary physician quality information available to members.[38] In other cases, the advocate can directly ask the physician how many cases similar to the one presented she or he has done and what the outcomes have been. It is also helpful to network from specialist to specialist to identify other experts in the particular field in different locations. Physicians employed by health plans in medical management roles and the plan's case managers can be of great assistance as advocates attempt to coordinate services and identify specific care providers.

MAKING CONNECTIONS ACROSS THE SPECTRUM OF CARE

Health advocates are skilled at making connections across multiple benefits programs, which both enhances their utilization and increases their value. To illustrate this point, consider the real case of a parent who called for assistance because she received a balance-due bill from an out-of-network emergency department physician who treated her 5-year-old son for an asthma attack at an in-network hospital. After obtaining a HIPAA-compliant release, the health advocate examined the physician's bill, the employer's health benefit documents, and how the plan paid the claim. In this case, the emergency department physician's services should have been processed at an in-network level of benefit because the employer's plan design stated that the participation status of the hospital would govern how bills from out-of-network physicians would be adjudicated. Correcting the mistake reduced the member's payment from $350 to $50, the amount of her emergency department copay, and ostensibly satisfied the parent's reason for calling. However, what about the child's underlying clinical needs? There was an opportunity to explore the circumstances that sent the child to the emergency department in the first place—his asthma. This is where the value of having a clinically experienced professional involved in the case demonstrates merit.

The advocate was able to seize the teachable moment and convince the mother to let her connect the child with the asthma management program offered by the health plan. Had no such program been available, the clinical advocate could have assumed the role of a case manager, provided the family with educational information about asthma, discussed common management strategies like how to avoid environmental triggers and properly use medications, scheduled the child for an appointment with his primary physician, and prepared the parent for the discussion with the doctor. The advocate could even have contacted the doctor's office in advance to alert the physician of the child's impending visit, history, and needs as well as coordinated any required lab tests or x-rays before the visit to make the physician encounter more useful.

Even in cases that present as seemingly straightforward claims or administrative issues, recognition of clinical opportunities establishes the value of advocacy services beyond any monetary accounting of a return on investment. Addressing these otherwise hidden clinical opportunities allows employers to maximize the true value of their benefit program, increasing the effectiveness of other care management programs they have put in place, while improving medical outcomes. Of course, there are also opportunities to save real dollars by providing navigational assistance and advocacy support to patients.

COORDINATING CARE ACROSS BENEFITS PROGRAMS

Employers, especially large employers with benefits programs typically involving a dozen or more vendors and touch points, position health advocacy and assistance programs in one of two ways. The most common approach is to view the program as a sort of safety net around the entire benefits program, serving individuals who might have tried to solve their problems or address their issues on their own, but did not reach the desired outcome.

The other approach is to use the advocacy program as a gateway to all of the other benefits programs and services offered. This "800-Call-Advocate" model has the obvious advantage of requiring that employees remember only one phone number. The health advocate can then discuss the case with the employee and link him or her to the correct service provider. By providing this personal, single point of contact, the advocate functions as a case coordinator, not only helping individuals to navigate the health system, but also providing them with help to navigate the benefits environment.

For example, an advocate could connect a 5-year-old asthmatic child to an asthma management program offered by a disease management company and subsequently link the child to an in-network allergist for evaluation. After the visit, the child's mother may call because the allergist ordered a nebulizer to administer her son's airway dilating medications and she is not sure of the authorization process. She may have questions about the plan's mail-order pharmacy program. The advocate can coordinate services with the health plan's case managers and speak to the plan-affiliated durable medical equipment supplier. Perhaps, during the child's illness, his mother would have to miss work. The advocate can contact the employer's benefits administrator and arrange for coverage for her under the Family and Medical Leave Act (FMLA).

It is easy to see how intertwined the system is, and how hard it can be for a patient struggling with a health issue to deal with it. This single, seemingly straightforward and common case could involve the child and his family, an emergency department physician, the hospital that operates the emergency department, the pediatrician, an allergist, a disease management nurse, the case manager at the health plan, a durable medical equipment provider, the company's benefits administrator for FMLA approvals, the carve-out pharmacy benefits administrator, and a query of the health plans' claims system. Is it any wonder that people find the healthcare system difficult to navigate?

CHANGING CONSUMER BEHAVIOR

It is fair to ask whether the purpose of providing consumers with help navigating the healthcare system is to change their future behavior, or merely to help them solve today's problem. Certainly, the stampede toward consumer-driven health care would suggest that many employers and plans believe that consumer behavior can be changed in ways that will lower costs and improve the quality of care. These models embrace the belief that consumers can be motivated or "activated" to assume greater responsibility for managing their own care, and that they can and will make smarter and more informed decisions about the care they receive and the professionals and hospitals that provide the care. However, as Alison Rein, a senior manager with AcademyHealth, pointed out in writing about consumer-driven health care, "Taken together these efforts may foster some improvements, but none of them constitute a big-picture 'fix' for the cost/quality problems ... nor do they introduce the elements of ease and continuity that are so lacking for consumers trying to get care in today's highly fractured health care sector."[39]

There is also ample evidence to suggest that those who function well in the consumer-driven, self-management process are different from the population of consumers at large. They appear to be more motivated or "activated" from the start, and so are innately better prepared to manage their own health.[23] The challenge is motivating the rest of the group to act in the same way. In the meantime, while we await the development of effective strategies for doing so, advocacy and assistance programs can do well by providing timely support to those who need help navigating the healthcare system.

CONCLUSIONS

As the United States struggles to reform its healthcare system, certain needs become obvious. The first is that the system of providing health benefits through employers will continue to struggle until some way of constraining the explosive increases in healthcare costs is found. Until then, employers will have no option but to increase the amount employees must pay for their health coverage. As a result, individuals will increasingly assume greater responsibility for managing their own health. Health advocacy and assistance programs provide support to help such individuals navigate the healthcare environment. By providing help at the consumer's moment of need, these programs have a great opportunity to help people make better care choices. Their interactions with individuals provide a framework to educate participants to make wiser medical and lifestyle decisions, which should both help to lower future costs and help people reach the best possible medical outcomes.

STUDY AND DISCUSSION QUESTIONS

1. What considerations are driving employers to redesign their health benefits programs?
2. How does a company's size influence the kind of health benefits it offers?
3. Compare the advantages and disadvantages of data-driven versus opt-in advocacy programs.
4. What can we learn from patterns of health advocacy program utilization?
5. What can be done to help consumers become wiser users of the healthcare system?

SUGGESTED READINGS AND WEB SITES

READINGS

Herzlinger RE, ed. *Consumer-Driven Health Care: Implications for Providers, Payers, and Policymakers.* San Francisco, CA: John Wiley & Sons, Inc.; 2004.

Herzlinger RE. *Market-Driven Health Care: Who Wins, Who Loses in the Transformation of America's Largest Service Industry.* New York, NY: Perseus Books; 1997.

Kaiser Family Foundation. *Healthcare Costs: A Primer.* Kaiser Family Foundation Web site. http://www.kff.org/insurance/7670.cfm. Published March 19, 2009. Accessed September 29, 2009.

Kaiser Family Foundation, *How Private Insurance Works: A Primer.* Kaiser Family Foundation Web site. http://www.kff.org/insurance/7766.cfm. Published April 21, 2008. Accessed September 24, 2009.

Kaiser Family Foundation, Health Research & Educational Trust, National Opinion Research Center. *Employer Health Benefits: 2009 Annual Survey.* Kaiser Family Foundation Web site. http://ehbs.kff.org/pdf/2009/7936.pdf. Published September 15, 2009. Accessed September 24, 2009.

WEB SITES

The Commonwealth Fund: http://www.commonwealthfund.org

Hospital Quality Compare: A quality tool provided by Medicare: http://www.hospitalcompare.hhs.gov/

The Kaiser Family Foundation: http://www.kff.org

The Leapfrog Group: http://www.leapfroggroup.org/

REFERENCES

1. Leibowitz A. The role of health advocacy in disease management. *Dis Manag.* 2005;8(3):141–143.
2. CIGNA introduces new service model that pairs individuals with a personal health advocate; making it easier to be healthy [news release]. Bloomfield, CT: CIGNA; July 24, 2008. http://newsroom.cigna.com/article_display.cfm?article_id=933&. Accessed September 28, 2009.
3. The Karis Group. The Karis Group Web site. http://www.thekarisgroup.com/index.html. Accessed September 29, 2009.
4. Medical Debt Help. Medical Debt Help Web site. http://www.medicaldebthelp.com/Negotiate_Medical_Debt.html. Accessed September 29, 2009.
5. Alderman L. After a diagnosis, someone to help point the way. *The New York Times.* September 11, 2009:B6. http://www.nytimes.com/2009/09/12/health/12patient.html?_r=1&scp=1&sq=patient%20advocates&st=cse. Accessed September 29, 2009.
6. Deblasi M. Someone on your side. *Bloomberg Personal Finance.* January 2003:71–73.
7. Kaiser Family Foundation. *Healthcare Costs, A Primer.* Kaiser Family Foundation Web site. http://www.kff.org/insurance/7670.cfm. Published March 19, 2009. Accessed September 29, 2009.
8. Docteur E, Berenson RA. How does the quality of U.S. health care compare internationally? Robert

Wood Johnson Foundation Web site. http://www.rwjf.org/qualityequality/product.jsp?id=47508. Published August 2009. Accessed September 29, 2009.

9. Young L. Advocates who help you negotiate health care. *BusinessWeek.* October 22, 2007:101–103.

10. Wells SJ. Health advocates: independent experts can help employees conquer mountains of medical paperwork, freeing HR to focus on other core concerns. *HR Magazine.* August 2006.

11. Kaiser Family Foundation, Health Research & Educational Trust, National Opinion Research Center. *Employer Health Benefits: 2009 Annual Survey.* Kaiser Family Foundation Web site. http://ehbs.kff.org/pdf/2009/7936.pdf. Published September 15, 2009. Accessed September 24, 2009.

12. Haynes VD. A premium sucker punch. *The Washington Post.* January 25, 2009:F1.

13. Arnst C. A secret wish for health reform. *BusinessWeek.* May 18, 2009:23.

14. Bloche MG. Consumer-directed health care. *NEJM.* 2007;355(17):1756–1759.

15. Mercer Human Resource Consulting. *Navigating the Pharmacy Benefits Marketplace.* California HealthCare Foundation Web site. http://www.chcf.org/documents/hospitals/NavPharmBenefits.pdf. Published January 2003. Accessed September 28, 2009.

16. Some MCOs say "best of breed" DM strategy offers high-quality, cost-effective design. *Inside Dis Manage.* February 3, 2006;2(3).

17. Blumenthal D. Employer-sponsored health insurance in the United States—origins and implications. *NEJM.* 2006;355(1):82–88.

18. Ray WA, Daugherty JR, Meador KG. Effect of a mental health "carve-out" program on the continuity of antipsychotic therapy. *NEJM.* 2003;348(19):1885–1894.

19. Goldman HH, Frank RG, Burnam MA, et al. Behavioral health insurance parity for federal employees. *NEJM.* 2006;354(13):1378–1386.

20. Stano M. Carve outs: comments on the workshop. *Am J Managed Care.* June 25, 1998;4:SP23–SP26.

21. Blumenthal D, Buntin MB. Carve outs: definition, experience, and choice among candidate conditions. *Am J Managed Care.* 1998;4:SP45–SP57.

22. Rosenthal MB. What works in a market-oriented health policy? *NEJM.* 2009;360(21):2157–2160.

23. Hibbard JH, Greene J, Tusler M. Plan design and active involvement of consumers in their own health and healthcare. *Am J Managed Care.* 2008;14(11):729–736.

24. Chernew ME, Newhouse JP. What does the RAND Health Insurance Experiment tell us about the impact of patient cost sharing on health outcomes? *Am J Managed Care.* 2008;14(7):412–414.

25. Siegel M. When doctors opt out. *Wall Street Journal.* April 17, 2009:A13.

26. Kravitz RL, Chang S. Promise and perils for patients and physicians. *NEJM.* 2005;353(26):2735–2739.

27. The Kaiser Family Foundation, Harvard School of Public Health. National survey on consumer experiences with and attitudes toward health plans [chart pack]. Kaiser Family Foundation Web site. http://www.kff.org/insurance/upload/National-Survey-on-Consumer-Experiences-With-Health-Care-Plans-Chartpack.pdf. Published August 2001. Accessed September 28, 2009.

28. Henry J Kaiser Family Foundation. *March/April 2004 Health Poll Report Survey.* Kaiser Family Foundation Web site. http://www.kff.org/kaiserpolls/upload/March-April-2004-Kaiser-Health-Poll-Report-Survey-Selected-Findings-on-the-Knowledge-and-Understanding-of-the-New-Medicare-Rx-Drug-Program-Toplines.pdf. Published April 2004. Accessed September 28, 2009.

29. Google. Google Web site. http://www.google.com/search?client=safari&rls=en&q=Health+advocate&ie=UTF-8&oe=UTF-8. Accessed October 1, 2009.

30. Health Information Privacy. US Department of Health & Human Services Web site. http://www.hhs.gov/ocr/privacy/. Accessed September 25, 2009.

31. Centers for Disease Control and Prevention. Ambulatory care use and physician visits. Centers for Disease Control and Prevention Web site. http://www.cdc.gov/nchs/fastats/docvisit.htm. Accessed October 1, 2009.

32. Andrews M. A new guide to the medical maze. *Fortune Small Business.* March 1, 2006;16(2): 87–88.

33. Rubinstein S. Finding a doctor is as easy as… *The Wall Street Journal.* August 3, 2006:D1.

34. Miller J. What employers want: As GE's global healthcare leader, Dr. Robert Galvin measures on value. *Managed Healthcare Executive.* July 1, 2006. http://managedhealthcareexecutive. modernmedicine.com/mhe/article/articleDetail. jsp?id=357673. Accessed October 1, 2009.

35. CIGNA. Myths and realities of health care. CIGNA Web site. http://newsroom.cigna.com/ section_display.cfm?section_id=51. Accessed September 29, 2009.

36. The Leapfrog Group. I want to compare hospitals on [comparison tool]. Leapfrog Group Web site. http://www.leapfroggroup.org/cp. Accessed October 1, 2009.

37. Hospital Quality Compare: A quality tool provided by Medicare. US Department of Health and Human Services Web site. http://www.hospitalcompare. hhs.gov/. Accessed October 1, 2009.

38. UnitedHealth Group. Unitedhealth premium physician designation. UnitedHealthcare Online Web site. https://www.unitedhealthcareonline. com/b2c/CmaAction.do?channelId=c5897affc 5ec4110VgnVCM1000007740dc0a. Accessed September 30, 2009.

39. Rein A. Navigating health care: why it's so hard and what can be done to make it easier for the average consumer. *Academy Health Issue Brief.* http://www.academyhealth.org/files/issues/ NavigatingHealthCare.pdf. Published October 2007. Accessed March 13, 2010.

CONTINUITY OF CARE

JOANNE REIFSNYDER, PhD, ACHPN, AND
THERESA P. YEO, PhD, MPH, MSN, CRNP

Executive Summary

Chronic care management is essential to population health management

Chronic medical conditions affect four out of five Americans aged 50 years or older[1] and their prevalence increases with advancing age. Medical care for chronic illness is a major contributor to healthcare costs under the present reimbursement system that rewards acute episodic care over chronic illness prevention and chronic care management. The ongoing care of patients with chronic diseases, including diabetes, hypertension, heart failure (HF), tobacco addiction, hyperlipidemia, chronic atrial fibrillation, arthritis, COPD, asthma, eye disease, and depression, accounts for most of the caseload in primary care practices. Evidence suggests that the majority of persons with chronic conditions are inadequately managed as a result of fragmentation of care, poor coordination of ancillary health services, and failure to adequately account for **case mix** factors such as varying severity of illness, cultural and/or individual patient characteristics, and nonadherence to self-management practices.[2] Many chronic conditions and their sequelae are largely preventable with lifestyle and behavioral choices; yet, current health care provides little incentive for self-management and personal accountability.

Chronic care management is the "coordination of care in order to reduce fragmentation and unnecessary use of resources, prevent avoidable conditions [complications] and promote independence and self-care."[3] Haphazard coordination of medical services is evident in the delivery of care for persons living with chronic debilitating conditions. Short-term and long-term clinical treatment and support are often provided by a multitude of medical and home care groups with the involvement of many different providers. Given these conditions, care easily becomes more fragmented and costly.

Continuity is essentially a patient-centered characteristic, referring to how individual patients experience health care. Successful chronic care management enhances continuity of care. There are three distinct types of continuity: informational continuity (medical information and knowledge of patient in the context of preferences and values), management continuity (consistent care with a consistent core of providers who agree on a management plan), and relational continuity (consistency that bridges past, current, and future care).[4] All three aspects of continuity must be present to provide chronic care management. Chronic care models that include these continuity factors and promote their use in the coordination of care, in addition to achieving cost control and promoting self-management, have been proposed by Bodenheimer, Wagner, Grumbach, and others.

The primary care setting has traditionally been considered the **medical home** because it has the potential to offer the full spectrum of care from preventive, acute, and episodic to long-term follow-up for chronic conditions.[5] Yet, the primary care setting is experiencing heightened strain, overwhelmed by the shifting demographics of the U.S. population, increased demand for health care, and reduced reimbursement for services. There have also been suggestions that as a result of these factors, many primary care practices are not managing chronic conditions adequately. Revised models of the primary care home concept are being developed and piloted, spurred on by an increasing aging population with multiple needs and a declining workforce of primary care providers.

This chapter presents an overview of the magnitude and impact of chronic conditions on the healthcare system, examines the evolution of models of care, and discusses current trends in the management of chronic conditions.

Learning Objectives

1. Elucidate the historical and contextual background of chronic care management.
2. Synthesize knowledge of the most common chronic conditions, medical expenditure data, and societal costs of chronic care.
3. Describe emerging models of chronic care management and delivery of care.

Key Words

accountable care organization	indirect costs
care management	medical home
case management	medical model
case mix	models of care
chronic care management	palliative care
chronic condition	Patient-Centered Medical Home (PCMH)
chronic disease	self-care agency
continuity	self-management
direct costs	social model

INTRODUCTION

The aging of the population in the United States and other developed countries has been well documented, and the implications for health care and other senior services are significant. The United State's aged population is expected to grow from 40 million in 2010 to 55 million in 2020—an increase of 36% in a single decade. By 2030, adults older than 65 years will comprise 19.3% of the population. The oldest old—those age 85 years and older—represented the most rapidly growing segment of this cohort between 2000 and 2010, and growth in this age group is projected to be 15% in the period between 2010 and 2020.[6]

In addition to aging of the population, changes in the distribution of ethnic and cultural characteristics are reshaping the demographics. Between 2007 and 2020, Caucasian elders will increase in number by 68% while minorities will increase by 184%, with the greatest growth among Hispanics (244%).[6] By 2020, minority elders will comprise 23.6% of the elderly, and for the first time in some communities, Caucasian elders will represent a minority. These dramatic population shifts, accompanied by a growing chronic illness burden, will significantly impact the required resources and costs of providing high-quality, culturally and linguistically appropriate care.

In the United States, an estimated 125 million persons have at least one **chronic condition**, and half of these persons have multiple chronic conditions.[7] This number is expected to rise to 157 million by 2020.[7] The prevalence of chronic disease increases with age; 82% of Medicare beneficiaries have one or more chronic conditions, and 25% have four or more conditions.[8–10] Seventy percent of all deaths are attributable to chronic illnesses, and medical care provided to this population accounts for more than 7% of the $2 trillion spent on health care in the United States.[11] Medicare beneficiaries with four or more chronic conditions are 99% more likely to be hospitalized[12] and they receive services from 14 different physicians (on average), accounting for 66% percent of Medicare spending.[7]

The term **chronic disease** refers to conditions that are generally ambulatory care-sensitive, meaning that effective outpatient management will reduce the likelihood of hospitalization.[13] Chronic conditions are generally classified as those illnesses and diseases that are expected to persist beyond one year and may lead to functional limitations, disability, and the need for long-term medical care. One quarter of persons with chronic disease are limited in their ability to perform basic activities of daily living (ADLs) including bathing, dressing, self-feeding, and toileting. Many more persons with chronic conditions struggle to perform those activities classified as instrumental ADLs (IADLs), such as preparing meals; performing household tasks (doing laundry, cleaning, paying bills); using technology, such as telephones, televisions, and computers; shopping; and adhering to medication and treatment schedules.[6] Data from the Medical Expenditure Panel Survey[6] (MEPS) indicate that people with chronic medical conditions require more inpatient hospital care, emergency department visits, and prescription medications, and they utilize more outpatient, community, and home health services than those without chronic conditions.

RISK FACTORS FOR CHRONIC DISEASE

According to data compiled by the National Center for Health Statistics, the average life expectancy for a person born in 2007 is 77.9 years.[14] Compared to a life expectancy of 47 years in 1900, such an increase in little more than a century is dramatic. Yet, if the major forms of cardiovascular disease (CVD) were eliminated, life expectancy would increase 7 years and increase another 3 years if all cancers were prevented.[15]

Of the most prevalent chronic diseases, CVD is significant in that it is the leading cause of death and is associated with the most modifiable risk factors. The lifetime probability of dying from CVD is 47%—significantly greater than the mortality risks associated with cancer (22%), accidental death (3%), diabetes (2%), and human immunodeficiency virus (HIV) infection (0.7%).[15]

Because all types of CVD taken together account for substantial morbidity and mortality, attenuation of the risk factors is of particular importance in improving population health. The major risk factors for the majority of the cardiovascular diseases are associated with lifestyle; they include elevated blood pressure, high blood cholesterol levels, overweight and obesity, current cigarette smoking, diabetes (in which the most prevalent form, Type 2 diabetes, is primarily attributed to lifestyle), and a sedentary lifestyle. Distribution of CVD varies by gender, race, and ethnicity. Blacks and African Americans have the highest prevalence of two or more risk factors (49%), followed by Native Americans and Alaska Natives (47%). Black and Mexican American women have been found to have a higher prevalence of CVD than comparable white women.[16] Despite campaigns by the American Heart Association and others, young women appear to not have modified high-risk behaviors leading to CVD. For example, in the 2000 Behavioral Risk Factor Surveillance Survey (BRFSS), women ages 18–24 years had the highest rates of current smoking (36%), and 30% reported sedentary behavior.[17] The importance of lifestyle and health was underscored by BRFSS self-report data from respondents age 18–74 years who were queried about healthy lifestyle indicators. Among those who reported the highest levels of health, 76% were non-smokers, 40% were at a healthy weight, 23% ate five fruits and vegetables per day, and 22% took part in regular physical activity.[17] Similarly, findings from a large European study provided strong evidence that development of diabetes, myocardial infarction, stroke, and cancer decrease progressively as the number of healthy factors (never smoking, body mass index (BMI) less than 30, 3.5 hrs/week of physical activity, and healthy diet) increases.[18]

OVERVIEW OF CHRONIC CONDITIONS

Five medical conditions have dominated medical spending from 1990 to 2010: heart disease, cancer, asthma, mental disorders, and trauma-related disorders.[19] In 2006, the mean healthcare expenditure per person was highest for persons with cancer ($5,176) followed by those with heart disease ($4,333).[6] Between 1996 and 2006, the prevalence of mental health disorders in the United States increased; this patient population also experiences the highest out-of-pocket expenses.

Three-quarters of the U.S. healthcare budget is spent on the care of persons living with chronic illness. An overview of common chronic medical conditions affecting Americans follows. Data on the incidence, prevalence, and associated direct and **indirect costs** are summarized in Table 4-1.

DIABETES

Diabetes is a group of glycemic conditions that includes type 1 diabetes, type 2 diabetes, gestational diabetes, genetic disorders, and prediabetes. All of these conditions are characterized by elevated blood glucose levels caused by defects in insulin production by the pancreas, impaired action of insulin, and cellular receptor-site resistance to insulin. Between 1980 and 2007, the number of persons aged 18–79 years suffering from diabetes nearly tripled, rising from 493,000 new cases of diabetes in 1980 to 1.6 million new cases in 2007 (roughly 7.8% of the population). This dramatic increase in diabetes prevalence can be explained almost entirely by lifestyle choices, most particularly obesity, sedentary lifestyle, and smoking.[20] The greatest rate of increase in the incidence of diabetes was observed in the 1990s, as rates of overweight and obesity started to skyrocket. The 1990s were a time of economic growth, rising incomes, and relocation to more suburban areas where services such as schools, churches, and shopping were not accessible by foot. People started to spend more time driving, had less physical activity, and ate more meals out of the home (often at fast-food restaurants).[21]

The combined direct and indirect costs associated with diabetes care are significant. In addition, 64% of adult diabetics age 18–79 years reported having had the condition for 10 years, indicating worsening chronicity of the condition.[20] Progression to type 2 diabetes from the prediabetic state is not inevitable. The Diabetes Prevention Program has demonstrated that lifestyle modifications in prediabetics, such as weight reduction and increased exercise, reduced the risk of type 2 diabetes 58% over 3 years and 71% in adults older than 60 years of age.[20] The combination of assessing daily glucose levels, monitoring long-term indicators of glycemic control (i.e., hemoglobin A1C levels [A1C]), and intensive insulin therapy is beneficial and cost-effective. Every percentage drop in the A1C level reduces eye, kidney, and neurological complications by 40% and lowers the risk of cardiovascular complications in diabetics.[20]

CANCER

Cancer remains the second leading cause of mortality in the United States, accounting for more than 560,000 deaths annually.[22] Because of the ongoing success of early detection strategies and improved treatment modalities, cancer is now considered both an acute and a chronic medical condition. More than 1.5 million new cases of all types of cancer are detected annually, adding to the growing number of cancer survivors estimated at more

Table 4-1 Incidence, Prevalence, and Costs of Selected Chronic Medical Conditions in the United States

Condition	Incidence	Overall Prevalence, Percent U.S. Population	Prevalence Age 20–65, Percent U.S. Population	Prevalence Age >65 Percent, U.S. Population	Direct Costs*	Indirect Costs*
Mental health disorders[19, 23–25]	44.3 million[23]	60 million[19] (26%)	75% of mental illnesses begin by age 24 years (45 million)[24]	20% >55 years[25]; declines over age 65 years[24]	$58 billion[19]	$193 billion[23]
Asthma[†14,26,27]	13.6 million[26]	20 million[26]	5–17 years: 9 million >20 years: 8.6 million[26]	1.4 million[27]	$6 billion[27]	$673 million[27]
Diabetes[20]	1.6 million, (persons >20 years)[20]	23.6 million (8%)[20] (includes 5.7 million undiagnosed cases)	23.5 million (11%)[20]	12.2 million (23%)[20]	$116 billion[20]	$58 billion[20]
Cancer[22,28]	1.5 million[28] <65 years, 221/100,000 >65 years, 2,134/100,000	11.1 million[28]	(6%) 20–59 years old[29]	(22%) 60–79 years old[15] (15%) >80 years old[29]	$72 billion[22]	$1,540 billion[22]
Arthritis[30,31]	‡	46 million (22%)[30]	18–64 years old (37%)[30]	>65 years (50%)[30]	$81 billion[31]	$47 billion[31]
Heart failure[32]	550,000[32]	5 million[32]	1 in 9 men, 1 in 6 women	10 per 1,000	$27 billion[73]	$3 billion
Coronary artery disease[32]	1.2 million	13.2 million[32]	after age 40, lifetime risk 49% for men, 32% for women		$75 billion	$67 billion
Angina[32]	400,000	6.5 million				
Myocardial infarction[32]	865,000	7.2 million[32]	98,000 women 284,000 men	372,000 women 410,000 men	$143 billion	
Hypertension[32]	1 in 3 adults	65 million[32] 59 million pre-hypertension (28 percent)	29% overall; more men than women until age 45–54 years		$48 billion	$16 billion
Stroke[32]	700,000	5.5 million	12%	38%	$37 billion	$21 billion
Total CVD[15,32]		71.3 million		27.4 million	$258 billion[15]	$146 billion

* Direct costs refer to medical expenditures; indirect costs refer to disability, lost earnings, and premature mortality associated with the condition.

† Incidence reported as rate per 1000 person-years.

‡ There is no national estimate of arthritis incidence because of the inability to know the disease status of everyone at the start of the period (CDC, 2009).

than 11 million persons.[28] The **direct costs** of cancer care account for 5% of spending for all medical treatment. The indirect costs and personal spending for cancer-related needs are also extremely high. Surgical treatment and adjuvant therapy with chemotherapy and/or radiotherapy for the leading sites of cancer (lung, colorectal, breast, and prostate cancer) account for the bulk of medical expenditures. The total cost for cancer care is further compounded by the costs of screening procedures.[33]

Estimates vary, but as many as 80% of cancers may be related to lifestyle and environmental factors.[34] For example, nearly all lung cancers could be prevented by smoking cessation and nearly all melanomas (a deadly form of skin cancer) could be prevented by protection from sun exposure. While the causes for many cancers are not fully understood, tobacco use, obesity, and environmental exposures (occupational exposures to carcinogens and air and water pollution) are believed to contribute to the development of lung cancer, colorectal cancer, breast cancer, prostate cancer, and pancreas cancer.[34]

CARDIOVASCULAR DISEASE

An estimated 71.3 million Americans suffer from at least one type of cardiovascular disease (CVD), of whom a large portion (27.4 million) are 65 years or older.[15] CVD is a broad term that encompasses coronary artery disease, which includes heart attack and angina, high blood pressure (HBP), heart failure (HF), stroke, heart rhythm disorders, and congenital abnormalities. CVD remains the leading cause of death for men and women in the United States, accounting for approximately 37.3% of all deaths in the United States each year, especially among the black population.

CVD is the most costly medical condition experienced by Americans, and the most prevalent and costly condition in the majority of developed, industrialized countries globally. The acquired risk factors for CVD are current cigarette smoking, high cholesterol, high blood pressure, the presence of diabetes, and increasing body mass index (BMI) greater than 26. In addition to these well-known risk factors, the incidence of heart disease and stroke is inversely related to education attainment, income levels, and poverty status.[16]

Heart Failure Heart failure is a significant source of morbidity and mortality, much of which could be avoided through prevention or control of high blood pressure.[1] While 75% of persons with HF have a history of high blood pressure (HBP), the strongest predictor is the presence of diabetes. Women who had diabetes, an elevated BMI, and/or decreased kidney function, had 7–13% incidence rates of HF when compared to women without these conditions.[35] HF is responsible for high rates of hospitalization as well as ambulatory care visits, which contribute to the rising expenditures for diagnosis and treatment.

Coronary Artery Disease More than 13 million persons suffer from coronary artery disease (CAD), including the millions who experience myocardial infarctions each year and those who have angina (cardiac chest pain). The presence of HBP is a significant predictor of coronary heart disease in blacks, while diabetes is a strong predictor in whites. Elevated cholesterol levels, overweight, obesity, and lack of physical activity predispose one to CAD.

High Blood Pressure   High blood pressure (HBP) affects 65 million Americans and directly accounts for 6% of CVD deaths. Prevalence of HBP is higher among blacks and African Americans compared to other races. The prevalence of HBP in American blacks is the highest in the world because it develops earlier in life.[15] The earlier development and increased severity of HBP-results in more HBP-related comorbidities. Data from the National Heart, Lung, and Blood Institute (NHLBI) indicate that only 38% of men and 23% of women age 80 years or older achieve the recommended level of blood pressure control.[36]

Atrial Fibrillation   Atrial fibrillation (AF) is a common heart rhythm disorder affecting more than 2.2 million persons and is becoming a significant population health issue. The incidence of AF increases with age (<1% younger than age 60 years, 9% of persons 80 years or older); therefore, both incidence and prevalence of AF is projected to increase as the number of persons older than 65 years continues to grow and as survival from other cardiovascular conditions improves. Poor control of AF can lead to stroke and the need for additional costly healthcare services.[37]

Hyperlipidemia   Elevated levels of total cholesterol and LDL ("bad") cholesterol are associated with an increased risk of CAD. In the United States, 99.9 million persons have elevated total cholesterol levels (>200 mg/dl). The average blood cholesterol levels for adults range between 204 and 199 mg/dl depending on race and ethnicity. Less than half of the persons who are candidates for cholesterol-lowering medications receive them[15] and only a third of patients taking lipid-lowering agents achieve their LDL goal. A 10% reduction in total cholesterol levels on a population-wide basis would result in a 30% reduction in coronary heart disease.[15] The impact of incremental change cannot be underestimated in striving for population health.

ASTHMA

Asthma is a chronic condition that often begins in childhood and is more common in males than females. Calculating the incidence and prevalence of asthma is complicated by misclassification of disease between asthma and chronic obstructive pulmonary disease in many studies. An estimate 5 million children age 5 to 17 years suffer from asthma. Prevalence estimates are more elusive in the adult population, with best estimates of 20 million adults living with asthmatic conditions. The direct costs of asthma treatment in children are approximately $1010 million or $401 per child and indirect costs, including parents' loss of productivity caused by school absent days, are estimated at $983.8 million.[38] Improved coordination of asthma prevention, **self-management** strategies, and education services could reduce the healthcare costs of asthma intervention and reduce morbidity associated with uncontrolled asthma.

MENTAL HEALTH DISORDERS

Mental health disorders are common, with approximately 26% of the U.S. adult population 18 years or older suffering from one or two diagnosable mental disorders.[23] Major depression is recognized as the second leading cause of disability days and lost productivity. Mental illness is a costly chronic condition in terms of both direct and indirect costs. Out-of-pocket payments for mental health care are the highest of any chronic condition.

IMPACT OF CHRONIC CONDITIONS

The impact of chronic illness is experienced at both individual and societal levels in terms of productivity, quality of life, morbidity and mortality, and healthcare costs. Chronic medical conditions typically progress to disability and additional comorbidities. For example, many individuals with advanced diabetes will experience chronic renal failure and partial or complete amputation of an extremity. Among Medicare-eligible patients, management of chronic conditions constitutes a disproportionate level of spending compared to the number of persons affected. For example, 14% of Medicare patients suffer from heart failure, yet 43% of all Medicare funding is spent on providing care to HF patients. Diabetes is another example of a chronic condition in which a relatively small proportion of Medicare patients (18%) utilize a disproportionate share of spending (32%).[39]

The need for **chronic care management** is one of the major challenges facing the U.S. healthcare system. As the longevity of Americans increases, so does the prevalence of people living with chronic disease. The lifestyle factors of tobacco use, physical inactivity, and weight gain also play a role in the increase in the development of chronic conditions at younger ages. Some persons with chronic conditions do not receive any health care or receive inadequate care; both result in poor disease control and unnecessary complications and disease morbidity. Improving the coordination of care and services and providing patients with the tools that will enable them and their families to participate in self-care management may decrease hospitalizations and emergency room visits.[40]

Patients without access to or dissatisfied with primary care services have drifted toward specialty care. The resultant multiplicity of providers increases complexity and fragmentation of health care, which increases the price without an adequate evidence base for improved disease status. While evidence of better outcomes is apparent when seeing a specialist for acute problems, the same has not proven true for chronic conditions.[41–43]

CARE DELIVERY VARIATION

Most persons with chronic illness receive care from multiple providers—care that is rarely coordinated and highly variable, which compromises its quality.[44] Variation in care may be explained as preference-sensitive (according to patients' preferences about options, as they understand them) and supply-sensitive (the supply of a resource is associated with volume).

Variations in supply-sensitive care are most often associated with geographic capacity and local payment policies. Regions with a greater number of physicians and more hospital beds have substantially greater utilization. For example, patients who live in the region with the lowest rates of supply-sensitive care were hospitalized on average for 6.1 days in their final 6 months of life, while those in regions with highest supply-sensitive care spent an average of 21.9 days hospitalized in their final 6 months. There is no evidence that those who received more care had better outcomes,[44] and the cost is staggering. Nearly 55% of all Medicare spending for beneficiaries in their final 2 years of life is in the acute care setting, where volume is more indicative of costs than price per unit. Costs may vary between the highest and lowest hospital referral regions (HRRs) by as much as $46,000 per patient.[44]

CHRONIC CARE MANAGEMENT

The terms care management, care coordination, disease management, and case management are often used interchangeably. **Care management** programs "apply systems, science, incentives, and information to improve medical practice and help patients manage medical conditions more effectively."[45] The goals of care management are to improve care quality, promote independence, and reduce unnecessary resource utilization. Models are classified along a continuum from social, to medical, to integrated. Hybrid, or integrated models, combine aspects of social and medical models, with a focus on linking individuals to services in their communities. These model types are discussed in the publicly funded home- and community-based services section of this chapter.

A number of payment and delivery models, such as managed care, health maintenance organizations (HMOs), and preferred provider organizations (PPOs) have attempted to serve as gatekeepers, as well as coordinators of care. A shared care model of primary care providers and specialists has been suggested and, for conditions such as depression and diabetes, may lead to better outcomes. However, studies demonstrating increased

---

BOX 4-1   COMPONENTS OF CARE MANAGEMENT

Components of care management include the following components (DMAA: The Care Continuum Alliance):

- population identification processes
- evidence-based practice guidelines
- collaborative practice models
- patient self-management education
- process and outcomes measurement
- routine reporting/feedback involving patients, physicians, health plan, and care team.

improvement in life expectancy and reduction of disability are lacking. Some patients suffer from overmedicalization,[46] while others receive limited care for similar conditions.

Chronic care management (CCM) is considered critical to health reform. Various approaches to care management have been explored; most notable were a series of Medicare demonstrations focused on the most complex and costly beneficiaries. Most recently, the Medicare Health Support demonstration authorized under the Balanced Budget Act (BBA) failed to produce the care improvements or cost savings that were projected. (See Chapter 14 for a discussion of Medicare demonstration projects and outcomes.) While the design, methodologies, and outcomes have varied somewhat among the various demonstrations, most failed to fundamentally change the quality or the cost of care delivery to multimorbid older adults. The barriers to successful care management appear to be challenges to enrollment and retention of participants, lack of buy-in from and coordination with the beneficiaries' primary physicians (and multitude of other physicians—on average, 14 unique physicians provide services to the Medicare beneficiary in a calendar year), nonadherence to evidence-based guidelines, single-disease focus as opposed to integrated approach, lack of personalization to the individual beneficiary, and failure to motivate the beneficiary to participate in chronic disease self-management.

SELF-MANAGEMENT OF CHRONIC CONDITIONS

The concept of self-management was initially described as **self-care agency** in the 1970s and the concept was further developed by Orem to include specific personal traits and capabilities necessary for the performance of self-care activities on one's behalf to maintain life and promote health and well-being.[47,48] Self-management of chronic conditions actually occurs on a widespread basis. For example, it has been well studied in relationship to diabetes care. When self-care agency characteristics are enhanced in diabetic patients through education techniques and training in self-care, the individual is more likely to perform diabetes care activities and to achieve glycemic control and reduce the development of diabetes-associated complications.[48,49]

CHRONIC DISEASE SELF-MANAGEMENT PROGRAM

This model was developed under a 5-year research grant to the School of Medicine at Stanford University. Unlike other models discussed in this chapter, the chronic disease self-management program (CD SMP) was developed to *complement* existing programs and treatment for persons with chronic disease, not as a stand-alone model. Developed under a conceptual model of self-efficacy, the research team utilized focus groups of persons with chronic illness to create the content of patient-directed training. Participants in the program receive their training in workshops that are facilitated by trained leaders; the latter group receives training from the Stanford team and certification in CD SMP. The workshops cover topics such as dealing with frustration, fatigue, pain, and isolation; exercises for improving strength, flexibility, and endurance; appropriate medication use;

effective communication with family and healthcare providers; proper nutrition; and how to evaluate new treatments.[50]

Researchers have found that the CD SMP improves patient outcomes. Participants in a randomized control trial with heart failure, lung disease, stroke, or asthma had fewer hospital days and a sustained cost-to-savings ratio estimated at 1:4.[51] Chronic disease self-management is included as a construct in the Wagner Chronic Care Model and has been integrated into numerous other models and interventions aimed at chronic care management.

THE WAGNER CHRONIC CARE MODEL

The Chronic Care Model[10] provides a useful conceptual framework for CCM. This model posits that a substantial amount of the care management takes place *outside of formal healthcare delivery systems.* The model emphasizes patient self-management, integration of community resources, and the use of health information technology (HIT) to drive decision support, evidence-based care, and coordination of care among multiple providers. The Chronic Care Model has been successfully applied in a variety of settings, including staff-model HMOs, large group practices, and community health settings.[45] While the entire model has not been rigorously tested, findings from a review of published studies that used components of the model to design interventions strongly suggest that integration of the model has the potential to improve care and reduce costs of care for individuals with chronic disease.[2]

One of the most significant barriers to implementation of the Chronic Care Model or similar models is the absence of meaningful financial incentives—that is, outside of capitated contracts or demonstrations, care coordination is not rewarded. In fact, effective care coordination can reduce utilization, which, in turn, reduces realizable revenue in a fee-for-service environment. Compared to providers, health plans have greater incentives to provide care management; however, their investment may be mitigated by concerns about enrollee loyalty (i.e., changing plans before the financial benefits of care coordination have been realized) and reputation as chronic illness "friendly" (i.e., adverse selection generated by public awareness of successful chronic care management). Wider adoption of the Chronic Care Model may not be realized until primary care providers, healthcare delivery systems, and health plans or government payers have aligned incentives to improve care coordination.[2]

PUBLICLY FUNDED HOME- AND COMMUNITY-BASED SERVICES

STATE HOME- AND COMMUNITY-BASED MODELS

Delivery of services to Medicaid beneficiaries in communities where chronic illness is prevalent accounts for an estimated 71% of Medicaid spending.[7] Therefore, states have a strong economic incentive to implement chronic care management programs. A number of **social models** for home- and community-based services have been developed and tested.

Interpreted differently by each state, social models have been primarily focused on management of long-term care services and the associated Medicaid dollars. Often structured as Medicaid waiver programs, social models provide a range of services that include information, referral, screening, assessment, care planning, authorization for other Medicaid-covered services, and monitoring. Some states employ personnel to manage home- and community-based services, while others contract with other agencies and providers such as local Area Agencies on Agency (the so-called "triple A's"). The limitation of social models is the lack of integration with medical services, leaving the beneficiary to self-coordinate services and multiple case managers and providers.[7]

Medical models for chronic care management have crossed over into state home- and community-based services. These newer models apply techniques and practices developed in the managed care environment, such as disease and complex case management, and apply these services to beneficiaries with complex illness who are at risk for hospitalization and adverse outcomes.[7] Such programs are more complicated to administer than purely social models, because states have less direct control over service provision (typically involving many medical specialists) and because Medicare, rather than Medicaid, is the primary payer for medical services provided to complexly ill individuals, most of whom are older adults. Similar to the social models, the effectiveness of medical models is limited by lack of integration with the necessary social and community supports to allow beneficiaries to self-manage in a healthy and safe home environment.

Newer **models of care** are emerging to bridge the gap between social and medical models for care management. Two principal arrangements are most prevalent: partially integrated models manage all services provided under state Medicaid assistance while Medicare services remain fee-for-service, and fully integrated models coordinate the full range of Medicare and Medicaid services.[7] In some states, Medicaid beneficiaries must enroll in a managed care organization for the Medicaid-authorized primary and acute services (e.g., Oregon), while other states manage acute and long-term care services for Medicaid beneficiaries (e.g., Arizona). In both examples, case managers work to coordinate social services with AAA and other state-funded programs with medical services provided by independent, community-based primary care and other physician providers. An example of a fully integrated model is the Program of All-Inclusive Care for the Elderly (PACE).

PROGRAM OF ALL-INCLUSIVE CARE FOR THE ELDERLY

The Program of All-Inclusive Care for the Elderly (PACE) model of care delivery traces its history to the 1970s, when an innovative, community-organized initiative was developed to provide services to older immigrants living in the Chinatown–North Beach area of San Francisco. Community health and social leaders formed a not-for-profit corporation, On Lok Senior Health Services, to address the long-term care needs of the immigrant group. Their model emphasized what has more recently been termed "aging in place"— that is, supporting seniors to live safely and fully in their communities when possible for as long as possible.[52] This central commitment inspired the PACE model, which is a federal/state partnership to support dually eligible, nursing home–eligible beneficiaries to live safely in their communities. PACE programs enroll eligible beneficiaries who are 55 years or older and meet nursing home eligibility requirements. PACE programs receive per member/per month payments under which they manage enrollees' comprehensive social and medical needs—including PACE center–based primary care and support services using an interdisciplinary model, adult day services, in-home support, home health care, medications, social services, and hospital or nursing home care when needed. In 2008, there were 61 PACE programs operating in 29 states. Outcomes associated with this model of comprehensive, community-based care management include avoidance of nursing home placement (just 7% of PACE enrollees reside in nursing homes);[52] evidence that interdisciplinary team performance is associated with better functional outcomes;[53] reduction in overall costs of care (16–38% lower than Medicare fee-for-service [FFS] populations and 5–15% lower than costs for similar Medicaid beneficiaries); and better self-reported health and quality of life when compared to non-PACE populations.[54]

Despite the success and appeal of the PACE model, enrollment has been slower than anticipated. The program was established as a permanent Medicare provision under the 1997 Balanced Budget Act (BBA); 40 new programs were authorized that year, and 20 programs were authorized in each successive year.[54] Several million adults are eligible for PACE, yet the 61 operating programs serve just a fraction of the population of potentially eligible adults. Despite numerous barriers, PACE remains a viable model for providing comprehensive, integrated social and medical services to frail older adults. Future development may include more flexible financing and reimbursement, program design changes that will support participation of community-based physicians, potential eligibility adjustments, and availability of PACE in rural settings where the population is less concentrated and, thus, less immediately available to a center base.[55]

PHYSICIAN PRACTICE-CENTERED MODELS

PATIENT-CENTERED MEDICAL HOME

The primary care setting has traditionally been considered a patient's "medical home" because it offers the full spectrum of care from preventive, acute, and episodic to long-term follow-up for chronic conditions[5] and management of terminal illness through death. Yet the primary care setting is experiencing heightened strain stemming from increased demand for health care, reduced reimbursement for primary care services, and primary care practitioner workforce shortages.

Some studies suggest that as a result of these factors, many primary care practices are not managing chronic conditions adequately. In a systematic review of the study findings, researchers found that having a high-quality and reliable usual source of care was associated with better health outcomes and lower mortality rates.[56] Additionally, higher ratios of primary care physicians in areas with high levels of income disparity resulted in decreased stroke, heart disease, and cancer mortality.[56] In 2004, Baicker and Chandra reported a linear decrease in Medicare spending when there was an increase in the supply of primary care physicians. The quality of care, assessed using 24 indicators of care for six common medical conditions, improved as well. In contrast, an increased supply of specialists was associated with more healthcare spending, but poorer care and outcomes.[57] Revised models of the primary care medical home concept are being developed and piloted, spurred by an increasing aging population with multiple needs and a declining workforce of primary care physicians and nurse practitioners to provide primary care.

While numerous visions and operating models for the **Patient-Centered Medical Home (PCMH)** exist, most are based on joint principles adopted in 2007 by four key medical groups. The principles that underlie the PCMH are described in Table 4-2.

The model has gained widespread attention as a potential physician-directed practice solution to poorly coordinated care, especially for those patients whose care needs are

Table 4-2   Joint Principles of the Patient-Centered Medical Home (PCMH)

Principle	Definition
Personal physician	Ongoing relationship with a physician who provides "first contact, continuous and comprehensive care."
Physician-directed medical practice	The physician is the leader of a team of care providers who, together, are responsible for the ongoing care of patients in the practice.
Whole-person orientation	The physician is responsible to provide for or arrange care to address all of the patient's needs, across all stages of life (acute care, chronic care, preventive services, and end-of-life care).
Care coordination/integration	Integration/coordination is across all settings where care is delivered as well as in the patient's community. Care is facilitated by information technology.
Quality and safety	Practices are patient advocates to support their attainment of optimal, patient-centered outcomes. The focus includes continuous quality improvement (QI), evidence-based medicine, and patient/family participation in decision making and QI.
Enhanced access	Scheduling, expanded hours, and other practices support access to care.
Payment	Payment structures recognize the added value of the PCMH, with appropriate adjustment for care management activities outside of face-to-face visits, IT platform, case-mix variation, and outcomes associated with continuous QI efforts.

Modified from: American Academy of Family Physicians, American Academy of Pediatrics, American College of Physicians, American Osteopathic Association. Joint principles of the patient-centered medical home. Patient-Centered Primary Care Collaborative Web site. http://www.pcpcc.net/content/joint-principles-patient-centered-medical-home. Published February 2007. Accessed March 14, 2010.

complex and costly. Numerous demonstration projects funded both by the federal government and by private health plans are under way to test the PCMH. Evidence supporting the role of primary care in health outcomes and costs includes the positive effects of access to primary care on reduced mortality, reduced use, and reduced health disparities. At the same time, policy experts caution against premature exuberance and have called for development of a broader consensus around the core components; feasible expectations for practice redesign elements, such as expanded staffing and electronic health records; and alternative payment policies to reward chronic care management over acute care utilization.[58] Additional challenges include the development and endorsement of a core set of standard measurement criteria, public perceptions of the concepts and terminology (e.g., the connotation of "home" and association with nursing home), and expectations around short-term cost savings or "business case" in the absence of concomitant system redesign that will align other stakeholders within the broader system.[59]

GUIDED CARE

Another primary care–based model has been proposed and studied by a team of physicians and nurses at Johns Hopkins University. Based on the Wagner Chronic Care Model, "Guided Care" is a model of comprehensive chronic care management in which specially trained registered nurses (RNs) collaborate with primary care physicians and their staff to meet the needs of multimorbid older adults with complex care needs and historically high medical costs.[60] The RN, who sees patients in the community to coordinate their care according to an evidence-based care guide that is developed for each patient, is an employee of the practice. Nurse performance is monitored and measured against performance targets. The eight activities of the Guided Care nurse include the following actions:

- assessing the patient at home—standardized questionnaire, goals for care identified
- creating an evidence-based care guide—merging patient data and goals with best practices guide
- monitoring the patient proactively—nurses are taught principles and practice of motivational interviewing
- empowering the patient for self-management
- coordinating care providers
- monitoring and managing transitions—visits hospital, etc., at time of admission and throughout to manage the transition back to home or to other location
- educating and supporting caregivers
- accessing community resources

There are several unique features of the Guided Care model. First, the Guided Care nurse is located in the primary care practice, an arrangement that facilitates teamwork between the RN and other team members. The Guided Care team applies the publicly available Medicare data–based Hierarchical Conditions Category (HCC) predictive model to identify patients who are multimorbid and have complex care needs and high expenditures. The depth, intensity, and duration of relationships between team members and nurse/patient are central to the success of the model, and care is provided longitudinally for as long as indicated—in fact, most patients receive it for life. The Guided Care nurse training is focused on the selected clinical activities that have been shown to improve outcomes of care. Finally, the practices use health information technology to generate care plans, reminders, and decision support. Findings from an early pilot study suggest improved quality of care and lower healthcare costs for those patients who received Guided Care.[60] Preliminary findings from an eight-site cluster-randomized controlled trial with 904 chronically ill individuals revealed that patients who received Guided Care were significantly more likely to rate their care highly after six months.[61] The study team will evaluate health outcomes, caregiver burden, and utilization and costs of services at 18 months (this analysis had not completed at the time of publication).

COMMUNITY-BASED, FEE-FOR-SERVICE MODEL: GERIATRIC CARE MANAGEMENT

Geriatric Care Management is a private-pay option for professionally guided system navigation, service procurement, and monitoring. The Geriatric Care Manager (GCM) assesses an individual's medical and social needs and then coordinates assistance from paid service providers and family/friends/community members to enable the individual to live safely, comfortably, and independently.[62] Typically, a GCM is a health and human services professional such as a social worker, nurse, psychologist, gerontologist, or other type of counselor. GCMs are usually licensed in their individual specialty by the state(s) in which they practice, and most work in solo or small group practices.

As previously discussed, the terms "care management" and "case management" are often used interchangeably. While the definitions are similar, **case management** is defined as a more "hands-on" and collaborative process that is often coordinated and reimbursed by a third-party payer, whereas in the Geriatric Care Management model, care management is a client-paid service that centers on effectively linking clients to needed services.

Four primary factors are driving the increasing prevalence of Geriatric Care Management, namely, the burgeoning group of older adults, evolution of the "aging in place" movement, separation (often by long distances) of older adults and their adult children, and the increasing complexity of the U.S. healthcare system. The latter factor has led to a recognized need for professional assistance with navigating the system and locating services and supports. As previously discussed, publicly funded programs (e.g., home- and community-based service programs, state or local Administration on Aging–funded in-home personal care providers) are primarily available to older adults with lower incomes and asset levels.

Thirty-four million Americans provide care to older family members, and 15% live an hour or more away from the relative to whom they provide care.[63] Perhaps most important to the growth of the GCM industry is this phenomenon of long-distance caregiving. In a survey of 1,130 self-identified long-distance caregivers, nearly 23% reported that they were primarily responsible for the older adult relative; nearly 75% were spending 22 hours per month or more helping with shopping, managing finances and other instrumental activities of daily living; and nearly 80% were working full- or part-time.[64] On average, caregivers lived 450 miles from the care recipient, requiring 7 hours of travel time. In addition to lost work productivity, caregivers' direct economic burden reached $392 to $674 per month for travel, and 10% of respondents paid for services at a rate of $490 to $751 per month.

PALLIATIVE AND END-OF-LIFE CARE

Beginning in 1967 with the dogged determination of a visionary healer, Dr. Cicely Saunders, the word "hospice" became associated with a new approach to care of the dying. St. Christopher's Hospice was founded in the United Kingdom in that year, and the work of Dr. Saunders and others to humanize care of the dying became a model that would be emulated throughout the world. In 1974, the first hospice was founded in the United States, and within just 8 years Congress had authorized expansion of the Medicare program to cover hospice care for persons approaching the end of life. Hospice began in the United States as a spiritually based grassroots movement, driven largely by volunteers with a vision and passion to ease the suffering of those whose lives were coming to a close. The hospice approach was, in many ways, in direct opposition to the expanding use of technology to prolong life. Hospice emerged as a "bridge" between healthcare goals focused narrowly on treatment, cure, and rehabilitation, as well as the needs of dying persons and their families. Hospice emerged as a philosophical and programmatic response to gaps, "(1) between treating the disease and treating the person, (2) between technological research and psychosocial support, and (3) between the general denial of the fact of death in our society and the acceptance of death by those who face it."[57] Hospice care in the United States in those early years was conceptually consistent with the tenets of Dr. Saunders, but differed in one important way. Unlike hospice care delivery in much of the United Kingdom, hospice in the United States largely developed as a home support program and was later codified as such under the Medicare Conditions of Participation for hospice. Thus, hospice grew up outside of the broader healthcare umbrella.

Hospice perhaps remains the best-kept secret in a fragmented and depersonalized healthcare system. It is unto itself a system of care in which terminally ill patients' and their families' worst fears are relieved, where suffering is eased, and where patient and family definition of quality of life is central. To its detriment, hospice care in this country developed as a parallel system of care characterized by little integration with "mainstream" (hospital and outpatient) health care. Most people, including healthcare providers, now know a little about hospice, although this was far from true at the outset. In the early years, hospice care was provided by mission-minded professionals and volunteers who were guided by compassion and commitment. The science underlying hospice care was all but absent, and there were few "experts" in this new model of care.

In 2007, there were 4,700 hospice programs that collectively provided care to an estimated 1.4 million individuals, nearly 39% of all deaths.[66] In the past two decades, as the broader umbrella encompassing care for persons with advancing illness and at end of life, **palliative care** has begun to develop an evidence base and has been embraced more widely. Between 2000 and 2005, the number of palliative care programs in hospitals grew by 96%, from 632 to 1,240.[67] More than 2,800 physicians have been certified in the subspecialty of hospice and palliative medicine[4] and there are more than 17,300 hospice and palliative care certified nurses and allied professionals.[68] Last year, the National Priorities Partnership named improving care for the dying as one of six priorities for reforming the healthcare system.[69] Despite the inroads and experience to date, there remains much work to be done to prevent and treat physical, psychosocial, and spiritual suffering experienced by those at end of life and their families. Most persons die in hospitals or, increasingly, nursing homes. Pain is often poorly treated, and patient and family wishes concerning end-of-life care are frequently not elicited, not recorded, or not communicated among the treating professionals. As noted previously, of the 2.4 million persons who died in 2007, just 39% received care from a hospice. Of those who did receive care from a hospice program in 2008, 30% died within a week of admission, and the median length of stay was just 20 days.[66] The most frequent refrain from families who received hospice care in 2007 was the same as in the early years: "We wish that we had known about you sooner."

The missing link and natural framework for palliative care is chronic care management. Currently, palliative care interventions remain siloed in hospital or home hospice settings. That is, the patient typically must be hospitalized to encounter a palliative care clinician, who frequently has no post-acute referral network or **accountable care organization** to which the patient can be referred for palliative care follow-up. Patient-Centered Medical Homes, should they be fully developed and reimbursed as care coordination models, may provide one solution to seamless care management that includes end-of-life care, although it will be difficult for most practices to extend their reach into the community to oversee and manage chronic illness care in the home.

A comprehensive approach to chronic care management should contain monitoring of disease projection, use of available decision support to predict decline, direct and supportive communication about feasible treatment goals, and advance care planning that considers the patient's and family's goals as central and matches goals to effective interventions. Such a model directly addresses the "elephant in the room"—downward illness trajectory and increasing likelihood of death—but does so in a way that matches how patients decline and live out their lives. There is no "bright line" that signifies when palliative care should begin—indeed, the newest conceptualizations of palliative care place it concurrent to disease-focused care at the time of diagnosis. How do we deliver high-quality palliative care to those individuals who need it most—for example, Medicare beneficiaries with multiple chronic illnesses who are within their final two years of life? Under the current model, palliative care and hospice care are introduced to patients as a care *alternative*. As chronic care management evolves, it is likely that providers will embed the palliative care approach in chronic care management—where the guiding principles can be integrated with high-quality, evidence-based illness management.

WORKFORCE NEEDS FOR AN AGING SOCIETY WITH INCREASING CHRONIC ILLNESS

The fragmentation of the U.S. healthcare system is frequently cited as a significant barrier to comprehensive management of chronic illness for older adults.[70] As discussed previously, both the population of older adults and their associated burden of chronic illness are projected to grow substantially in coming years. Projected shortages of primary care practitioners to support this burgeoning population have been well documented.

Both the American College of Physicians (2006 position paper on Advanced Medical Home)[71] and the American Academy of Nurse Practitioners (2007 position paper)[72]—the bodies representing physicians and nurses who provide much of the primary care in the United States—point to the need for coordinated primary health care that is patient-centered, directed by a single provider, evidence-based, and focused on quality and safety. Both groups cite the Patient-Centered Medical Home as a viable model for providing such care, although they differ on the type of practitioner that should be considered. While the American College of Physicians advocates that the central figure should be a personal physician who works with a team of healthcare professionals, the American Academy College of Nurse Practitioners argues that NPs have demonstrated their ability to provide high-quality, cost-effective primary care and must be included in design, development, and provision of increased primary care to meet the nation's needs.[72] Importantly, both organizations advocate for a structure that:

- uses evidence-based medicine and clinical decision support tools to guide decision making at the point of care based on patient-specific factors;
- organizes the delivery of that care according to the Chronic Care Model, but leverages the core functions of the Chronic Care Model to provide enhanced care for all patients with or without a chronic condition;
- creates an integrated, coherent plan for ongoing medical care in partnership with patients and their families;
- provides enhanced and convenient access to care, not only through face-to-face visits, but also via telephone, email, and other modes of communication;
- identifies and measures key quality indicators to demonstrate continuous improvement in health status for individuals and populations treated;
- adopts and implements technology to promote safety, security, information exchange, and portals for patients to access their health information; and
- participates in programs that provide feedback and guidance on the overall performance of the practice and its clinicians.

Improving the health of the population hinges on better coordination of care, and future reform efforts will be stymied without increased numbers of primary care providers.

CONCLUSIONS

There is a growing recognition among policy makers and clinicians that healthcare delivery system reform hinges more on rethinking the way that we *manage chronic illness* than overhauling an entire system.[70] The mismatch between the chronic care needs of the population and the acute care orientation of the healthcare delivery system is spurring reform.[60] More than anything else, reforming chronic care will require us to break out of our provider-centric and disease-focused silos to take a whole-person approach to care management.[62] The 2001 Institute of Medicine (IOM) report: *Crossing the Quality Chasm: a New Health System for the 21st Century* outlined critical areas for healthcare delivery re-design.[73] These areas include: basing health care on continuous relationships with healthcare providers, customizing patient care based on the needs of the individual, and sharing of health illness information through electronic medical records (EMR). Chronic care management will be enhanced by the incorporation of population health data into the delivery system.

Taken together, the aging of the population, prevalence of chronic illness, and payment models that focus on acute/episodic illness rather than chronic care management, pose significant threats to the sustainability of the healthcare system. Much of the cost of health care is related to chronic disease and much of chronic disease prevalence is modifiable—if there were better models for population health management that emphasized illness prevention and comprehensive care management. The predominant conceptual model for chronic care management developed by Wagner and colleagues has guided development of numerous approaches and interventions. However, not until payment is reformed will there be sufficient incentives to adopt new approaches to chronic care management. Successful care management models will bridge social and medical needs; integrate services across settings; rely on electronic exchange of data that are predictive, accessible, and shared; recognize the role of the patient and empower self-management; and address needs across the care continuum, including death.

STUDY AND DISCUSSION QUESTIONS

1. Discuss the risk factors and circumstances that lead to the development of chronic diseases.
2. Compare and contrast models for chronic care management. What are their relative strengths and weaknesses?
3. Where does chronic disease self-management fit into an overall approach to chronic care?
4. What are the barriers and facilitators to chronic disease self-management?
5. Does the Chronic Care Model provide a framework for healthcare reform? If so, how?

SUGGESTED READINGS AND WEB SITES

READINGS

Boult C, Giddens J, Frey K, Reider L, Novak T, eds. *Guided Care: A New Nurse–Physician Partnership in Chronic Care.* New York, NY: Springer Publishing Company; 2009.

Institute of Medicine. *Retooling for an Aging America: Building the Health Care Workforce.* Washington, DC: The National Academies Press; 2008.

Lorig K, Sobel D, Gonzalez V, Minor M, Holman H, Laurent D. *Living a Healthy Life With Chronic Conditions: Self-Management of Heart Disease, Arthritis, Diabetes, Asthma, Bronchitis, Emphysema, and Others.* 3rd rev ed. Boulder, CO: Bull Publishing Company; 2006.

Morrison RS, Meier DE. *Geriatric Palliative Care.* New York, NY: Oxford University Press; 2003.

WEB SITES

AARP Public Policy Institute: http://www.aarp.org/research/ppi/

Agency for Healthcare Research and Quality: http://www.ahrq.gov

Centers for Disease Control and Prevention: http://www.cdc.gov/

DMAA: The Care Continuum Alliance: http://www.dmaa.org/

Medical Expenditure Panel Survey: http://www.meps.ahrq.gov

National Chronic Care Consortium: http://www.nccconline.org

Partnership for Solutions: http://www.partnershipforsolutions.org

Patient-Centered Primary Care Collaborative: http://pcpcc.net

REFERENCES

1. AARP. *Chronic Care: A Call to Action for Health Reform.* Washington, DC: AARP Public Policy Institute. http://assets.aarp.org/rgcenter/health/beyond_50_hcr.pdf. Accessed October 20, 2009.

2. Bodenheimer T, Wagner EH, Grumbach K. Improving primary care for patients with chronic illness. *JAMA.* 2002;288(14):1775–1779.

3. Collins SR, Schoen C, Doty MM, Holmgren AL, How SK. Paying more for less: older adults in the individual insurance market: findings from the Commonwealth Fund Survey of Older Adults. Issue brief. *Commonw Fund.* 2005;841:1–12.

4. Haggerty JL, Reid RJ, Freeman GK, Starfield BH, Adiar CE, McKendry R. Continuity of care: a multidisciplinary review. *BMJ.* 2003;327(7425):1219–1221.

5. Grumbach K, Bodenheimer T. A primary care home for Americans—putting the house in order. *JAMA.* 2002;288:889–893.

6. Administration on Aging. *A Profile of Older Americans: 2008.* Washington, DC: US Department of Health and Human Services. http://www.aoa.gov/AoARoot/Aging_Statistics/Profile/2008/docs/2008profile.pdf. Published 2008. Accessed March 15, 2010.

7. Mollica RL, Gillespie J. Care coordination for people with chronic conditions. Partnership for Solutions Web site. http://www.partnershipforsolutions.org/solutions/index.html. Published January 2003. Accessed December 17, 2009.

8. Machlin SR. Trends in health care expenditures for the elderly age 65 and over: 2006 versus 1996. http://www.meps.ahrq.gov/mepsweb/data_files/

publications/st256/stat256.pdf. Medical Expenditure Panel Survey Statistical Brief #256. Published August 2009. Accessed December 17, 2009.

9. Hoffman C, Rice D, Sung HY. Persons with chronic conditions. their prevalence and costs. *JAMA.* 1996;276(18):1473–1479.

10. Wagner EH. Meeting the needs of chronically ill people. *BMJ.* 2001;323(7319):945–946.

11. Chronic Disease Prevention and Health Promotion. Centers for Disease Control and Prevention Web site. http://www.cdc.gov/NCCdphp/overview.htm#top. Accessed March 15, 2010.

12. Wolff JL, Starfield B, Anderson G. Prevalence, expenditures, and complications of multiple chronic conditions in the elderly. *Arch Intern Med.* 2002;162(20):2269–2276.

13. Bindman AB, Grumbach K, Osmond D, et al. Preventable hospitalizations and access to health care. *JAMA.* 1995;274(4):305–311.

14. QuickStats: average life expectancy at birth, by race and sex—United States, 2000, 2006, and 2007. *MMWR.* 2009;58(42):1185. http://www.cdc.gov/mmwr/preview/mmwrhtml/mm5842a7.htm. Accessed December 17, 2009.

15. Thom T, Haase N, Rosamond W, et al, for American Heart Association Statistics Committee. Heart disease and stroke statistics—2006 update. A report from the American Heart Association Statistics Committee and Stroke Statistics Subcommittee. *Circulation.* 2006;113(6):e85–e151. http://circ.ahajournals.org/cgi/content/abstract/CIRCULATIONAHA.105.171600v1. Accessed December 17, 2009.

16. CDC. Racial/ethnic and socioeconomic disparities in multiple risk factors for heart disease and stroke—United States, 2003. *MMWR.* 2005;54(5):113–117.

17. Reeves MJ, Rafferty AP. Healthy lifestyle characteristics among adults in the United States, 2000. *Arch Intern Med.* 2005;165(8):854–857.

18. Ford ES, Bergmann MM, Kroger J, Schienkiewitz A, Weikert C, Boeing H. Healthy living is the best revenge: findings from the European Prospective Investigation Into Cancer and Nutrition-Potsdam study. *Arch Intern Med.* 2009;169(15):1355–1362.

19. Soni A. The five most costly conditions, 1996 and 2006: estimates for the U.S. civilian noninstitutionalized population. http://www.meps.ahrq.gov/mepsweb/data_files/publications/st248/stat248.pdf. Medical Expenditure Panel Survey Statistical Brief #248. Published July 2009. Accessed March 15, 2010.

20. 2007 National diabetes fact sheet: general information and national estimates on diabetes in the United States [fact sheet]. Atlanta, GA: US Department of Health and Human Services, Centers for Disease Control and Prevention; 2007. http://www.cdc.gov/diabetes/pubs/factsheet07.htm. Accessed March 15, 2010.

21. Vandegrift D, Yoked T. Obesity rates, income, and suburban sprawl: an analysis of US states. *Health Place.* 2004;10(3):221–229.

22. American Cancer Society. Statistics for 2008. American Cancer Society Web site. http://www.cancer.org/docroot/STT/stt_0_2008.asp?sitearea=STT&level=1. Accessed October 20, 2009.

23. National Institute of Mental Health. The numbers count: mental disorders in America. National Institute of Mental Health Web site. http://www.nimh.nih.gov/health/publications/the-numbers-count-mental-disorders-in-america/index.shtml. Updated August 10, 2009. Accessed December 17, 2009.

24. Mental illness exacts heavy toll, beginning in youth [news release]. Bethesda, MD: National Institute of Mental Health; June 6, 2005. http://www.nimh.nih.gov/science-news/2005/mental-illness-exacts-heavy-toll-beginning-in-youth.shtml. Accessed March 15, 2010.

25. Department of Health and Human Services. Mental health: a report of the Surgeon General. http://www.surgeongeneral.gov/library/mentalhealth/home.html. Published December 2009. Accessed March 15, 2010.

26. Moorman JE. National surveillance for asthma—United States, 1980–2004. MMWR. 2007; 56 (SS08):1–14;18–54. http://www.cdc.gov/mmwr/preview/mmwrhtml/ss5608a1.htm. Updated October 5, 2007. Accessed March 15, 2010.

27. Smith DH, Malone DC, Lawson KA, Okamoto LJ, Battista C, Saunders WB. A national estimate of the economic costs of asthma. *Am J Respir Crit Care Med.* 1997;156(3 Pt 1):787–793.

28. American Cancer Society. *Cancer Facts & Figures, 2009.* Atlanta, GA: American Cancer Society;

2009. http://www.cancer.org/downloads/STT/500809web.pdf. Accessed December 17, 2009.

29. Surveillance Epidemiology and End Results (SEER). Browse the SEER Cancer Statistics Review 1975–2006. http://seer.cancer.gov/csr/1975_2006/browse_csr.php?section=2&page=sect_02_table.18.html. Accessed March 15, 2010.

30. CDC. National and state medical expenditures and lost earnings attributable to arthritis and other rheumatic conditions—United States, 2003. *MMWR.* 2007;56(1):4–7.

31. Yelin E, Murphy L, Cisternas MG, Foreman AJ, Pasta DJ, Helmick CG. Medical care expenditures and earnings losses among persons with arthritis and other rheumatic conditions in 2003, and comparisons to 1997. *Arthritis Rheum.* 2007; 56(5):1397–1407.

32. American Heart Association. Heart Disease and Stroke Statistics—2009 Update. Dallas, TX: American Heart Association: 2009. http://www.americanheart.org/downloadable/heart/12402509 46756LS–1982%20Heart%20and%20Stroke%20Update.042009.pdf. Accessed December 17, 2009.

33. National Cancer Institute. Cancer trends progress report—2007 update. National Cancer Institute Web site. http://progressreport.cancer.gov/doc_detail.asp?pid=1&did=2007&chid=75&coid=726&mid. Updated November 16, 2007. Accessed December 17, 2009.

34. Nelson N. The majority of cancers are linked to the environment. *BenchMarks.* 2004;4(3):1–4. http://www.cancer.gov/newscenter/benchmarks-vol4-issue3/page1. Accessed December 17, 2009.

35. Bibbins-Domingo K, Lin F, Vittinghoff E, et al. Predictors of heart failure among women with coronary disease. *Circulation.* 2004;110(11): 1424–1430.

36. Lloyd-Jones DM, Evans JC, Levy D. Hypertension in adults across the age spectrum: current outcomes and control in the community. *JAMA.* 2005;294(4):466–472.

37. Lee WC, Lamas GA, Balu S, Spalding J, Wang Q, Pashos CL. Direct treatment cost of atrial fibrillation in the elderly American population: a Medicare perspective. *J Med Econ.* 2008;11(2): 281–298.

38. Wang LY, Zhong Y, Wheeler L. Direct and indirect costs of asthma in school-age children. *Preventing Chronic Disease.* 2005;2(1): 1–10. http://www.cdc.gov/pcd/issues/2005/jan/04_0053.htm. Accessed December 17, 2009.

39. Linden A, Adler-Milstein J. Medicare disease management in policy context. *Health Care Financ Rev.* 2008;29(3):1–11.

40. Hsiao CJ, Boult C. Effects of quality on outcomes in primary care: a review of the literature. *Am J Med Qual.* 2008;23(4):302–310.

41. Harrold LR, Field TS, Gurwitz JH. Knowledge, patterns of care, and outcomes of care for generalists and specialists. *J Gen Intern Med.* 1999; 14(8):499–511.

42. Greenfield S, Rogers W, Mangotich M, Carney MF, Tarlov AR. Outcomes of patients with hypertension and non-insulin dependent diabetes mellitus treated by different systems and specialists: results from the medical outcomes study. *JAMA.* 1995;274(18):1436–1444.

43. Greenfield S, Kaplan SH, Kahn R, Ninomiya J, Griffith JL. Profiling care provided by different groups of physicians: effects of patient case-mix (bias) and physician-level clustering on quality assessment results. *Ann Intern Med.* 2002;136(2): 111–121.

44. Wennberg JE, Fisher ES, Goodman DC, Skinner JS. Tracking the care of patients with severe chronic illness. The Dartmouth Atlas of Health Care, 2008. http://www.dartmouthatlas.org/atlases/2008_Atlas_Exec_Summ.pdf. Accessed December 17, 2009.

45. Mechanic D. The rise and fall of managed care. *J Health Soc Behav.* 2004;45 Suppl:76–86.

46. Bentzen N. *WONCA Dictionary of General Family Practice.* Copenhagen, Denmark: Laegeforeningens Forlag, 2003.

47. Taylor SG. Dorothea E. Orem: self-care deficit theory of nursing. In: Toomey AM, Alligood MR, eds. *Nursing Theorists and Their Work.* St. Louis, MO: Mosby; 2006:267–291.

48. Sousa VD, Zauszniewski JA, Zeller RA, Neese JB. Factor analysis of the Appraisal of Self-care Agency Scale in American adults with diabetes mellitus. *Diabetes Educ.* 2008;34(1):98–108.

49. Boren SA, Gunlock TL, Schaefer J, Albright A. Reducing risks in diabetes self-management: a systematic review of the literature. *Diabetes Educ.* 2007;33(6):1053–1077.

50. Stanford School of Medicine. Chronic Disease Self-Management Program. Stanford Patient Education Research Center Web site. http://patienteducation.stanford.edu/programs/cdsmp.html. Accessed December 17, 2009

51. Lorig KR, Sobel DS, Stewart AL, et al. Evidence suggesting that a chronic disease self-management program can improve health status while reducing utilization and costs: a randomized trial. *Med Care.* 1999;37(1):5–14.

52. National PACE Association. What is PACE? National PACE Association Web site. http://www.npaonline.org:80/website/article.asp?id=12. Accessed December 23, 2009.

53. Mukamel DB, Temkin-Greener H, Delavan R, et al. Team performance and risk-adjusted health outcomes in the Program of All-Inclusive care for the Elderly (PACE). *Gerontologist.* 2006;46(2):227–237.

54. Petigara T, Anderson G. Program of all-inclusive care for the elderly. Health Policy Monitor Web site. http://www.hpm.org/en/Surveys/Johns_Hopkins_Bloomberg_School_of__Publ._H_-_USA/13/Program_of_All-Inclusive_Care_for_the_Elderly.html. Published 2009. Accessed March 2010.

55. Hirth V, Baskins J, Dever-Bumba M. Program of all-inclusive care (PACE): past, present, and future. *J Am Med Dir Assoc.* 2009;10(3):155–160.

56. Starfield B, Shi L, Macinko J. Contribution of primary care to health systems and health. *Millbank Q.* 2005;83(3):457–502.

57. Baicker K, Chandra A. Medicare spending, the physician workforce, and beneficiaries' quality of care. *Health Aff.* 2004;Suppl Web Exclusives:W184–W197.

58. Berenson RA, Hammons T, Gans DN, et al. A house is not a home: keeping patients at the center of practice redesign. *Health Aff.* 2008;27(5):1219–1230.

59. Rittenhouse DR, Shortell SM. The patient-centered medical home: will it stand the test of health reform? *JAMA.* 2009;301(19):2038–2040.

60. Boult C, Karm L, Groves C. Improving chronic care: the "Guided Care" model. *Permanente J.* 2008;12(1):50–54.

61. Boult C, Reider L, Frey K, et al. Early effects of "Guided Care" on the quality of health care for multimorbid older persons: a cluster randomized controlled trial. *J Gerontol A Biol Sci Med.* 2008;63(3):321–327.

62. Stone R, Reinhard SC, Machemer J, Rudin D. Geriatric care managers: a profile of an emerging profession. http://www.careersinaging.com/careersinaging/geriatric_care_managers.pdf. Published November 1, 2002. Accessed December 17, 2009.

63. National Alliance for Caregiving, AARP. *Caregiving in the U.S.* http://www.caregiving.org/data/04finalreport.pdf. Published April 2004. Accessed March 15, 2010.

64. National Alliance for Caregiving, Zogby International. Miles away: the MetLife study of long-distance caregiving. http://www.caregiving.org/data/milesaway.pdf. Published July 2004. Accessed March 15, 2010.

65. Wentzel KB. *To Those Who Need It Most, Hospice Means Hope.* Boston, MA: Charles River Books; 1981.

66. National Hospice and Palliative Care Organization. *NHPCO Facts and Figures: Hospice Care in America.* http://www.nhpco.org/files/public/Statistics_Research/NHPCO_facts_and_figures.pdf. Published 2009. Accessed September 19, 2009.

67. Kuehn BM. Hospitals embrace palliative care. *JAMA.* 2007;298(11):1263–1265. http://jama.ama-assn.org/cgi/content/full/298/11/1263. Accessed September 19, 2009.

68. American Academy of Hospice and Palliative Medicine. Certification. American Academy of Hospice and Palliative Medicine Web site. http://www.association-office.com/ABHPM/etools/publicdir/search.cfm. Accessed September 15, 2009.

69. National Priorities Partnership. *National Priorities and Goals: Aligning Our Efforts to Transform America's Healthcare.* Washington, DC: National Quality Forum; 2008.

70. Dentzer S. Reform chronic illness? Yes, we can. *Health Aff.* 2009;28(1):12–13.

71. American College of Physicians. The advanced medical home: a patient-centered, physician-guided model of health care. http://www. acponline.org/advocacy/where_we_stand/ policy/adv_med.pdf. Published January 30, 2006. Accessed September 15, 2009.

72. Fellows of the American Academy of Nurse Practitioners. *Nurse Practitioners: Promoting Access to Coordinated Primary Care.* http://www.aanp .org/NR/rdonlyres/26598BA6-A2DF-4902-A700-64806CE083B9/0/PromotingAccessto CoordinatedPrimaryCare62008withL.pdf. Published December 5, 2007. Accessed March 15, 2007.

73. Institute of Medicine. *Crossing the Quality Chasm: A New Health System for the 21st Century.* Washington, DC: National Academy Press; 2001.

POPULATION HEALTH QUALITY AND SAFETY

SUSAN DESHARNAIS, PhD, MPH, AND
VALERIE P. PRACILIO, MPH

Executive Summary

Population health quality and safety—pillars of a culture of wellness

Quality and safety are integral to advancing population health. Achieving population health requires improving the current system, where measuring quality and safety at the population level is a real challenge. Poor access to care and information highlights the disintegration of our current system, which focuses more on illness than on wellness. The tradition of delivering "sick" care, rather than "health" care, must be changed. We have a shared responsibility, and we must develop a shared vision for achieving a system that meets the needs of populations and is founded on effective collaboration, coordination, and teamwork; where resources are available for quality improvement; and where everyone is accountable for quality. Looking at models that have been proven effective, we can strive to create an "epidemic of health and wellness." Utilizing Avedis Donabedian's matrix, we provide a framework for achieving population health quality and safety. Throughout this chapter, we present successes and failures of integrating care at this level, as well as policy implications.

Learning Objectives

1. Explain why it is difficult to monitor healthcare quality and safety at the population level.
2. Conceptualize how to measure quality and safety at a population level, using Donabedian's matrix.
3. Explain the cause of variations in practice patterns across communities.
4. Describe how to address quality and safety issues in an ideal situation, using available data in a specified community.

Key Words

culture	relational coordination
outcome	safety
process	structure
quality	teamwork

INTRODUCTION

Quality, as defined by the Institute of Medicine, is "the degree to which health services for individuals and populations increase the likelihood of desired health outcomes and are consistent with current professional knowledge."[1] Delivery of health services implies that the provider is responsible for good quality care that meets the patient's expectations. **Safety** is "freedom from accidental injury" and is a necessary component of quality.[2] The responsibility does not rest solely on providers; consumers are also part of the healthcare team. While safety can be achieved without quality, quality cannot be achieved without safety. Quality and safety are integral to advancing population health.

Safety is a shared responsibility; providers influence the processes through which care is delivered and patients have responsibility for providing information, adhering to instructions, and complying with recommendations. In a population-based system, healthcare providers would need to focus on meeting the needs of populations, while healthcare consumers would be their own advocates.

When healthcare quality and safety are viewed from a population perspective, we currently find an unsatisfactory situation. The health care in virtually all communities in the United States is *not* delivered through integrated systems, where communication is clear, **teamwork** is the norm, and all healthcare providers collaborate to provide safe, quality care. Instead, there are a variety of providers, both public and private, who operate independently. Physicians primarily work in their offices and/or clinics, spending a small portion of their time in hospitals; hospital personnel work in separate institutions that compete with one another; divisions of health departments, both state and local, work independently, often providing care to indigent people in the community, but also providing other services to the populations living in a given area; pharmacists often work for "chains," each with different record systems; and many people in the community are uninsured, receiving only emergency care. Given this situation, how can we begin to measure the quality and safety of the health care provided to a given population?

Care is fragmented, and there is no single information system on which we can rely to tell us what is happening. There are few public records available other than birth and death certificates and the registries for some diseases that are, by law, reportable, such as HIV and cancer. The tradition has been one in which healthcare services are delivered to individual patients by providers who practice individually in a system that supports individual "sick" care, rather than population-based health care. The types of data collected have been defined by the way that healthcare providers are reimbursed, rather than on the quality and safety of the care provided. However, using claims data and other reimbursement records to measure the quality and safety of the care provided has significant limitations.

Complexity is inherent in the healthcare system. More than 45% of Americans suffer from one or more chronic conditions.[3] Poorly coordinated treatment of chronic conditions is a true quality and safety concern in our current healthcare system and is a symptom of the current system structure. On average, an American patient will spend 5.5 days in the hospital annually, during which she or he will encounter numerous healthcare providers.[4] While quality and safety efforts tend to focus on hospitals, the majority of healthcare services are provided in outpatient settings. Of the annual 1.1 billion ambulatory care visits, 57.5% are visits to primary care providers who monitor and manage chronic conditions.[5–7] The greatest opportunity for improvement in population health relies on better management of chronic conditions; however, management of these conditions is as complex as the system in which health care is delivered. Patients have encounters with primary care physicians, specialists, nurses, pharmacists, and hospitals as well as other healthcare providers; the expectation is that they are all communicating and working collaboratively to provide the best that the healthcare system has to offer. The unfortunate truth is that in our fragmented system, this expectation is often unmet. Everyone is a healthcare consumer. All consumers have expectations that must be achieved as they seek preventive care as well as curative care. However, it is not solely the provider's role to meet consumer expectations. To advance population health, providers and patients must have a "shared responsibility" for quality and safety. A system that primarily provides curative care is not sustainable because it does not encourage quality and safety monitoring or foster continuity of care. If the airline industry were "curative," airplanes would only be inspected when something went wrong, rather than before each flight. The result would be an unsafe system with endangered, dissatisfied consumers, not unlike the current U.S. healthcare system.

ADVANCES IN QUALITY AND SAFETY

While progress has been made in raising awareness of the challenges healthcare providers face in providing high-quality and safe care, there is still a lot of work to be done. Healthcare reform is on the national agenda, and change is imminent. There is an opportunity to reflect on what has brought about the current challenges and redefine the system, building on demonstrated successes and eliminating inefficiencies. In order to bring this vision to reality, we need to focus on populations rather than individuals.

The current reality has been described as the "first curve," or the so-called craft age. Our vision would create the "second curve," or information age, designed to meet the needs of populations founded on collaboration, coordination, and teamwork, with resources available

> ### BOX 5-1 THE FOUR TENETS OF POPULATION HEALTH QUALITY AND SAFETY
>
> - Healthcare delivery is focused on what will benefit the majority, meaning it is population based.
> - Providers and patients must have shared responsibility for quality and safety.
> - Chronic care management is a natural place to start focusing on population health quality and safety improvement.
> - Population health quality and safety create a framework for advancing health and wellness.

for quality improvement, in a place where everyone is accountable for quality and safety.[8] (See Figure 5-1.) A shared commitment to reaching the second curve will rely on addressing four dimensions of quality: access, technical performance, interpersonal performance, and continuity.[9] It will also require movement toward wellness and away from "curative" care. In preserving health, emphasis will need to be placed on four tenets of population health quality and safety (PHQS).

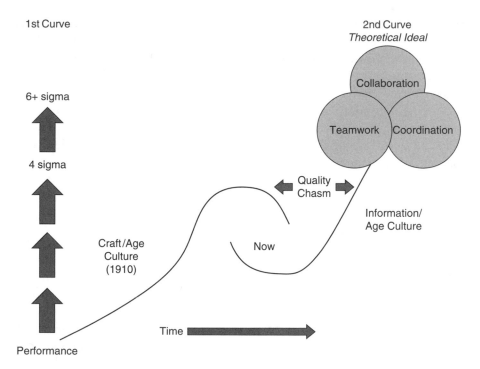

Figure 5-1 Moving from the 1st curve of process improvement to the 2nd curve of process re-engineering.
Adapted from Morrison I. *The Second Curve: Managing the Velocity of Change.* New York, NY: Random House Publishing Group; 1996.

To achieve wellness, our fragmented system that rewards high-cost, intensive medical intervention over higher value primary care, preventive medicine, and the management of chronic illness will need to build on a foundation of success.[10]

WHAT HAS WORKED

The success of a few key healthcare organizations that share this vision provides a framework for advancing quality and safety and promoting health and wellness. In Minnesota, a consumer-governed nonprofit healthcare organization helped 72% of all adults receive appropriate preventive screenings in 2006.[11] In Michigan, more than 100 hospitals implemented checklists for five practices that were cited to cause safety concerns, resulting in 1,500 lives saved in an 18-month period.[11] In Pennsylvania, the Transitional Care Model was developed to facilitate a partnership between advanced-practice nurses and the healthcare team to identify patients at risk for poor post-discharge outcomes and create discharge plans through communication with the patient, the healthcare team, and the family.[11] Identifying themes that led to the success of these organizations and initiatives will inform an agenda for population health management. There are three core components that emerged from these successes and influence quality and safety: (1) the organization, (2) the coordination, and (3) the **culture**. These components provide a starting point for population health efforts.

The National Quality Forum convened key thought leaders to address the challenges of our healthcare system through a partnership aimed at identifying priorities.[11] This collaboration signaled a shared sense of responsibility to transform health care. Similarly, leaders in healthcare organizations must share responsibility for the quality and safety of care.[12] Everyone has the capacity to be a leader. Those individuals directly involved in the process or system that needs improvement are perfectly positioned to be engaged in the efforts. **Relational coordination** is a must. Shared goals, knowledge, and mutual respect define relational coordination, a concept that manages the interdependencies between people performing the tasks necessary to deliver safe, quality health care.[13] This concept is in alignment with teamwork, which is as integral to healthcare quality as the wings are to an aircraft. Teamwork is learned in practice, with each team member bringing unique skills and experience to his or her work. The collective efforts of an interprofessional team will do more to achieve health and wellness than any one individual.

Underlying the organization and coordination of healthcare delivery is culture, which affects behavior and performance.[14] Culture relates to perceptions and the organization's belief system, which influences individuals and teams. An organization that values quality and safety and institutes supportive mechanisms that foster teamwork, communication, and coordination will likely be successful. To achieve transformational change called for by the National Priorities Partnership and required to reach the second curve, the organization, coordination, and culture of the American healthcare system must advance quality and safety to ultimately create an environment where health and wellness can flourish.

REDUCING FRAGMENTATION

If meaningful and sustainable improvements are to be accomplished, a conceptual model is needed. In the 1960s, Dr. Avedis Donabedian recognized that healthcare quality is embedded in, and influenced by, the external environment in a given community.[15] Donabedian described how the processes of care (the manner in which professionals practice) are primarily by-products of the resources available in the environment and the structure by which they are allocated. Similarly, the outcomes of care (the condition of patients following treatment and recovery) are a result of both the structure of resources and the processes of care, i.e., the manner in which professionals practice in that community.

The **structures** and **processes** are the inputs that help explain the large variations in both practice patterns and patient **outcomes** that are apparent across the United States.[16] The obvious explanation for variation is the structural differences between communities, including available resources, insurance coverage, the community's cultural values and beliefs about health, and provider decision making, often a reflection of the culture. The physician population is not homogeneous. Differences in where and when they were trained contribute to variation in processes of care, in addition to geography and differences in traditions between and among local hospitals and integrated delivery systems.

Donabedian attempted to organize thinking about healthcare quality and safety by providing a structure that allows us to analyze inadequacies and plan for improvement. Analyzing inadequate outcomes will inform a strategy to repair the structure of the delivery and the processes of care that produced such outcomes.[15]

A FRAMEWORK FOR ACHIEVING HEALTH AND WELLNESS

Donabedian's framework for analyzing quality is broadly applicable from the small office practice that is a comparatively simple setting to a community representing a seemingly more complex situation. In addition to classifying measures into domains of structure, process, and outcome, Donabedian further categorizes according to four aspects of quality: access, technical performance, interpersonal performance, and continuity. These classifications have been organized into a table that demonstrates the aspects of health care that must be considered when discussing quality and safety in the following section.

QUALITY AND SAFETY MEASUREMENT: THE CONSUMER'S PERSPECTIVE

As stated previously, everyone is a healthcare consumer. Some are internal consumers within a system (the providers of healthcare services), while others are external consumers (the patients). As external consumers, we have two primary expectations we want met during our encounters with providers: access to the care needed and effective care. Quality of care can be defined in terms of a provider's technical performance and whether that care meets patients' expectations.[9] Provision of quality services by delivery systems is necessary to earn the population's trust. Without trust, healthcare consumers will turn to the health system only when they are in dire need of curative care.[9]

A CONSUMER'S VIEW OF QUALITY AND SAFETY

Healthcare consumers utilize the healthcare system when in need of preventive care or curative care. Regular checkups, health screenings, and pharmaceutical needs draw consumers into the system from time to time; however, the majority only utilize healthcare services when feeling ill. No matter what the cause, healthcare consumers deserve to receive a standard level of service, just as one would expect when purchasing services from any other industry. Table 5-1 describes the standard that a healthcare consumer would expect in a system that addresses population needs.

It is evident from this example that a number of measures would be interesting from the consumer's perspective. Simplistic measurements would not be adequate. It is essential to understand consumer needs and develop operational definitions with supportive data to address and measure the many different aspects of quality and safety that the consumer values.

Table 5-1 Measures of Quality and Safety from the Healthcare Consumer's Perspective

Components of Quality	Structure	Process	Outcome
Access	• Were the hours of operation convenient? • Did I have adequate transportation to get to see my provider? • Was the parking and/or shuttle simple to use and free? • Was there sufficient signage within the building to find the place I needed to be?	• What was the waiting time? • Did this provider take my insurance?	• Am I satisfied with various aspects of access to this provider? • Were my health outcomes and safety problems worse because of access problems? • Was the waiting time acceptable to me?
Technical performance	• Are the providers properly trained to treat my conditions? Do they do a lot of these procedures? • What are the mortality and complication rates at this place for the procedures I need? • Are procedures in place and people trained to protect my safety?	• Was the waiting area clean and was hand sanitizer available? • Did the provider correctly diagnose my conditions? • Did the provider wash hands before examining me? • Were safety procedures followed?	• Do I feel confident in this provider's knowledge? • Are my health outcomes optimal? • Am I satisfied with my health outcomes? • Did I suffer any preventable injury during my care?

Table 5-1 Measures of Quality and Safety from the Healthcare Consumer's Perspective (Continued)

Components of Quality	Structure	Process	Outcome
Interpersonal performance	• Is my language spoken? • Is the area where I am treated private, or are other people too close to ensure privacy and confidentiality?	• Did the provider allow time for me to ask questions? • Did the provider make sure I understood how I should take my medicine? • Is my privacy protected when I speak to people who are providers? • Were evidence-based treatment alternatives discussed with me? Did I understand the choices?	• Do I trust this provider to do what is best for me? • Do I feel respected by this provider? • Would I return to this provider for care in the future? • Did I understand what I should do to follow instructions and comply with recommendations for care?
Continuity	• Are there procedures in place so that I can easily bring information from my other providers to this provider? • Will information from this encounter be available to my other providers?	• Were appropriate referrals made? • Will this provider help me set up appointments with the providers to whom I am referred? • Are future appointments with this provider easy to set up?	• Were safety problems minimal during handoff? • Am I satisfied with the way that referrals and transfers are handled?

AN INSTITUTION'S VIEW OF QUALITY AND SAFETY

Donabedian's framework can also be applied to institutions or hospitals to measure, assess, and improve quality and safety. In this situation, the institution typically is focused on the population of patients they treat. The measures of interest may arise from the marketing and financial needs of that institution, demands of external regulatory and quasi-regulatory agencies, and feedback from consumers. Table 5-2 describes a number of infrastructural and provider-focused measures that can be used to assess quality and safety at the institution's level. Availability of services at the institution, the expertise of the healthcare providers, and their ability to work as a team to provide safe, effective care to the patients at the point of care and during transitions are examples of measures used to assess providers, institutions, and the populations they serve.

Table 5-2   Measures of Quality and Safety from the Institution's Perspective

Components of Quality	Structure	Process	Outcome
Access	Range and scope of services provided in the institution and associated outpatient and inpatient facilities (within a system).	Waiting times for appointments in various departments.	Are consumers satisfied with their access to care?
Technical performance	Credentialing of physicians; standards for hiring nurses and other professionals.	Error rates for certain procedures; compliance rates of providers with guidelines.	Complication rates for various defined procedures; infection rates for defined groups of patients.
Interpersonal performance	Training of personnel in cultural sensitivity, communication skills.	Time spent with patients; ability of providers to deal effectively with patients in different ethnic groups.	Patient reports about whether they trust the providers and believe they are respected.
Continuity	Availability of procedures for transferring patients and information across units within the facility, and, when necessary, to other facilities.	Are the adopted procedures followed? Do systems for transferring patients and patient information work efficiently?	Are patients satisfied with the manner in which transfers and referrals are handled?

CREATING AN EPIDEMIC OF HEALTH AND WELLNESS

EPIDEMIOLOGICAL FACTORS

There are a number of epidemiological factors that contribute to disease. Many of these factors can be affected by community action, whether at the local, state, or national level; therefore, consideration must be given to these environment, nutrition, behavior, immunological, genetic, social, and spiritual factors, as well as healthcare services, in refocusing the system on health and wellness.

For the purposes of our discussion of quality and safety, the focus will remain on healthcare services as a possible danger to the community. This topic has been explored in detail in the Institute of Medicine (IOM) report, *To Err Is Human*,[2] which aimed a national spotlight on the health system's shortcomings. Getting healthcare consumers into the system is a challenge, but keeping them safe while they are in the system is equally challenging. The dangers of the American healthcare system have been reaffirmed in the literature and in the media with alarming frequency. Josie King is among a number of recognized names that have experienced unfortunate encounters while receiving health-care services. At just 18 months old, Josie was the victim of a treatment error, dying from severe dehydration and misused narcotics while under the care of a well-trained and well-regarded medical team at Johns Hopkins Medical Center in 2001.[17] Josie's mother, Sorrel, has turned the direct harm to Josie and her family into positive energy to improve medical care safety through a foundation established in Josie's name.

While the complications from Josie's treatment cannot be corrected, many healthcare consumers can avoid a similar experience if systems and communication improve. Kilo and Larson describe the taxonomy of harm from healthcare services: direct harm to the patient affects the patient's physical and emotional health, and indirect harm includes wasteful healthcare expenditures.[18] When expenditures are excessive or of low clinical value, meaning the costs outweigh the benefits, misallocation of resources, which carries opportunity costs, can result. Both types of harm, direct and indirect, have an impact on the health of the community.

A population health focus warrants different metrics and different types of data for measurement. Instead of measuring what happens to those who receive care in the facilities, it is necessary to focus on all of the members of the population in a given community, the well, the high risk, and those who are ill but not receiving care. Table 5-3 focuses on community-level aspects of healthcare quality and safety.

A population approach is challenging because the necessary data on communities typically are not available. Given the complexity, lack of coordination, and poorly integrated data collection systems in any community, it is necessary to develop a systematic method for analyzing the population-level quality and safety and a repository for maintaining data. The development of such a system may seem to be insurmountable—neither feasible nor affordable to create or to implement.

Sufficient resources are not always available for quality and safety improvement in many healthcare institutions and communities. Dougherty and Conway, in an article describing the transformation needed in U.S. health care, commented that, "Successful quality improvement interventions by clinicians or health care delivery systems are often not rewarded or may even lose money if they result in decreased use of services. This challenge is beginning to be addressed by building the infrastructure for transparency about quality and price and by developing incentive systems consistent with the principles of value-based competition. In the future, purchasers, employers, clinicians, patients, communities, and policy makers must be involved in developing an environment that is committed to a shared solution."[19] The lack of obvious return on investment creates yet another barrier to improving quality and safety in some communities.

ACHIEVING HEALTH AND WELLNESS

In order to achieve a population health focus on healthcare delivery and an epidemic of health and wellness, a shared solution is needed to address quality and safety. Five steps

Table 5-3   Measures of Quality and Safety from the Community's Perspective

Components of Quality	Structure	Process	Outcome
Access	Level of concern about quality and safety among both the public and private institutions in the community.	Are providers taking actions toward prevention and/or early detection of health problems that can be addressed effectively if the problems are discovered early? This includes outreach programs for people who do not ordinarily seek care.	What are the rates in the community of events that can be prevented if patients get early care or preventive care?
Technical performance	Level of training and experience regarding quality and safety among the providers in the community.	Are safe practices followed by healthcare providers in the community? Are providers educating people in the community about healthy and safe practices?	What are the infection rates and complication rates for preventable problems? What types of preventable unsafe events are occurring in the community? What is the health status of people in the community?
Interpersonal performance	Culture and leadership regarding quality and safety within the community of healthcare providers, especially regarding communication and teamwork.	How well are the providers working to encourage patients to ask questions and to understand their problems and treatments?	Are people in the community able to trust the providers? Is compliance with prescribed care adequate?
Continuity	Connections (among the healthcare providers in the community) that allow communication, transfer of information, and transfer of patients.	How well are the providers working together to make efficient handoffs/transfers of patients and information?	Are people in the community able to move from one provider to another, with assistance in getting referrals and having information transferred?

have been identified that will lead health care closer to health and wellness, employing the following strategies to focus efforts and measure improvements.

Step 1: Adapt Donabedian's Model to Apply to Population-Based Measurement of Healthcare Quality and Safety

Based on best available information, such as infection rates or obesity rates, population-level problem areas should be prioritized. As the healthcare delivery system broadens its interest to include wellness, the needs of the population, indicated by health risks, must be considered in choosing a starting point when setting priorities. Questions that must be addressed include: (1) What are the relevant indicators of health status? and (2) What are the most important population-wide issues related to the quality and safety of the health care provided to the population living in that community? Utilizing the Donabedian matrix, indicators to address community needs could be defined and developed. For example, if preliminary information reveals that the acquired infection rate in one community is higher than the rates in other similar communities, high priority might be assigned to that problem. After the priorities are set, measures are established by three actions:

- Develop operational definitions of community indicators.
- Evaluate indicators for validity, reliability, acceptability, and cost.
- Develop instruments and identify data sources.[20]

After they are defined, the measures are put to use in an effort to bring the community a step closer to providing high-quality and safe care that can generate healthier populations.

Step 2: Measure Potential Problem Areas

For indicators to be useful, they must be well defined and easily understood. A clear definition of the numerator and denominator is a starting point. In the denominator, attention must be given to questions such as inclusion and exclusion criteria related to the population of interest, as well as enumeration of the population at risk for the outcome under study. Questions may arise pertaining to whether the persons in the numerator are selected from the population in the denominator and if the numerator includes all outcomes occurring in the denominator population.

After the indicators have been established, data sources must be identified and instruments for data collection developed. Acceptability of gathering the needed data and the cost of data collection and interpretation must be considered. Protecting individual patient information is of utmost importance when assessing the quality and safety of care and in getting "buy in" from providers to release the data needed to get a clear picture. Kazandjian points out that "a rate in itself is not very informative unless it is compared to another rate."[20] Here, the need for transparency is highlighted because making comparisons is necessary to understand good versus poor quality, safety, or performance. As demonstrated in the example of healthcare-acquired infections, details related to the classification scheme and coding of medical records and billing systems must be understood to make fair comparisons and identify the magnitude of the problem.

Step 3: Understand the Sources of Quality and Safety Errors (Analysis of Errors) in Problem Areas

After information has been gathered from healthcare providers in the community, on healthcare-acquired infections, for example, the cause of infection can be determined. To understand the root cause of errors, a number of tools can be utilized. Flowcharts are useful because they provide a visual description of a process, fishbone diagrams help identify potential causes leading to a problem, and the Pareto chart helps identify potential sources of defects (see the Institute for Healthcare Improvement Web site). These three tools are among the seven basic tools of quality control; others include the histogram, check sheet, control chart, and scatter diagram.

Data points can be compared among groups in similar communities, as suggested by Kazandjian, and stratified by type of infection (e.g., urinary tract, central line, respiratory), age, principal diagnosis, or other relevant characteristics. Identified differences help inform priority setting and provide benchmarks against which progress can be measured. If a peer group has a relatively low infection rate, your goal should not necessarily be to achieve the same low rate, but to achieve a rate of zero. The peer group serves as a comparison to measure progress, rather than an ultimate goal.

Step 4: Attempt to Improve Healthcare Quality and Safety in a Defined Community

After the problems are identified, they should be shared among providers to allow analysis and feedback in an attempt to understand potential causes of the problems. Understanding the problems is the first step toward solving them. The question is, after the problem is understood, how should the delivery system be held accountable for remediating it? Who is the responsible community authority, and how will the authority ensure that the providers of care will analyze the situation and address the problem effectively? How will we know if process improvements occurred and if subsequent outcomes improved? This is a serious limitation in trying to address a safety problem at the community level. How can this improvement be done without having a legal mandate and authority to manage or monitor improvement, or risking the loss of the cooperation of providers in a voluntary situation? Public reporting is a tricky proposition. Will it cause improvement or destroy a voluntary alliance to improve healthcare quality and safety?

Step 5: Remeasure and Sustain Improvement (Stabilize Changes to System)

Achieving improvement is an important step to raising quality, but it is only the beginning in many respects. Frequent remeasurement is necessary to verify that the improvement is sustained. It is easy to halt efforts after an improvement is realized, but hard work is needed to make sure the improvement is not reversed. While a longitudinal approach to quality and safety is the most effective, it is often unrealistic given time and resource constraints. Often, only a few cycles of remeasurement are feasible and the sustainability of the improvement is up to the team closely engaged in the efforts.

If followed, these five steps will go a long way to achieving quality care and patient safety. National efforts, such as the National Priorities Partnership, in collaboration with the National Quality Forum, the Agency for Healthcare Research and Quality, and others will provide guidance, but community members (consumers) and their healthcare providers will chart the course. The confluence of new strategies to improve quality and safety supported by health profession education that addresses teamwork and communication is imminent. But it will only lead to transformational change if it requires a sense of shared responsibility and willingness to work across silos to ultimately achieve health and wellness.

CONCLUSIONS

An integrated system, where communication is clear, teamwork is the norm and all health-care providers collaborate to provide safe, quality care is the vision. The reality is that while progress has been made in raising awareness of the challenges healthcare providers face, there is still a lot of work to be done. In this chapter, we have argued that a transformational change is needed to deliver population health through safe and quality healthcare products and services. The current healthcare delivery system is fragmented and decentralized, which lends itself to silos in which the various aspects of healthcare delivery take place. A population health approach calls for management across silos to change the way care is delivered to benefit many instead of the few the current system reaches.

While the larger issues of health insurance coverage and data systems to support collection and management of information that will allow us to understand the health of our communities require resources and infrastructural support, there are steps that we can take immediately to advance the population health agenda. We all have a role to play as healthcare consumers and healthcare professionals in making this vision a reality. The first step is the integration of the principles of communication, teamwork, and collaboration through interdisciplinary curricula focused on population health quality and safety. We share the responsibility to identify community needs, prioritize them, and identify strategies to address them. Donabedian's framework, as described in this chapter, provides a mechanism for practical application of these concepts. As health professionals, students, and members of the community, we must move the population health agenda forward. It is up to us to create an epidemic of health and wellness.

STUDY AND DISCUSSION QUESTIONS

1. What are the three core components that emerged from successes that influence quality and safety?
2. How can a focus on population health quality and safety be achieved?
3. How can quality and safety be measured at the population level?
4. Whose responsibility is it to create a focus on health and wellness?

SUGGESTED READINGS AND WEB SITES

READINGS

Cohen MR, ed. *Medication Errors: Causes, Preventions, and Risk Management.* Sudbury, MA: Jones and Bartlett Publishers; 2000.

Institute of Medicine. *Crossing the Quality Chasm: A New Health System for the 21st Century.* Washington, DC: National Academy Press; 2001.

Institute of Medicine. *To Err Is Human: Building a Safer Health System.* Washington, DC: National Academy Press; 2000.

McLaughlin CP, Kaluzny AD. CQI, transformation, and the "learning" organization. In: *Continuous Quality Improvement in Health Care: Theory, Implementation, and Applications.* 2nd ed. Gaithersburg, MD: Aspen Publishers, Inc.; 1999:179.

Nash DB, Goldfarb NI, ed. *The Quality Solution: The Stakeholder's Guide to Improving Health Care.* Sudbury, MA: Jones and Bartlett Publishers; 2006.

Varkey P; and American College of Medical Quality. *Medical Quality Management: Theory and Practice.* Sudbury, MA: Jones and Bartlett Publishers; 2009.

Wachter RM. *Understanding Patient Safety.* New York: The McGraw-Hill Companies, Inc.; 2008.

WEB SITES

Agency for Healthcare Research and Quality (AHRQ): http://www.ahrq.gov/qual/

AHRQ PSNet: Patient Safety Network: http://www.psnet.ahrq.gov/

American Hospital Association (AHA): Hospitals in Pursuit of Excellence: http://www.hpoe.org

Institute for Healthcare Improvement (IHI): http://www.ihi.org/ihi

Institute for Healthcare Improvement: Tools: Quality Resources: http://www.ihi.org/IHI/Topics/Improvement/ImprovementMethods/Tools/#Quality Resources

National Committee for Quality Assurance (NCQA): http://www.ncqa.org/

National Patient Safety Foundation (NPSF): http://npsf.org/

National Quality Forum (NQF): http://www.qualityforum.org/Home.aspx

REFERENCES

1. Institute of Medicine. *Crossing the Quality Chasm: A New Health System for the 21st Century.* Washington, DC: National Academy Press; 2001.

2. Institute of Medicine. *To Err Is Human: Building a Safer Health System.* Washington, DC: National Academy Press; 2000.

3. Partnership to Fight Chronic Disease. *Almanac of Chronic Disease 2009.* Partnership to Fight Chronic Disease; 2009. http://fightchronicdisease.org/index.cfm. Accessed July 2, 2009.

4. American Hospital Association. Chartbook: trends affecting hospitals and health systems. American Hospital Association Web site. http://www.aha.org/aha/research-and-trends/chartbook/ch3.html. Accessed September 14, 2009.

5. Kovner AR, Knickman JR, eds. *Jonas & Kovner's Health Care Delivery in the United States.* 9th ed. New York: Springer Publishing Company; 2008.

6. Anderson GF, Knickman JR. Chronic care. In: Kovner AR, Knickman JR, eds. *Jonas & Kovner's Health Care Delivery in the United States.* 9th ed. New York: Springer Publishing Company; 2008:223.

7. National Center for Health Statistics. *Health, United States, 2008.* Washington, DC: US Government Printing Office; 2009:374–603. http://www.cdc.gov/nchs/data/hus/hus08.pdf#094. Accessed September 14, 2009.

8. Morrison I. *The Second Curve: Managing the Velocity of Change.* New York, NY: Random House Publishing Group; 1996.

9. Brown LD, Franco LM, Rafeh N, Hatzell T, eds. *Quality Assurance of Health Care in Developing Countries.* Bethesda, MD: Quality Assurance Project; 1997.

10. Shih A, Davis K, Schoenbaum S, Gauthier A, Nuzum R, McCarthy D. Organizing the U.S. health care delivery system for high performance. The Commonwealth Fund Web site. http://www. commonwealthfund.org/Content/Publications/ Fund-Reports/2008/Aug/Organizing-the-U-S-- Health-Care-Delivery-System-for-High-Perfor- mance.aspx. Published August 2008. Accessed September 16, 2009.

11. National Priorities Partnership. *Aligning Our Efforts to Transform America's Healthcare: National Priorities & Goals.* Washington, DC: National Quality Forum; 2008. http://www.national prioritiespartnership.org/uploadedFiles/NPP/ 08-253-NQF%20ReportLo%5B6%5D.pdf. Accessed September 16, 2009.

12. McLaughlin CP, Kaluzny AD. CQI, transforma- tion, and the "learning" organization. In: *Continu- ous Quality Improvement in Health Care: Theory, Implementation, and Applications.* 2nd ed. Gaith- ersburg, MD: Aspen Publishers, Inc.; 1999:179.

13. Gittell JH. *High Performance Healthcare: Using the Power of Relationships to Achieve Quality Effi- ciency and Resilience.* New York, NY: McGraw- Hill; 2009.

14. Ogrinc GS, Headrick LA. *Fundamentals of Health Care Improvement: A Guide to Improving Your Patients' Care.* Oakbrook Terrace, IL: Joint Commission Resources; 2008.

15. Donabedian A. Evaluating the quality of medical care. *Milbank Mem Fund Q.* 1966;44(suppl): 166–206.

16. The Dartmouth Institute for Health Policy & Clinical Practice. The Dartmouth Atlas of Health Care. The Dartmouth Atlas Web site. http://www. dartmouthatlas.org/. Published 2008. Accessed March 18, 2010.

17. King S. *Josie's Story: A Mother's Inspiring Crusade to Make Medical Care Safe.* New York, NY: Atlantic Monthly Press; 2009.

18. Kilo CM, Larson EB. Exploring the harmful effects of health care. *JAMA.* 2009;302(1): 89–91.

19. Dougherty D, Conway PH. The "3T's" road map to transform US health care: the "how" of high-quality care. *JAMA.* 2008;299: 2319–2321.

20. Kazandjian VA. *The Epidemiology of Quality.* Gaithersburg, MD: Aspen Publishers, Inc.; 1995:15–16.

Chapter 6

RISK MANAGEMENT AND LAW

HENRY C. FADER, ESQ.

Executive Summary

Legal counsel—working to meet the patient's, healthcare provider's, and institution's goals

This chapter discusses the role that legal risk plays as new directions in patient care are developed to better foster the health of patient populations. An inherent requirement to understanding risk is to incorporate an appreciation for the laws that govern healthcare policy and healthcare delivery. This necessitates the development of a relationship between legal counsel and risk management.

To understand how laws, regulations, and court opinions impact population health initiatives, one must consider constitutional boundaries and their impact on reaching an organization's and society's collective goals. Understanding how laws govern healthcare policy and delivery is instrumental in developing a framework for population health. Through a review of a few specific risks, as they relate to protected populations, medical errors, safety concerns, licensure, professional liability, privacy and tax laws, and employer wellness, this chapter provides a review of legal considerations for addressing population health.

Learning Objectives

1. Learn how legal counsel works with risk managers in a collaborative environment.
2. Appreciate how the U.S. Constitution and state constitutions provide for the separation of powers essential to promulgating and enforcing laws and regulations.
3. Discuss specific areas of the law that are anticipated to be part of the emergence of population health strategies.

4. Describe how lawyers assist providers with reduction of risk in potential litigation arising from errors and how an "apology" program might be best utilized.

5. Learn how employee benefits have developed with tax-advantaged approaches and the role employee wellness initiatives may play in implementing population health strategies.

Key Words

American Recovery and Reinvestment Act (ARRA)	Health Insurance Portability and Accountability Act (HIPAA)
apology laws	Medicare Advantage (MA)
breach notification rules	negligence
Employee Retirement Income Security Act of 1974 (ERISA)	Nurse Licensure Compact
	risk management
Health Information Technology for Economic and Clinical Health (HITECH) Act	tax-exempt status
	tort system

INTRODUCTION

This chapter demonstrates the impact of legal risk as an innovation and method for how new directions for the health of patient populations are initiated. It focuses on the provider's role in caring for patients and resultant risks; how risks can be mitigated; and the necessary partnerships that must be formed among lawyers, healthcare institutions, and individual providers. Legal risk can be quantified in financial loss, but it also can be professionally damaging to providers when it results in a lost or suspended license or damaged reputation. There are inherent legal risks in the provision of quality healthcare services, especially under new models of care, and risk must be considered when new approaches to patient care are introduced.

An understanding of laws that govern healthcare policy and healthcare delivery is instrumental in developing a framework for refocusing on population health. Lawyers especially provide guidance on the application of law and, when required, challenge the status quo by initiating legal actions in tribunals on behalf of providers and healthcare institutions as advocates, resulting in better outcomes for patients. Risk managers also play an important role in loss prevention at the provider and institution levels. Through identification and prevention of potentially high-risk situations and timely mitigation, risk managers can prevent unnecessary loss from unfavorable situations as they arise.

The partnership among healthcare providers, lawyers, and risk managers is not only useful when an event occurs that requires guidance from legal counsel, but also prevents such events from occurring through training and **risk management**. The area of legal risk management assesses the relative risks of a particular activity under the applicable laws, regulations, and court decisions within the jurisdiction of the patient or provider, as the case may be.[1] While consultation from legal counsel is not required, it is preferred to ensure appropriate and complete mitigation of risk. Because our U.S. legal system is based upon legal argument of precedent and interpretation of complex laws, risk managers are wise to engage legal counsel to prepare for the expected challenge to the providers' actions. In a planning context, legal counsel can provide insight into how the proposed implementation of new concepts or ideas meets or exceeds current legal guidelines and protections expressed in court decisions and written laws and regulations.

Healthcare services are so highly regulated in the United States that introducing approaches that focus on populations can add exposures. When change in the manner of care impacts a particular population, there will be other stakeholders who may attempt to modify or stop the chosen initiative through legal action, regulatory change, or legislation. When a healthcare delivery change is made, proactive anticipation and response to the potential reactions of all of the impacted stakeholders will contribute to reduction of risk.

This chapter will touch on many important areas of the law that impact education in population health, but space does not permit a review of all possible areas. The law literally changes every day as courts make rulings, new directives are issued, administrative tribunals issue decisions, and legislators seek compromise solutions to community-wide problems. After a brief review of the role law plays on behalf of patients, providers, and healthcare institutions, some of the key legal risk areas in population health will be discussed. Finally, developing approaches to legal risk management and avoidance or mitigation will be illustrated.

THE ROLE OF LAW

One of the important teachings of the field of population health is to move away from an individual patient focus to an emphasis on the needs of a particular community, such as those with a particular disease or characteristic.[2] When introducing initiatives that impact population health, policy makers must consider how a proposed action will impact the overall health of the targeted population. Because our legal system focuses on provider identification and mitigation of risk for populations, one must understand how the laws of the United States operate and the challenges they present to devise strategies to adequately address them.

Under the U.S. Constitution and most state constitutions, government is organized into three branches: legislative, executive, and judiciary, all of which have influence over any changes to the focus, structure, and delivery of care as we know it today.[3] The legislative branch passes laws after deliberating the views of various stakeholders to proposed legislation. The executive branch regulates and licenses professionals and facilities and issues regulations as required by state and federal law. Enforcement of all laws and regulations also falls to the executive branch of government. The judicial branch is represented by the state and federal court system. Under the U.S. Constitution, the jurisdiction of certain legal proceedings is mandated to the federal courts and others are left to state courts, an important distinction because state and federal courts have different political constituencies. In health care, important constitutional issues are typically part of any mechanism of change, so a thorough understanding of U.S. and state constitutional law is essential. All three branches play an important role in creating and enforcing regulations that protect healthcare providers and patients in the provision of healthcare services.[3]

Laws, regulations, and court decisions at the institution level affect how care is delivered by that institution, while laws, regulations, and court decisions at the provider level affect how providers practice. At the patient level, laws, regulations, and court decisions serve to protect the rights of the patient in all matters related to receiving healthcare services. All such restrictions and directives have an effect on the provider's practice and the patient's ability to receive safe care that is timely, efficient, and equitable. While laws and regulations are necessary for protection and risk mitigation, it is ultimately behaviors that have an effect on outcomes.

Many policy makers believe that appropriate incentives can change the behaviors of patients, providers, and institutions and will guarantee improved clinical results. Healthcare risk managers can play an important role in developing and implementing safe and effective patient care practices, preserving financial resources, and maintaining safe working environments.[4] The American Society for Healthcare Risk Management (ASHRM) provides support in this area. While they typically play a role in policy making and regulation at the institution level, risk managers are often engaged in training and education efforts to mitigate risk within an institution or particular provider group and can serve as patient advocates.[4] In a perfect world, all professionals would be properly trained, similarly aligned, and agree upon the same goals. Because this is not the case, strategies must be devised to administer incentives with the interests of the institution, providers, and especially the patients in mind.[5]

The population health agenda includes providing comprehensive care and treatment for chronically ill patients, which has been changing the way patients are treated by their physicians over the years. This trend prompted the **Medicare Advantage (MA)** program, which provides bundled payment incentives for insurance companies to sell managed care products to Medicare beneficiaries.[6] The primary aim of Medicare Advantage was to provide plans with an incentive for providers to better coordinate care; it remains unclear whether a bundled payment provides sufficient compensation to impact results. Moreover, it also is not clear whether incentives truly improve outcomes, which has led some researchers to consider whether penalties may be more effective. One example of the limitations of incentives is the past failure of physicians to adopt electronic medical records in medical office practices. Legislation enacted in 2009, including the **American Recovery and Reinvestment Act (ARRA)**,[7] and **Health Information Technology for Economic and Clinical Health (HITECH) Act**,[8] provides that physicians will be incentivized to implement, and then penalized financially if they fail to adopt, electronic health records in the coming years. Given competing concerns about the adequacy of the physician workforce, policy makers must consider whether a penalty will influence physicians to make the investment required or drive them to leave medical practice. Regardless of the decision to impose an incentive or penalty, we must not lose sight of what is best for the population as a whole. While incentives may not be the answer, penalties run the risk of leaving institutions without enough resources for improvement activities.

Another approach to consider is a combination of both incentives and penalties aimed at achieving the desired changes and deterring inefficient or lower quality practice. To have a true picture of the impact of an incentive or penalty, these should be applied as community-based standards across the broad population. As U.S. health reform efforts focus on what levels of care and provider behaviors are appropriate for different population groups, incentives and penalties could play an important role. As a critically important component of policy analysis, leaders will have to determine the associated legal risks arising from each.

PATIENT ADVOCACY

Regardless of what motivates behavior change, there is still an inherent need for advocacy at the patient, provider, and health institution levels. Risk managers serve to mitigate risk at each of these levels, and lawyers advocate for the best interests of their respective clients.

All three branches of government are sensitive to the need to protect the most vulnerable populations. Not only does government display compassion for those less fortunate, but there are also affirmative protections for those who cannot otherwise protect themselves. Populations with mental or physical disabilities, those with AIDS or who are HIV positive, and individuals with drug and alcohol addictions have been protected under the umbrella of state and federal laws and court opinions for decades.[9] These areas of protection most recently have been extended to the patient's information in medical and pharmaceutical records and the prevention of mining such data at the individual level.[10] Appropriate attention to training and compliance with laws is necessary to protect institutions and providers from legal risk in determining treatments applicable to particular patient populations.

While an analysis of each protection afforded for special populations under laws, statutes, regulations, and court cases is not within the purview of this chapter, most federal and state laws and agencies that oversee special protected populations have sought to expand these laws widely to encompass the most vulnerable populations. While protection is not guaranteed to all special populations, regulation affords protection to many more individuals than would have received it otherwise. Constitutional law and congressional action have played a significant role in advocacy for and expansion of health care and legal protections afforded these special populations.

In addition to risk mitigation at the government level, risk managers within institutions also serve as patient advocates. Internal to the organization, risk managers have an understanding of the patient population and are sensitive to their needs. When high-risk situations present themselves, the risk manager is available for consultation, and when error occurs, timely mitigation is provided. Risk managers track and trend errors and other occurrences and work closely with legal counsel for guidance on the law with the ultimate goal of ensuring safe patient care.

PROVIDER ADVOCACY

Handling of delicate situations associated with provider behaviors requires careful thought and, in most cases, legal consultation. When a medical error occurs, procedures are usually in place to mitigate risk either through error reporting systems that document the occurrence or through policies that direct the healthcare provider to the institution's risk management officer for anonymous error reporting.

Risk managers within institutions also serve as provider advocates. Internal to the organization, risk managers have an understanding of the provider and institution and are sensitive to their needs. When high-risk situations present themselves, the risk manager is available for consultation, and when error occurs, timely mitigation is provided. Risk managers work closely with legal counsel for guidance on the law with the ultimate goal of minimizing loss from unintentional or poor outcomes.

Heightened awareness of medical errors has caused institutional providers to change their behavior to embrace compliance and codes of ethics. Fear of remediation, as well as threats to licensure and certification, have led such providers to be more cognizant of their behavior and how they handle poor outcomes. Education on reporting poor outcomes and compliance with safety initiatives has progressed significantly over earlier attempts. While being forthright about a medical error may not always result in avoidance of penalty, it demonstrates the provider's obligation to patients and dedication to the role of advocate. As patients are increasingly being expected to actively participate in their health care, open, honest conversations with individual providers will be the cornerstone of the physician–patient relationship and a two-way dialogue will hopefully emerge.

Professional Licensure   Many observers believe that a national certification and licensing system for all professionals is a vital element to establishing a system of health care that focuses on the health of the general population and distinct population subsets. Today, most professionals must be licensed under the state laws where they practice, and while reciprocity is common, it is more focused on basic requirements than actual skills and certification of competency. Numerous national societies and associations provide national certification across state lines, but have no standing under licensing laws. The nursing profession has made the most progress in national licensure, developing an approach of a federal compact (like a driver's license) that would permit nurses to practice across state lines. Today, 23 states are part of the **Nurse Licensure Compact** for registered nurses.[11,12] However, progress and change in the area of professional licensing and accreditation is stymied by state police power advocates' insistence that state law govern professionals within their borders.

As we work toward reforming health care to focus on collaboration and population-based approaches, we must consider the procedures currently in place that prepare health-care providers for practice. Licensure is one example of an archaic system that has been used for centuries to demonstrate knowledge and competency based on standards. Processes of training, discipline, retraining, and accreditation need to give way to a new look at how professionals are licensed. Traditional licensing procedures do not support a culture of safety in healthcare systems. Currently, professionals are investigated and disciplined by peers, which presents concerns about disrupting collegiality and referral patterns, as well as questioning superiors on a medical staff.[13] A population health agenda is emerging that includes reviewing the procedure for licensing. As the expectations for health professionals change, so should the procedures and legal sanctions that enforce their licensure and certification. The legal implications to such a dramatic shift will require the cooperation of many stakeholders, including the licensed professionals and their representative bodies, to remediate years of constitutional decisions under state and federal law.

Professional Liability and Negligence   A new look at the focus of America's health system usually calls for reform of the country's **tort system,** which defines what constitutes injury and the circumstances under which the responsible party should be held accountable.[14] This discussion typically places providers and healthcare institutions on one side and patients' rights advocates on the other. The current tort system encourages practicing "defensive medicine," which significantly drives healthcare costs. Providers argue that without placing financial limits on the current tort system, expenses incurred for unnecessary testing and procedures will continue to increase the cost of care.[15]

The tort system also provides an opportunity to correct the "wrongs" that result from professional **negligence**. In order for negligence to be determined, injury must have occurred, typically physical, and the provider must have breached the duty to perform a procedure or make a diagnosis and direct treatment correctly. Negligence is typically governed by the standards developed in a particular jurisdiction, which causes duties, standards, and definitions of injury to vary from one jurisdiction to another.[16]

When a misadventure (an error or adverse event) occurs in a hospital or other healthcare facility, the medical staff and risk management departments often investigate the facts and circumstances, as well as the professional competency of the individual involved. In the past, the professional peer review process has been relied upon to improve quality of care in institutions and to assist physicians and other professionals to improve their skills. To allow this process to serve both professionals and the community, special statutes are in place to protect internal, peer review proceedings from discovery in litigation.[17] Today, serious misadventures need to be reported to state licensing boards and patient safety authorities. In some states (e.g., Minnesota), misadventures are also publicly reported.[18] This shift in the direction of greater transparency and accountability continues to highlight the evolution of the relationship between individuals and their healthcare providers.

The issue of standard of care is also evolving. Many courts require that expert testimony on the standard of care be related not only to the standard of practice in the state, but to the community where the injury occurred.[19] As a result, determinations of whether the standard of care was met are inconsistent, depending upon the particular jurisdiction where the incident occurred. Expert witnesses have to be considered qualified (under special evidentiary rules that vary by jurisdiction) to comment upon local practice in providing care in the community in which the alleged malpractice occurred, notwithstanding the possibility that a higher level of care and treatment may be provided by medical professionals in another geographic location in an adjoining state or county. What should be the standard of care for professional negligence? Options for consideration include development of a set of standards by (1) national boards or clinical experts, (2) subgroups reflecting local practice differences associated with the patient's location in a rural community or in a region of the county with a lower experience level for a particular approach, or (3) some other standard.

Many healthcare professionals and institutions argue that because of defensive medicine practices and the costs of defending lawsuits, the current tort system adds a huge financial burden and negatively impacts the relationship of professional and patient when procedures or treatment do not go as planned. There is a movement afoot to reform the tort system and to develop an alternative. One of the alternatives adopted in some states that is being discussed in many legal jurisdictions are the so-called the **"apology" laws.**[20–23] Under today's tort system, making an admission of error is an enormous gamble for an individual professional or institution because it is an admission against interest, purely voluntary, that can be used as evidence in a court of law. The apology movement requires that the professional and institution provide the specifics of what happened to the patient and the patient's family immediately after discovering the problem—such action would typically be carried out with the involvement of the institution's risk manager. They would apologize for the misadventure and describe the steps they were taking to avoid a recurrence. They might agree with the patient and the patient's family not to charge for the costs of the procedure or medical treatment in exchange for patient agreement not to sue for damages. The notion is one of respect for the patient and the family. Again, the goal would be to reduce the incalculable costs of litigation impacting healthcare delivery.

To many, it seems essential that to reduce the costs of defensive medicine and the real and threatened liability payouts for judgments against doctors and institutions, tort reform must be a part of any change in care delivery. Without an alternative, professionals may continue to migrate to jurisdictions where tort laws have less impact, to the detriment of communities where tort reform is not a tenable option.

Healthcare Privacy Laws   All providers are required to protect patient information through privacy laws. Healthcare privacy laws will have an impact on new programs directed at preventive and chronic care treatment in a population health framework. An examination of the ethical and licensure standards that professionals are bound to follow is germane to the discussion of privacy. These ethical and legal standards are generally applicable to professionals such as physicians, nurses, and other skilled clinicians. Prior to 1996, the "right to privacy" primarily referred to legal decisions and laws designed to control the media and its invasion of private lives; it did not specifically outline the special status of health information in our society.

In 1996, the **Health Insurance Portability and Accountability Act (HIPAA)** was enacted by Congress to protect health information held by providers and employers.[24] Regulations implementing HIPAA were issued in 2000.[25] HIPAA's purpose was to protect all electronic health records, but it was soon interpreted to cover all records in any format, including printed records. Under HIPAA provisions, state law protections preempt federal law where HIPAA requirements are less stringent.[26] While institutions and medical providers generally became compliant with the privacy protections of HIPAA, concerns still remain over breakdowns in the security and protection for health records, especially related to electronic information. One important use of patient information, provided patient health information is de-identified (i.e., stripped of those elements that would permit a viewer to determine the identity of the individual) is that researchers are permitted to utilize available data to follow trends and conduct comparative effectiveness studies in population health.[27] In February 2009, the American Recovery and Reinvestment Act (ARRA) included a number of changes to HIPAA and its regulations to tighten the security requirements for data stored by providers.[7] ARRA changed who is covered, what is covered, and how the interaction with state law will operate. It also set forth new rules for compliance and enforcement of HIPAA generally. The HIPAA regulations under ARRA will continue to expand the focus on the protection of health information.

ARRA introduced a new focus on physicians' widespread use of electronic health records, or EHRs. To meet the new provisions, physicians will need to buy vendor-developed systems that have sufficient privacy and security protections built into them. All providers will be subject to **breach notification rules** and will have to meet more stringent standards for security as well.[28]

As electronic data become more commonplace in health care, compliance with healthcare privacy laws will continue to emerge as a high-risk area. Actions are being brought in both the state and federal courts when there are breaches or failures to properly secure the information.[29] While there is still no federal private right of action for violations of HIPAA, the U.S. Department of Justice, Office of Civil Rights is taking on new responsibilities for breach notification and other alleged violations of HIPAA and privacy and security laws.[30] Personal responsibility of physicians, physician practices, and institutions to properly protect this information will continue to develop.

ADVOCATING FOR POPULATION HEALTH AND WELLNESS

Two important areas of the law that require consideration as the healthcare system focus is redirected to population health are (1) provider tax status and (2) employer-based health insurance.

TAX STATUS

The development of acute care hospitals as not-for-profit and charitable organizations with a mission-based approach is one of the unique characteristics of the U.S. hospital system. This may be evidenced by hospitals serving large numbers of uninsured patients without payment and the creation of clinics and outreach programs out of a sense of service. Others have criticized the not-for-profit sector as being as profit-motivated as the for-profit sector.[31] As a result, more and more scrutiny has fallen on the not-for-profit sector since 2006 in terms of governance, executive compensation, and the level of community benefit provided in order to maintain their tax-exempt status.[31]

The key to the existence of any not-for-profit organization is a determination of **tax-exempt status** by the Internal Revenue Service (IRS) under a myriad of complex requirements.[32] The more complicated the healthcare corporate structure under examination, the more complex the requirements for continuing obligations to maintain that tax exemption. Not-for-profit status granted by the IRS exempts the organization from payment of taxes on earnings derived from its operations and investments.[32] Furthermore, tax-exempt organizations have an additional significant advantage in that they are permitted to finance capital and operating expenses through tax-exempt indebtedness that is sold to the public and large financial institutions at low rates. IRS tax exemption also translates into state and local tax exemptions, providing relief from state income and sales taxes as well as local real estate and business taxes.

Studies that compare the level of care and treatment provided by not-for-profit organizations to that provided by for-profit organizations have not produced conclusive evidence that one is better than the other. For-profit organizations consistently bemoan the fact that they do not have the tax and financing opportunities provided to not-for-profits, especially when not-for-profits directly compete with for-profit organizations.[31] Under universal access, depending upon the level of payment associated with particular groups of patients, not-for-profit status could continue to work to the financial benefit of not-for-profit providers because reform legislation would require certain levels of "community benefit" in return for retained tax-exempt status. If a decision was made to eliminate tax-exempt status for acute care hospitals, it could directly impact the resources available for the delivery of care and the general health of the population that is currently served by those institutions.

EMPLOYER-BASED HEALTH INSURANCE

Another important area of the tax law relates to employer-provided employee benefits. Aside from the Medicare and Medicaid programs and other federal and state payment programs, the majority of individuals receive coverage through private plans provided by employers. These plans are regulated by the federal **Employee Retirement Income Security Act of 1974 (ERISA)**.[33] State laws also govern private employer plans in the areas of insurance regulation, state mandates, and required coverage that must be offered to employees by employers in their benefit plans. These are extremely technical and highly regulated areas of federal and state law jurisdiction. Employers have traditionally provided options that employees can choose along a spectrum from health maintenance organizations (HMOs), to so-called Preferred Provider Organizations (PPOs), to Health Savings Accounts (HSAs), the latter with high deductibles and copays. Employers have always been fearful of being too involved in their employees' care. For this reason, many large employers have sought to establish employer-funded ERISA "qualified plans."[33] These ERISA self-insured plans can shield employer sponsors against malpractice actions that can lead to damage awards for pain, suffering, lost earnings, and costs of future medical care as a result of withholding care or treatment. Another benefit to ERISA self-insured plans is that they typically are able to bypass state-mandated benefits, one of the cost drivers of higher healthcare costs for employees.[33]

Most ERISA plans, as well as plans that meet state law requirements, are structured in such a way that payments are made directly to providers for only the care rendered to the beneficiaries. This keeps medical costs lower for self-funded plans because they do not have to pay the costs for other community members they do not employ or fund under the plan. Private insurers and third-party administrators are permitted to take into account the medical condition of the participants in the employer's plan when making their underwriting decisions. This practice has changed the way that plans are written, from a community-wide basis to a medical underwriting model. Abuses associated with the medical underwriting model, such as dropping participants from coverage after the fact and denying coverage for pre-existing conditions, have led many to call for federal laws to protect against such practices.

The growth of employer-sponsored health plans is also rooted in taxation. The primary benefit of employer sponsorship is the ability granted to employees to exclude the cost of health coverage from their income when determining their federal and state income taxes.[34] As costs have continued to rise in this area, and as a result of the recession that dates back to December 2007, these tax laws have exacerbated the need for change.

Many employers who are dedicated to improving employee health and limiting the increases in employee healthcare costs have overcome some of their fears about being involved in their employees' healthcare management. An emerging area of reform is an employer-based approach to prevention and greater personal responsibility for wellness.[35–38] Putting aside concerns about malpractice liability, employers are experimenting with incentives for their employees to take better care of their health. Employer-sponsored fitness memberships and monitoring of health indicators such as blood pressure, blood sugar, and weight, as well as smoking cessation and other lifestyle issues, are not uncommon today. It is still not clear how the court system and regulators will view these changes. Will they support employers' efforts, or will they feel that such involvement in employee health is an invasion of privacy? For example, employees could bring charges under claims that employers discriminated against those who did not meet health-related goals or that, as disciplinary measures, employers used private information about their employees' genetic makeup, inability to stop smoking, or inability to lose weight. While employees may consent to this intrusion into their lives, the question is whether they participate because they perceive a need for this assistance or whether they feel intimidated that if they do not join these wellness initiatives, they would be reprimanded or terminated from their employment.

Tax law, especially tax-exempt status and employee benefits for health insurance coverage, are in need of reexamination. The success of the population health agenda rests on having support, rather than impediments for better health and wellness.

CONCLUSIONS

The United States has a great opportunity to impact the health of its population. This chapter has been devoted to how the law intersects for patients, providers, and institutions, as well as the management of risk. Any reform to the fragmented and complex healthcare system must give careful consideration to the legal concepts that provide guidance and oversight. As many change advocates have learned over the years, the U.S. healthcare system is tremendously complex; its growth and transitions over the years have been sensitive to balancing myriad legal concepts. As a result, any attempt to refocus delivery of health care on populations must be guided by a thorough understanding of the prevailing laws and regulations.

STUDY AND DISCUSSION QUESTIONS

1. Describe how legal counsel should work with a risk manager at an institution to achieve a collaborative environment for both professionals.
2. Provide a schematic diagram of the separation of powers under the U.S. Constitution and describe how each branch impacts healthcare providers.
3. Select one area of the law and describe how population health innovations will be implicated.
4. From an employee's viewpoint, describe how wellness initiatives would impact his or her employer's health plan. What legal pitfalls do you perceive?

SUGGESTED READINGS AND WEB SITES

READINGS

Antieau CJ, Rich WJ. *Modern Constitutional Law.* Vol 1-3. 2nd ed. New York, NY: Thomson West Publishers; 2009.

Dunkle DS. *VEBAs and Other Self-Insured Arrangements (Portfolio 395).* Arlington, VA: BNA Tax & Accounting; 2009.

Gue DG, Fox SJ. *Guide to Medical Privacy & HIPAA.* Washington, DC: Thompson Publishing Group, Inc.; 2009.

Humo T. *Employer's Guide to Self-Insuring Health Benefits.* Washington, DC: Thompson Publishing Group, Inc.; 2009.

Journal of Law, Medicine & Ethics. Boston, MA: American Society of Law, Medicine & Ethics.

Sanbar SS; American College of Legal Medicine, ed. *Legal Medicine.* 7th ed. Philadelphia: Mosby; 2007.

Scheutzow SO. State medical peer review: high cost but no benefit—is it time for a change? *Am J Law Med.* 2009;25(7).

Teitelbaum JB, Wilensky SE. *Essentials of Health Policy and Law.* Sudbury, MA: Jones and Bartlett Publishers; 2007.

WEB SITES

American Health Lawyers Association: http://www.ahla.org

American Society for Healthcare Risk Management: http://www.ashrm.org/

Center for Studying Health System Change: http://www.hschange.org

The Joint Commission: http://www.jointcommission.org

Legal Solutions in Health Reform Project: http://www.law.georgetown.edu/oneillinstitute/national-health-law/legal-solutions-in-health-reform/index.html

REFERENCES

1. Teitelbaum JB, Wilensky SE. *Essentials of Health Policy and Law.* Sudbury, MA: Jones and Bartlett Publishers; 2007:153.

2. Kindig D, Stoddart G. What is population health? *Am J Public Health.* 2003;93(3):380–383.

3. Teitelbaum JB, Wilensky SE. *Essentials of Health Policy and Law.* Sudbury, MA: Jones and Bartlett Publishers; 2007:14–15.

4. American Society of Healthcare Risk Management. American Society of Healthcare Risk Management Web site. http://www.ashrm.org. Accessed December 7, 2009.

5. American Society for Healthcare Risk Management. Data for safety: turning lessons learned into actionable knowledge. *Monograph;* 2008. http://www.ashrm.org/ashrm/education/development/monographs/Mono_ActionKnowledge.pdf. Accessed December 7, 2009.

6. Centers for Medicare & Medicaid Services. Medicare Advantage Plans. US Dept of Health and Human Services Web site. http://www.medicare.gov/Choices/Advantage.asp. Published December 7, 2009.

7. American Recovery and Reinvestment Act of 2009 Pub L No. 111-115, H.R. 1, 123 Stat 115.

8. The Health Information Technology for Economic and Clinical Health Act § 13, Pub L No. 111-115, H.R. 1 (2009), codified at 42 USC § 300jj et. seq.

9. Teitelbaum JB, Wilensky SE. *Essentials of Health Policy and Law.* Sudbury, MA: Jones and Bartlett Publishers; 2007:148–150

10. *IMS Health, Inc. and Verispan, LLC v Kelly A. Ayotte,* 550 F3d 42 (1st Cir 2008), *cert denied,* 77 USLW 3708 (2009).

11. Nurse Licensure Compact Administrators. Nurse Licensure Compact (NLC) implementation. Nurse Licensure Compact Administrators Web site. http://www.ncsbn.org/158.htm, Updated October 2009. Accessed December 7, 2009.

12. Nurse Licensure Compact Administrators. Nurse Licensure Compact (NLC) implementation. Model NLC legislation. Nurse Licensure Compact Administrators Web site. http://www.ncsbn.org/1100.htm. Accessed December 7, 2009.

13. Miller RD. *Problems in Health Care Law*. 9th ed. Sudbury, MA: Jones and Bartlett Publishers; 2006:251–270.

14. Miller RD. *Problems in Health Care Law*. 9th ed. Sudbury, MA: Jones and Bartlett Publishers; 2006:587–622.

15. American Medical Association. Health System Reform Bulletin—Sept. 10, 2009. American Medical Association: Health System Reform Web site. http://www.ama-assn.org/ama/pub/health-system-reform/bulletin/10sept2009.shtml. Accessed December 9, 2009.

16. US Chamber of Commerce. Medical liability reform. US Chamber of Commerce Web site. http://www.uschamber.com/issues/index/health/medliability. Accessed December 9, 2009.

17. Bremer WD. Scope and Extent of Protection from Disclosure of Medical Peer Review Proceedings Relating to Claim in Medical Malpractice Action, American Law Reports 5th, 2009; 69(559).

18. Minnesota Adverse Event Reporting Law, 144.7065 Minn Stat (last revised 2009).

19. Pearson JO Jr. Modern Status of "locality rule" in Malpractice Action Against Physician Who Is Not a Specialist, American Law Reports 3rd. 2009;99(1133).

20. Segal J, Sacopulos MJ. Apology laws: a variety of approaches to discussing adverse medical outcomes with patients and others. *AHLA Connections*. 2009;13(11):26–29.

21. Apology laws in Maine: Me. Rev Stat Ann § 2907(2).

22. Apology laws in Colorado: Colo Rev Stat Ann § 13-25–135(1).

23. Apology laws in Vermont: Vt Stat Ann title 12 § 1912(a).

24. Pub L No. 104–191 (1996).

25. *Fed Regist*. 2000;65(82):461. *Fed Regist*. 2002; 67(53):181.

26. Miller RD. *Problems in Health Care Law*. 9th ed. Sudbury, MA: Jones and Bartlett Publishers; 2006:440–452.

27. Miller RD. *Problems in Health Care Law*. 9th ed. Sudbury, MA: Jones and Bartlett Publishers; 2006:452–455.

28. Breach notification rules, *Fed Regist*. 74(42):740 pursuant to Section 13402 of HITECH (February 17, 2009) codified at 45 CFR § 160 et. seq.

29. Conn J. Breach law uncovers shortfalls: experts say problems exist keeping data secure. *Mod Healthc*. 2009;39(49):10, 12.

30. New penalties and procedures under HIPAA were issued by the Department of HHS by interim final rule, 74 *Fed Regist*. 2009;74(56): 123–56, 131.

31. Furrow BR, Greaney TL, Johnson SH, Jost TS, Schwartz RL. *Furrow, Greaney, Johnson, Jost and Schwartz' Health Law: Cases, Materials and Problems*. Abridged 6th ed. New York, NY: Thomson West Publishers; 2008:498–504.

32. 26 USCA. § 501(c)(3).

33. 29 USCA Title I, § 1132 (preemption of state law) and § 1144 (exclusive federal court jurisdiction) relating to exemptions applicable to employee benefit plans

34. Fronstin P, Salisbury D. Health insurance and taxes: can changing the tax treatment of health insurance fix our health care system? *EBRI Issue Brief*. 2007;(309):1–25.

35. The Leapfrog Group. The Leapfrog Group Web Site. http://www.leapfroggroup.org/. Accessed December 7, 2009.

36. Partnership for Prevention. Partnership for Prevention Web site. http://www.prevent.org. Accessed December 9, 2009.

37. US Chamber of Commerce. Chamber backs wellness program. Free Enterprise: US Chamber of Commerce Web site. http://www.uschamber magazine.com/article/chamber-backs-wellness-programs. Published January 2008. Accessed December 9, 2009.

38. Flaherty R. Unlocking corporate wellness programs. *Business Strategies Magazine*. August 2006; 10–13.

THE BUSINESS OF HEALTH

Chapter 7

MAKING THE CASE FOR POPULATION HEALTH MANAGEMENT: THE BUSINESS VALUE OF BETTER HEALTH

RONALD R. LOEPPKE, MD, MPH, FACOEM, FACPM

Executive Summary

Good health is good business

The **health** of our population is inextricably linked to the health of our economy. Health-care costs consume one-sixth of our nation's gross domestic product, accounting for some $2.3 trillion annually in medically related expenditures and significantly more in health-related **productivity** losses. Good health is the engine that fuels our growth, and poor health can likewise derail profitability and viability of business and industry. Therefore, it is time to focus on the "health" as much as the "care" in health care and prioritize population health improvement as the ultimate goal of our healthcare system.

In the recent rhetoric on healthcare reform, there has been an unprecedented emphasis on finding ways to improve healthcare quality, expand access, and lower costs. However, we will be unable to achieve real, sustainable savings or improve individual lives unless and until we reduce the burden of illness and health risks in an effort to improve the health status of the nation as a whole.

The United States faces a stark reality: the tectonic plates of our healthcare system and our economy are colliding and we are experiencing the seismic repercussions of the inefficiencies and expenditures of our current medical care model combined with compelling demographic and economic trends in our society. In addition, a perfect storm is on the horizon with the transition of 80 million baby boomers into their age of entitlement, which will likely produce a "silver tsunami" impact upon the Medicare system, the Social Security system, and the medical care ecosystem. Furthermore, the rising tide of ill-fated lifestyles throughout our population is producing a tidal wave of health risk and chronic illness that is also unleashing its fury across the inadequate levees of our "sick care system" and threatening our economic sustainability.

Chronic disease now affects more than 133 million Americans with no signs of abatement. Indeed, 63% of healthcare cost increases over the past five years are related to a rise in chronic illness.[1,2] The burden of providing healthcare services for chronic conditions, from depression to obesity and heart disease to diabetes, is draining the profitability of employers and the fiscal future of the nation as a whole.

Poor health has had a financial impact on business, industry, and our economy that has largely lurked beneath the surface and may not be recognized until the damage is done. Medical and pharmaceutical expenses are just the tip of the iceberg that is threatening to sink many corporate ships. There is a growing recognition that health-related productivity loss such as substandard performance on the job (**presenteeism**), as well as employee absences caused by illness, injury, and other factors (**absenteeism**) add compelling cost burdens to employers. In fact, recent studies show that for every dollar of medical and pharmacy costs, employers are burdened with two to three dollars in health-related productivity losses (presenteeism and absenteeism).[3]

The fundamental business value proposition of population health management is simple: Good health is good business. Employers need to realize that health promotion can minimize health risks while excessive health costs follow excessive health risks. Therefore, finding ways to manage risk by improving health status makes sound economic sense. To bring about real change to the corporate bottom line, employers must look beyond healthcare benefits as a cost to be managed toward the benefits of good health as investments to be leveraged.

There is an emerging body of evidence proving the business value of health that links health, productivity, and economic improvements. It defines a new business case to invest in a more proactive, wellness-oriented, true "health system"—built on the pillars of **prevention** to form the foundation of population health improvement. It is clear that this is not only a fiscal and clinical imperative—it is a moral imperative.

Learning Objectives

1. Provide scientific and economic data to support the business case for good health.
2. Highlight the value of an organization's human capital.
3. Describe the roles of the health plan, purchaser, consultant, and specialty vendor in population health improvement.
4. Identify strategies to promote good health to decrease both presenteeism and absenteeism.
5. Provide an overview of key population health improvement solutions.

Key Words

absenteeism	prevention
health	productivity
Health Risk Assessment (HRA)	value-based benefit design
health-related productivity	wellness
presenteeism	

INTRODUCTION

More than 133 million Americans have one or more chronic health conditions ranging from heart disease to diabetes. Obesity, a precursor to metabolic illnesses such as heart disease and diabetes, now costs $147 billion a year in pharmacy and medical expenses alone, which amounts to one-tenth of all healthcare spending.[4]

The increasing burden of illness and health risk is leading to increased healthcare costs and reduced productivity in the United States at a time when employers and the nation are struggling to retain financial viability in an increasingly global economy.

While individual health and wellness programs (HWP) and integrated health improvement initiatives are achieving remarkable results in some areas, there remains much concern about the overall health of the nation. It is estimated that 80% of heart disease and stroke, as well as 40% of all cancers, are preventable.[1,2] Caring for just one diabetic patient over a lifetime costs $400,000 in medical and drug expenditures alone. Better health and lifestyle choices, such as diet, exercise, and smoking cessation, could readily save billions of dollars in medical expenses and make great strides toward regaining productivity and absenteeism losses. Therefore, the question for individuals, providers, employers, health plans, communities, and the nation is simply, "Why aren't we focusing more on the 'health' in health care?"

Clearly, a variety of reasons exist for our lack of progress, from funding to gathering the collective will to encourage personal accountability. In reality, one entity cannot accomplish change alone. Each constituency in the health delivery system plays a key role in creating and implementing programs that will improve individual health and ultimately reduce healthcare costs.[5] (See Figure 7-1.) Both risks and rewards are attached to such participation. Employers are ultimately responsible for creating a healthy workplace environment and culture of health, including the development of a balanced **value-based benefit design**. Not doing so risks higher rates of workplace injury and illness, increased employee turnover rates and decreased business performance. Rewards to employers include the following benefits:

- optimal health and business performance
- greater employee satisfaction
- ability to attract and retain great employees
- improved productivity and greater financial viability

While population health is key to refocusing on health, at some point, it is up to the individual to take responsibility to transform his or her health, to put down the cigarette, to start an effective exercise regime, or to lose weight.

Individuals on their own often have difficulty achieving these goals. Government assurances that their healthcare benefits are portable and engaging and will not be precluded, limited, or terminated would be foundational. Patients also need committed providers focused on prevention and quality care. In striving to reach these goals, population health

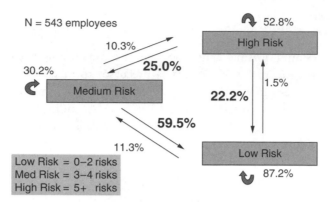

Figure 7-1 Examples of Health Improvement Program Impact on Health Risk Reduction
Courtesy of *Population Health Management*. 2008;11(6):287–296.

management strategies can play a critical role in ensuring global success for individuals, employers, and the nation.

THE BUSINESS CASE FOR GOOD HEALTH

RELATIONSHIP BETWEEN HEALTH AND PRODUCTIVITY

The U.S. economy makes investment in productivity-related health a critical and economically essential initiative. Without effective population health management programs, the profitability and viability of American businesses will be further eroded. According to PricewaterhouseCoopers, healthcare costs are projected to increase 10% for employers and even more for employees by the end of 2010.[6] Within just a few short years, such increases will be unsustainable for even the most financially sound employers.

We are spending nearly 18% of our GDP on health care. The healthcare sector is consuming 8 times more than the U.S. government spends on education, 87 times more than the amount spent on the water supply, and 830 times the amount spent on energy conservation.[7]

However, in analyzing the root cause of the increases in healthcare costs between 2002 and 2007, Thorpe revealed that 63% of the increases were caused by an increase in the burden of chronic illness and health risk, leading to higher utilization costs. Only 37% of the increase was related to other reasons like new drugs, technology, or unit costs of procedures or services.[1,2] We can't afford to have unrealistic expectations about how the costs will be covered; the fact is, we must share the responsibility. We all need to invest in our personal health now, or we will be paying for it the rest of our lives. As a famous Pogo cartoon once said, "We have met the enemy and he is us."[8]

Because the costs of care are so daunting, we can't be confident that the problems will fix themselves. In fact, all the profits of the health insurance companies in the United States would only offset the costs of American health care for four days. All the profits of the 10 largest pharmaceutical companies would pay for only seven days of the present level of healthcare expenditure. Even the total profits of all the companies in every industry in America would defray less than five months of healthcare costs in the United States.

Even more troubling than the overwhelming costs associated with health care in the United States is the poor value for the money we spend. The United States spends twice as much as other wealthy nations on health care. Receiving health care does not always yield better health, as evidenced by life expectancy in the United States, which is lower than 41 other countries; we often rank near the bottom on other key health indicators.

The crisis will only grow worse as the nation's global business competitiveness continues to be undermined. It is vital that the business community recognizes that the health of its workforce is inextricably linked to the productivity of the workforce and, therefore, the health of the bottom line for corporate America. Employers should see their employees as human capital and the benefits of better health as investments to be leveraged, rather than the expense of the health benefit as a cost to be managed. Improving the health assets of human capital can improve the economic assets of the financial capital and enhance enterprise value.

However, in their quest to manage costs, some employers are seeking to offset healthcare increases through cost-sharing or program reductions. Copays and coinsurance have increased considerably over the past decade. Some employers are cutting or eliminating health and wellness programs.

However, such cost-saving strategies will not work—healthcare costs cannot be balanced on the backs of employees or consumers. For example, studies show that decreases in prescription utilization are leading to excessive emergency department visits and hospitalizations. Employers and health plans must recognize that as health risks increase, costs for absenteeism, presenteeism, and disability also increase.

IMPACT OF PRODUCTIVITY ON BUSINESS

Presenteeism and absenteeism represent major hidden costs that are often misunderstood or overlooked, despite being the most critical components of medical expenditures. The result is that employers experience several consequences:[9]

- **average productivity loss:** 115 hours per employee per year as a result of illness
- **absenteeism:** 10 days per year per person with chronic illness
- **avoidable sick days:** 400 per year per 1,000 employees

But burdensome costs are not associated only with being absent; for every absent employee (absenteeism), three more employees are present but not maximally productive because of illness (presenteeism). In total, 69 million workers reported missing days at work because of illness, resulting in a total of 407 million lost work days. In addition, 55 million workers reported a time when they were unable to concentrate at work because of their own illness or that of a family member, equating to another 478 million lost days.[9]

Such costs place considerable burden on employers and must be factored into any accurate and comprehensive economic analysis. Recently, a multi-employer study[3] covering more than 150,000 employees sought to better quantify the actual costs of presenteeism and absenteeism. The key finding of the study was that health-related productivity costs are two to three times higher than medical and pharmacy costs. For every dollar spent on medical costs, two to three dollars are spent on total **health-related productivity** loss. The same study also showed that health conditions with the highest absenteeism– presenteeism costs are often overlooked because they do not generate the highest medical costs, yet they drive total health-related expenditures.

Pharmacy and medical costs for cancer (other than skin cancer), back–neck pain, chronic pain (other than back–neck pain), high cholesterol, and depression are highest. When health-related productivity costs were measured with medical and pharmacy costs, the top five chronic health conditions driving overall health costs shifted significantly to depression, obesity, arthritis, back–neck pain, and anxiety. When developing healthcare programs, employers and plan sponsors must factor these realities into their design of benefits and health-related programs. Increasingly, the science of evidence-based benefit design can provide helpful guidance.

Chronic Illness Leads to Absenteeism and Presenteeism

While it is vital that employers understand the economic implications of absenteeism and presenteeism, it is of equal importance to address the underlying causes. The extent to which chronic disease affects a workforce has a direct impact on the employers' bottom line.

According to a 2008 study by the Milken Institute, an independent economic think tank, the current and future treatment and lost productivity costs for the seven most prevalent chronic diseases—cancer, diabetes, hypertension, stroke, heart disease, pulmonary diseases, and mental disorders—are $1.3 trillion annually.[10] Overall, chronic disease accounts for 70% of all deaths and 83% of all medical and prescription costs; chronic disease affects 45% of the population. (See Table 7-1.)

Future generations of consumers and workers face significant challenges. Childhood obesity is at near-epidemic levels, with costs estimated at $14 billion annually.[11] Today's youths may be the first American generation to have a shorter average life span than their parents.

To remain viable and competitive in a global marketplace, managing healthcare costs and improving productivity for society, as a whole, is critical. Achieving this goal continues to place undue burdens on employers. According to a survey by Watson Wyatt and the National Business Group on Health, employers spent $7,173 per employee for health care in 2008.[12]

Even profitable companies face challenges in keeping pace with healthcare costs. A company with a net profit of 10% must have a minimum of $200K in sales per employee to cover the total cost of healthcare expenditures and losses.[13]

Table 7-1 The Responsibilities, Risks, and Rewards of Key Stakeholders

Employees—Consumers

Responsibilities	Risks	Rewards
• Health management	• Nutrition	• Improved health
• Disease management	• Physical activity	• Incentive-based rewards
• Job performance	• Substance abuse	• Enhanced performance

Providers—Clinicians/Health Plans

Responsibilities	Risks	Rewards
• Outcomes management	• Medical costs	• Performance-based incentives
• Quality management	• Care–health management	• Efficiency–effectiveness
• Cost management	• Data-driven information	• Improved outcomes
• Disability management	systems	

Employers—Purchasers/Government

Responsibilities	Risks	Rewards
• Corporate culture of health	• Impact of poor health on total health cost	• Optimal health and business performance
• Investment in prevention–safety	• Impact of benefit design on total health cost	• Employee satisfaction
• Healthier workplace environment	• Employee turnover	• Employee retention
• Value-based benefit design	• Increased premiums	• Improved bottom line
	• Decreased business performance	

Courtesy of *Journal of Occupational and Environmental Medicine.* 2006;48(5):533–537.

WORKFORCE ISSUES

When it comes to healthcare benefits, employers and employees agree on one simple fact: Both want a healthy workforce. Healthy employees are typified by the following attributes:

- **healthy:** Employees demonstrate optimal health status as defined by positive health behaviors, minimal modifiable risk factors, and minimal illnesses, diseases, and injuries.
- **productive:** Employees function to produce the maximum contribution to achievement of personal goals and organizational mission.
- **ready:** Employees possess an ability to respond to changing demands, given the increasing pace and unpredictable nature of work.
- **resilient:** Employees adjust to setbacks, increased demands, or unusual challenges by bouncing back to optimal "well-being" and performance without incurring severe functional decrement.[13]

While good health is clearly a goal for both employers and employees, a number of workforce issues must be addressed while on the journey toward achieving it.

Most employees want a strong, quality, and affordable healthcare benefit—particularly if they suffer a chronic illness. However, most workers are not willing to be accountable for their health and well-being. The majority of workplace programs today do not provide the personal support necessary to help drive meaningful and sustainable changes to poor health behaviors.

Leading employers with effective integrated health improvement initiatives use **Health Risk Assessments (HRAs)** to develop a blueprint for action and to prioritize more targeted and personalized programs. Many employers offer financial incentives to complete HRAs; some employers additionally offer incentives for participation in health improvement programs. However, in a study of more than 120 employers regarding workforce participation rates in completing HRAs, researchers found that an organization's commitment to creating a culture of health and integrated ongoing communications about the health improvement initiatives were stronger influences on employee participation than cash incentives. In fact, to achieve a 50% employee participation rate on the HRA, employers without a culture of health and good communication strategies had to pay $120 per person in incentives. However, employers with a culture of health and effective communications had to provide only $40 per person in incentives to yield an HRA completion rate of at least 50%.[14]

Some employers are concerned that employees will not remain at the company long enough for the organization to realize the benefits of their health improvement strategies. The average worker employed in nonretail or in the food service industry works for a single employer for approximately five years.[15] Health management companies note that it can take three years or longer for an employer to recoup investments in population health programs— if they consider only medical and pharmaceutical costs as the net savings. However, many employers are moving beyond medical cost savings as the only measure of return on investment (ROI). In addition, they are including leading performance indicators, such as health risk reduction, productivity improvement, and shareholder value to more broadly define the value of their investment (VOI). In fact, health risks can be reduced and productivity can be improved significantly within just one year. Health risks and productivity are, therefore, leading indicators of positive returns, while medical costs are actually lagging indicators.[16]

In addition, employers that provide innovative, integrated health improvement programs are looked upon as "employers of choice" in their communities, attracting and retaining employees. Their employee job satisfaction goes up and their turnover rates go down.[17]

The appropriate question for employers is, "What is the full value I get from investing in improving an employee's health?"

ACCESS TO CARE AND DISPARITIES

While there is much recognition and support for health and wellness programs today, significant barriers and disparities to care remain in our current healthcare system. (See Box 7-1.) According to the 2008 National Healthcare Disparities Report,[18] patients in general receive

BOX 7-1 DISPARITIES IN THE CURRENT U.S. HEALTHCARE SYSTEM

- Minorities are more likely to be diagnosed with late-stage breast cancer and colorectal cancer compared with whites.
- Patients of lower socioeconomic position are less likely to receive recommended diabetic services and more likely to be hospitalized for diabetes and its complications.
- When hospitalized for acute myocardial infarction, Hispanics are less likely to receive optimal care.
- Many racial and ethnic minorities and persons of lower socioeconomic position are more likely to die from HIV. Minorities also account for a disproportionate share of new AIDS cases.
- The use of physical restraints in nursing homes is higher among Hispanics and Asian–Pacific Islanders compared with non-Hispanic whites.
- Blacks and poorer patients have higher rates of avoidable hospital admissions (i.e., hospitalizations for health conditions that, in the presence of comprehensive primary care, rarely require hospitalization).[18]

evidence-based, quality care only about half of the time, and diabetics, for example, receive quality care only 45% of the time.

Today's healthcare system is often typified by poor care coordination, inadequate adherence to recognized evidence-based clinical guidelines, greater health disparities between socioeconomic groups, and shortages of primary care physicians and nurses. To achieve better health for the nation, health plans, legislators, and providers must collaborate to find solutions and recognize that we cannot place the health of the nation's consumers "in boxes"; that is, we must provide some flexibility and recognize differing standards for employer, government, and other sponsored health plans.

KEY PLAYERS IN POPULATION HEALTH MANAGEMENT

THE PURCHASER'S ROLE

To develop a truly effective healthcare system, the goals and incentives for all participants, regardless of the payer, must be aligned. Achieving optimal health is a shared responsibility among individuals, providers, employers, and health plans. While all participants play an important part, the employer-purchasers retain a critical role in the current marketplace. As the buyers of benefits and services, they are ultimately the drivers of change.

Health plan purchasers must adopt those programs that provide the greatest value to employee populations at a cost that ensures economic viability. In terms of the healthcare benefit, value is defined as cost-effective, affordable, comprehensive, integrated, engaging, and sustainable.

Purchasers must also recognize that maintaining a healthy workforce goes beyond returning people to work after an illness or injury. To ensure sustainable success, employer-purchasers are interested in moving their populations toward a preventive model that includes three types of prevention:

- **primary prevention:** Keep healthy people healthy and reduce health risks of those at risk through health promotion and wellness.
- **secondary prevention:** Screening and biometric testing lead to early detection and diagnosis of health conditions.
- **tertiary prevention:** Early intervention and evidence-based treatment reduces morbidity, mortality, and disabilities.

However, it is equally important that employers provide more integrated person-centric healthcare benefit models that will deliver better access, availability, and adherence to health improvement programs, with an emphasis on seamless, proactive, longitudinal treatment and self-care.

THE HEALTH PLAN'S ROLE

The health plan's role is to provide the expertise, structure, technology, and capabilities to help plan sponsors develop and implement healthcare benefit programs that best meet their needs. Health plans' specific responsibilities include improving the health of the members while ensuring that copays, coinsurance, and overall plan design are affordable and appropriate for all employees. The health plans are also responsible for developing a benefit design that encourages **wellness**, prevention, and evidence-based quality care compliance through value-based benefit design with aligned incentives. In addition to these activities, health plans should ensure the quality of care delivered while engaging providers in pay for performance and other incentive programs focused on rewarding clinical outcomes and health improvements rather than just volume of services.

THE HEALTHCARE CONSULTANT'S ROLE

Consultants' expertise, as well as the dedication and knowledge of vendors, can help ensure the development of successful population health management programs. Consultants are responsible for familiarizing themselves with vendors and the specific needs of their clients.

They must strive to ensure that their opinions are based on experience and fact and are not colored by personal bias. Consultants should also provide assurances that they have only one goal—to help their clients find the health plans or specialty vendor partners to improve the health and productivity of the workforce and generate the greatest value for the investment.

One of the key services consultants can provide is the development of the request for proposal (RFP) criteria. Criteria need to focus on depth of expertise, past history, recommendations, qualifications of staff, technology, reporting capabilities, account team, and other factors that will help the organization select the most appropriate vendors to meet their needs. The RFP should also be carefully designed so that plan sponsors are truly comparing potential vendors on an "apples to apples" basis.

Consultants should also strive to help their clients understand the comprehensive range of issues—the "big picture" of value-based benefit design—with the ultimate value being improved health status of the population. Even when key factors remain similar, cost alone is not sufficient to gauge the ability of a vendor. Vendors that can bring value-added services to clients, including technology, program development, and high-level clinical support may ultimately provide the best service.

THE SPECIALTY VENDOR'S ROLE

Specialty vendors, such as organizations with a broader continuum of health management services or those that may have a more limited focus on one end of the spectrum (e.g., wellness or disease management), play a number of key roles in population health management. They typically are the entities with the most knowledge and experience in development and implementation of targeted programs.

The specialty vendor can help health plans and employers identify areas of need by conducting in-depth HRAs and by developing other targeted self-reporting productivity measurements. Utilizing self-reporting tools augments the analysis of medical, laboratory, and pharmacy claims data and is the foundation for any population health management program. Data generated by these tools are particularly enlightening for the majority of covered lives that do not generate a claim in a given year. For example, obesity rarely shows up in medical claims and yet we know from both objective and subjective data that prevalence is high in most populations today.

Employers need these types of data because there are significant rates of presenteeism and absenteeism related to obesity. Specialty vendors can help interpret HRA findings about conditions such as obesity and identify functional outcomes related to productivity. In addition, they may help identify when certain clinical recommendations have unintended health consequences. In one example, a health plan had promoted the use of regular antihistamines (e.g., diphenhydramine) for patients with seasonal allergies because they are much less expensive than non-sedating antihistamines (e.g., loratadine). While the drug costs went down, the full costs to the employer went up—because of the sedating side effects of the cheaper antihistamines causing more on-the-job injuries and lost productivity. These are important insights that specialty vendors, working in conjunction with employers and health plans, can help to identify and communicate to ensure optimum program development.

Specialty vendors can also assist employers in quantifying their value of investment (VOI) in health improvement strategies. Under a VOI approach, a wide range of performance indicators, such as the following, are examined:[15]

- participation and active engagement in health improvement initiatives progressing positively
- improved adherence to prevention guidelines and evidence-based screening

- reduced health risks
- improved health and functional status of the population
- improved adherence to medications and to the completion of clinical process indicators associated with improved outcomes
- fewer emergency department visits and hospitalizations
- reduction of absenteeism
- increased productivity

THE VALUE OF POPULATION HEALTH MANAGEMENT STRATEGIES

The good news about employers' adoption of successful population health management strategies is that, when well designed and properly implemented, the strategies can produce significant results. A 2007 study, by Watson Wyatt, of 355 large employers showed that organizations with strong wellness programs achieved remarkably lower total healthcare costs than other employers with shorter sick leaves, reductions in short- and long-term disability, and improved general health coverage.[12]

More specifically, a study documented the financial impact of population health strategies using absenteeism as the endpoint to indicate that participants averaged three fewer sick days per year, translating to a cost savings of $15.60 for every dollar spent on the program.[19] While more research is needed, the literature highlights that reduced healthcare costs and improved productivity are the by-products of well-thought-out and well-implemented health management programs.[20]

The potential exists for better global population health programs. According to the Milken Institute,[10] with modest improvements in treating chronic disease, the United States could avoid 40 million cases of chronic disease, decrease costs by $218 billion, reduce economic impact of disease by $1.1 trillion, and increase GDP by $908 billion. (See Table 7-2.)

MAKING THE BUSINESS CASE

When making the business case for good health, it is important to ensure that health plan and benefit executives present "hard data" relevant to a business leader's focus on the bottom line. As an example, an enlightened human resources manager and chief financial officer (CFO) at one large employer presented a business case to its executive team by estimating the company's total health-related costs (including medical, pharmacy, presenteeism, and absenteeism costs). The data showed that the employer was likely experiencing eight days of lost health-related productivity (absenteeism and presenteeism) per full-time equivalent employee (FTE) per year, at a cost of $2,598 per employee. When multiplied by the number of FTEs in that workforce, the modeled health-related productivity cost for that employer totaled $153 million per year. With an integrated health enhancement program, data showed that if the same employer could reduce health-related productivity loss by one

Table 7-2 Health Costs to Employers Rising

For Every 100 Employees

- 60 are sedentary
- 25 smoke
- 10 have diabetes
- 50 have high cholesterol
- 24 have high blood pressure
- 50 are distressed or depressed
- 27 have active cardiac disease
- 20% of healthcare expenditures are attributable to preventable illness
- 40% of healthcare expenditures are attributable to modifiable risk
- 11,500 hours of productivity per year are lost due to health conditions

Source: U.S. Department of Health and Human Services, 2005.

day per FTE per year, it would add $18.8 million to the bottom-line earnings before income tax, depreciation, and amortization (EBITDA). Furthermore, the CFO translated the impact of this on the market value of the company by multiplying this figure by the ratio of earnings to stock price. Through this calculation, the $18.8 million improvement in earnings (EBITDA) would translate into a $244.4 million increase in market cap valuation. When divided by the 292 million shares outstanding, this bottom line contribution would yield an astonishing $0.84 value per share improvement.[16] (See Table 7-3.)

Table 7-3 Wellness Program Benefits to Companies

Companies with Highly Effective Health and Productivity Programs:

- Yield 20% more revenue per employee
- Demonstrate a 16.1% higher market value
- Deliver 57% higher shareholder returns

Have Cost Increases That Are:

- 5 times × lower for sick leave
- 4½ times × lower for long-term disability
- 4 × times lower for short-term disability
- 3½ × times lower for general health coverage

Source: Watson Wyatt/National Business Group on Health, 2007/2008. *International Journal of Workplace Health Management.* 2008;1(2).

CONCLUSIONS

Since the early 1950s, America's health system has been designed to care for the sick. Now is the time to move toward a true health and wellness system. Good health is not only of great value to individuals and populations, but also to industry and society. Healthy employees experience higher productivity and lower overall healthcare costs—thus contributing to the bottom-line business performance.

Wellness works and prevention pays. Therefore, it is important for all stakeholders to look beyond healthcare benefits as costs to be managed and toward the benefits of good health as investments to be leveraged. Achieving this goal requires a healthcare system that provides standardized quality care with an individualized approach to help employees become healthier and stay healthier. The statement "employees are your greatest asset" must move beyond a simple platitude to become a fundamental guiding principle designed to ensure the health and well-being of employees and the economic viability of employers.

STUDY AND DISCUSSION QUESTIONS

1. What is the relationship between health and productivity?
2. What are the barriers to achieving a healthier population?
3. What can health plans and employers do to overcome these barriers?
4. What role do absenteeism and presenteeism have on the employer's health-related costs?

SUGGESTED READINGS AND WEB SITES

READINGS

Loeppke R. The value of health and the power of prevention. *Int J Workplace Health Manage.* 2008;1(2):95–108.

Loeppke R, Nicholson S, Taitel M, Sweeney M, Haufle V, Kessler RC. The impact of an integrated population health enhancement and disease management program on employee health risk, health conditions, and productivity. *Popul Health Manag.* 2008;11(6): 287–296.

Loeppke R, Taitel M, Haufle V, et al. Health and productivity as a business strategy: a multiemployer study. *J Occup Environ Med.* 2009;51(4):411–428.

Serxner S, Gold D, Meraz A, Gray A. Do employee health management programs work? *Am Health Promot.* 2009;23(4):1–8.

Taitel MS, Haufle V, Heck D, Loeppke R, Fetterolf D. Incentives and other factors associated with employee participation in health risk assessments. *J Occup Environ Med.* 2008;50(8):863–872.

Watson Wyatt Worldwide. *Building an Effective Health & Productivity Framework: 2007/2008 Staying@Work Report.* New York, NY: Watson Wyatt Worldwide; 2007:1–23. http://www.watsonwyatt.com/research/deliverpdf.asp?catalog=2007-US-0216&id=x.pdf. Accessed November 30, 2009.

WEB SITES

American College of Occupational and Environmental Medicine: www.acoem.org
Institute for Health and Productivity Management: www.ihpm.org
Integrated Benefits Institute: www.ibiweb.org
National Business Group on Health: www.businessgrouphealth.org

REFERENCES

1. Thorpe KE, Florence CS, Howard DH, Joski P. The impact of obesity on rising medical spending. *Health Aff.* 2004;Suppl Web Exclusives: W4-480–486.
2. Thorpe KE. The rise in health care spending and what to do about it. *Health Aff.* 2005;24(6): 1436–1445.
3. Loeppke R, Taitel M, Haufle V, et al. Health and productivity as a business strategy: a multiemployer study. *J Occup Environ Med.* 2009;51(4): 411–428.
4. Pollan M. Big food vs. big insurance. *New York Times.* September 10, 2009:A43. http://www.nytimes.com/2009/09/10/opinion/10pollan.html. Accessed March 21, 2010.
5. Loeppke R. The 3R's of health care: responsibilities, risks and rewards. *Health Prod Manag.* 2002:15–19.
6. PricewaterhouseCoopers' Health Research Institute. Behind the numbers—medical cost trends for 2010. PricewaterhouseCoopers' Health Research Institute; 2009. http://www.pwc.com/us/en/healthcare/publications/behind-the-numbers-medical-cost-trends-for-2010.jhtml. Accessed September 9, 2009.
7. Goldhill D. How American health care killed my father. *The Atlantic Online,* September 2009. http://www.theatlantic.com/magazine/archive/2009/09/how-american-health-care-killed-my-father/7617/. Accessed March 21, 2010.
8. Kelly W. *Pogo: We Have Met the Enemy and He Is Us.* New York, NY: Simon and Schuster; 1987.
9. Serxner SA, Gold DB, Bultman KK. The impact of behavioral health risks on worker absenteeism. *J Occup Environ Med.* 2001;43(4):347–354.
10. DeVol R, Bedroussian A. *An Unhealthy America: The Economic Burden of Chronic Disease: Charting a New Course to Save Lives and Increase Productivity and Economic Growth.* Santa Monica, CA: The Milken Institute; 2007. http://www.milkeninstitute.org/pdf/chronic_disease_report.pdf. Accessed November 30, 2009.
11. Marder WD, Chang S. *Childhood Obesity: Costs, Treatment Patterns, Disparities in Care, and Prevalent Medical Conditions.* http://www.medstat.com/pdfs/childhood_obesity.pdf. Thomson Medstat Research Brief. Published 2006. Accessed November 30, 2009.
12. Watson Wyatt Worldwide. *Building an Effective Health & Productivity Framework: 2007/2008 Staying@Work Report.* New York, NY: Watson Wyatt Worldwide; 2007:1–23. http://www.watsonwyatt.com/research/deliverpdf.asp?catalog=2007-US-0216&id=x.pdf. Accessed November 30, 2009.
13. Loeppke R. Good health is good business. *J Occup Environ Med.* 2006;48(5):533–537.
14. Taitel MS, Haufle V, Heck D, Loeppke R, Fetterolf D. Incentives and other factors associated with employee participation in health risk assessments. *J Occup Environ Med.* 2008;50(8):863–872.
15. Bureau of Labor Statistics. Bureau of Labor Statistics Web site. http://www.bls.gov. Accessed November 30, 2009.

16. Loeppke R. The value of health and the power of prevention. *Int J Workplace Health Manage.* 2008;1(2):95–108.

17. Loeppke R, Nicholson S, Taitel M, Sweeney M, Haufle V, Kessler RC. The impact of an integrated population health enhancement and disease management program on employee health risk, health conditions, and productivity. *Popul Health Manag.* 2008;11(6):287–296.

18. US Department of Health and Human Services. *National Healthcare Disparities Report 2008.* Rockville, MD: Agency for Healthcare Research and Quality; 2009. AHRQ Publication No. 09-0002.

19. Aldana SG, Merrill RM, Price K, Hardy A, Hager R. Financial impact of a comprehensive multisite workplace health promotion program, *Prev Med.* 2005;40(2):131–137.

20. Serxner S, Gold D, Meraz A, Gray A. Do employee health management programs work?" *Am Health Promot.* 2009;23(4):1–8.

THE BUSINESS CASE FOR CULTURAL CHANGE: FROM INDIVIDUALS TO COMMUNITIES

MARIO MOUSSA, PhD, MBA, AND
JENNIFER TOMASIK, MS

Executive Summary

A return to the fundamentals

Chronic and preventable conditions, such as obesity and type 2 diabetes, account for the vast majority of healthcare costs. While population health programs have demonstrated their financial and clinical effectiveness in the treatment of these behavior-related conditions, the reimbursement system encourages hospitals and physicians to focus instead on the acute-care crises of individual patients. This perverse situation will last until policy makers overcome a profound cultural bias that shapes the current debate over healthcare expenditures, focusing attention on individual rather than population health. We propose an agenda for cultural change that promotes five alternative ways of framing the debate: populations vs. patients, preventive care vs. reactive care, chronic conditions vs. acute conditions, integrated healthcare teams vs. physicians, and communities vs. individuals.

Learning Objectives

1. Discuss the financial implications of leaving population health needs unaddressed.
2. Gain insight into the perverse incentives, brought about by transaction-based financing, which drive up the cost of health care.
3. Identify viable alternatives to the current acute-care healthcare delivery system.

Key Words

accountable care organization (ACO)
chronic care management
cultural change

disease management (DM)
integrated healthcare delivery system
prevention

INTRODUCTION

WHAT IS THE COST?

America, think twice before you grab that supersized burger and soda! Your "value" meal, like other items on our national list of fast-food favorites, is costing us billions of dollars. So do other voluntary choices we make every day. Do they really, you may ask, cost billions of dollars? Yes, at least. Consider the facts.

- **Expanding waistlines equal expanding costs.** Our widespread addiction to the high-fat, sugar-laden fare served at mass-market restaurant chains has fueled an obesity epidemic. One-third of the U.S. population is obese, and a stunning two-thirds are overweight. Ground zero for the obesity catastrophe may be Huntington, West Virginia. A pediatrician there recently saw an 8-year-old child who is 80 pounds overweight and has already developed type 2 diabetes. Unable to contend with all of the ailing child's complications, the doctor could offer only compassion—he prayed by his patient's bedside.[1] Emotional costs apart, in terms of dollars and cents the price tag for our collective binge is huge. According to one study, the annual direct healthcare costs associated with obesity in the United States are $80 billion. The report estimates that, if current trends continue, 43% of U.S. adults will be obese by 2018, adding nearly $344 billion to the nation's annual direct healthcare costs and accounting for more than 21% of healthcare spending.[2]
- **Obesity and smoking are factors in many costly chronic conditions.** Smoking is the number one cause of preventable illness in the United States. Smoking and obesity are contributing factors for many people who suffer from chronic conditions, including diabetes, heart disease, and cancer, to name a few. Direct and indirect costs for diabetes total nearly $138 billion, while cardiovascular disease imposes an even greater burden: nearly $300 billion.[3] Total healthcare expenditures for common chronic conditions represent approximately $1.8 trillion of the $2.2 trillion total U.S. healthcare bill, which in turn represents about 16.2% of the U.S. GDP.[4] This percentage is likely to grow unless, as policy makers say, reformers succeed in *bending the cost curve.* This will almost certainly require large-scale, population-based efforts to encourage people to adopt healthy behaviors.
- **Unhealthy behavior drives skyrocketing costs.** Employers who feel the pinch of ballooning costs have started to respond with their own programs. Safeway's CEO,

Steven A. Burd, has undertaken a one-man campaign to draw attention to the behavioral causes of our healthcare cost problem. Citing numerous studies, he has built his case around two statistics: 70% of all healthcare costs are attributable to behavioral choices, such as opting for that fatty hamburger instead of a green salad; and 74% of all costs are related to four chronic conditions—cardiovascular disease, cancer, diabetes, and obesity—all of which, to a large degree, can be attributed to behavioral or environmental factors.[5]

Together, these facts add up to an astounding cost. Our unmet population health needs account for approximately $1 trillion in healthcare spending.[6] Disregard, for the moment, ethical concerns for the well-being of our fellow citizens. For financial reasons alone, population health needs to become a topic in the national healthcare debate.

A focus on population health would represent a fundamental change, leading policy analysts, legislators, and administrators to reconsider the allocation of resources, as well as the structure of the reimbursement system. We think the change begins with a shift in perspective that emphasizes five components:

- populations vs. patients
- preventive vs. reactive care
- chronic conditions vs. acute conditions
- integrated healthcare teams vs. physicians
- communities vs. individuals

Not only do these alternatives have financial implications, they also reflect basic beliefs about the very nature of healthcare delivery. Adopting a population health perspective, therefore, requires a **cultural change**. We acknowledge this is no small accomplishment.

In the following sections, we discuss each alternative, highlighting its potential impact on healthcare costs. We conclude with reflections on the cultural barriers to discussing healthcare financing in terms of population health.

POPULATIONS VS. PATIENTS

Adopting a population health perspective is like going "back to the future." Because medical science in the late 19th and early 20th centuries had only a rudimentary grasp of the underlying causes of disease, health issues were then seen in largely socioeconomic terms.[7] As a result, policy makers targeted factors that, in today's terms, had to do with "lifestyle:" sanitation, crowded housing conditions, food quality, and nutrition. The social problems were massive. Yet policy-driven reforms led to dramatic improvements in health and mortality.

Advances in medical science brought a whole new understanding of illness and disease—oriented more toward individuals and biological processes than to environment, social, and behavior factors. With this understanding came a new health policy perspective, which sociologist Irving Zola describes as "medicalized."[6] According to this point of view, individuals have health problems that are best treated by a medical system accessed through physicians and other health professionals. The medicalized mind-set focuses on diagnostic tests that identify illness, procedures, or other interventions to treat it—one person and one illness at a time. As a consequence of this dominant cultural bias, over time, policy discussions gravitated toward addressing the problem of ensuring that *individuals* have access to the care they need as opposed to looking at the needs of the population. This bias has led to dramatic cost increases and a crushing financial burden on the government and employers.

Healthcare spending has reached the point where policy makers agree something must be done to rein in the escalating costs. "Health care is one of the fastest growing expenses in the federal budget," said President Obama as he announced the nomination of Governor Kathleen Sebelius as secretary of health and human services, "and it's one we simply cannot sustain." Health policy discussions reflect the tension between ensuring access to care for individuals and allocating the limited resources available to care for the population as a whole.

A current tenet of the healthcare debate claims that government bureaucrats will ration care—in other words, limit access, force healthcare providers "to do what they are told," and disrupt the privileged relationship between the individual patient and his or her physician.[8] This focus on obtaining individualized care has led to an imbalance in overall healthcare spending: 95% of healthcare dollars go to direct medical services, while only 5% are devoted to **prevention**. These figures suggest that the problem of access to healthcare services, important as it may be, has overshadowed broader questions about the health of communities and even our society.

Some employers are ahead of the curve, recognizing the importance of health and wellness and supporting such related initiatives in the workplace. Lessons can be learned from a few employers who have started to bring national attention to broader questions, seeking to shift the terms of policy debate away from the individualistic or medicalized perspective. With an eye on the bottom line, Safeway, Dow Chemical, Pitney Bowes, USAA, Caterpillar, Black and Decker, and several other companies have begun to build their health benefit strategies around population health principles. Initial efforts have yielded promising results. In fact, the findings of a study that examined 42 work-based health initiatives revealed, on average, the following benefits:

- a 30% reduction in workers' compensation and disability management claims costs
- a 26% reduction in health costs
- a 28% reduction in sick leave absenteeism
- a $5.93-to-$1 return-on-investment ratio[9]

Safeway's Healthy Measures program is built on two of the key components of the cost conundrum: behavior and chronic conditions (cardiovascular disease, cancer, diabetes, and obesity). This program represents a population health perspective in seeking to manage the total health of its "population" of employees. Like other company programs, Healthy Measures uses data-tracking tools that reveal health patterns and trends among the employees and suggests wellness strategies to prevent illness and disease and avoid acute health crises. It also helps to reduce the cost of treatment when it becomes necessary.

Although Healthy Measures resembles the **disease management (DM)** programs that became popular in the 1990s, it differs from them in several important ways. Like Healthy Measures and other recently established employer programs, DM targets specific conditions that patients have already developed. Often, the conditions are chronic and generate most of the healthcare costs. Population-oriented programs, such as Healthy Measures, are different in that they seek to influence or manage participants' total health. The goal is to avoid getting sick in the first place or avoid experiencing the complications associated with chronic conditions. Such programs represent more of a wellness approach. Participants can take advantage of fitness centers and healthy food options available within company cafeterias. They also have access to care management counseling and a 24-hour nurse helpline. If treatment is needed, access to healthcare providers is available.

One of the most innovative aspects of population-oriented programs, like Healthy Measures, is the emphasis on incentives. Many programs provide rewards in the form of reduced premiums for eating healthy foods, exercising regularly, and avoiding unhealthy behaviors like smoking. These incentives encourage a lifestyle that promotes health and wellness, helping to reduce the number of doctor appointments, medical procedures, and prescriptions needed. In this respect, "rationing" occurs naturally because participants have reasons to make choices that reduce the need for acute medical care. If a family does not exhibit signs or symptoms of the four leading chronic conditions, they receive a discount on their premium, saving as much as $1,560. Individuals can save up to $780.[5] This is a win-win situation for participants, the employer, and those professionals who provide services that promote healthy lifestyles. The payoff for Safeway: For the past four years, healthcare costs have been flat. Most companies have seen increases of nearly 40%.[5] Because most companies like Safeway self-insure, this saving can go right to their bottom line, providing them with a competitive advantage.

Pitney Bowes, now a nationally recognized leader and innovator in health benefits design, has done more than keep costs flat. They have actually started to bend the cost curve. Michael Critelli, the company's executive chairman and a leader deeply committed to finding ways to increase employees' participation in managing their own health, described the fundamental change in Pitney Bowes's thinking related to healthcare costs: "In the old days we were very generous in paying for people's medical bills. Today we'd like to be very generous in helping people be healthy, but at a lower cost."[10] Their programs, some of which include onsite comprehensive health clinics and fitness centers, cafeterias with redesigned food services and prices, incentives for employees to better manage their health, and low-cost drugs for chronic diseases, have resulted in $40 million in savings over the last nine years. This includes a 50% reduction in disability days for employees with diabetes and a 6% reduction in total medical costs.[11]

Pitney Bowes's passion for health improvement led it to partner with other like-minded, Fortune 500 companies that are successfully experimenting with ways to increase employee engagement in health improvement and cost-reduction. These companies, including Walmart, Cardinal Health, BP America, and several others, came together to create Dossia—a consortium that provides members' employee populations with access to lifelong portable electronic personal health records. Dossia's vision: *To transform the U.S. health care system by reducing waste and facilitating better care by developing and making widely available a lifelong personally-controlled health record.*[12] The Dossia consortium has recognized the daunting challenge individuals face in tracking and updating their medical information, which they need to manage their health.

This is not a problem that can be solved one person at a time. By creating this population of tens of thousands of employees, Dossia has been able to finance and deliver something that has not yet been possible on a national scale. So what is the payoff for the country? Steven Burd, CEO of Safeway, estimates that the United States could save as much as half a billion dollars by employing innovative strategies that companies have piloted.[5]

One might be tempted to dismiss Burd's claims as exaggerations. But many studies have reached similar conclusions about the potential savings in population-oriented programs and policies. According to a study done in the 1980s, annual medical costs for people with chronic conditions averaged $3,074. The costs associated with those treated for acute conditions alone were dramatically lower: $817.[13] The gap would almost certainly be higher today.

The financial implications of a shift toward population-oriented programs and policies are stunningly large. Then why are policy makers not rushing to embrace population health? Many would agree that the current "sick care" system does not yet support prevention as much as it does treatment.

PREVENTIVE VS. REACTIVE

Today's individualized, medicalized healthcare system is "reactive." As a nation, the United States essentially waits for people to become ill and then spends healthcare resources to diagnose and treat those illnesses. This is the fundamental philosophy that influences the delivery of care and, perhaps more important, the payment scheme that finances care. Physicians and hospitals are paid when they treat sick patients. And, by and large, the more they do (e.g., tests, visits, procedures, etc.), the more they are paid. Keeping people healthy has not been the focus. As we noted, only 5% of healthcare resources (and maybe less) are currently directed toward prevention.[7]

But what exactly is prevention? Prevention can be thought of in many different ways. There is prevention in the sense of promoting public health. This includes access to clean water, clean air, and safe communities, among other things. There is prevention in the sense of promoting healthy behavior, encouraging people to stop smoking, eat the right foods, and exercise regularly. Finally, there is prevention in the sense of good clinical practice: screening and detecting disease to enable early treatment or to help people with chronic disease slow the progress of their illness.[14]

Managed care organizations were some of the first to tackle prevention on a large scale. They lauded prevention as part of their philosophical core, and their products were designed to incorporate many different types of prevention strategies. Their assumption was that increasing health would decrease cost. They attempted to do this in a number of ways, such as by offering discounted gym memberships to encourage members to increase their activity levels, creating smoking cessation programs, and enrolling members in disease management programs to reduce the cost of care associated with their most expensive populations (e.g., asthmatics and diabetics). In particular, disease management programs were expected to greatly increase the quality of care that chronically ill members would receive, along with decreasing the cost of this care overall.

In the early days, managed care was heralded for driving cost out of the system and for its efforts to increase quality across the board. Although efficiency gains were initially made through primary care gatekeepers and strict controls on what was deemed appropriate care by the insurers, the overall impact of early managed care experiments was not so successful. Fragmented networks of providers made it difficult to truly manage cost. Patients also rebelled against the gatekeeping of their care, which was viewed largely as being directed by insurers and not their physicians. As the power of the gatekeepers declined, so too did the insurers' ability to rein in costs.[15]

Disease management programs, which were widely believed to deliver high-quality care at lower cost, have now been proven in some cases to increase cost.[16] Still, it would be wrong to conclude that population-oriented prevention is ineffective. For one thing, research shows that disease management programs have fulfilled their promise of increased quality and better outcomes. Their high cost is not surprising, given that the care targets those who are already ill. With a focus on resources to treat the sick and to manage the chronically ill, few resources are left to invest in prevention. But the evidence gathered by the most recent studies shows that investing in prevention efforts for healthy people could pay great dividends.

Dee Edington and his colleagues at the University of Michigan Health Management Research Center, who have done extensive research assessing the costs associated with workplace wellness and prevention programs,[17] have demonstrated that investing in prevention makes good business sense. Edington and his team study health risks, including factors like alcohol consumption, blood pressure, physical activity, safety belt usage, smoking, and stress, to name a few. People are categorized as being low, medium, or high risk, depending on the number of risks they self-report in a Health Risk Assessment (HRA). The research shows that the cost of someone in a high-risk category greatly exceeds those individuals with a lower health risk. This means that cost follows risk. Moreover, the cost of care for individuals who move from a low-risk to a high-risk category is actually greater than the costs associated with high-risk individuals who are able to improve their health status.[18] Overall, these important results demonstrate in real dollars and cents the value of managing health in a preventive rather than a reactive way.

Of course, investing in prevention has to be balanced with dollars for **chronic care management** and the delivery of care to those who are acutely ill. Because the healthy population largely exceeds those who are ill, it does make sense to look for a return on investment for those efforts to keep the healthy well. Doing so will help employers, health plans, and communities target those interventions that have the biggest impact on their populations and will help create a shift in thinking from reactive to preventive investments.

CHRONIC CONDITIONS VS. ACUTE CONDITIONS

The bottom line reality is that the current reimbursement system in the United States pays for procedures, not prevention. Apart from employers, who shoulder a large percentage of healthcare costs, and to some degree patients, who are taking on an increasing percentage of those costs, there is little systemwide incentive to attend to population health needs. To put it bluntly, healthcare providers are paid for quantity, not quality. Atul Gawande recently visited one of the most expensive healthcare markets in the country: McAllen, Texas. In conversations with local physicians and hospital administrators, Gawande repeatedly heard the same point: Reimbursement incentives lead to an overemphasis on acute-care procedures, which drive revenue.[19]

As one of McAllen's surgeons observed, "Medicine has become a pig trough here."[19] The trough is a reimbursement system[19] that pays on a fee-for-service basis using a diagnostic and procedural coding system. Those codes that are reimbursed at the highest level tend to be delivered, to the greatest extent, in healthcare delivery systems. One example is treatment of gallstones. Generally, if there are no complications, patients should be educated about the condition and encouraged to moderate their diet. After they make the recommended changes in their eating habits, a gallstone may dissolve on its own or shrink to the point that it no longer causes symptoms. Nonetheless, the choice to operate immediately is becoming increasingly common. This has several advantages: Operating increases revenue, satisfies patients' desire for a physician to take action, and reduces the need for the patients to take the initiative to change their own behavior, the challenges of which are described in Chapter 2. It is simply easier and more lucrative to perform a procedure than to counsel a patient to adopt a healthier lifestyle. Even if a physician does not explicitly recognize that he or she is making this choice, the incentives are stacked up in a way that encourages this decision.

This situation is not unique to McAllen, Texas. Working in tandem, the government and private reimbursement systems have created a healthcare industry that virtually ignores wellness and prevention and emphasizes the diagnosis and treatment of individual symptoms and physiological abnormalities. For example, the insurance system will reimburse a hospital for amputating a limb afflicted with gangrene caused by diabetes-related complications. But it pays little or nothing to help a patient avoid developing diabetes, which would have eliminated the cost of amputation. Moreover, no insurance incentives are available for tracking or managing the health of an entire population or community, many of whose members have chronic conditions like diabetes.[13] Billing occurs at the individual patient level, a reflection of what the system presently values. This is like watching a soccer match through a pinhole: You see a single player kicking the ball downfield, but you are blind to the strategy and dynamics of the larger game.

INTEGRATED HEALTHCARE TEAMS VS. PHYSICIANS

The alternative to a reimbursement system that encourages individual doctors to treat individual patients is one that supports team-based, holistic management of entire communities or populations of patients. There are a few efforts taking place across the country that demonstrate the value of such an approach.

Integrated healthcare delivery systems, such as the Mayo Clinic, reveal the stunning potential of collaborative healthcare efforts. These systems take a more holistic view of the patient and feature incentives aimed at promoting health rather than increasing transactions. The Mayo Clinic, like other integrated systems, such as Intermountain Healthcare and Geisinger, is finding creative strategies to increase quality and decrease costs. The integrative model consists of interdisciplinary, shared decision making and a holistic view of the patient that focuses not only on physical and mental functioning, but also on well-being.[20] The integrated model promotes increased communication between physicians and other healthcare professionals, as well as between doctors and patients; recognition of the variety of health determinants, such as culture and environment; and a decreased focus on transaction-oriented procedures.

One of the most significant benefits of an integrated model is that it encourages health providers to give people one of the most effective treatments: thoughtful attention. In a visit to the Mayo Clinic, Gawande observed: "There was no churn—no shuttling patients in and out of rooms while the doctor bounces from one to the other."[19] One patient suffering from colon cancer and other complex issues enjoyed a full hour with her physician who, at one point, requested a visit from the cardiologist for a consultation. The two physicians took their time in discussing the next steps. No doubt, the Mayo Clinic has been able to maintain low costs for a number of reasons, but most importantly it has created a compensation structure that has fostered a culture of team-based collaboration among all kinds of specialists.

COMMUNITIES VS. INDIVIDUALS

So far, we have discussed four alternative ways of framing the complex web of issues associated with healthcare delivery, outcomes, costs, and financing: populations vs. individuals, preventive vs. reactive care, chronic conditions vs. acute conditions, and integrated health-care teams vs. individual doctors. Each one requires a fundamental shift in the way policy makers, legislators, and administrators think about health care. Our fifth alternative—communities vs. individuals—may require the biggest shift of all. It concerns the ethical fabric of American society.

In 1933, U.S. health expenditures had climbed to 4% of the gross domestic product (GDP). Policy makers feared that this level of spending would threaten the country's ability to recover from the economic downturn that later became the Great Depression.[21] Today, national health spending is expected to reach $2.5 trillion in 2009, accounting for nearly 18% of the U.S. GDP. This trend is expected to continue, increasing to $4.4 trillion by 2018[22]—a figure more than double 2007 national health spending.[23] At the same time, increasing costs have not produced concomitant improvements in outcomes or quality care. A 2009 policy brief by Elliott Fisher and his team summed it up well: "Perhaps the most counter-intuitive finding is that higher spending does not necessarily lead to better access to health care or better quality of care."[24]

In large part, the cost–benefit problem seems to result from providing and financing transaction-oriented care for individual patients. This has perverse consequences for the system as a whole. In many cases, a hospital may actually receive more money for a patient whose care was delivered poorly than for one who received the right treatment at the right time with a good outcome.

Take this common scenario of a young, otherwise healthy female who enters a hospital for an appendectomy. While in surgery, a small, unnoticed surgical sponge is left inside her abdominal cavity. Shortly after the surgery, she spikes a fever and experiences acute pain—more than would be considered normal during postsurgical recovery. She then develops an infection and a scan reveals that the sponge was left behind, resulting in a second surgery and more days in the hospital. Depending on how the hospital is paid, it could actually receive *more* money for this patient than for one who experiences a successful course of treatment and returns home as expected. Until recently, Medicare presumed that hospitals were doing everything possible to prevent complications. As a result, taxpayers and patients bore the cost when such complications occurred.[25]

The costs associated with preventable complications are astounding.[26] The additional payment for hospital-acquired infections averages $19,480—a stunning 42% of total payments. Postoperative hip fractures and skin ulcers average $12,196.[27] No doubt, a greater focus on these types of costs and the quality and patient safety issues associated with them has started to spark change, but the changes are made within the "medicalized" model of treatment for individuals. This model has broad implications.

In effect, health care is "supply driven"; the greater the supply of medical resources, the more unnecessary care is delivered. Differences in Medicare spending in 2006 varied more than threefold across U.S. hospital referral regions and the differences in spending were not explained by quality. Research shows that those differences are almost entirely explained by differences in the volume of healthcare services received by similar patients.

This supply-driven model goes a long way toward explaining why the healthcare costs in the United States are the highest in the world and growing at a rate that poses a serious threat to patients, employers, and the nation.

As the United States spends more on health care, it will have less to spend on other public goods, like education, defense, and infrastructure. Spending on health care has out-paced spending in other areas of consumer goods nearly threefold since 1980. Companies have concluded that escalating healthcare costs threaten their survival. In 2004, General Motors reported that it spent more for medical benefits than for steel. Starbucks spends more on health care than coffee. Safeway CEO Steven Burd became a passionate voice in the healthcare reform debate after learning that expenditures on health care exceeded the grocery chain's net profit.[5]

It seems only natural to ask: Can the United States afford the current healthcare system? Yet the current terms of the healthcare debate make it difficult to even raise this question. As a society, one of our deepest cultural values is individual responsibility and choice. The focus on the individual as the most important ethical value has led to a situation where few people are assessing the healthcare system's overall performance at the macro level in terms of its finances, perceived value, and clinical outcomes. In essence, the responsibility for performance devolves to the individual provider and patient. Virtually no one is accountable for the health of the U.S. population or the effectiveness of the healthcare system.

Because most health outcomes are produced outside of the "medical" context, policy makers and healthcare leaders need to focus on community-based prevention—reducing smoking rates, obesity, cholesterol levels, and other key markers. In their book, *Connected*, Nicholas Christakis and James Fowler observe that smoking has decreased from 45% among adults in the United States to 21% in the past 40 years. They found that people tend to quit together—in effect, as a community of friends and acquaintances. Social ties have an impact on obesity as well. Weight gain might even be "contagious" in that it can spread from person to person.[28] This research provides additional evidence that a community-based approach to the problems of smoking and obesity could have a major benefit. At the same time, it would require a new way of thinking about how to improve the health, as opposed to the health care, of the population. Which brings us back to the big question: Who should be accountable for population health, and how should it be financed or compensated?

We believe the ideal system, like integrated delivery systems, would be held accountable for the health of its communities, or populations. This makes sense in terms of both expenditures and outcomes, because prevention methods generate the greatest cost savings and the best results. Some forward-thinking organizations are already moving in this direction. They are making this leap—not necessarily to see a short-term return on investment for their own bottom line, but to make an impact on the long-term health of their communities.

An emerging model to make this kind of accountability to communities possible on a broader scale is the **accountable care organization (ACO)**. The underlying principle behind the ACO is to hold providers accountable for the overall quality and cost of care for the populations they serve. Forcing better integration of care and encouraging that integration through reimbursement schemes, ACOs seek to mitigate or eliminate the fragmentation and perverse incentives that exist in the current healthcare system. Policy analysts predict that over time, ACOs will also reduce the overall cost of care delivery.[29] The ACO model represents a stark cultural contrast to how care is typically financed and delivered today. In many ways, it embodies a community-oriented "ethical principle" that guides the allocation of *health resources* across an entire population as opposed to delivering medical services at the individual patient level alone.

CONCLUSIONS

The current system of healthcare financing is built on incentives that encourage patients, physicians, hospitals, and even policy makers to take a narrow, individualistic, transactional view of health care. This has led to a "tragedy of the commons," in Garret Hardin's terms, where the failure to pursue common goals leads to disappointing outcomes for all individuals.[30] Everyone would benefit if public and private healthcare organizations applied a population health perspective. As a nation, we would likely spend less on medical care, enjoy healthier lives, and have more to invest on other collective goods. The problem is that most healthcare organizations have business models whose success relies on performing as many transactions as possible, especially the more profitable procedures, because the current system rewards quantity rather than quality.[19]

The healthcare market has failed to deliver what every individual consumer wants—the best product for the lowest price. Ironically, to achieve this goal, the healthcare system would need some entity, or group of entities, to manage the health of entire communities. Don Berwick, CEO of the Institute for Healthcare Improvement, calls this entity an "integrator."[31]

As Berwick and his colleagues note, the barriers to creating an integrator are political rather than technical. There are simply too many entrenched interests in maintaining the existing system for anyone to break the current gridlock. Moreover, as we have emphasized, there are also cultural barriers that have to do with the deeply ingrained individualistic bias of American medicine and culture. Therefore, despite a growing body of evidence that a highly integrated, prevention-oriented healthcare system would be both less expensive and more effective, we expect that policy makers will not implement one any time soon, much as we would like to see it become a reality.

At the same time, we take heart in the many incremental improvements that are being made. Small-scale innovations are occurring across the country—at the Mayo Clinic, Geisinger, and Intermountain Healthcare, as well as at employers like Pitney Bowes, Dow Chemical, Safeway, Quad/Graphics, and Black and Decker. These innovators have shown there is a way to reduce spending on healthcare costs. The solution lies in spending more on health.

STUDY AND DISCUSSION QUESTIONS

1. What are the financial implications of not addressing population health? What are the differences between long-term and short-term implications, and how should the approach differ for each type of implication?
2. Who is responsible for decreasing the soaring costs of health care, and who has the authority to change the fundamental culture of both our healthcare system and our national code of ethics?
3. What are some of the ways in which a shift from individual- to population-oriented care would lead to better overall outcomes?
4. Discuss some strategies to encourage the shift from a transaction-based, individual-focused system to one that emphasizes the integrated care of populations. What are some examples of organizations that have already made this transition?

SUGGESTED READINGS AND WEB SITES

READINGS

Brownlee S. *Overtreated: Why Too Much Medicine Is Making Us Sicker and Poorer.* New York, NY: Bloomsbury USA; 2007.

Encinosa WE, Hellinger FJ. The impact of medical errors on ninety-day costs and outcomes: an examination of surgical patients. *Health Serv Res.* 2008;43(6):2067–2085.

Gawande A. The cost conundrum: what a Texas town can teach us about health care. *The New Yorker.* June 1, 2009.

Lantz PM, Lichtenstein RL, Pollack HA. Health policy approaches to population health: the limits of medicalization. *Health Aff.* 2007;26(5):1253–1257.

WEB SITES

Centers for Medicare & Medicaid Services: National Health Expenditure: NHE Fact Sheet: http://www.cms.hhs.gov/NationalHealthExpendData/25_NHE_Fact_Sheet.asp
Dossia: http://www.dossia.org/about-dossia/mission-and-vision
Partnership for Prevention: http://www.prevent.org/

REFERENCES

1. Witchel A. The minister of food. *The New York Times.* 2009;50.
2. Thorpe KE; and United Health Foundation, American Public Health Association, Partnership for Prevention. *The Future Costs of Obesity: National and State Estimates of the Impact of Obesity on Direct Health Care Expenses.* www.americashealthrankings/2009/spotlight.aspx. Updated November 2009. Accessed November 20, 2009.

3. Stone RE. Improving health and reducing the costs of chronic diseases. In: Herzlinger RE, ed. *Consumer-Driven Health Care: Implications for Providers, Payers, and Policymakers.* San Francisco, CA: Jossey-Bass; 2004:643–650.

4. Partnership for Prevention. America's health rankings finds advances in disease treatment, but not disease prevention: preventable chronic diseases threaten access & affordability of medical care. Partnership for Prevention Web site. http://www.prevent.org/content/view/285. Updated November 17, 2009. Accessed November 17, 2009.

5. Burd SA. How Safeway is cutting health-care costs: market-based solutions can reduce the national health-care bill by 40%. *The Wall Street Journal.* June 12, 2009:A15. http://online.wsj.com/article/SB124476804026308603.html. Accessed November 15, 2009.

6. Lantz PM, Lichtenstein RL, Pollack HA. Health policy approaches to population health: the limits of medicalization. *Health Aff (Millwood).* 2007;26(5):1253–1257.

7. Thompson TG. Health promotion & prevention—a new priority. Sports Medicine & Science Institute Web site. http://www.esportsmedicine.org/healthcare.html. Updated June 2003. October 23, 2009.

8. Ralston RE. Shrugging off government health care. Americans for Free Choice in Medicine Web site. http://www.afcm.org/shruggingoffgovernmenthealthcare.html. Updated August 30, 2009. Accessed November 18, 2009.

9. Chapman LS. Meta-evaluation of worksite health promotion economic return studies. *Art of Health Promotion.* 2003;6(6):1–10.

10. Smerd J. How Pitney Bowes is turning its innovative health care practices into a new business. *Workforce Manag.* 2007;1,12–17.

11. Mahoney JJ. Role of employer and health plan in disease management. Paper presented at: National Business Coalition on Health. January 19, 2006.

12. Dossia. Mission and vision. Dossia Web site. http://www.dossia.org/about-dossia/mission-and-vision. Accessed November 20, 2009.

13. Gruman JC, Gibson, CM. A disease management approach to chronic illness. In: Herzlinger RE, ed. *Consumer-Driven Health Care: Implica-*

tions for Providers, Payers, and Policymakers. San Francisco, CA: Jossey-Bass; 2004:561–569.

14. Pronk NP, ed. *ACSM's Worksite Health Handbook: A Guide to Building Healthy and Productive Companies.* 2nd ed. Champaign, IL: Human Kinetics; 2009.

15. Herzlinger RE. Consumer-driven health care: taming the health care cost monster. *J Financial Serv Professionals.* 2004;58(2):1537–1816.

16. Fireman B, Bartlett J, Selby J. Can disease management reduce health care costs by improving quality? *Health Aff (Millwood).* 2004;23(6):63–75.

17. Edington DW. *Zero Trends: Health as a Serious Economic Strategy.* Ann Arbor, MI: Health Management Research Center; 2009.

18. Cross M. Spend money on healthy people! *Manag Care.* 2004;13(8)20–26.

19. Gawande A. The cost conundrum: what a Texas town can teach us about health care. *The New Yorker.* June 1, 2009.

20. Boon H, Verhoef M, O'Hara D, Findlay B. From parallel practice to integrative health care: a conceptual framework. *BMC Health Serv Res.* 2004;4(1):15.

21. Falk IS, Rorem CR, Ring MD. *The Costs of Medical Care: A Summary of Investigations on the Economic Aspects of the Prevention and Care of Illness.* Chicago, IL: University of Chicago Press; 1933.

22. Sisko A, Truffer C, Smith S, et al. Health spending projections through 2018: recession effects add uncertainty to the outlook. *Health Aff (Millwood).* 2009;28(2):w346–w357.

23. Centers for Medicare & Medicaid Services. NHE fact sheet. US Department of Health & Human Services Web site http://www.cms.hhs.gov/NationalHealthExpendData/25_NHE_Fact_Sheet.asp. Updated August 7, 2009. Accessed August 7, 2009.

24. Fisher E, Goodman D, Skinner J, Bronner K. Health care spending, quality, and outcomes: more isn't always better. The Dartmouth Institute for Health Policy & Clinical Practice Web site. http://www.dartmouthatlas.org/atlases/Spending_Brief_022709.pdf. Updated February 27, 2009. November 25, 2009.

25. Milstein A. Ending extra payment for "never events"—stronger incentives for patients' safety. *N Engl J Med.* 2009;360(23):2388–2390.

26. Reinhardt UE. Healthcare crisis: who's at risk? Public Broadcasting Service Web site. http://www.pbs.org/healthcarecrisis/Exprts_intrvw/u_reinhardt.htm. Updated November 2, 2000. Accessed November 1, 2009.

27. Encinosa WE, Hellinger FJ. The impact of medical errors on ninety-day costs and outcomes: an examination of surgical patients. *Health Serv Res*. 2008;43(6):2067–2085.

28. Christakis NA, Fowler JH. *Connected: The Surprising Power of Our Social Networks and How They Shape Our Lives*. New York, NY: Little, Brown and Co.; 2009.

29. Fisher ES, McClellan MB, Bertko J, et al. Fostering accountable health care: moving forward in Medicare. *Health Aff (Millwood)*. 2009;28(2):w219–w231.

30. Hardin G. The tragedy of the commons. *Science*. 1968;162(5364):1243–1248.

31. Berwick DM, Nolan TW, Whittington J. The triple aim: care, health, and cost. *Health Aff (Millwood)*. 2008;27(3):759–769.

9

INFORMATION TECHNOLOGY

JOHN K. CUDDEBACK, MD, PhD, AND
DONALD W. FISHER, PhD

Executive Summary

Good data are the cornerstone of population health management

Electronic health records (EHRs) are critical for assessing and managing population health. This chapter describes the role of EHRs in the care of individual patients, the use of disease registries for surveillance and tracking in population health, and aggregation of data from EHRs and other patient-level systems, such as physician and hospital billing systems, in a data warehouse. We discuss the analytic potential of large databases for quality improvement and **comparative effectiveness research (CER)**—and some implications for the way data are captured in source systems. We describe the coding systems commonly used in **health services research**. Finally, we return to patient-level systems, examining lessons learned regarding implementation of EHRs; government incentives for adoption and "meaningful use" of EHRs and e-prescribing; expectations for interoperability; and some unintended consequences of introducing information technology into the very complex work environment of a healthcare organization. Our main focus is on information systems within provider organizations, from small physician practices to large integrated networks, with reference to public health informatics and observations on the different perspectives of payers and providers when creating longitudinal records that reflect the process of care and health outcomes.

Learning Objectives

1. Appreciate the benefits of capturing structured data in an electronic health record (EHR) for the care of individual patients, for assessing and managing population health, for quality and performance improvement, and for research and policy.
2. Discuss the relationship between point-of-care systems (e.g., EHRs), surveillance and tracking systems (e.g., disease registries), and retrospective analytic systems (e.g., data warehouses).

3. Describe some common sources of data for health services research. Understand the strengths and weaknesses of various data sources.

4. Explain critical success factors for EHR implementation and some unintended consequences of inserting information technology into healthcare workflows.

Key Words

accounts receivable

alert fatigue

claims data

clinical decision support

comparative effectiveness research (CER)

computable data

computerized physician order entry (CPOE)

controlled vocabulary

data warehouse

diagnosis codes

diagnosis-related groups (DRGs)

discrete field

disease registry

electronic health record (EHR)

genomic profile

health information exchange

Health Level 7 (HL7)

health services research

inferential gap

meaningful use

national provider identifier (NPI)

Nationwide Health Information Network (NHIN)

Office of the National Coordinator for Health Information Technology (ONC)

ontology

patient accounting

personal health record (PHR)

pharmacovigilance

point-of-care systems

practice management system

procedure codes

prospective payment

regional health information organization (RHIO)

registry

risk adjustment

structured data

transaction systems

INTRODUCTION

Nearly 20 years after the Institute of Medicine's landmark report, *The Computer-Based Patient Record: An Essential Technology for Health Care,*[1] adoption of electronic records and **clinical decision support** at the point of care remains astonishingly low. In recent surveys, only 4% of physicians in the United States had a fully functional **electronic health record (EHR)**, and an additional 13% had a basic one.[2] Only 17% of U.S. hospitals had computerized medication order entry by prescribers in all units.[3] Health care lags far behind other information-intensive industries in its use of information technology (IT). Broad adoption and "**meaningful use**" of EHRs is recognized as essential for substantially improving quality and reducing the overall cost of health care. Effective use of IT has become a key area of focus for U.S. health policy and healthcare reform.

Healthcare organizations have used information technology for decades, but as in other industries, IT was initially used for administrative functions such as patient registration, billing, and financial management. Ironically, the extreme fragmentation and complexity of healthcare payment in the United States has forced providers to continue investing in administrative systems in order to protect their financial stability, deferring implementation of clinical systems that could actually improve the quality and efficiency of the core business—promoting health and providing care to patients.

Systems were developed as early as the 1970s for managing workflow and quality control within hospital "ancillary" departments such as laboratory, radiology, and pharmacy. Many of these systems were quite sophisticated, but they seldom extended beyond the walls of the respective department. In the 1980s, order communication systems on nursing units replaced slips of paper in pneumatic tubes, but most were designed for use by clerical staff to enter orders, not to assist physicians in deciding what to order. One commercial software vendor pioneered **computerized physician order entry (CPOE)** in the early 1970s,[4] but the majority of vendors did not offer workable CPOE until much later, initially in systems for hospitals. It was not until the late 1990s that comprehensive EHR products were introduced for ambulatory care. That, of course, is where the vast majority of healthcare encounters occur and where EHRs are particularly valuable for supporting continuity of care over time. Other pioneering EHR systems were developed within university settings and at the Veterans Health Administration, whose system, called VistA, was developed for its 1,500 facilities nationwide, including hospitals, rehab centers, and ambulatory clinics.[5] This comprehensive system is in the public domain, which may reduce some of the costs of EHR acquisition. However, successful EHR implementation involves much more than simply purchasing hardware and software.

FROM PAPER MEDICAL RECORDS TO THE EHR

Traditional paper medical records have many shortcomings, from illegible handwriting to a lack of templates to guide clinicians in consistently documenting critical information in specific clinical situations. Paper records can be used in only one place at a time, and they can be misplaced or lost. They cannot provide alerts, reminders, or context-sensitive reference material to assist clinicians in caring for individual patients. For population health, the critical shortcoming of paper records is that patient-level data cannot be aggregated to form a clear picture of the population, their care, and the outcomes of that care.

It's easy to be misled by the word *record* in the term *EHR*, which suggests simply translating the traditional paper record into electronic form. In fact, an EHR is much more than a record. At the patient level, it is a dynamic tool that enables a new approach to clinical workflow, evidence-based decision making, and team-based care. At the population level, it enables both care and learning—*care* in the sense of identifying patients who may be at risk for poor outcomes because they have not received treatment or tests that are indicated, according to current evidence, and *learning* in the sense of using aggregate data

BOX 9-1 EHR AND EMR—THE SAME OR DIFFERENT?

Note on terminology: Many people use the terms *EHR* (electronic health record) and *EMR* (electronic medical record) interchangeably, but according to definitions commissioned in 2008 by the Office of the National Coordinator for Health Information Technology (ONC), the two terms are distinguished by standards-based interoperability. An EHR is defined as "an electronic record of health-related information on an individual that conforms to nationally recognized interoperability standards and that can be created, managed, and consulted by authorized clinicians and staff across more than one healthcare organization." An EMR is defined similarly, but within a single healthcare organization.

to refine and expand the evidence base, to enhance our understanding of what interventions are most effective (and cost-effective) for certain subsets of patients within a population.

INFERENTIAL GAP

This dual role of the EHR can best be understood in terms of a two-fold "**inferential gap**" in health care—the nonapplication of relevant existing evidence in the care of individual patients and the lack of evidence germane to a particular clinical situation.[6,7] Two classic studies illustrate these problems. First, in a thorough survey conducted in 1999 and 2000, McGlynn et al. found that U.S. adults received only 55% of recommended preventive care, acute care, and care for chronic conditions such as hypertension (high blood pressure) and diabetes.[8] EHRs can address this gap at the patient level by ensuring that a patient's chronic conditions are addressed and that appropriate preventive care is provided on every visit, even if the visit is for a minor acute condition. **Disease registries** address the gap at a population level by allowing a provider organization to identify patients who need follow-up or preventive care but are not scheduled for or have missed an appointment.

Second, Boyd et al. reviewed current clinical guidelines for common chronic diseases and found that they generally fail to account for multiple comorbid conditions.[9] The strict application of existing guidelines to a hypothetical elderly patient with five chronic conditions yielded a medication regimen so complex it would be unmanageable. In practice, physicians often make thoughtful compromises when treating complex patients. Capturing data from these "natural experiments" allows us to develop optimized protocols for specific patient populations by aggregating the data for those patients, then studying the relationships between the actual process of care and the resulting outcomes.

STRUCTURED DATA

To fully appreciate the importance of EHRs and how they are implemented, we must consider both sides of the inferential gap. To improve the care of individual patients through clinical decision support, EHRs must contain sufficient clinical detail about an individual patient to apply increasingly elaborate therapeutic guidelines and generate relevant alerts. For example, the EHR should contain a patient *problem list* with the patient's symptoms and diagnoses coded, so the software can apply guidelines that recognize and adjust for specific comorbid conditions. The patient's allergies and intolerances should also be coded, so the EHR's decision support logic can recognize, for example, that the first-line therapy for a new diagnosis is a drug in the same class as one to which the patient has had an allergic reaction in the past. The EHR could then suggest using an alternative drug that is not likely to cause an allergic reaction.

This type of decision support requires that information about the patient's allergies be captured in "structured" form, that is, selected from a pull-down list of drugs and drug classes, rather than entered as error-prone free text. Human caregivers could easily interpret *penicillin* or *PCN* entered as free text in an allergy field or in a sentence about allergies in a narrative note, and computers can, of course, be programmed to recognize obvious abbreviations and misspellings. But the information is more usable for clinical decision support—and can even be interpreted by humans with less ambiguity and risk of error—if it has been entered in structured form. This is a basic principle of data capture: If the coding scheme is known in advance, encoding should be done as close to the source as possible by the person with the greatest knowledge of the situation.

There are two key aspects of **structured data**: (1) a **discrete field**, or data element, for each concept, and (2) a standard set of codes, or a **controlled vocabulary**, for expressing the data in each field. A narrative (free text) note may contain information about current and past medications, allergies, and intolerances, but it may be difficult to interpret the information correctly and unambiguously, depending on sentence structure, verb tenses, and use of negation. This is particularly true for computerized "natural language processing" algorithms. Capturing data in discrete fields within the EHR reduces the risk of misinterpretation by human caregivers and makes the information accessible to computerized clinical decision support algorithms at both the patient and the population levels. Therefore, structured data are sometimes referred to as **"computable" data**.

From this perspective, it is easy to understand the benefits and limitations of various approaches to implementing an EHR with varying levels of "structure" in data capture. At the lowest level of structure, simply scanning handwritten visit notes (and indexing them by patient, with reference to the registration system) eliminates the risk that the record will be lost and enables the record to be accessed by multiple people in different locations at the same time. But the scanned record can still suffer from illegible handwriting, and, more significantly, it does not contain discrete data, such as the patient's blood pressure measurements over time or a list of the patient's diagnoses, that could be used to drive clinical decision support.

For example, current guidelines for managing hypertension recommend treatment if the patient's blood pressure is over 140/90, *unless* the patient has diabetes, in which case blood pressure should be controlled to 130/80 or lower.[10] An EHR that contains discrete blood pressure readings, a patient problem list (symptoms and established diagnoses), and a current medication list can alert clinicians during a visit (1) if the patient's blood pressure exceeds the applicable threshold, depending on whether the patient has diabetes; (2) if the patient's blood pressure is trending upward over time, despite prescribed therapy; and (3) in an e-prescribing system that receives updates from pharmacies, whether the patient is refilling his or her prescriptions for antihypertensive medications on schedule. The EHR can also remind clinicians to screen for diabetes periodically in patients with blood pressure between 130/80 and 140/90.

PATIENT- AND POPULATION-LEVEL CLINICAL DECISION SUPPORT

Individualized alerts and reminders, delivered via an EHR at the point of care, when a patient is being seen, can be valuable in ensuring that each patient receives appropriate care. But provider organizations must devote attention to fine-tuning the alert criteria in their EHRs to ensure their effectiveness and to avoid "**alert fatigue**." Alerts must also be appropriate for the setting. Nearly all the patients a nephrologist sees may have some degree of renal failure, so an alert about an elevated creatinine level, which could be useful to a primary care physician, would not provide new information to a nephrologist and would simply impede workflow. Physicians may come to resent inappropriate alerts and reminders, clicking through them without thinking carefully about each one and potentially overlooking an alert about something important. Most organizations monitor the level of alerts generated in their EHRs, and there is art in achieving the right balance. The more data that are captured in structured form, the more precisely alerts and reminders can be tailored to the patient's situation and the physician's practice.

In addition to clinical decision support in the care of individual patients, EHRs can play a vital role in population management, because data from the electronic records of an organization's entire patient population with a particular chronic condition are aggregated in a disease registry. The **registry** allows the organization to look across this patient population and determine which patients are overdue for screening, periodic testing, follow-up care, or prescription refills for chronic conditions. In addition to this "surveillance" function, registries may support patient outreach, not only identifying patients who need to be contacted, but offering a mechanism to track phone calls and patient interactions. Ideally, a note is interfaced back to the EHR, giving clinicians a complete view of all patient interactions. The registry may be a separate system or a module of an EHR, with a database optimized for a population view. Some registry systems use interactive voice-response technology to place automated phone calls to patients, reminding them about needed follow-up or preventive care.

In more advanced registries, predictive models are applied to the data to identify patients who are at risk for poor outcomes in the future or unusually high resource use over, say, the coming year. Proactive interventions range from outreach and *care coordination* for all patients with a particular chronic illness to aggressive, individualized *case management* for patients who appear to be headed for hospitalization in the near term.

EHRs and disease registries are complementary. EHRs provide alerts and reminders to ensure appropriate care for patients who are being seen. Registries identify patients who are not being seen, but should be.

SYSTEMS AND DATA SOURCES OTHER THAN THE EHR

We will now consider other IT systems that healthcare provider organizations typically have, with an emphasis on those that provide a view of the process of care or of patient outcomes—information that is essential for population management. Choices made in selecting and implementing various IT support systems—and the way they work together—determine the degree to which an organization can truly transform care to improve quality, safety, and efficiency for individual patients and for populations.

ADMINISTRATIVE SYSTEMS

A core system within every provider organization is *patient registration,* the system that maintains a record of every patient who receives care and cross-references the way each patient is identified in the organization's systems. Ideally, a provider organization has only one "medical record number" for each patient, but mergers among providers are common, so multiple sets of numbers may need to be consolidated or cross-referenced. If an organization has older ("legacy") systems with different ways of identifying patients, an enterprise master patient index (EMPI or MPI) may be used to translate among the patient identifiers used in different systems. Identifying patients can be quite complex because a person's name may change over time, as is the case with marriage or adoption, and other data, including address, phone number, driver's license number, and insurance coverage, can also change. Patients may provide inconsistent information or data may be entered incorrectly, compounding the challenge.

Consistent training of registration personnel and retrieval of any paper records prior to patient arrival are critical for promoting safety. Still, errors occur, so systems must accommodate changes in patient identification. Merging records and teasing apart an "overlay," created when two individuals are erroneously assigned the same identifier, must be supported. These practical challenges of patient identification should be kept in mind when using datasets obtained from provider organizations.

Patient registration is viewed as the front end of a "revenue cycle" that culminates in sending bills to patients and claims to third-party payers (insurance companies or government programs such as Medicare, Medicaid, and workers' compensation). In hospitals, the system that generates bills or claims is called **patient accounting**. Physician practices typically have a system that includes patient registration, appointment scheduling, and billing, called a **practice management system**. These systems also manage the collections process, which is called patient **accounts receivable**.

Patient accounting and practice management systems are distinguished from general financial systems, which mirror the management systems used in any business: general ledger, human resources, payroll, and materials management. These systems support operational processes within the organization, rather than the care of individual patients, but they are often specialized for healthcare organizations. For example, many industries use staff scheduling systems, but a hospital staff scheduling system may forecast demand for nurses and other direct care personnel based on the current and projected patient census and scheduled surgeries. Materials management systems may have specialized modules for pharmaceuticals, surgical supplies, custom orthopedic implants, and other features of supply chain management peculiar to health care, including interfaces to implant logs within surgery systems. These are only a few examples of the systems that may be found within a healthcare organization. General financial systems hold a wealth of information about organization processes that support care delivery, but they generally do not contain information about the care of individual patients.

SYSTEM ARCHITECTURE

Healthcare provider organizations vary in size and complexity from solo physician practices to large, integrated delivery networks. Smaller organizations tend to use software from a single vendor that provides adequate functionality across all categories of systems. This is often called a "monolithic" architecture, with all functions built on a single, shared database. Many larger organizations have chosen systems from different vendors providing different functionality for each department's needs. In this "best-of-breed" architecture, systems are typically integrated using a messaging standard called **Health Level 7**, or **HL7**.[11] The term refers to the seventh, or highest, layer of an international standard for open systems integration. Lower layers establish the connection between two systems; the seventh layer is where the information is transmitted. HL7 messaging is widely used to exchange information among systems within a provider organization and with other providers via a **health information exchange**. Message flow is managed by a system called an *interface engine* or *integration engine*. System-to-system communication processes can be quite complex, but HL7 standards and integration engines simplify their management.

CLAIMS DATA

In the absence of data from an EHR, the series of claims for each patient provides a useful, albeit stylized, picture of the care process, filtered through billing rules that depend on the way providers are organized and the nature of the patient's insurance coverage. Yet claims have the substantial advantage of being structured data, with discrete fields (specified by transaction standards) and common code sets.

Each claim includes one or more **diagnosis codes** and one or more **procedure codes**. Diagnoses are coded using ICD-9-CM, the International Classification of Diseases, 9th Revision, Clinical Modification. The World Health Organization is responsible for the ICD system. ICD-9-CM provides codes for both diagnoses and procedures. All claims require ICD-9-CM procedure codes, specifying surgical and other procedures that were performed. (Professional fee claims use the same diagnosis codes, but a different procedure coding system.) In addition to these procedure codes, institutional claims also define broad categories of services, such as "room and board" for various kinds of hospital units or levels of care (e.g., acute care, intensive care), diagnostic tests, surgical services, etc. Nursing care is included in the daily charge for each hospital unit, the main distinction among units being the intensity of nursing care provided.

Since the 1980s, Medicare and many commercial insurance plans have paid hospitals a fixed amount for each admission, established in advance, depending on the patient's diagnoses and any surgical procedures performed. This is called **prospective payment**. Each hospital admission is classified into one of about 500 categories called **diagnosis-related groups (DRGs)**, and a fixed payment rate is established for every patient in each DRG, with some adjustments for very costly cases, called "outliers." Centers for Medicare and Medicaid Services maintains the DRG system and sets the rates for Medicare, but hospitals typically negotiate rates with commercial insurers. The software that assigns cases to DRGs is called a grouper. Modified versions of the DRG system are used for certain state Medicaid programs and for other payers in some states. DRGs are convenient, and the system continues to be improved, but dividing the entire spectrum of hospital care into just 500 categories yields relatively coarse groupings, particularly for pediatrics and other low-volume populations. The patients and the care provided within some DRGs may be quite heterogeneous. It is also important to remember that DRGs were designed for payment, so they group patients by overall cost of hospital resources consumed (excluding professional fees), which may not be correlated with clinical outcomes.

Two additional coding systems that are increasingly being used for clinical work include SNOMED-CT (Systematized Nomenclature of Medicine–Clinical Terms) and LOINC (Logical Observation Identifiers Names and Codes). Neither appears on claims, but datasets from EHRs are likely to include these codes. LOINC defines standard names for many types of "observations." It is used chiefly for laboratory tests, but the system includes codes for vital signs, EKG findings, and even patient satisfaction surveys. SNOMED-CT evolved from a system developed to encode findings in anatomic pathology, adding concepts that are important in frontline clinical practice. It differs in an important way from the ICD diagnosis codes. ICD is a hierarchical system for classifying diseases, organized roughly by body system. Each condition appears in only one place in the hierarchy, although the assignment of certain diseases to body systems is somewhat arbitrary. Because ICD was developed mainly for public health reporting, it provides far more granularity for common conditions than for rare conditions. In contrast, SNOMED-CT is not a classification system but a nomenclature, a controlled vocabulary of terms, with rules for combining them so that virtually any concept can be expressed through a compound term.

Longitudinal Patient Records   The importance of aggregating data from multiple patients to create a population view has been discussed. At the patient level, there is also a need to assemble data from a series of encounters to create a longitudinal record reflecting the patient's health and health care over time. Occasionally, we may need only a cross-sectional view, for example, to study a particular service provided to patients during a hospital stay, but we are usually interested in care processes and patient outcomes that evolve over time, which requires longitudinal records.

Not only does a longitudinal record give the sequence and timing of acute illnesses and healthcare services, but accumulating diagnoses over time is often the only way to gain a complete picture of a patient's chronic conditions. The diagnosis codes on a claim for an individual encounter do not necessarily reflect all of the patient's diagnoses, only those that were treated, or that affected treatment, during the corresponding encounter. Consider a patient with diabetes, hypertension, and congestive heart failure. Owing to limited time, the physician may document only the principal condition addressed during each office visit, perhaps diabetes during one visit and heart failure during another. Only with a longitudinal record that spans several visits can we be reasonably certain to see diagnosis codes for all of the patient's chronic conditions.

Algorithms have been developed to identify *episodes of illness,* using longitudinal **claims data**, distinguishing acute episodes from ongoing care for one or more chronic conditions. In evaluating resource utilization for a patient with chronic illness, it is important to distinguish whether a hospital admission is likely to have resulted from suboptimal treatment of a chronic condition or if it was due to an unrelated acute illness. These algorithms are imperfect, partly due to limitations of the source data, but as payers attempt to evaluate physicians on the quality and resource efficiency of the care they provide, it is important to characterize—and properly attribute to physicians—care for distinct episodes of illness. Moving from discrete hospital admissions to longitudinal patient records may seem like a subtle transition, but it has far-reaching implications for the design of databases and analytic models.

Combining Clinical and Claims Data   Even when clinical data are available, the sequence of billable events constitutes a standardized "framework" for a longitudinal patient record. Because they are pervasive and standardized, claims data are used for many purposes beyond payment. For example, many payers have developed disease management programs, using predictive algorithms based on claims data to identify patients who are at risk for developing more serious conditions or for increased utilization (of healthcare services) over the coming year.

The recent growth in pharmacy benefits as a routine component of health insurance has provided an important new source of information for understanding care processes because medications are often a crucial part of therapy. Moreover, claims reflect the actual dispensing of medications, so claims data indicate whether patients are refilling their prescriptions on schedule. This can reveal several kinds of problems with pharmaceutical therapy, for example, that a patient (1) has stopped taking a prescribed medication, (2) is taking it on a different schedule than was prescribed, (3) is continuing to refill a prescription that the physician had meant to discontinue, or (4) is taking duplicate or conflicting medications prescribed by different physicians and/or dispensed by different pharmacies.

Of course, claims data reflect only prescription medications for which patients used their pharmacy benefit. Neither over-the-counter medications nor agents classified as "nutriceuticals" are included, so while a pharmacy claims database reflects whether a patient is on clopidogrel, a prescription antiplatelet agent, it cannot indicate whether the patient is also taking aspirin or omega-3 fatty acids, both of which can have an additive effect. Moreover, patients may choose not to use their pharmacy benefit for prescriptions filled through low-cost generic programs, so these drugs would not be reflected in pharmacy claims for specific patient populations. (Advanced e-prescribing systems provide physicians with a patient's prescription fill history. This information is usually based on dispensing, rather than claims. It still excludes over-the-counter items, but for prescription medications, it may be more timely and more complete than the data available to payers.)

Laboratory results are important in indicating whether certain risk factors, such as cholesterol, are being managed effectively. Claims data show that a laboratory test was done, but the claims dataset does not include the test result. Increasingly, claims data are being combined with lab results obtained from large national laboratory providers to track whether risk factors like cholesterol are being successfully managed. These data may be used by insurers to target patients for disease management and also to profile physician performance.

As pharmacy claims illustrate, a major shortcoming of claims data is that they are blind to noncovered services, for which no claim is generated. Another critical blind spot is the contrast between physician office visits, which are typically reflected in claims data, and activities such as care coordination, visit planning, patient outreach, patient education, and health coaching. These are often critical to achieving good outcomes, yet they are seldom reflected in claims data because they are seldom reimbursed.

THREE MAJOR CATEGORIES OF SYSTEMS

The systems within a typical healthcare provider organization can be grouped into three major categories: (1) **transaction systems**, (2) disease registries, and (3) data warehouses. These categories are distinguished by the business functions they support and the level of data aggregation, from individual patients to broad populations. Figure 9-1 illustrates major "logical" systems within each category, that is, functions that must be performed, whether by discrete software systems or by modules within a "monolithic" system, as well as some typical data types.

First we will discuss the two extremes, transaction systems and data warehouses. Then we will address registries, which are a hybrid of the two.

TRANSACTION SYSTEMS

Systems that support granular business processes, including systems used at the point of care, are considered transaction systems. An EHR focuses on a series of patient care events,

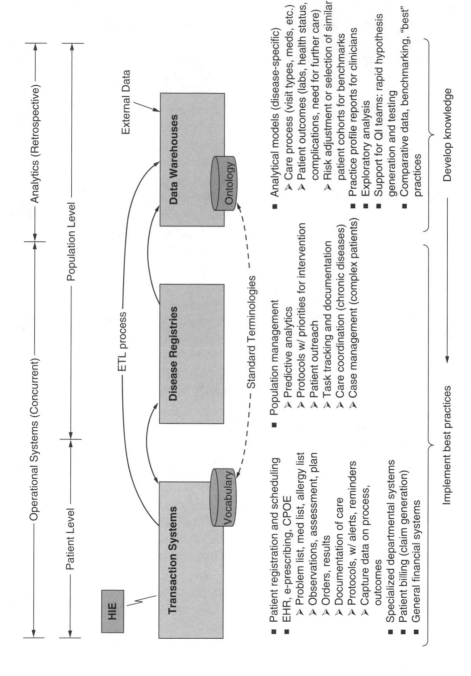

Figure 9-1 Three Major Categories of Systems

one patient at a time. A patient scheduling system arranges individual appointments. These systems usually involve some natural data aggregation, such as patient problem lists and medication lists in an EHR, or a scheduling system view showing all patient appointments with a given provider on a given day. Patient billing systems accumulate data about discrete services provided to patients and group them into invoices or claims. Still, the focus of these systems is not data aggregation, per se, but carrying out a business process at a granular level.

DATA WAREHOUSES

At the other end of the spectrum, a **data warehouse** assimilates data from multiple transaction systems. It facilitates analysis across an entire patient population and offers diverse ways to "drill down" to specific subsets of patients, clinical services, or parts of an organization. Patient billing systems and EHRs can summarize all services for a given patient over time, but they generally cannot identify all patients who received a given service. That requires a different "slice" through the data. Transaction systems typically enable rapid access to a particular view of the data, usually by patient. Data warehouses have much broader datasets, and they enable many different views into the data.

For example, no single transaction system allows us to analyze the use of imaging in patients with low back pain. The radiology system has information about patients who had imaging studies, but for this analysis, we also need to know about the patients with the same diagnoses who did not have imaging studies. And we need to understand the full picture for both groups of patients—their other diagnoses and the sequence of visits, medications, and other services provided before and after the imaging. We would want to correlate the care following the procedure with the clinical picture and the findings of the procedure. In some cases, the radiology system may have more details about the procedure than the information reflected in the final report sent to the EHR. For this kind of study, it is easy to recognize the advantages of collecting data from multiple transaction systems in a data warehouse, organized to support these queries.

Many EHR vendors now offer a disease registry module, and physicians may access a registry at the point of care. Logically, however, an EHR remains a transaction system, designed mainly for caring for individual patients. Registries and data warehouses are designed for a population view.

DISEASE REGISTRIES

Registries are a hybrid type of system, designed for surveillance (case finding) and tracking. Like data warehouses, they aggregate data about an organization's patients, usually a specific patient population, such as patients with diabetes, asthma, or heart failure. Common queries related to surveillance may be built in. Like transaction systems, registries identify individual patients who may require intervention, such as follow-up care or periodic prevention or screening. In an EHR, a patient's record is usually accessed when the patient calls or comes in for an office visit. In contrast, a registry looks at a population of patients and identifies all the patients who meet certain criteria indicating a need for intervention.

This use of the term *registry* refers to an operational system used by provider organizations for active management of a defined patient population, so it may be called a *disease registry* or *patient registry*. It is a basic tool of population management. The term *registry* is also used for a more passive system used to collect a standardized dataset, over time, on a defined patient population, such as patients who have received a specific drug, implanted device, or surgical procedure, or patients who have been diagnosed with cancer.[12] These registries focus on obtaining a specific dataset and periodic follow-up on each patient, and they are used primarily for outcomes research, rather than active population management. For example, most hospitals maintain a "tumor registry," in which they collect annual follow-up on patients who received treatment for cancer.

CREATING DATA WAREHOUSES

Data warehouses may be created at multiple levels, within an organization and across organizations. The term may be applied to any database that aggregates and organizes data from multiple source systems with a defined process for keeping it current and an ability to query the system in ways that were not (fully) anticipated when the system was designed. A data warehouse may be optimized for certain types of queries, but all warehouses should permit some degree of "exploratory" analysis.

Data warehouses often bring in external data. For example, each patient's home address may be combined with census data to impute an education level to the patient based on the median education level within the area. This approach may be used for a variety of factors, such as degree of urbanization, local availability of certain healthcare services, and driving distance to various facilities. These imputed variables are not specific to an individual patient, but they can be useful in population-level analyses to inform strategic decisions, such as where to locate new specialty practices. They can also inform operational processes. Analysis may reveal that patients who live more than a certain distance from a clinic are significantly less likely to keep follow-up appointments. With this knowledge, an organization may decide to provide additional appointment reminders to patients who live in certain areas.

MAPPING TO COMMON TERMINOLOGY

A terminology system that provides names for concepts within a certain domain and defines relationships among the concepts is called an **ontology**. Most ontologies specify certain hierarchical relationships, mapping detailed terms to one or more higher-level classes. For example, drugs available in the United States are identified by a National Drug Code (NDC). NDCs serve as universal product identifiers for human drugs. The Food and Drug

Administration (FDA) assigns a unique NDC to each drug (or combination), dosage form, and strength, from each manufacturer. These very granular codes are useful for supply chain management and for tracking adverse reactions (which could be caused by the drug itself or caused by the manufacturing process). But this is too much detail for an ambulatory e-prescribing system or an inpatient CPOE system. There, the generic name of the drug and the available dosage forms and strengths are important, but not the manufacturer.

Consider a retrospective analysis to determine whether certain patients are receiving a beta-blocker upon discharge from the hospital. It would be unwieldy to construct a query that names every drug in this class, let alone every dosage form, strength, and manufacturer. Rather, data elements that involve drugs are loaded into a data warehouse at multiple levels of granularity: the NDC (and in some cases, lot number) that was dispensed by a particular pharmacy for a particular patient at a particular time; all forms of a given drug (e.g., a certain beta-blocker); and all medications that fall into a given class (e.g., all beta-blockers). Medications are often grouped into classes such as this, but the classes are not strictly hierarchical because some drugs may be used for multiple purposes and thus fall into multiple therapeutic classes.

Mapping data to a common ontology as they are loaded into a data warehouse can be a painstaking process, given the many ways that data are represented in different source systems. Yet mapping is essential in order to enable practical clinical and business questions to be addressed efficiently, with sufficiently rapid turnaround to keep clinicians engaged in quality improvement initiatives. Although it would be ideal to have all medications mapped in full detail, the time required and cost would be substantial. A large organization may have literally hundreds of separate entries in various source systems that refer to something as simple as aspirin and aspirin-containing compounds. With more than 20,000 distinct prescription drugs available in the United States (not counting over-the-counter, complementary, and alternative medications),[13] it is impractical for most organizations to map everything before they start to use a data warehouse. Increasingly, data warehouse developers are being selective about detailed mapping, driven by analytical needs. This approach can limit the spontaneity of exploratory analyses, but it makes it feasible to capture richer detail in areas of particular interest.

Enabling Data-Driven Improvement   Are some physicians more likely than others to prescribe insulin for type 2 diabetes patients who are having trouble controlling their blood glucose? What are the outcomes and the overall cost of medications for such patients who are on insulin, compared to those who remain on multiple oral agents? Such questions are critical for understanding how an organization is caring for specific patient populations, and they are fundamental to quality and performance improvement.

Physicians and provider organizations are often "graded" by payers or in public accountability initiatives on how consistently they follow accepted guidelines for treating a certain condition and the outcomes their patients achieve. Most pay-for-performance

(P4P) plans are also based on such measures. A common "process" measure is the proportion of a physician's diabetic patients being tested periodically for glycated hemoglobin (HbA1c) to evaluate their long-term blood glucose control. A corresponding "outcome" measure is the fraction of patients who are (known to be) in good control. Such measures provide a high-level view of current performance, but they give little guidance for improvement. To make the data actionable for improvement, we must examine processes of care at a detailed level, including how various subsets of the patient population experience those processes. Such an *exploratory analysis* typically requires data from multiple transaction systems, integrated in a data warehouse.

Several analytical issues must be addressed in order to establish the credibility of the data and to engage clinicians in quality improvement (QI). Physicians may think, "Those aren't my patients," so it's critical to have a transparent and reasonable method for attributing patients to physicians. Physicians may think, "My patients are sicker," so it's important to be able to characterize each physician's attributed patients in terms of age, severity of illness, and comorbid conditions or overall disease burden. (On average, half the physicians who think their patients are sicker are probably right.) Many factors other than quality of care can influence outcomes, such as the severity or complexity of the patient's disease, lifestyle, and compliance with prescribed therapies, level of education, socioeconomic status, family and other support systems, and even values and beliefs that cause some patients to opt for aggressive therapy where others may choose a more conservative course. Seldom do secondary datasets include information about all of these, but if outcomes are to be interpreted as reflecting quality of care, we must try to account for all factors other than quality that can affect outcomes.

Risk adjustment refers to statistical methods used to account for patient factors associated with a greater risk of certain outcomes. There are two general approaches to using a large database for risk adjustment. One is to develop a multivariate regression model that reflects the contribution of each (measured) factor to the patient's risk of a particular outcome. The regression equation is then used to estimate risk for individual patients, which can be done without further reference to the database. The other general approach is to identify, within the data warehouse, a cohort of patients who are similar to the measured population in terms of patient factors, and compare outcomes in the measured population to those in the "matched" cohort. Regardless of approach, risk must be evaluated separately for each outcome. A patient who is at risk for high resource consumption may or may not be at greater risk for a particular clinical complication. For credibility with clinicians and comparative fairness, it is important to acknowledge these subtleties, including the fact that some important patient factors may not be reflected in the available data. No approach to risk adjustment is without disadvantages, but simply having a thorough and open discussion about the selected approach can be an important step toward a culture of data-driven quality and performance improvement.

Risk adjustment is more critical for measures published as "quality report cards" or used as a basis for payment or for directing patients to particular providers (i.e., through tiered copayments). Without credible risk adjustment in these settings, providers may be reluctant to accept high-risk patients, and this can create a barrier to access for the sickest patients. Statistical risk adjustment is often used in hospital performance measures, but measures for physicians typically focus on process elements that everyone agrees should apply to all patients (e.g., that HbA1c should be measured periodically for all diabetic patients) or on a subset of the patient population (e.g., applying targets for HbA1c levels and blood pressure control only to patients younger than a certain age). Patient attribution is also important. Measures reflecting a given physician's management of chronic conditions typically include only those patients whose pattern of visits indicate that the physician is responsible for managing their chronic care.

Risk adjustment is less critical when data are used for internal QI within a provider organization, where there is less tendency to think in terms of damage control. Variation in care processes or patient outcomes—across an organization, across multiple organizations, or over time—often suggests an opportunity for improvement. This is not to say that patients with the "best" outcome or the lowest resource use should be the benchmark for all patients, only that variation may point to fertile ground for improvement. The more successful we are in accounting for patient factors that contribute to variation, the more likely the remaining variation points to real opportunity.

For QI, we must move beyond whether a physician's patients are sicker, to ask if there might still be some opportunities to improve care for this challenging population. Can we separate patients who are achieving good outcomes from others who may need more attention? Are other physicians or other care teams treating similar patients and achieving better outcomes at lower cost? Exploring the data in these ways usually shifts physicians and other clinicians out of a defensive mind-set and stimulates hypothesis generation about how care could be improved, or at least which aspects of care might be contributing to poor outcomes or high cost.

The transition to creative thinking about improvement is a critical step in engaging clinicians in QI, and it requires the ability to analyze the data in ways they find meaningful. Having timely data from multiple transaction systems integrated in a data warehouse is crucial for rapid turnaround on these analytical questions, and rapid turnaround is essential for maintaining the interest of busy clinicians. Integrating patient-reported health status and the results of patient, physician, and employee satisfaction surveys add important dimensions. It's also important to include data about the providers, such as gender, languages spoken, and years in practice, because these factors may be helpful in understanding interactions with certain patients, or for identifying comparable patient–provider relationships for comparison, within a data warehouse.

As noted in Figure 9-1, EHRs and registries play an essential role in implementing what is learned (from data warehouses and improvement initiatives) about which care processes work best for each patient population. EHRs and registries ensure that improved care processes are carried out consistently for the right patients and populations. Within a provider organization, the return on investment for a data warehouse may seem "soft," compared with transaction systems that enable essential business and clinical processes. However, by engaging clinicians in a culture of improvement and by promoting data-driven decision making, a data warehouse and the analytics it enables can be the key to *improving* these processes, rather than just carrying them out.

CHALLENGES IN CREATING DATA WAREHOUSES

We have learned that there is great value in data warehouses, particularly those that span multiple provider organizations and thus are likely to reflect a variety of approaches to care and the corresponding outcomes, as well as differences in the overall cost of achieving those outcomes. Among the broadest and most useful data are Medicare fee-for-service claims, which CMS makes available to health services researchers. CMS has created a Chronic Condition Warehouse (CCW) that combines claims, enrollment, and assessment data for Medicare beneficiaries who have any of 21 chronic conditions and are covered by Parts A (hospital care), B (professional services), and D (prescription drugs) of the Medicare program (Parts B and D are optional). The CCW permits creation of longitudinal patient records, subject to strict privacy controls. These are very rich datasets, but they suffer from the limitations previously described for all claims data. There is also a delay of up to two years between the time care is provided and the data become available. And, of course, their main focus is Medicare beneficiaries, that is, people 65 years of age and older. Other public data resources include Medicaid data, whose content and availability varies by state, and datasets resulting from various state requirements for hospitals and other institutional providers to report de-identified, patient-level data.

Several provider groups have developed initiatives for sharing detailed clinical data, also subject to strict privacy controls. Many academic medical centers that are members of the University HealthSystem Consortium (UHC) share patient-level data from their teaching hospitals and their community affiliates. Hospitals and integrated networks that are members of the Premier healthcare alliance also share data on hospital quality measures, resource utilization, and operational efficiency. The Institute for Healthcare Improvement (IHI) and the American Medical Group Association (AMGA) conduct best-practice collaboratives in which participants share specific datasets on care processes and patient outcomes.

The methods used in these improvement collaboratives differ from those of traditional health services research, where historical data are analyzed, often using elegant statistical methods to overcome the limitations of observational data. In contrast to this static approach, collaboratives involve a cyclic process in which organizations combine analytical findings with clinicians' experience and intuition to design incremental changes in care processes, study the results of these changes, refine the interventions, and repeat the cycle, seeking further improvement. Data and analytics are essential, but they are only one step in a dynamic process that refines and ultimately validates the participants' collective understanding of best practices. Collaboratives also address the challenges of disseminating best practices and incorporating them into routine clinical practice.

PUBLIC HEALTH INFORMATICS

Applied epidemiology is the foundation of public health. From tracking patterns of disease and population needs for health services to prioritizing interventions and evaluating their results, data are essential. It must be remembered, however, that the "population view" assembled in typical provider or payer data warehouses reflects the *patient* population, that is, those persons who have received care. It is not a view of the population as a whole. Thus, public health informatics also relies on *survey data,* including census data and several surveys conducted by the National Center for Health Statistics, which is part of the Centers for Disease Control and Prevention. Most states also maintain registries for pediatric immunizations, which serve the same functions as the provider-based disease registries previously discussed. Some state-level registries exchange data with providers' internal registries or EHRs via HL7 messages.

Surveillance is an important theme in public health, tracking everything from risk factors, like obesity and smoking, to influenza epidemics and patterns of infection with methicillin-resistant Staphylococcus aureus (MRSA). Since September 11, 2001, surveillance for bioterrorism has also become very important. Data sources range from "reportable diseases," which providers are required by various state laws to report, to real-time data shared voluntarily by emergency departments and other frontline care providers. More effective surveillance has been touted as a major benefit of the Nationwide Health Information Network (discussed later in this chapter), providing data that are both broader and richer than those currently available.

An important application of active surveillance is **pharmacovigilance**, aimed at detecting, understanding, and preventing adverse effects of drugs and biologic products. As previously noted, clinical trials typically involve a few thousand patients at most, so uncommon side effects and adverse reactions may not be known when a drug enters the market. Manufacturers report to the Food and Drug Administration (FDA) any adverse events that are reported to them, but patients and providers may fail to recognize the connection to the drug. A potentially powerful method is to use very large databases, assembled from claims and EHRs, to detect patterns of adverse events among patients taking a new drug. The FDA's Sentinel Initiative is the focus of considerable effort to create suitable federated databases and to develop statistical methods for "signal" detection.[14,15]

PRACTICAL ISSUES OF EHR IMPLEMENTATION AND ADOPTION

Most large, multispecialty medical groups are using advanced EHRs, disease registries, and e-prescribing, but these technologies are rare in small physician practices. Small practices seldom have the time or money to undertake a disruptive IT implementation, and having relatively few support staff limits their potential to gain efficiencies through workflow redesign. There is often no one within the practice to manage on-site servers and software, or to fine-tune alerts and reminders for clinical decision support. The ambulatory EHR market has also been relatively fluid, making vendor selection quite challenging. In the past, these factors created a greater risk of implementation failure in small practices.

Fortunately, EHRs and practice management systems are becoming available through remote hosting, called an "application service provider" (ASP) or "software as a service" (SaaS) model, eliminating the need for physician practices to install software and to maintain servers. It is easier to manage a secure internal network; also, end-user devices have improved considerably as hardware prices have dropped. Today's EHR products are substantially more mature than those that were available 10 or 15 years ago, when many large groups initially adopted them. Small practices will still have difficulty creating data warehouses, but EHRs increasingly include reporting tools that provide valuable summary and trend data.

There is still room for improvement in EHRs, but it must be understood that championing an EHR in the mid-1990s took far more courage and vision than are required today.

IMPORTANCE OF PROCESS REDESIGN AND COGNITIVE SUPPORT

Clinical and operations leadership is the most critical factor for a successful EHR implementation, but redesign of care processes to take advantage of IT is the most important step in realizing potential efficiencies. Distributing documentation tasks among care team members and using the system for worklists and messaging within the practice are common areas of emphasis.

With the explosion of new information in the medical literature and increasingly nuanced practice guidelines, routine medical care is beginning to exceed the limits of human cognition. Decision support and access to context-appropriate reference material will soon be essential, as therapies begin to be tailored for each patient's **genomic profile**. Still, these features will require careful calibration to ensure that important issues are addressed without creating alert fatigue. This will require new organizational functions for "knowledge management" to maintain clinical content within the system. There are also many choices to make about which data are captured in structured form (rather than dictated notes) and how they are encoded. The benefits of this extra work for providers accrue mainly downstream—to the same caregiver when seeing the patient in follow-up, to other caregivers who see the patient, in administrative processes that are simplified, and in enhanced quality and patient safety.

One of the benefits most useful to physicians is having full access from a remote location to medical records and to e-prescribing when on call. Yet, as an organization becomes dependent on an EHR, it emphasizes the need for technical support and backup mechanisms to ensure the availability and reliability of the system and the data it contains.

A 2009 report from the National Research Council indicated just how far we have to go, based on site visits to some of the nation's most advanced hospitals: "IT applications ... appear designed to automate tasks or business processes for administrative efficiency and ... provide little support for the cognitive tasks of clinicians. IT-based systems for health care are often designed in ways that simply mimic existing paper-based forms and workflow and do not take advantage of human–computer interaction principles."[16]

IMPACT OF ORGANIZATIONAL CULTURE

At a strategic level, it makes sense for most provider organizations to implement an EHR, but observers of such initiatives often say that "culture eats strategy for lunch." It is important to recognize the scope and depth of the transformation that implementing a modern EHR entails, making explicit issues that would otherwise never have surfaced. It is not uncommon for physicians within a practice to take different approaches to treating a certain condition, but the differences may not be recognized when using paper medical records. However, designing decision support rules to implement the practice's "standard protocol" for the condition brings the issue to light. Even more basic is the fact that physicians may be uncomfortable with the visibility that an EHR or a data warehouse gives every clinical decision. Some may feel that they are "practicing in public," or that elaborate documentation is required to justify each decision. It is, of course, a healthy discipline to document one's rationale, including the patient's role in shared decisions. But the visibility of individual decisions and particularly of patterns of care may expose fundamental issues of trust among clinical colleagues.

To gain the full benefit of an EHR, provider organizations must develop a sustainable capability for continuous improvement. They must continue incremental improvement beyond the initial implementation. For many provider organizations, this is not only a substantial investment—it's also a big change in organizational culture. Some elements are necessary to achieve and sustain the kind of fundamental transformation that implementing an EHR entails. Implementation of EHRs must be viewed not as a technology project, but a clinical and operational transformation in order to leverage IT. Organizations often have an unrealistic view of such initiatives, thinking the most difficult decision involves selecting the right vendor. Many organizations have succeeded with vendors and products that have been at the center of failures in other organizations. While certain vendors and products may be a better match for some organizations than for others, success is much more than simply "making the right choice." Major systems typically remain in place for 10 to 20 years, so the ongoing relationship with a vendor may be more important than a detailed analysis of current product functionality.

Implementation is sometimes viewed simply as a matter of good project management—maintaining disciplined focus and avoiding "scope creep." Those processes are important, but organizations should approach the initiative with an open mind, anticipating experimentation and mutual learning, as discussed later in this chapter.

INCENTIVES FOR E-PRESCRIBING AND "MEANINGFUL USE" OF EHRs

In the HITECH (Health Information Technology for Economic and Clinical Health) Act, passed in 2009 as part of the economic stimulus legislation, the American Recovery and Reinvestment Act (ARRA), Congress authorized CMS to provide substantial financial incentives for eligible professionals and hospitals who achieve "meaningful use" of "certified" EHRs. Incentive payments begin in 2011 and gradually decrease, providing a benefit to organizations that have been early adopters. Starting in 2015, providers who have not achieved "meaningful use" may be subject to financial penalties under Medicare.

The focus on meaningful use recognizes that improved health and health care do not result simply from adoption of IT, but from using the technology to inform clinical decisions, to enhance efficiency and patient safety by ensuring that relevant information is not forgotten or overlooked, to engage patients and families, to monitor and improve quality and cost-efficiency, and to reduce health disparities among minorities and disadvantaged populations. CMS has defined criteria for meaningful use that represent increasing expectations for these outcomes in 2011, 2013, and 2015. The meaningful use criteria are entirely consistent with the themes outlined in this chapter and, in fact, they explicitly address the population health perspective.

The HITECH incentives require the use of a "certified" EHR, in recognition of the growing importance of certification, both in driving industry expectations and in giving guidance to providers who wish to acquire an EHR. In response to this requirement, the Certification Commission for Health Information Technology (CCHIT) has stratified its criteria, offering a baseline level of certification to ensure that a product can meet the meaningful use requirements and an advanced certification to recognize leading-edge products that advance the industry as a whole.

In addition to the HITECH incentives, CMS will offer separate cash incentives through 2013 for use of an e-prescribing system that meets certain criteria. These incentives have captured the attention of providers and are generally viewed as effective policies for encouraging providers to make the transition to EHRs and e-prescribing. HITECH also solidified in statute the **Office of the National Coordinator for Health Information Technology (ONC)** within the Department of Health and Human Services. ONC was established by executive order in 2004.

INTEROPERABILITY

From the outset, ONC has focused not just on EHR adoption, but also on defining a vision for an interoperable, standards-based **Nationwide Health Information Network (NHIN)**, assembled by connecting regional health information exchanges (HIEs), generally operated by **regional health information organizations (RHIOs)**. As is apparent from the previous discussion of code sets for capturing data in structured form and the issues involved in aggregating data to create data warehouses, we have a long way to go before this vision can be fully realized, but it is never too early to begin adopting the standards that it will require.

The HIPAA transaction standards established a **national provider identifier (NPI)** for individual and institutional healthcare providers, but it stopped short of establishing a national patient identifier. Most observers believe this concept is not politically feasible in the United States, given our national culture, but the lack of a uniform patient identifier imposes a substantial burden on any regional HIE and particularly on the NHIN. These systems are forced to use secondary identifiers and probabilistic matching methods (e.g., assigning more significance to a match on an uncommon name than to a match on a common name).

Meanwhile, many providers are offering "patient portals" that provide secure, Web-based access into the organization's EHR. Features vary, but most allow patients to view part or all of their own medical record, as maintained by providers; to enter information that can be viewed by providers; to communicate with providers; and to conduct administrative transactions such as requesting or scheduling appointments. Communication with providers ranges from simply replacing phone calls with secure messaging (similar to e-mail) to formal "e-visits" that replace office visits for non-urgent problems, for which providers receive payment.

Personal health records (PHRs) that are separate from providers' EHRs are also being introduced, both as stand-alone products (Google Health, Microsoft HealthVault) and as employer-sponsored initiatives (Dossia). These systems are developing interfaces to EHRs, and ideally they will integrate data from multiple providers for a single patient. PHRs are also developing interfaces to various home monitoring devices, from electronic scales for patients with congestive heart failure to blood glucose meters for patients with diabetes.

It is important to be realistic about the benefits we expect from connecting EHRs. There has been a focus on care coordination, consistent with the concept of creating a "medical home" for each patient. However, achieving effective care coordination in our fragmented delivery system can be a staggering challenge. A recent analysis of detailed physician survey data and Medicare claims revealed that a typical primary care physician has 229 other physicians working in 117 practices with whom care must be coordinated for his or her patients.[17] Clearly, it is not realistic to expect that simply connecting EHRs, even through a sophisticated HIE, will cause independent practices to spontaneously coalesce into medical homes. Multispecialty medical groups have learned that even with a single, shared EHR and a strong corporate culture, they need to hire, train, and equip people whose job it is to provide care coordination and disease (population) management for patients with chronic conditions and to provide case management for complex patients.

PRIVACY AND SECURITY

The HIPAA Privacy and Security Rules, which were extended and modified by HITECH, have had a profound effect on management of health information, including its use for research. The HIPAA Privacy Rule applies to all individually identifiable health information, regardless of form, and the Security Rule applies to information in electronic form. For more about HIPAA, refer to Chapter 6.

UNINTENDED CONSEQUENCES

Adoption of EHRs and other **point-of-care systems** should be viewed not as a technology project, but as a strategic change-management initiative, with attention to the sociology and psychology of behavior change. Fortunately, there is a growing body of research to inform these initiatives. Some organizations have observed unintended adverse consequences of implementing CPOE and EHR systems, including more work or new work for clinicians; unexpected changes in workflow, communication patterns, and the "power structure;" and generation of new kinds of errors.[18,19] For example, entering medication orders via pull-down lists eliminates the problems of illegibility and ambiguity, but it provides the opportunity to mistakenly select an adjacent item from the pull-down list.[20] This suggests that system designers should use techniques such as highlighting likely choices, given the clinical situation, or lettering that emphasizes differences between similar or adjacent entries.

More fundamentally, there is a growing recognition of the complex nature of clinical work:

> There is quite a large mismatch between the implicit theories embedded in these computer systems and the real world of clinical work. Clinical work, especially in hospitals, is fundamentally interpretative, interruptive, multitasking, collaborative, distributed, opportunistic, and reactive. In contrast, CPOE systems and decision support systems are based on a different model of work: one that is objective, rationalized, linear, normative, localized (in the clinician's mind), solitary, and single-minded. Such models tend to reflect the implicit theories of managers and designers, not of frontline [clinical] workers.[21]

Fortunately, the industry as a whole is assimilating these lessons into software design and system implementation methods. We still have a long way to go, but there is reason to be optimistic that we will continue to progress toward effective use of systems and data to improve health and health care for individuals and populations.

CONCLUSIONS

Data are essential for provider organizations, research, and policy. Growing adoption of EHRs promises to enable better decision making in the care of individual patients and also in managing population health. Research based on richer, more real-time data will inform policy decisions in all parts of the healthcare system. This chapter provided a foundation for wise interpretation of data for any use—an understanding of the source systems and the frontline care processes where the data originate, as well as the mechanisms by which they are aggregated and analyzed.

STUDY AND DISCUSSION QUESTIONS

1. Ideally, disease registries are populated with structured data captured in an EHR as a by-product of providing care. However, suppose your organization has no EHR but wants to assess and improve its management of patients with diabetes. What are some source systems that you might use to populate a disease registry?

2. How does a third-party payer's view of a patient's care and outcomes differ from the view of a medical group that provides much of the patient's care and has an advanced EHR? Would the payer, the medical group, or both together be likely to have sufficient data to address all of the aspects of outcomes that are important to the patient's employer?

3. What measures would you use, as the manager of an EHR, to detect or monitor "alert fatigue" caused by alerts or reminders in your system?

4. Which aspect of the "inferential gap" do you believe has the greatest impact on population health status and the overall cost of health care in the United States? Will this change over the next 10 to 20 years?

5. How would you design an observational study to evaluate the effectiveness of clinical decision support in an EHR, in terms of patient outcomes? What data sources would be required? What clinical decisions would you focus on? How would you identify a credible point of comparison?

SUGGESTED READINGS AND WEB SITES

READINGS

Han YY, Carcillo JA, Venkataraman ST, et al. Unexpected increased mortality after implementation of a commercially sold computerized physician order entry system. *Pediatrics.* 2005;116(6):1506–1512.

Rapid learning. *Health Aff.* 2007;26(2):w107-w118. http://content.healthaffairs.org/cgi/content/full/hlthaff.26.2.w107/DC2. Published January 26, 2007. Accessed January 3, 2010.

Sittig DF, Singh H. Eight rights of safe electronic health record use. *JAMA.* 2009;302(10):1111–1113.

Wears RL, Berg M. Computer technology and clinical work: still waiting for Godot. *JAMA.* 2005;293(10):1261–1263.

WEB SITES

AcademyHealth (health services research): http://www.academyhealth.org
Agency for Healthcare Research and Quality: http://www.ahrq.gov
American Medical Informatics Association: http://www.amia.org

Clinical Informatics wiki: http://www.informatics-review.com/wiki
Health Information Technology: http://www.healthit.hhs.gov
Healthcare Information and Management Systems Society: http://www.himss.org
National Library of Medicine (NLM): http://www.nlm.nih.gov/

REFERENCES

1. Institute of Medicine. *The Computer-Based Patient Record: An Essential Technology for Health Care.* Revised ed. Washington, DC: National Academies Press; 1997.

2. DesRoches CM, Campbell EG, Rao SR, et al. Electronic health records in ambulatory care: a national survey of physicians. *N Engl J Med.* 2008;359(1):50–60.

3. Jha AK, DesRoches CM, Campbell EG, et al. Use of electronic health records in U.S. hospitals. *N Engl J Med.* 2009;360(16):1628–1638.

4. Bates DW. Computerized physician order entry and medication errors: finding a balance. *J Biomed Inform.* 2005;38(4):259–261.

5. Office of Enterprise Development. *VistA-HealtheVet Monograph 2008–2009.* Washington, DC: Department of Veterans Affairs; 2008. www4.va.gov/vista_monograph. Accessed October 24, 2009.

6. Perlin JB, Kupersmith J. Information technology and the inferential gap. *Health Aff.* 2007;26(2): w192–w194.

7. Stewart WF, Shah NR, Selna MJ, Paulus RA, Walker JM. Bridging the inferential gap: the electronic health record and clinical evidence. *Health Aff.* 2007;26(2):w181–w191.

8. McGlynn EA, Asch SM, Adams J, et al. The quality of health care delivered to adults in the United States. *N Engl J Med.* 2003;348(26):2635–2645.

9. Boyd CM, Darer J, Boult C, Fried LP, Boult L, Wu AW. Clinical practice guidelines and quality of care for older patients with multiple comorbid diseases: implications for pay for performance. *JAMA.* 2005;294(6):716–724.

10. US Department of Health and Human Services; National Institute of Health; National Heart, Lung, and Blood Institute; National High Blood Pressure Education Program. *The Seventh Report of the Joint National Committee on Prevention, Detection, Evaluation, and Treatment of High Blood Pressure.* Bethesda, MD: US Department of Health and Human Services; 2004:25. NIH Publication No. 04–5230.

11. Health Level Seven International. Health Level Seven International Web site. http://www.hl7.org. Accessed January 3, 2010.

12. Gliklich RE, Dreyer NA, Eds. *Registries for Evaluating Patient Outcomes: A User's Guide.* Rockville, MD: Agency for Healthcare Research and Quality; 2007. AHRQ Publication No. 07-EHC001-1.

13. US Food and Drug Administration. National drug code directory. US Food and Drug Administration Web site. http://www.fda.gov/Drugs/InformationOnDrugs/ucm142438.htm. Updated April 5, 2010.

14. US Food and Drug Administration. FDA's Sentinel Initiative. US Food and Drug Administration Web site. www.fda.gov/Safety/FDAsSentinelInitiative. Accessed January 3, 2010.

15. Foundation for the National Institutes of Health. Observational Medical Outcomes Partnership Web site. http://omop.fnih.org. Accessed January 3, 2010.

16. Stead WW, Lin HS; and Committee on Engaging the Computer Science Research Community in Health Care Informatics, National Research Council. *Computational Technology for Effective Health Care: Immediate Steps and Strategic Directions.* Washington, DC: National Academies Press; 2009.

17. Pham HH, O'Malley AS, Bach PB, Saiontz-Martinez C, Schrag D. Primary care physicians' links to other physicians through Medicare patients: the scope of care coordination. *Ann Intern Med.* 2009;150(4):236–242.

18. Campbell EM, Sittig DF, Ash JS, Guappone KP, Dykstra RH. Types of unintended consequences related to computerized provider order entry. *J Am Med Inform Assoc.* 2006;13(5):547–556.

19. Ash JS, Sittig DF, Poon EG, Guappone K, Campbell E, Dykstra RH. The extent and importance of unintended consequences related to computerized provider order entry. *J Am Med Inform Assoc.* 2007;14(4):415–423.

20. Koppel R, Metlay JP, Cohen A, et al. Role of computerized physician order entry systems in facilitating medication errors. *JAMA.* 2005;293(10):1197–1203.

21. Wears RL, Berg M. Computer technology and clinical work: still waiting for Godot. *JAMA.* 2005;293(10):1261–1263.

DECISION SUPPORT

MATTHEW C. STIEFEL, MPA

Executive Summary

Measurement provides decision support and drives innovation

This chapter focuses on the measurement and analysis tools used to support decision making in population health. The tools and methods used depend on the kinds of decisions needing support. The three main purposes of measurement in population health—improvement, accountability, and research—provide the overarching framework for how to develop a strategy. The Measurement for Improvement section provides an overview of the Model for Improvement[1] and the useful tools associated with it. Predictive modeling is another decision-support mechanism that contributes to effective population health management. The Measurement for Accountability section describes a framework for assessing value in health care, including metrics for the triple aims of population health, per capita cost, and care experience. The chapter concludes with a brief discussion of measurement for research, the distinctions between efficacy and effectiveness research, and comparative and cost-effectiveness. Decisions in the areas of improvement, accountability, and research require different types of decision support.

Learning Objectives

1. Distinguish among the three purposes of population health measurement.
2. Describe the Model for Improvement and associated tools.
3. Learn about the key metrics for the Triple Aim.
4. Provide a framework for assessing value in population health.
5. Learn about the major types of population health and health services research.

Key Words

comparative effectiveness research (CER)	predictive modeling
cost-effectiveness	Quality-Adjusted Life Years (QALY)
effectiveness	return on investment (ROI)
efficacy	Triple Aim
efficiency	value
healthy life expectancy	

INTRODUCTION

THREE MAIN PURPOSES FOR MEASUREMENT IN POPULATION HEALTH

Improvement, accountability, and research are the three main purposes of measurement.[2] Approaches to measurement differ according to the purpose. In measurement for improvement, the general strategy is to measure just enough to learn. This approach is characterized by limited data and small, sequential samples. Hypotheses are flexible and are apt to change as learning takes place. Trend data are typically analyzed, and the data are used by those doing the improvement.

Measurement for accountability focuses on reporting, oversight, comparison, choice, reassurance, or motivation for change. It is not about hypothesis testing, but evaluation of current performance. It is important to make adjustments to reduce bias in comparisons, and important to collect all available, relevant data.

Measurement for research seeks to discover new knowledge that may have broad application, where the standard of evidence is beyond doubt. In the research context, tests are carefully blinded and controlled and the experimental design seeks to eliminate bias. Hypotheses are fixed, with a single, large test that typically employs traditional statistical techniques.

Because the purpose of measurement should determine the methods, mismatching purposes and methods can have adverse consequences. For example, applying traditional research methods in an improvement setting can slow down the learning process, and more importantly, set the bar for statistical significance too high to detect potentially useful changes. Alternatively, applying improvement methods to research questions can lead to inappropriate generalization of findings. While there are three main purposes of measurement, there are many differences in the methods used for each purpose (Table 10-1).

MEASUREMENT FOR IMPROVEMENT

THE MODEL FOR IMPROVEMENT

Measurement for improvement is built on a rich tradition of quality improvement measurement methods dating back to the early 1900s, led by the pioneering work in the science of improvement by Deming, Shewhart, and Juran. The Model for Improvement, developed by Associates in Process Improvement, is a simple but powerful tool to

Table 10-1   The Three Purposes of Measurement

Aspect	Improvement	Accountability	Research
Aim	Improvement of care	Comparison, choice, reassurance, spur for change	New knowledge
Methods: Test observability	Test observable	No test, evaluate current performance	Test blinded or controlled
Bias	Accept consistent bias	Measure and adjust to reduce bias	Design to eliminate bias
Sample size	"Just enough" data, small sequential samples	Obtain 100% of available, relevant data	"Just in case" data
Flexibility of hypothesis	Hypothesis flexible, changes as learning takes place	No hypothesis	Fixed hypothesis
Testing strategy	Sequential tests	No tests	One large test
Determining if a change is an improvement	Run charts or Shewhart control charts	No change focus	Hypothesis, statistical tests (t test, F test, chi-square), p values
Confidentiality of the data	Data used only by those involved with improvement	Data available for public consumption and review	Research subject's identities protected

Adapted from Solberg L, Mosser G, McDonald S. The three faces of performance measurement: improvement, accountability, and research. *Jt Comm J Qual Improv.* 1997;23(3):13–147.

Provost L, Murray S. *The Data Guide: Learning from Data to Improve Health Care.* Austin, TX: Associates in Process Improvement; 2007. Used with permission of authors.

accelerate improvement that incorporates many of the tools and techniques originally developed by these pioneers.[1] The Model for Improvement consists of two parts. The first part focuses on three basic questions to frame the improvement journey:

- What are we trying to accomplish?
- How do we know that a change is an improvement?
- What change can we make that will result in an improvement?

The second part consists of continuous cycles of Plan-Do-Study-Act to test and implement changes in real-world settings.

A clear goal statement is essential to answer the first question concerning what we are trying to accomplish. A useful technique for developing goal statements is to make them "S.M.A.R.T.": Specific, Measurable, Attainable, Realistic, and Time-bound.

The tools of statistical process control were developed in large part to answer the question of whether or not a change is an improvement. In general, the process involves plotting data over time and applying tests to determine if there has been a change in the underlying results of a process. The first step is to gather data on performance. The data collection tool does not need to be sophisticated, but should include basic information about the process and outcomes, and observations about barriers or new ideas to test. The data should then be plotted in a run chart, which is a trend graph that includes a median line. Simple rules have been developed to analyze the data in a run chart to determine special cause variation as opposed to common cause variation, or chance. These rules are illustrated in Figure 10-1.

The control chart is a more sophisticated version of a run chart that is used to detect special cause variation. This chart adds upper and lower control limits to a run chart and additional rules about the behavior of the data in relation to the control limits to determine if a process is in control. After the run or control charts are developed, it is important to prominently display them for review by all those in the process, and to include the charts in the improvement process.

Armed with the tools to determine improvement, the next logical step is to identify process changes that will result in an improvement. The PDSA (Plan, Do, Study, Act) cycle has become a time-tested framework for generating and testing ideas for improvement. The Plan step involves developing objectives, predictions, and plans to carry out the cycle. The Do step involves carrying out the plan and documenting data and observations. The Study step involves analyzing the data, comparing results to predictions, and summarizing what was learned. The Act step involves determining the changes to be made in the next cycle, and the cycle repeats. A key feature of the Model for Improvement is the rapid and repeated use of the PDSA cycle. In significant contrast to measurement for research, PDSA cycles might be measured in days or even hours.

The driver diagram, a tool developed by the Institute for Healthcare Improvement, is another useful tool for designing changes that will result in an improvement. This diagram organizes the theory of improvement for a specific project, visually connecting the outcome or aim, key drivers, design changes, and measures. Typical key drivers include performance of a component of the system, an operating rule or value, or some element of system structure. A driver diagram template is shown in Figure 10-2.

PREDICTIVE MODELING

Predictive modeling is another powerful set of tools for performance improvement. In general, this approach relies on mathematical modeling to predict the probability of an outcome. It is used in many industries other than health care, including archeology and geology (e.g., to predict the likelihood of archeological sites or mineral deposits), insurance (e.g., to predict cost), and marketing (e.g., to predict what consumers will buy). Within the context of health care, predictive modeling is typically used to predict such outcomes as cost, resource utilization, or mortality by population segments. The ultimate goal of using a predictive model is the delivery of tailored interventions and resources to a specific population segment based on their specific needs. Predictive models in health care are used for a variety of purposes, including identification of individuals at risk for adverse health outcomes, high resource utilization, hospital stays/days/readmissions, expensive or risky procedures, large healthcare-related costs, or disenrollment from a health plan.

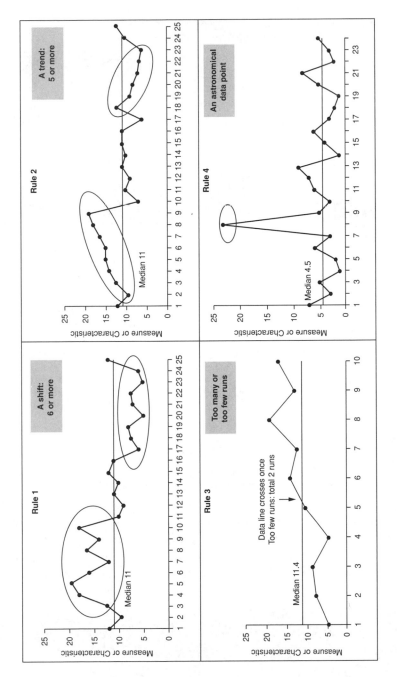

Figure 10-1 Indicators of Non-Random Patterns

Source: Provost L, Murray S. *The Data Guide: Learning from Data to Improve Health Care.* Austin, TX: Associates in Process Improvement; 2007:3–10.

Definition: A driver diagram is used to conceptualize an issue and determine its system components, which will then create a pathway to get to the goal.

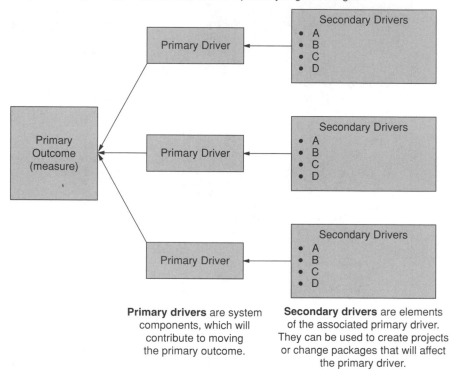

Primary drivers are system components, which will contribute to moving the primary outcome.

Secondary drivers are elements of the associated primary driver. They can be used to create projects or change packages that will affect the primary driver.

Figure 10-2   Driver Diagram Template
Source: Institute for Healthcare Improvement (used with permission)

The traditional approach to population care management has been to intervene with those individuals who historically have the worst outcomes or the highest utilization. This "threshold" approach assumes that members with poor outcomes this year are the most likely to have poor outcomes next year. Accuracy of predictions depends on correlation between outcomes now and outcomes in the future. However, this assumption of correlation has two major shortcomings. First, natural progression of disease or the impact of treatment tends

BOX 10-1   KEY PREDICTIVE MODELING QUESTIONS

Modeling questions include:

- What are you predicting?
- Why are you predicting it?
- How accurate is your prediction?
- What actions are taken based on the prediction?

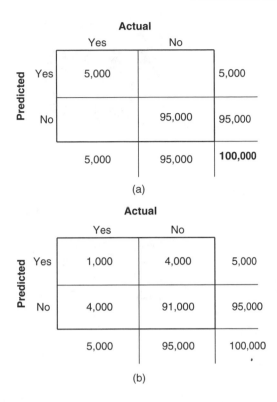

Figure 10-3   (a) Perfect Sensitivity and Specificity; (b) Realistic Sensitivity and Specificity

to cause people to get better over time, unless they have a progressively deteriorating condition. Second, the statistical phenomenon of regression toward the mean causes outliers in one period to move closer to the mean in the next period as a result of stochastic or random variation. Because of these two phenomena, most high utilizers in a general population are likely to have *lower* utilization in the next period, even in the absence of any intervention. The predictive modeling approach addresses this problem by looking retrospectively at patterns. The model is typically built with data from a prior period and applied to current data in order to forecast future patterns.

The quality of predictive models is assessed through the performance metrics of sensitivity and specificity. Sensitivity, or the true positive rate, measures the percentage of high-risk individuals who are correctly identified by the model. Specificity, or the true negative rate, measures the percentage of individuals *not* at high risk who are correctly identified by the model. The examples in Figure 10-3 illustrate the concepts of sensitivity and specificity. In a population of 100,000 people, 5,000 end up having a given condition, and 95,000 end up not having the condition. In Figure 10-3a, the predictive model correctly predicts all 5,000 individuals who end up with the condition (100% sensitivity) and correctly identifies all 95,000 individuals who do not end up with the condition (100% specificity). Figure 10-3b

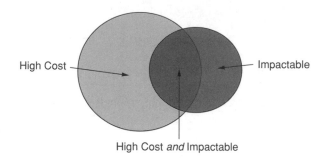

Figure 10-4 Impactability

presents a more realistic example of predictive model performance. In this case, the model correctly predicts 1,000 of the 5,000 people who actually end up with the condition (20% sensitivity) and correctly predicts 91,000 of the 95,000 people who do not end up with the condition (96% specificity). In this case, there are 4,000 false positives, and 4,000 false negatives.

The performance of a predictive model depends on the threshold selected for identifying those at risk for a condition, as well as population demographics and data quality. Sensitivity and specificity are *competing* objectives. Ensuring that everyone with the condition is included (higher sensitivity) increases the likelihood that people without the condition are incorrectly predicted to have the condition (lower specificity). If the model identifies the entire population (specificity = 0%), then no high-risk members will be overlooked (i.e., sensitivity = 100%). If the model identifies no one in the population (sensitivity = 0%), then there will be no false positives (i.e., specificity = 100%). A perfect model would have sensitivity *and* specificity equal to 100%. In reality, there are no perfect models.

The main challenge with predictive modeling is identifying the individuals who can be helped among those identified as high risk. This challenge is known as impactibility, or targeting people with the highest probability of benefit from an intervention. Figure 10-4 illustrates the impactibility question.

In a predictive model identifying high-cost individuals, the cost trajectory can only be influenced for a subset of them. It is, therefore, necessary to not only predict high-cost individuals, but also those individuals with known evidence-based and cost-effective interventions that can reduce their cost trajectory.

MEASUREMENT FOR ACCOUNTABILITY

MEASURING THE TRIPLE AIM

While measurement is the first step in identifying needs, the second is determining accountability in order to take action. The Institute for Healthcare Improvement's (IHI) **Triple Aim** provides a useful framework for measuring accountability.[3] This initiative

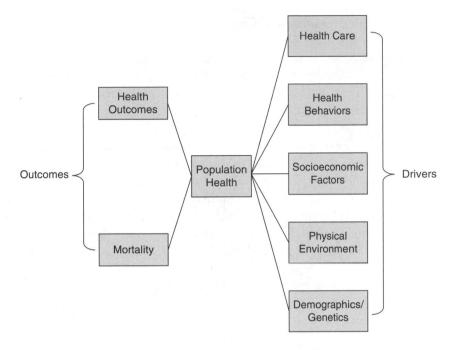

Figure 10-5   Population Health Measurement Driver Diagram

focuses on three main components—improving population health, per capita cost, and the care experience. This section will cover measurement of each of the three aims and discuss how they can be combined to assess overall value.

Measuring Population Health   The driver diagram, as previously discussed, is a useful tool to help understand the measurement of population health (Figure 10-5).

The drivers, or determinants, of population health are shown on the right side of the diagram, and the outcome measures are shown on the left side. The drivers and outcome measures can become increasingly more specific through further branching of the diagram.

Population health outcomes include both the mortality and health status of the population. These measures can be combined to create a measure of a population's **healthy life expectancy**, which has become a standard in the world for measuring population health at the national level. The World Health Organization measures a variant of healthy life expectancy for 193 countries around the world and the European Union has established a measure of healthy life expectancy as a key structural indicator for all member states.[4,5] According to Réseau Espérance de Vie en Santé (REVES), the international network on health expectancies and the disablement process, healthy life expectancy, sometimes referred to as *health expectancy,* is a general term referring to "the entire class of indicators expressed in terms of life expectancy in a given state of health. Health expectancies are indicators of current health and mortality conditions."[6] Health expectancies can be created using a variety of different measures of health, such as disease status, disability, perceived health, or other concepts.

Health status measures range from objective measures of physiologic, disease, and functional status (such as the ability to climb a flight of stairs) to subjective measures of self-perceived health. They also range from single-question, global assessments of health status to assessments across multiple domains of health, aggregated by preference-weighted scoring. The single-question methods are used most frequently in national or state surveys for population health surveillance because they are shorter and easier to include in more general population surveys. However, the multiple-domain methods provide a more complete assessment of health for both individuals and populations and are more often used in clinical applications.

Healthy life expectancy (HLE) has a number of valuable measurement properties. Compared to mortality and morbidity rates, HLE is a more intuitive and meaningful measure of health for both individuals and populations; people care greatly about living long *and* healthy lives. Age standardization is already embedded in the HLE measure, so populations with different age distributions can be compared directly without further adjustment.

HLE has two different and important interpretations. It is a valuable stand-alone measure of individual and population health; it is also fundamentally important when expressed as a percentage of overall life expectancy. The change in the ratio of HLE to LE over time is a measure of *compression* or *expansion* of morbidity in a population, or the extent to which increasing life expectancy is accompanied by an increase or decrease in the burden of ill health.

Evans and Stoddart developed a framework, shown in Figure 10-6, describing the conceptual relationship between the determinants and outcomes of health in a landmark paper in 1990.[7]

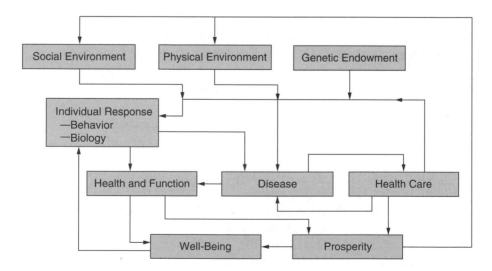

Figure 10-6 Health Determinants and Outcomes
Evans RG, Stoddart GL. Producing health, consuming health care. *Soc Sci Med.* 1990;31(12):1347–1363.

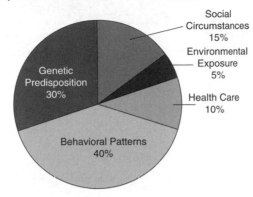

Proportional Contribution to Premature Death

Figure 10-7   Determinants of Health
Adapted from McGinnis JM, Williams-Russo P, Knickman JR. The case for more active policy attention to health promotion. *Health Aff (Millwood)* 2002;21:78–93.
Source: Schroeder SA. Shattuck lecture. We can do better—improving the health of the American people. *N Engl J Med.* 2007;357(12):1221–1228.

They expanded on the narrow relationship between health care and disease by describing the broader determinants of health, including genetics, physical and social environment, and behavior. They also broadened the concept of health beyond the absence of disease to include well-being and prosperity. Kindig and Stoddart later added the important dimension of the *distribution* of health in a population to differentiate it from individual health.[8] McGinnis et al. estimated the relative impacts of the various determinants of health described by Evans and Stoddart.[9] These impacts are shown in Figure 10-7.

A provocative conclusion of their analysis is the relatively small contribution of health care to population health compared to the behavioral, environmental, and genetic determinants. Kindig later operationalized this framework in a measurement system ranking the counties in Wisconsin on both the determinants and outcomes of population health, as shown in Figure 10-8.[10]

Measuring the Care Experience   In its landmark report, *Crossing the Quality Chasm,* the Institute of Medicine articulated broad aims of making health care safe, effective, patient-centered, timely, equitable, and efficient.[11] These aims can be thought of as a broad framework for improving care, and specific measures of each dimension can be developed to create a dashboard of care experience measures. The overall experience of care is best assessed by those receiving care—the patients. The Consumer Assessment of Healthcare Providers and Systems (CAHPS) program is a public–private collaboration sponsored by the U.S. Agency for Healthcare Research and Quality (AHRQ) to support the assessment of consumers'

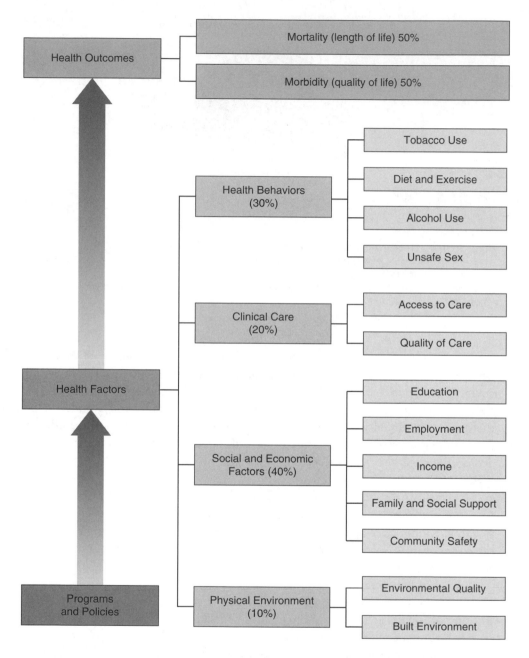

Figure 10-8   Determinants and Outcomes of Population Health in Wisconsin
County Health Rankings model ©2010 UWPHI

experiences with health care. In addition to questions about specific aspects of care, the CAHPS survey includes a global question on their overall experience of health care: "Using any number from 0 to 10, where 0 is the worst health care possible and 10 is the best health care possible, what number would you use to rate all your health care in the last 12 months?"[12] Wasson developed another widely utilized tool for consumers to assess their overall experience of care. Consumers are asked to answer the following question on a five-point Likert-type scale: "When you think about your health care, how much do you agree or disagree with this statement: 'I receive exactly what I want and need exactly when and how I want and need it'?"[13]

Measuring Per Capita Cost   Per capita cost, like population health, requires a population denominator for measurement. However, separation of healthcare delivery and financing in most of the United States makes it difficult to identify the population served by the delivery system and, therefore, difficult to calculate per capita cost. The concept, however, is straightforward. It includes the total healthcare costs per person in the defined population. In addition to direct healthcare costs, some argue for the need to include indirect costs, such as productivity and time away from work, in the total cost equation. One attractive feature of the person as the unit of cost measurement is that it enables costs to be disaggregated in the same way as people: by geography, demographics, conditions, or other characteristics. Direct costs can also be disaggregated by type of healthcare service, such as hospital care, primary care, specialty care, and ancillary services, and further by volume versus unit cost drivers.

The National Committee for Quality Assurance (NCQA) has recently developed a new set of Healthcare Effectiveness Data and Information Set (HEDIS) measures in the general category of relative resource use, for several chronic and acute conditions.[14] These relative resource use measures are calculated at the per capita level, but use standard unit costs to control differences in prices for services to facilitate comparisons across health plans.

The *Dartmouth Atlas*, which has been measuring geographic variation in health system performance across the United States for more than 20 years, has developed an innovative method for imputing a population denominator for more than 300 hospital referral regions in the United States, based on regional patterns of utilization.[15] The *Dartmouth Atlas* uses these population denominators to calculate population-based rates for costs and utilization for the Medicare population and has consistently shown dramatic geographic variation in per capita costs, made more dramatic by their lack of correlation with quality measures.

If a healthcare system doesn't serve a defined population, then it is not able to use population-based measures such as per capita cost. Instead, episode-based costing is in widespread use. The unit of analysis is the episode of care, defined as "a series of temporally contiguous health care services related to the treatment of a given spell of illness or provided in response to a specific request by the patient or other relevant entity."[16]

Episode-based cost analysis is used in insurance underwriting as well as provider profiling to compare resource utilization performance by provider.

MEASURING VALUE AND EFFICIENCY

Value and return on investment are important to those purchasing health care for a population. A common definition of **value** is: "worth, utility, or importance in comparison with something else."[17] This definition includes an important characteristic of value—that it is relative. Value is more than finding something desirable. It requires a determination of what would be given up in exchange for something. For market goods, value is indicated by the amount of money a person would pay. The ultimate test of value is choice—people "vote with their feet" if given an opportunity. Another key characteristic of value is that it is subjective. There is no one right answer, and different stakeholders will have different perspectives on value. IHI's Triple Aim—improving population health, per capita cost, and the care experience—provides a useful framework for assessing value. Value can be seen as the optimization of these three objectives. Tradeoffs among the objectives, however, will be made differently by different stakeholder groups. While all three aims are important, purchasers must place a priority on cost, consumers care about health outcomes and the care experience (and increasingly about cost because they bear an increasing responsibility for costs), and clinicians care greatly about the quality of care and service provided. Health plans have the challenge of developing products that balance these aims in order to compete successfully in the marketplace.

Efficiency is a concept related to value in the accountability measurement domain; the term has been both hotly debated and loosely defined in recent years. The AQA Alliance developed a useful definition of efficiency in health care, subsequently endorsed by the National Quality Forum: "Efficiency of care is a measure of the relationship of the cost of care associated with a specific level of performance measured with respect to the other five IOM aims of quality."[18] In the context of the Triple Aim value framework, efficiency defined in this manner can be seen as a combination of two elements of the Triple Aim: cost and care experience.

Return on investment (ROI) for health care is a concept related to value that is especially important from the purchaser's perspective. Return on investment describes the size of a return relative to an investment. However, the ROI measure has some important limitations. Projects with the same return on investment can have very different total savings. For two projects, the one with the lower return on investment may actually have the higher total savings. This issue is especially important to purchasers evaluating disease management programs. For example, a program costing $1 million and returning $3 million in savings has a 3:1 ROI and $2 million in net savings. In contrast, a program costing $10 million returning $20 million in savings has a 2:1 ROI and $10 million in net savings. Of course budget constraints are relevant, but the program with the lower ROI in this case produces $8 million more in savings. For this reason, the DMAA: The Care Continuum Alliance recommends net savings over ROI in the evaluation of disease management programs.[19]

MEASUREMENT FOR RESEARCH

A full review of research methods for health services and population health research is beyond the scope of this chapter, although there are many excellent texts on health services research methods (see Suggested Readings and Web Sites). One important high-level topic for decision support is the distinction between efficacy and effectiveness research. Both are focused on whether a particular intervention works. **Efficacy** refers to whether an intervention can work under ideal conditions. On the other hand, the pragmatic question of whether an intervention works in routine clinical care relates to **effectiveness**.

Clinical trials are examples of efficacy research. They are designed to isolate the effect of a particular intervention, by controlling, to the extent possible, for other factors of potential influence. However, in real life, these factors *do* intervene and influence the effectiveness of the intervention. For example, patients in clinical trials usually have no health problems other than the ones under investigation, and compliance is carefully controlled. However, patients in routine clinical practices often have multiple conditions and may fail to follow medical advice. Efficacy research focuses on whether an intervention works under ideal conditions, whereas effectiveness research focuses on whether an intervention works in practice. The questions are both important and complementary, but it is important to be clear which question is being addressed in a research study.

In the area of effectiveness research, comparative effectiveness and **cost-effectiveness** are two related and important types of health services research. The Institute of Medicine defines **comparative effectiveness research (CER)** as:

> the generation and synthesis of evidence that compares the benefits and harms of alternative methods to prevent, diagnose, treat, and monitor a clinical condition or to improve the delivery of care. The purpose of CER is to assist consumers, clinicians, purchasers, and policy makers to make informed decisions that will improve health care at both the individual and population levels.[20]

Cost-effectiveness research adds economic considerations in relation to effectiveness. It is a construct closely related to efficiency, measuring the cost of a program or intervention associated with a given level of effectiveness. In health services research, the measure of individual health most commonly used in cost-effectiveness analysis is termed **Quality-Adjusted Life Years**, or QALYs. It is the individual health building block of the population health measure of healthy life years, which was previously discussed. It is defined as a year of life lived in less-than-perfect health as compared to a year of life in perfect health. For example, a year lived with blindness may be equated to half a year in perfect health. Healthcare regulatory agencies in many countries, such as the National Institute for Health and Clinical Excellence in the United Kingdom, use cost-effectiveness analysis explicitly in their evaluation of new drugs and technologies. In the context of the Triple Aim value framework previously described, cost-effectiveness can also be seen as a combination of two elements of the Triple Aim: cost and health.

CONCLUSIONS

Decision support tools and methods used in population health depend on the kinds of decisions needing support. Decisions in the areas of improvement, accountability, and research require different types of decision support. The distinctions have been highlighted in this chapter for clarity of presentation. However, the boundaries are not as distinct in practice, and it is important to consider how they fit together into an integrated analytic and evaluation system. Local improvement efforts frequently reach a point where a large investment or change is required for widespread implementation. At that point, more tightly controlled research methods may be required to enhance confidence in the investment decision. As clinical information systems and electronic medical records become more widely used, there is increasing opportunity to thoughtfully design data systems that can be used for all three purposes of process improvement, external reporting, and research. In such an integrated decision-support infrastructure, it is possible to envision improvement projects generating ideas for research, research findings more quickly implemented in practice, and reporting requirements fulfilled through automated extractions from electronic data systems. Data could seamlessly roll up to the board of directors and external reporting agencies for accountability, down to frontline teams for improvement, and over to research teams to generate new knowledge and insights.

STUDY AND DISCUSSION QUESTIONS

1. What are the three main purposes of population health measurement?
2. What are the three basic questions in the Model for Improvement?
3. What are the primary outcome measures of population health?
4. What are the key determinants of population health?
5. How can value and efficiency be measured in population health?
6. How do key stakeholders' perspectives differ?

SUGGESTED READINGS AND WEB SITES

READINGS

Aday LA, Begley CE, Lairson DR, Balkrishnan R. *Evaluating the Healthcare System: Effectiveness, Efficiency, and Equity.* 3rd ed. Chicago, IL: Health Administration Press; 2004.

Berwick DM, Nolan TW, Whittington J. The triple aim: care, health, and cost. *Health Aff.* 2008;27(3):759–769.

Evans RG, Barer ML, Marmor TR, eds. *Why Are Some People Healthy and Others Not? The Determinants of Health of Populations.* Hawthorne, NY: Aldine De Gruyter; 1994.

Evans RG, Stoddart GL. Producing health, consuming health care. *Soc Sci Med.* 1990;31(12):1347–1363.

Langley GJ, Moen RD, Nolan KM, Nolan TW, Norman CL, Provost LP. *The Improvement Guide: A Practical Approach to Enhancing Organizational Performance.* San Francisco, CA: Jossey-Bass; 2009.

McGinnis JM, Williams-Russo P, Knickman JR. The case for more active policy attention to health promotion. *Health Aff.* 2002;21(2):78–93.

Mullner RM, ed. *Encyclopedia of Health Services Research.* Thousand Oaks, CA: SAGE Publications; 2009.

Murray CJL, Evans DB, eds. *Health Systems Performance Assessment: Debates, Methods and Empiricism.* Geneva, Switzerland: World Health Organization; 2003.

Solberg LI, Mosser G, McDonald S. The three faces of performance measurement: improvement, accountability, and research. *Jt Comm Qual Improv.* 1997;23(3):135–147.

WEB SITES

Dartmouth Atlas of Health Care: http://www.dartmouthatlas.org/
Healthy People 2020: The Road Ahead: http://www.healthypeople.gov/HP2020/
REVES: http://reves.site.ined.fr/en/home/about_reves/
University of Wisconsin Population Health Institute: http://uwphi.pophealth.wisc.edu/

REFERENCES

1. Langley GJ, Moen RD, Nolan KM, Nolan TW, Norman CL, Provost LP. *The Improvement Guide: A Practical Approach to Enhancing Organizational Performance.* San Francisco, CA: Jossey-Bass; 2009.
2. Solberg LI, Mosser G, McDonald S. The three faces of performance measurement: improvement, accountability, and research. *Jt Comm Qual Improv.* 1997;23(3):135–147.
3. Berwick DM, Nolan TW, Whittington J. The triple aim: care, health, and cost. *Health Aff.* 2008;27(3):759–769.
4. World Health Organization. *World Health Statistics 2009.* Geneva, Switzerland: World Health Organization; 2009. http://www.who.int/whosis/whostat/EN_WHS09_Full.pdf. Accessed May 31, 2009.
5. European Commission. Healthy life years. European Commission's Directorate for Public Health and Risk Assessment Web site. http://ec.europa.eu/health/ph_information/indicators/lifeyears_en.htm. Accessed May 20, 2009.
6. REVES. What are the health expectancies? REVES Web site. http://reves.site.ined.fr/en/DFLE/definition/. Accessed May 20, 2009.
7. Evans RG, Stoddart GL. Producing health, consuming health care. *Soc Sci Med.* 1990;31(12):1347–1363.
8. Kindig D, Stoddart G. What is population health? *Am J Public Health.* 2003;93(3):380–383.
9. McGinnis JM, Williams-Russo P, Knickman JR. The case for more active policy attention to health promotion. *Health Aff.* 2002;21(2):78–93.
10. Taylor KW, Athens JK, Booske BC, O'Connor CE, Jones NR, Remington PL. *2008 Wisconsin County Health Rankings.* Madison, WI: University of Wisconsin Population Health Institute; 2008.
11. Institute of Medicine. *Crossing the Quality Chasm: A New Health System for the 21st Century.* Washington, DC: National Academies Press; 2001.
12. Agency for Healthcare Research and Quality. *CAHPS Pocket Reference Guide for Adult Surveys.* US Department of Health and Human Services Web site. https://www.cahps.ahrq.gov/content/products/PDF/PocketGuide.htm. Accessed December 14, 2009.
13. FNX Corporation, Trustees of Dartmouth College. How's Your Health Web site. http://www

.howsyourhealth.org/. Accessed December 14, 2009.

14. New HEDIS® measures allow purchasers, consumers to compare health plans' resource use in addition to quality [news release]. Washington, DC: National Committee for Quality Assurance; February 22, 2006. http://www.ncqa.org/tabid/362/Default.aspx. Accessed December 14, 2009.

15. The Dartmouth Institute for Health Policy & Clinical Practice. The Dartmouth Atlas of Health Care. The Dartmouth Atlas Web site. http://www.dartmouthatlas.org/. Accessed May 18, 2009.

16. Hornbrook MC, Hurtado AV, Johnson RE. Health care episodes: definition, measurement and use. *Med Care Rev.* 1985;42(2):163–218.

17. Merriam-Webster Word Central. value. Word Central Web site. http://www.wordcentral.com/cgi-bin/student?value. Accessed December 15, 2009.

18. AQA Alliance. *AQA Principles of "Efficiency" Measures.* AQA Alliance Web site. http://www.aqaalliance.org/files/PrinciplesofEfficiencyMeasurement.pdf. Revised June 2009. Accessed December 14, 2009.

19. DMAA: The Care Continuum Alliance. *DMAA Outcomes Guidelines Report.* Washington, DC: DMAA: The Care Continuum Alliance; 2008. Vol 4:80.

20. Institute of Medicine. *Initial National Priorities for Comparative Effectiveness Research.* Washington, DC: National Academies Press; 2009.

Chapter 11

MARKETING AND COMMUNICATION: METHODS FOR REACHING POPULATIONS

WILLIAM HAGGETT, EdD

Executive Summary

Communication is the key to reaching populations and imparting knowledge

Marketing approaches can be used to generate awareness, solicit interest, build consumer engagement, and communicate with populations through a variety of media outlets. Marketing and communication in health care must account for the unique aspects of the field. Consumers often do not view themselves as users of services (e.g., chemotherapy, hospitalizations). However, they are engaged in multiple channels of communication, including doctor to patient, manufacturer to consumer, and disease organization to the general public. The purposes of engaging consumers and patients are broad (e.g., behavior change, basic content understanding), further complicating traditional marketing and communication approaches. Marketing approaches to consumers continue to evolve, as evidenced by the changes observed in disease management efforts since 2000. With the introduction of electronic and social media, targeting specific messages to specific consumers is advancing at a quickened pace. Output and outcome measures to assess the impact of communication strategies are becoming more sophisticated as real-time feedback and data analytic methodologies evolve. Unlike other industries or sectors that are seeking interactions for specific products or services, the healthcare sector interacts with broad cross-sections of consumers at various stages of their lives, with communication objectives changing over time.

Learning Objectives

1. Explain how marketing and communication are defined in health care.
2. Describe the components of communication plans and strategies.
3. Appreciate the role of communication objectives, tailored approaches, targeted audiences, and outcome measures in successful communication strategies.

Key Words

communication objectives   health literacy
communication outcome measures   stratification

INTRODUCTION

Gaining the attention of the public is vitally important to consumer engagement and, ultimately, to the success of population health interventions. Marketing approaches can be used to generate awareness, solicit interest, build consumer engagement, and communicate with populations through a variety of media outlets. The American Marketing Association defines marketing as activities and processes for creating, communicating, delivering, and exchanging offers that have value for customers, clients, partners, and society at large. Marketing is not just one technique (e.g., advertising); rather, it is a broad set of relationship-building methods that extend to product conception, pricing structure, distribution channels, customer service orientation, public relations, and overall strategic planning.

The application of marketing techniques to health care can be complicated, expensive, and even intimidating. Because many consumers often find it difficult to see themselves as consumers of healthcare services (e.g., hospitalizations, surgeries, chemotherapies), traditional marketing practices of communicating brand images and benefits are often ineffective in the healthcare setting.[1] The numerous communication paths—ranging from doctor to patient, from disease organizations to the general public, and from insurers to their members—increase the complexity and create the challenges to successfully communicating important health-related messages to targeted audiences.

ENGAGING THE CONSUMER

Healthcare communication approaches and strategies have been used extensively in the field of disease management (DM). Since the 1980s, the disease management industry has been evolving as a key driver of efforts to prevent and manage disease among specific populations. Most commonly deployed through employee health benefits, strategies have evolved from a focus on specific diseases to a "whole person" orientation. Dee Edington, director of the Health Management Research Center at the University of Michigan and author of the Future of Population Health: Moving Upstream section at the end of this text, states "disease management is one of the three necessary strategies in total population management, which is needed to arrive at the total value of health for an employee population or any defined population. Acute care and wellness management are the other two components."[2]

Highlighting the importance of communication in the overall value proposition, Bob Ihrie, from the Lowe's Companies, Inc., puts it simply: "Participation is the key to DM programs; we're only effective if we can reach people."[2]

The disease management industry changed considerably between 2000 and 2010, during which a transition from a disease focus to population health has been observed.[3] Consequently, many DM companies have refocused their efforts more broadly to supporting wellness and managing those with multiple chronic illnesses. Outreach strategies have evolved as well. For example, Health Dialog, a provider of care management services, uses a variety of methods to identify and engage targeted consumers. Ranging from predictive modeling, to application of findings from cause and effect research, and "whole person," nurse-based coaching with a shared decision-making approach, the company also applies sophisticated outreach tools in its quest to impact health among the identified population.[4] Data-driven **stratification** of the targeted population supports identification of subsets of consumers with comparable healthcare needs. Outreach uses selection methods to reach and engage members with similar needs. A number of techniques, including outbound phone calls, general mailings, electronic communications, and clinical phone consultations—all support the **communication objectives** of educating, motivating, and engaging consumers to manage, maintain, and improve their health status.

COMMUNICATION STRATEGIES FROM OTHER INDUSTRIES

While unique in many ways, the healthcare sector's communication challenges are nonetheless shared by other industries. Many industries have employed similar consumer outreach strategies, relationship-building activities, and consumer-friendly applications. For example, Southwest Airlines, an acknowledged innovator in the airline industry, was an early and effective user of the Internet to build relationships with customers through weekly newsletters and special offer emails.[5] The airline encouraged online bookings that were significantly more cost-effective at $1 for reservations made online, in comparison to $10 for reservations made with the assistance of a travel agent. Additionally, customers were given incentives to purchase other items—rental cars, hotels, attraction tickets—through convenient, user-friendly tools.

Like healthcare institutions, financial institutions are heavily regulated. Both industries offer relatively universal services and work to combat stereotypes of providing impersonal service and having self-serving agendas.[6] Since 1997, banks have been mandated to meet the requirements of the Community Reinvestment Act. According to the provisions of the Act, compliance assessments were made to determine whether community banks were meeting the credit needs of their entire community. Innovative banks capitalized on this mandate, viewing it as an opportunity for promotion and brand enhancement, rather than simply another requirement. Rooney reports on several such institutions that took their positive results to the media—ranging from reinvestment results to media images of employees and officials contributing to the community.[6] Some innovative healthcare companies have used similar strategies. For example, several Blue Cross and Blue Shield plans have state requirements as the insurer of last resort. Many use this service to their communities in marketing, advertising, and promotional activities.

The hotel industry invests significantly in destination marketing and uses techniques that could be applied to healthcare settings. "You won't see a dog-eared *People* magazine in the lobby of a Hyatt Hotel. But you will see slick brochures for other Hyatt properties, services, amenities, and loyalty programs," says Rob Rosenberg from Springboard Brand and Creative Strategy.[1] Physicians and healthcare organizations could adapt this strategy to capitalize on the time patients spend in waiting areas. Healthcare consumers are a captive audience while in a waiting area, providing an opportunity for education, assessment, and promotion of other services offered by the institution or organization.

The technologies and functionalities used in other industries are also infiltrating the healthcare market. Health systems are utilizing reservation system technology to schedule recurring appointments and to create reminders for needed services (e.g., lab work, mammography, and immunizations). Decision-support tools built into electronic systems are proving helpful to both providers and patients. Sponsored social networking tools and blogging are increasingly being used in the health sector to promote supportive relationships among patients dealing with similar health concerns or conditions. Social matchmaking sites are also being adapted to promote the physician–patient relationship and matching. Many of these technologies are built on a common platform for promoting products, but how they are marketed is determined by the industries in which they are utilized.

While adoption of electronic information technology is rapid in some areas (e.g., integrated delivery system use of electronic medical records), it remains scattered and disjointed; adoption is slow in most others (e.g., real-time claims processing, e-prescribing). Throughout the healthcare system, expense, interoperability, and workflow barriers are well documented. Despite these barriers, communication efforts supported by technology for health-related topics is growing and expanding rapidly. In 2000, the state of the art focused on single diseases, mass communication techniques, and high-level data sources. Today, sophisticated predictive modeling and integrated approaches encompass all disease states, addressing complete healthcare needs as well as gaps in care.

Communication tools range from the traditional targeted mailings to timed electronic communications that coincide with time-sensitive reminders to obtain targeted services. In fact, several companies are experimenting with interactive monitors (e.g., blood pressure, weight, sleep tools) that both send and receive electronic information, allowing real-time monitoring and influencing of desired behaviors. Numerous techniques to reinforce patients' continuous engagement in managing their health status rely on electronic information technologies.

WHY COMMUNICATE? WHAT IS THE COMMUNICATION OBJECTIVE?

The goal of marketing and communicating is to engage and retain participation, influence behaviors of the targeted consumers, and impart knowledge and content. In population health, improved health status is the ultimate desired outcome across all segments of consumers identified as the target audience. Communicable disease outbreaks are one example of an urgent need for issue-specific population health outreach. For example, the 2009 H1N1 flu outbreak required swift action to educate and direct behavior among the general public, healthcare providers, public health government officials, schools, and high-risk segments of the population—all of which were targeted with information from the Centers for Disease Control and Prevention. Regular hand washing and the correct methods of managing coughs and sneezes were reinforced through public service announcements, television, Web-based demonstrations, and signage in public locations. While managing the H1N1 outbreak remains a significant *clinical* challenge, it also posed a population health challenge in communicating appropriate and accurate information to the public. Effective communication was imperative to promote widespread awareness and to prompt behavior change, such as social distancing to limit the spread of the disease.

In health care, there is no single set of communication objectives—rather, the objectives vary by target audience. For consumers, the communication objective may be to inform, to motivate, and to cause action. For health plans, the communication objective may be to educate, to promote, to remind, or to change behavior. Similarly, for government payers such as state Medicaid or federal Medicare programs, the objective is to provide information to assist members in understanding their eligibility for benefits and managing their health. For employers, the communication objective may be to reinforce a company's commitment to its employees through benefits programs or to encourage active engagement by their employees in available health benefit and service offerings. For healthcare providers, the communication objective may range from content to coaching, educating, and motivating. Examples range from the brochures on healthy eating found in many physicians' offices to closed-circuit videos running in facility waiting rooms and electronic visits employed by select doctors to social networking sites used by some hospitals. In population health, the objectives are similar—to educate, to inform, to engage, to retain, and to influence behavior. To successfully achieve these primary objectives, a variety of traditional strategies and approaches are in place and new techniques are emerging.

WHO IS THE AUDIENCE?

Effective communication strategies target messages and modes of delivery to the selected audience. Think for a moment about the best way to communicate with two diabetic consumers. One is a 25-year-old, recently diagnosed, otherwise healthy Hispanic male.

The second is a 53-year-old diabetic female who has lived with her diabetes for 30 years. Understanding the needs and desires of the audience is the key to developing a successful, "personalized" communication strategy. In this example, a number of questions must be considered, including: Are the communication objectives the same for both consumers? What communication approaches would be effective for both audience members? What language should be utilized in the communication? Are the same diabetes brochures, which contain basic facts about the disease, useful to both audience members? Would Internet resources or social networks for diabetic users work for both consumers? Would the 53-year-old consumer respond to a short text message or, likewise, would the 25-year-old consumer find value in a booklet sent via snail mail?

In addition to understanding the needs of the consumers and the challenge of designing effective communication strategies with their needs in mind, segmentation filters add complexity to communicating with healthcare consumers. A number of factors that impact effective communication strategies must be considered; chiefly, you should consider ethnicity, language, sex, gender, geography, age, health status, reading level, and economic status. Individuals employed in large companies often benefit from human resource departments that promote tailored, health-related programs; offer incentive programs; and serve as a resource for health matters. Small companies or individuals purchasing insurance on their own often do not have access to those benefits—impacting communication strategies of insurers and providers alike.

One of the segmentation filters, gender, has been associated with openness to communication. Women tend to be more open and accepting of a variety of communication approaches related to health issues.[7] Women reported value in interventions such as phone calls where they could ask questions of a nurse, Internet-based programs tailored to specific health needs, pharmaceutical company discount programs, and pharmacy offerings that include a complete listing of medications. While men indicated positive levels of interest in similar programs, women's attitudes and receptivity were significantly higher.

Segmentation by ethnicity requires an understanding of the needs of the specified ethnic or racial group. The aforementioned questions were answered by a survey, which found that Asians, Hispanics, and African Americans were more likely to report that their physician did not understand the needs of their ethnic–racial group. African American women were found to be more likely to use brochures in physicians' offices and more likely to use insurance company materials as sources of information than other ethnic–racial groups. Asian women reported high levels of reliance on friends and family; health food and nutrition store sales representatives used government-related Internet sites for health information. Finally, Caucasian women reported needing less help and advice than other groups in managing health matters.

Age is associated with consumers' online navigation approaches and the information on which they act.[8] Consumers 65 years of age and older are concerned about the accuracy of Internet content, while those from "Generation Y" explore online content out of curiosity. While more than 81% of consumers reported visiting a health-related Web site, the purpose and acceptance of information varied significantly across age groups.

In population health, the target audience for specific messages is often selected based on health status. A number of methods for stratifying the population by health status have been suggested. Bigalke, Keckley, and Underwood[9] stratified the general population into six discrete categories for health management purposes—healthy, at risk for development of a chronic illness, acute illness, chronic illness, catastrophic illness, and end of life. Many health plans have adopted this methodology and regularly stratify their membership into similar categories to target interventions more precisely. In addition to risk stratification approaches, companies also target members by diagnosis or life cycle events (e.g., messages generated by the birth of a child and messages targeted by age group and gender for age-appropriate screenings). A review of dozens of health plan brochures, electronic messages, newsletter articles, and other promotional pieces completed by the author revealed two common communication strategies—providing health- or disease-related content and a call to action to change behaviors to align with evidence-based clinical guidelines. Examples include reminders for diabetic patients to receive an annual retinal exam, the importance of medication compliance, immunization schedules for parents of newborns, updated clinical information on congestive heart failure guidelines, and general messaging on the benefits of routine screenings. While similar content is readily available through a wide range of sources, delivering it to the right consumers, with the right message, for their specific needs at the right time is the ongoing communication challenge.

From the physician's perspective, the communication challenge is different. The traditional communication method of providing content and influencing behavior is often face-to-face and of short duration. While these interactions are an optimal method for successful communication, their effectiveness varies by the physician's knowledge, communication style, and overall "bedside manner." Physician–patient interactions are now supported through the more recent development of clinical alerts. Health plans use alerts to electronically communicate to providers, distributing time-sensitive clinical information that requires attention (e.g., gaps in care, medication noncompliance). In some cases, alerts may be sent to plan members as well. Rosenberg and colleagues demonstrated that clinical alerts sent to both patients and physicians produced significant increases in compliance with the guidelines connected to the alerts.[10]

Interaction between consumers and personnel at pharmacies is short in duration, similar to interaction with physicians. In contrast, pharmacists and other pharmacy personnel routinely provide educational information when prescription drugs are refilled. The presence of trained health professionals in pharmacies offers yet another communication opportunity. This opportunity not only benefits the patient when education and consultation are provided, but also benefits the pharmacy when such interventions are regarded as a value-added service that enhances consumer loyalty.

WHAT IS THE MESSAGE?

Messaging in population health has two main objectives—content delivery and behavior change. Thousands of sources of clinical information are available through academic institutions, private companies, disease advocacy organizations, and Internet blogs. Despite the plethora of resources, questions of accuracy and reliability are a growing concern with new technologies affording anyone the opportunity to create content. However, trusted sources such as the URAC Web site accreditation program are a strong national effort to identify and certify acceptable health content sources on the Internet.[11]

Content messages range from basic facts to sophisticated analyses of intervention outcomes. For the general public, messages are usually general in nature, provided through mass media outlets, and offered free of charge. Consider the numerous charity events held in communities throughout the country in support of cancer research or, specifically, breast cancer awareness. The messaging about the cause is focused on promoting general awareness and increasing engagement across broad population groups. To attract a specific audience, media approaches must target segments of the population with more detailed and comprehensive content. The disease management industry has experienced success with targeted outreach and engagement of members utilizing messages focused on the specific needs of those members. In contrast to such tailored approaches, a general brochure would likely produce limited impact.

After consumers become aware of an issue through the content delivered, they must engage in behavior change to affect outcomes. Gaining the attention of the public is vitally important to initiate engagement and drive the success of population health interventions. As a tool, marketing is essential to build the awareness that can lead to the engagement of consumers in activities to improve their health.

Health literacy issues must be considered when designing messages that are both linguistically and culturally appropriate. Engaging members of the communities where the messages will be used is immensely helpful in ensuring appropriateness of the content and the level of sophistication. Health literacy was defined by Healthy People 2010 as "the degree to which individuals have the capacity to obtain, process and understand basic health information and services needed to make appropriate health decisions."[12] According to research studies, persons with limited health literacy skills are more likely to forgo important preventive activities such as mammograms, Pap smears, and flu shots.[13] When compared to those with adequate health literacy skills, studies have shown that patients with limited health literacy skills enter the healthcare system when they are sicker.[14] Coupled with well-documented disparities in health status among racial and ethnic groups, addressing the challenge of improving health literacy across all segments of healthcare consumers is a critical component of population health strategies.

HOW SHOULD YOU COMMUNICATE?

There are many strategies for communication available today, and consumers are being flooded with marketing materials from a variety of companies and organizations that all want their messages to be heard. While health plans, providers, or disease management companies are actively communicating with their customers, so too are the cellular companies, food and drink producers, politicians, direct response marketers, and news media, as well as our "friends and family." Understandably, consumers express that they are inundated with messages and have difficulty discerning the most important content worthy of their attention. With so much exposure, how can plans, providers, and other companies maximize the likelihood that their message is heard?

Direct marketers using traditional mailing techniques consider a 5% response rate successful. Web advertisers celebrate the thousands of "hits" their messages receive. Television outlets report share numbers that count impressions in the hundreds of thousands. Traditional data measures are being challenged and new approaches are being developed. Trusov, Bucklin, and Pauwels[15] evaluated the impact of electronic word-of-mouth marketing through an assessment of electronic referrals from other users on an Internet social networking site. That study reported significantly higher impact through this relatively new word-of-mouth endorsement when compared to traditional approaches. Moreover, this channel continued to impact new customer registration for as long as 3 weeks, compared to just 3 to 7 days for traditional marketing approaches.

Social networks are a fairly new communication category that is gaining traction across many consumer segments. Largely aligned with a young consumer market, outlets such as Facebook, Twitter, blogs, and Wikipedia are increasingly being used by traditional companies as a strategy for reaching select demographics in different ways. Swaminathan[16] suggests that organizations need to rethink their communication strategies and marketing approaches because of the significant impact of social media. Strategies, such as using video to deliver messages across all segments, are being applied, especially for such hard-to-reach audiences as low literacy groups, recently diagnosed patients, and elderly consumers. The traditional company Web site was developed as an expansive gateway to gain access to organizational information. The intent was to drive traffic to the organization's site, which has an effect on the site's ranking in a Google search. Theoretically, as the number of people who access the site increases, the number of consumers who purchase products and services grows as well. With the increased adoption of social media, content placed on sites outside the organization's Web site produces a connection that expands the reach. For example, a healthcare system could sponsor a nutritional video for diabetics. Rather than burying the content on the organization's Web site, a savvy company would also make it available on the company blog, Facebook, and YouTube pages.

With the expansion of social media into the healthcare market, a number of tools have become available. It is important to understand the usefulness of each of the tools to determine which would benefit the organization. (See Box 11-1.) Based on the perceived

> ### BOX 11-1 SOCIAL NETWORK MEDIA TYPES
>
> Sarasohn-Kahn effectively summarized the various social network media types:
> - "Blogs enable users to record text, graphics and video and to share them with others.
> - Online forums allow people to post opinions on subjects of personal interest.
> - Podcasts help people create and share audio files.
> - Really Simple Syndication (RSS) rapidly disseminates new information.
> - Social network services use software for communities of people to share and explore their interests with others. These Web-based services can involve chat, messaging, email, video, file-sharing and discussion groups.
> - Wikis enable a group of people to record, edit and verify knowledge on a particular subject collectively."[17]

value of the content, emerging evidence demonstrates that consumers may consider paying for health-related content.

The Corporate Research Group[10] found that Internet-based healthcare social networking is scattered across many outlets—Facebook, Twitter, blogs—but growing significantly. While smaller when compared to other social networking sites, healthcare Web sites tend to attract women 35 to 55 years of age with above-average income and education. Several not-for-profit organizations, such as the American Cancer Society, Diabetes Hands Foundation, and the Mayo Clinic, sponsor such social network sites. Questionnaires or assessments connected with health information Web sites can be tremendously helpful in understanding population needs. Arnquist[18] described a Web site that allows patients to report information about their health and stores it in databases that can be mined for observations and trends from the participants' contributions. So-called "crowd-sourcing" research allows patients to control their data and build bridges among themselves, their doctors and researchers. With the growing use of the Internet by consumers seeking health-related information, the number of Web resources can be expected to grow as well.

WHAT WORKS?

Assessing the effectiveness of population health communication strategies is equally as complex as developing and delivering the message. Success might take many forms, such as receiving thousands of exposures from a billboard promoting smoking cessation, increasing the percentage of compliant patients with routine labs for diabetes, or reducing the incidence of a given disease state in a geographic area. Each of these examples denotes a potentially successful communication strategy.

Communication effectiveness is often viewed from two perspectives: *outputs* and *outcomes*. Outputs are measures of activities, such as the number of TV ads placed, brochures distributed, emails sent, or Web sites visited. Outcomes, on the other hand, focus on moving the targeted audience toward specific attitudes, behaviors, or actions. For proactive population health analysis and intervention, **communication outcome measures** need to extend beyond basic media impressions or brochures mailed and assumed read. Structuring outcome measures should be directly tied to the health outcome measures desired, such as increased compliance, reduced disease prevalence, or reduced costs.

As communication strategies are developed, it is critical that both output and outcome measures be established in the planning stages. Measurement techniques are advancing and technology is becoming less expensive. Traditional mail surveys are being replaced by online "pulse checks," which are almost real-time reactions to questions or issues posed via electronic means. In-person focus groups are being augmented by online counterparts that allow more timely and less expensive participation across broader geographies and customer segments.

Successful communication strategies require measurement against defined goals and objectives. While output measures are important, there are process measures that drive the outcomes, such as behavioral change and improved health status, that the communications were created to achieve. Measurement should strive to document specific process indicators and outcomes.

CONCLUSIONS

Marketing and communication in health care involves a complex set of messages and approaches to reach defined audiences. The content of messages covers a broad array of clinical, behavioral, and motivational topics for audiences who are not likely to actively seek the intended messages. The unique needs of each targeted consumer can vary dramatically as her or his health status changes. From a population health perspective, reaching broad audiences is achieved by use of both traditional methods as well as newer technology. Like other sectors, the continued and accelerating use of new social media is transforming the health communication dynamic. Unlike some other industries or sectors that are seeking interactions for specific products or services, the healthcare sector interacts with broad cross-sections of consumers at various stages of their lives, whose communication objectives change over time. Further, the opportunities for communications are being altered as more retail medicine outlets provide care traditionally offered by physicians, as more primary care is provided in emergency departments, and as pharmacists are often the most frequently encountered clinicians for many patients. Measures of successful communications will increasingly focus on desired outcomes—changes in health status—rather than output measures that focus on activity levels. Efficiency and cost-effectiveness of communication strategies will also be monitored as the overall cost of health care continues to escalate.

STUDY AND DISCUSSION QUESTIONS

1. What is marketing and what are several specific examples of marketing in the health-care environment? How is this similar or different in other industries?
2. Describe how the targeted audiences for communications can change the approach used by an organization. Suggest some effective methods for specific audiences.
3. What are the major purposes of marketing in population health?
4. Suggest approaches for individuals to validate health information available from the ever-growing information highway.
5. What are the differences between outcome and output measures?
6. Prepare a marketing plan that targets newly diagnosed diabetic patients.

SUGGESTED READINGS AND WEB SITES

READINGS

Aase L, Schroeder S, Hooverson A, Patchin S. *Not Ur Parents' Healthcare Anymore: The 411 on Selling Health via New Media.* Manasquan, NJ: Health Intelligence Network; 2007.

Chung A, Mercurio C; for Corporate Research Group. *Profits from Health 2.0: The Emerging Social Networking Revolution in Healthcare.* New York, NY: Corporate Research Group; 2009.

Journal of Management and Marketing in Healthcare. Henry Stewart Publications.

Nash DB, Manfredi MP, Bozarth B, Howell S. *Connecting with the New Healthcare Consumer: Defining Your Strategy.* Sudbury, MA: Jones and Bartlett Publishers; 2001.

WEB SITES

Health Dialog: http://www.healthdialog.com

Health Engagement Barometer: http://engageinhealth.com/docs/EdelmanHealthEngagement Barometer_Deck012709.pdf

URAC Health Web Site Accreditation: www.urac.org/consumers/resources/accreditation. aspx

REFERENCES

1. Shaw G. Department focus: marketing—lessons from the field. Media Health Leaders Web site. http://www.healthleadersmedia.com/content/215014/topic/WS_HLM2_MAG/Department-Focus-MarketingLessonsfrom-the-Field. html. Published 2008. Accessed on September 9, 2009.

2. Managed Healthcare Executive. 2008 leaders in disease management. Managed Healthcare Executive Web site. http://managedhealthcareexecutive.

modernmedicine.com/mhe/article/articleDetail. jsp?id=549839. Published September 1, 2008. Accessed June 25, 2009.

3. Todd WE, Nash D, eds. *Disease Management: A Systems Approach to Improving Patient Outcomes.* Chicago, IL: American Hospital Publishing, Inc.; 1997.

4. Health Dialog. Health Dialog Web site. http:www. Healthdialog.com. Accessed June 25, 2009.

5. Levinson M. Southwest Airlines does web business right. The CIO Web site. http://www.cio. com/article/30722/southwest_Airlines_Does_ Web_Business_Right. Published December 1, 2001. Accessed June 25, 2009.

6. Rooney K. Consumer-driven healthcare marketing: using the web to get up close and personal. *J Healthc Manag.* 2009;54(4):241–251.

7. Benini D, Whitcup MS, Dudley F. Multi-cultural marketing of health and wellness to women. *Guideline Inc. Trend Report.* June 2007:11.

8. Snyder J, Johnson C, Tesch B. *How Different Generations Use Online Health Research.* Cambridge, MA: Forrester Research Inc.; 2007:1–7.

9. Deloitte Center for Health Solutions, *Disease Management and Retail Pharmacies: A Convergence Opportunity.* Washington, DC: Deloitte Center for Health Solutions; 2008:4–13. http://www.deloitte. com/assets/Dcom-UnitedStates/Local%20Assets/ Documents/us_chs_RetailPharmacyandDM Convergence.pdf. Accessed June 12, 2009.

10. Rosenberg SN, Shnaiden TL, Wegh AA, Juster IA. Supporting the patient's role in guideline compliance: a controlled study. *Am J Manag Care.* 2008;14(11):737–744.

11. URAC. URAC health Web site accreditation. URAC Web site. http://www.urac.org/consumers/ resources/accreditation.aspx. Accessed June 12, 2009.

12. US Department of Health and Human Services. *Healthy People 2010.* http://www.healthypeople. gov. Accessed April 14, 2010.

13. Scott TL, Gazmararian JA, Williams MV, Baker DW. Health literacy and preventive health care use among Medicare enrollees in a managed care organization. *Med Care.* 2002;40(5):395–404.

14. Bennet CL, Ferreira MR, Davis TC, et al. Relation between literacy, race, and stage of presentation among low-income patients with prostate cancer. *J Clin Oncol.* 1998;16(9): 3101–3104.

15. Trusov M, Bucklin RE, Pauwels K. Effects of word-of-mouth versus traditional marketing: findings from an Internet social networking site. *J Marketing.* 2009;73(5). http://www.atypon-link. com/AMA/doi/abs/10.1509/jmkg.73.5.90?cooki eSet=1&journalCode=jmkg. Accessed September 22, 2009.

16. Swaminathan KS. Just shut up and listen? *Outlook.* 2009;21(3).

17. Sarasohn-Kahn J; for California HealthCare Foundation. *The Wisdom of Patients: Health Care Meets Online Social Media.* Oakland, CA: California HealthCare Foundation; 2008:4.

18. Arnquist S. Research trove: patients' online data. *The New York Times.* August 25, 2009: D1. http://www.nytimes.com/2009/08/25/ health/25web.html. Accessed August 25, 2009.

MAKING POLICY TO ADVANCE POPULATION HEALTH

POLICY IMPLICATIONS FOR POPULATION HEALTH: HEALTH PROMOTION AND WELLNESS

TRACEY MOORHEAD, JEANETTE C. MAY, PhD, MPH, AND KIP MACARTHUR

Executive Summary

A system of health and wellness must consider whole person, whole population needs

Increasing costs and prevalence of chronic conditions among various segments of the U.S. population have caused policy makers to seek alternative models of care to address the needs of at-risk and chronically ill populations. Indeed, in 2009, the new Obama administration, congressional leaders, interest groups, and others declared healthcare delivery system reform a top priority for the 110th Congress. Both the administration and Congress outlined potentially sweeping changes in the nation's healthcare delivery system and quickly began consideration of reform packages that aimed to provide coverage for uninsured Americans and to increase the quality and efficiency of healthcare delivery. Various options for expanding insurance coverage, coupled with delivery and reimbursement system reforms, could result in expansive new opportunities and population health strategies. This chapter outlines key players in federal policy making (both enactment and implementation); experiences from early disease management demonstrations and pilot programs enacted at the federal level; specific proposals considered during the 2009 healthcare reform debates; and key components for consideration in developing policy to advance population health activities.

Learning Objectives

1. Describe the factors that play a role in the shift to population health management.
2. Identify the key players and their roles in federal policy making for population health.
3. Appreciate the components of population health under the Medicare program and how Medicare policy has shaped commercial insurance.

Key Words

accountable care organization (ACO)	fee-for-service
computerized physician order entry (CPOE)	health information technology (HIT)
discretionary spending	mandatory spending

INTRODUCTION

Population health management programs have evolved considerably to better address the needs and resources of the populations and providers served. This evolution includes a significant transformation through adoption of multiple intervention modalities that are both additive and complementary to the traditional call center model. Today, leading industry organizations are deploying proven health promotion, prevention, and chronic care management services spanning an entire population's continuum of health, that is, healthy, at risk, and chronically ill. The industry has developed more collaborative and innovative models of care delivery to fully integrate services with practicing physicians and to support individuals in adherence to physician-led care plans. Significant new opportunities for the population health management industry are being contemplated by ongoing federal activities to enact healthcare reform legislation. Congressional leaders and the Obama administration have strongly emphasized the importance of prevention and wellness activities, sought to improve access to care coordination, and promoted the widespread adoption of health information technologies to collect, share, and analyze health-related data. These proposals and others clearly recognize the importance of a total population management approach to healthcare delivery.

KEY PLAYERS IN FEDERAL POLICY MAKING

There are many players that affect healthcare policy at both the federal and state levels. These players include the U.S. Congress, congressionally mandated independent organizations, and cabinet-level agencies and offices. This section includes an overview of each.

The federal government influences policy and population health directly as one of the largest purchasers of health care and indirectly as an influencer of private sector healthcare purchasing and delivery. As one of the largest employers and purchasers of healthcare services, the federal government finances and provides coverage to nearly 129.8 million government employees; the poor, disabled, and elderly; active duty and former military personnel and their dependents; and Native Americans and other populations.[1] Given this role, federal government purchasing and healthcare delivery policies can often be expected to "trickle down" to other purchaser and provider populations. For example, independent health plans and providers who participate in federal programs, such as

Medicare **fee-for-service** or the military-focused TRICARE program, may impose payment and rate policies similar to those imposed by large government-managed programs on nongovernment clients. Private sector purchasers, especially those seeking coverage options for thousands of employees, dependents, or retirees, may seek to negotiate, through annual contract negotiations, rates similar to those paid by government programs. As such, government coverage and payment policies extend beyond government-managed programs and can directly impact coverage and rate policies for other purchasers, as well as payment policies for healthcare practitioners.

The U.S. Congress plays a key role in establishing healthcare policy and will directly influence population health management in the context of broader health policy and healthcare reform. Several Congressional committees, in both the U.S. House of Representatives and the U.S. Senate, share jurisdiction over portions of the healthcare delivery and payment systems at the federal level. In the House, the Education and Labor Committee, the Energy and Commerce Committee, and the Ways and Means Committee have jurisdiction over healthcare delivery and payment systems for the private sector, as well as government programs. The Education and Labor Committee considers legislation relating to employer-sponsored health benefits. The Energy and Commerce Committee handles public health, Medicaid, pharmaceutical, and other national health insurance issues, while the Ways and Means Committee has authority over bills and matters pertaining to health programs under the Social Security Act and many public health programs. There are two Senate committees with jurisdiction over healthcare policy. The Senate Finance Committee considers healthcare programs under the Social Security Act, including Medicare, Medicaid, and other health programs financed by certain taxes or trust funds. The Senate Health, Education, Labor and Pensions Committee (HELP) handles legislation that impacts other health programs not governed by the Social Security Act.

Congressional legislative efforts to enact policy changes are informed by numerous sources, including a variety of congressionally mandated, independent organizations. Among these organizations, Medicare Payment Advisory Commission (MedPAC) and the Congressional Budget Office (CBO) are integral to advancing the population health agenda.

The Medicare Payment Advisory Commission (MedPAC) was created by the Balanced Budget Act of 1997 (BBA 97) as an independent congressional agency. The 17-member Commission, comprised of health policy experts, healthcare providers, and academicians, provides the U.S. Congress with analyses, recommendations, and reports on issues affecting the Medicare program, including payment, access, and quality. MedPAC convenes publicly several times annually to review staff research and to seek comment and input from healthcare researchers, providers, and beneficiary advocates on financing and delivery, as well as other trends affecting the Medicare program. Congressional leaders and their staff rely heavily on MedPAC analyses for close examination of existing policy and case studies to understand the impact of potential policy or payment changes.

Since 1997, MedPAC has studied models of care coordination in treating those with chronic disease and the feasibility of applying these models to a broader Medicare population.

These care coordination efforts are expected to foster better patient understanding and compliance with various treatment regimens, as well as drive patients to more appropriate and less costly care settings rather than emergency departments. Care coordination and appropriate utilization are key components of any successful population health management program.

In its June 2009 Report to Congress, the Commission reiterated concerns that poor care coordination combined with a growing prevalence of beneficiaries with chronic disease will continue to put a strain on Medicare resources. A 2003 MedPAC analysis of Medicare fee-for-service beneficiaries found that a Medicare beneficiary saw, on average, five different physicians each year. For those who were diagnosed with at least three common chronic conditions, the number increased to 10 or more per year.[2] When viewed from a population health perspective, fragmented access to care is inefficient and ineffective.

The report goes on to review several Medicare pilots and demonstration projects that address chronic conditions and cost in the fee-for-service Medicare population. These pilots and demonstrations, which have influenced care delivery and population health management program development, are discussed later in the chapter. In addition, the Commission analyzed the feasibility of developing a Medicare Chronic Care Practice Research Network to continue testing models of care coordination for the Medicare population. These findings can help move population health forward through the testing and validation of various models designed to address whole person, whole population needs.

The Congressional Budget Office (CBO) was established in 1974 as an objective, non-partisan entity to provide data, estimates, and analyses on the fiscal implications of congressional proposals and federal spending on the economy. For legislative proposals reported out of a Congressional committee or upon request, the CBO is required to produce estimates on the impact of both **discretionary spending** (budget authority that is provided and controlled by appropriation acts and the outlays that result from that budget authority) and **mandatory spending** (budget authority provided and controlled by laws other than appropriation acts and the outlays that result from that budget authority).[3] Increasing healthcare costs and expanding public sector program populations have caused great emphasis to be placed on CBO's scoring reports for healthcare reform and policy proposals.

Current CBO models have not attributed savings to proposed prevention and wellness programs. The models continue to present challenges to the population health management industry in demonstrating cost savings associated with disease prevention. In its December 2008 analysis of key issues in health insurance proposals, the CBO stated that while initiatives to improve people's health, such as adopting healthy lifestyles, obtaining preventive screenings, and implementing programs to better manage chronic disease, led to better quality of life, they don't necessarily reduce healthcare spending. Yet, they still may be worthwhile. However, the CBO has questioned whether certain types of initiatives save enough to cover the cost. As of 2010, the CBO has concluded that the clinical and economic impact of prevention services is not sufficiently well understood to precisely estimate costs and benefits.

Several reports dispute the CBO's assertion that prevention will not reduce healthcare spending. In a white paper commissioned by the Partnership to Fight Chronic Disease, economists James Capretta and Michael J. O'Grady suggest that there are limitations to the

CBO's cost estimating practices. Because they don't forecast beyond a 10-year budget window, they are not able to capture the long-term savings associated with preventing chronic disease.[4] Ingenix recently produced a study titled "Potential Medicare Savings Through Prevention and Health Risk Reduction," which aimed to identify the relationship between cost and risk.[5] In the study, researchers developed models to better understand how cost would be affected if the population were able to shift to a lower risk category and/or maintain a low-risk status longer. The models suggest that the Medicare program could save $65 billion annually, which is approximately $650 billion over 10 years, by increasing the number of low-risk individuals who are 65 years of age and reducing the health risk progression by 10%.

Cabinet-level agencies and other offices are also key players in policy making who are primarily responsible for implementing legislative policy on healthcare issues. Most prominent, the Centers for Medicare and Medicaid Services (CMS), formerly known as the Health Care Financing Administration (HCFA), is an office of the U.S. Department of Health and Human Services (HHS). CMS was established as the regulatory agency for federal healthcare programs, including Medicare, Medicaid, and the Children's Health Insurance Program (CHIP). CMS administers all aspects of these programs, including covered healthcare services and benefits, eligibility, enrollment, and provider participation. In 2009, approximately 100 million people were covered under the Medicare, Medicaid, and CHIP programs.[1] As discussed earlier, the federal government has a significant role in the financing and delivery of health care, developing health policy, and managing population health as one of the largest administrators and purchasers of healthcare services.

The Office of the National Coordinator for Health Information Technology (ONC) is the principal federal agency charged with the coordination of national efforts to implement the use of **health information technology (HIT)** and the electronic exchange of health information. The ONC is engaged in promoting the development of a nationwide health information technology infrastructure that will lead to interoperability of health information.

HIT plays an important role in population health management and is a key strategy for achieving population health improvement. HIT improves patient safety and the overall quality of care as well.[6] Technology, such as **computerized physician order entry (CPOE)**, decreases the incidence of medication errors and adverse drug events.[7] Patients, particularly those with chronic conditions, often see multiple healthcare providers; health information technology, like electronic health records (EHRs), allows each provider access to the same information. HIT increases access to information and improves transparency among healthcare providers, leading to improved delivery of healthcare services and population health management.

OVERVIEW OF HISTORICAL DEMONSTRATIONS AND PILOTS

The expected growth of the Medicare population, with the prevalence and costs associated with the treatment of chronic illness, has caused policy makers to seek alternative models of care to address the needs of chronically ill beneficiaries. Passage of the Medicare Modernization Act of 2003 gave CMS the authority to explore other care delivery models for the fee-for-service Medicare population through demonstrations and pilot programs.

Demonstrations and pilots are requested by Congress and carried out by CMS for the purpose of testing the viability and feasibility of new models. Results from previous demonstrations and pilots are used to shape new models for testing and have already begun to impact population health. This is an exercise that is integral to population health, building on previous successes to achieve more success and advancing the agenda to achieve high-quality, affordable, coordinated care.

Initially, population health management has shown strong results in commercial and other government programs and can be successfully adapted and implemented in the Medicare environment. Pilots that are testing these strategies on Medicare-managed populations include both Medicare Advantage plans and Special Needs Plan for Chronically Ill populations. Both may provide some insight and experience of care coordination with the Medicare population. Preliminary results suggest that a population health management strategy that includes disease management, case management, and care coordination may improve outcomes and reduce costs.[8]

In contrast to the commercial and public sector managed care markets, identifying ideal health management models for Medicare fee-for-service beneficiaries is only in the early stages of development. Despite the fact that the promotion of wellness and the reduction of health risks are crucial components of population health, prevention and wellness solutions have not yet been tested in fee-for-service Medicare populations. Roughly three-quarters of Medicare beneficiaries receive care through original fee-for-service Medicare, under which the provider of services is paid for each unit of service. Original Medicare consists of Part A (inpatient hospital, skilled nursing facility, and hospice) and Part B (medical insurance like doctor's visits, outpatient care, and some preventive services). Medicare Advantage or Medicare Part C (formerly known as Medicare+Choice), permanently authorized as part of the Balanced Budget Act of 1997, is a type of managed care that is run by private health plans approved by CMS. Part C provides coverage granted through Parts A and B, which often (varies by plan) includes additional benefits not covered by Medicare fee-for-service, such as vision and hearing aids. Medicare Advantage is an alternative for Medicare-eligible individuals whereby enrollees are encouraged to seek care with participating providers. In many cases, Medicare Advantage plans charge premiums, in addition to the Part B premium, to account for enrollees receiving benefits that are beyond those of traditional Medicare coverage.

Medicare currently provides healthcare benefits and coverage to more than 40 million Americans; the vast majority of these beneficiaries are older than 65 years of age. A growing number of Medicare beneficiaries with multiple chronic conditions are responsible for the greatest percentage of healthcare expenses. These beneficiaries are likely to have more provider visits, see multiple clinicians, fill more prescriptions, and have far more hospitalizations. Care coordination and wellness and disease management programs offer these populations crucial support services to assist with the management and mitigation of diseases and risk factors. These programs have repeatedly demonstrated value in public sector programs at the state Medicaid level and in numerous private sector programs. As such, care coordination and disease management are among the approaches now being tested for Medicare fee-for-service beneficiaries. The Medicare Health Support program and the Medicare Care Management Performance Demonstration were just two of the large studies established to identify models of care appropriate for this population. The main purpose of demonstrations and pilots is testing programs in a small cohort that will later be applied to a larger population, after it is determined to achieve desired results. This is an important concept in population health management, despite the fact that it can't be simply assumed that what works in one group of patients can be broadly applied to a larger population. Testing through demonstrations and pilots are an important part of the evolving population health strategy. Great effort should be taken to conduct pilots using a representative sample of the larger population to which the studied effort would be applied if proven successful.

Medicare Health Support (MHS) represented the first large-scale attempt to demonstrate the effect of disease management services provided to Medicare fee-for-service beneficiaries. Launched through eight contractor organizations beginning in 2005, MHS was originally designed to provide services for more than 250,000 beneficiaries over a period of three years. Interim evaluation results from the MHS program did not provide resounding evidence of the financial impact of disease management, leading CMS to end the program prematurely. MHS organizations outlined several design flaws that contributed to difficulties experienced in the pilot, most specifically, the need to utilize dynamic predictive modeling, the availability of and access to real-time data, better provider engagement, and a collaborative evaluation model to improve outcomes of future programs.

The Medicare Care Management Performance Demonstration was authorized in the Medicare Modernization Act in 2003 as a three-year demonstration to establish incentive payments to encourage physicians to achieve better outcomes, promote coordination of care, and reduce emergency department visits and hospitalizations. In addition to quality reporting requirements, the demonstration provided additional incentive payments for reports electronically submitted through a nationally certified electronic health record. The program was launched in 2007 in four states (Arkansas, California, Massachusetts, and Utah) and involved 800 small to medium physician practice groups. In August 2009, CMS released initial results from the program indicating that financial incentives can increase quality of care. Almost all of the participating physician practices received the incentive payments for reporting; however, only 23% of the practices were able to report electronically with certified EHRs. A full report to Congress describing the findings from this program is required by the summer of 2011.

STATE CASE STUDIES IN DISEASE MANAGEMENT

Early on, states recognized the value of disease management programs as a strategy to improve quality and control the increasing costs of healthcare delivery, especially to those with chronic illnesses. In the late 1990s, states began to implement disease management programs for chronically ill Medicaid patients in an effort to address the rising costs associated with treatment. By the early 2000s, nearly all 50 states had implemented disease management or care coordination programs for some segment of the Medicaid population. Federal policy allowed many states to develop and implement various approaches to care management, resulting in case studies demonstrating the potential for care management in public populations. In effect, states were permitted exceptional flexibility in the design and implementation of such programs, going far beyond interventions tested in the Medicare populations.

The state of Missouri transformed its Medicaid program from a provider-centered model to an individual-centered, outcomes-focused model by combining primary care case management, care coordination, and disease management services offered through targeted disease state and risk assessment.[9] The expectation was that the newly designed program would improve adherence, increase appropriate service utilization, increase provider use of electronic tools, and improve both participant and provider satisfaction. It led to improvements in outcomes, such as adherence, service utilization, and cost for participants who had a variety of chronic conditions. For participants with diabetes, adherence to recommended diabetic testing and screening improved. Other outcomes that improved included lipid panel compliance for both the diabetic and coronary artery disease (CAD) populations, as well as improved medication adherence for asthma and chronic obstructive pulmonary disease (COPD) populations. Lastly, both emergency department (ED) visits and costs decreased substantially for the population enrolled in the program.

In Pennsylvania, a pay-for-participation (P4P) program was instituted in 2003 with selected providers in an effort to reduce inpatient admissions and emergency department visits by Medicaid beneficiaries. Incentives were paid to those providers who practiced guideline-based care and ensured that patients who received certain interventions experienced improved health outcomes. Results demonstrated that Medicaid beneficiaries associated with a provider receiving pay-for-participation incentives had fewer inpatient admissions and emergency department visits than those beneficiaries receiving care from a provider not receiving additional payments.

KEY CONSIDERATIONS IN POLICY DEVELOPMENT

Policy makers acknowledge the impact of chronic illness on the Medicare population and are seeking solutions to improve health outcomes and prevent avoidable healthcare costs. There is universal acknowledgement of the need to better manage and prevent chronic illness through whole person, whole population management. Organizing care, information, and services around the health needs and desires of individuals is a concept that all healthcare stakeholders have embraced. For policy makers, redesigning care delivery models to meet these goals requires understanding existing barriers to management and prevention, recognizing innovative delivery models, and identifying key components that contribute to the success of delivery models. Further complicating the challenge of care delivery redesign is the need to align financing and payment models with new delivery approaches.

Current financing and payment mechanisms are focused on the outdated fee-for-service model and present a significant hurdle for team-based, wellness-focused care.

Population health management continues to move toward collaborative models of care delivery and it has become clear that no single model is appropriate for all settings or populations. Rather, flexible models developed and aligned with the needs of the target population and existing services have demonstrated considerable success. Many models seek to transform provider practice design, integrate health information technology, and develop partnerships among interdisciplinary healthcare teams. As these new models and collaborations evolve, population health management strategies can provide significant support and expertise based on experiences in service delivery and outcomes improvement.

Population health management strategies and components are essential solutions for policy makers to consider at both the federal and state level. Population health management aims to improve the health status of the entire population through prevention, wellness, chronic condition support, and advanced care management services. Key components of population health management are identification of population strategies and processes; comprehensive needs assessments that include physical, psychological, economic, and environmental components; proactive health promotion programs that increase awareness of the health risks associated with certain personal behaviors and lifestyles; patient-centric health management goals and education that may include prevention, behavior modification programs, and support for concordance between the patient and the primary care provider; self-management interventions aimed at influencing behavior change; routine reporting and feedback that may include communications with the patient, caregivers, providers, health plan, and ancillary providers; and evaluation of clinical, humanistic, and economic outcomes on an ongoing basis.

A review of successful commercial and public sector programs offers key design principles for consideration in the implementation of future population health management programs in Medicare fee-for-service. These principles would include:

- appropriate use of data and analytic capabilities to target populations most appropriate for intervention;
- the availability of care coordination and coaching resources for targeted populations;
- widespread adoption of interoperable health information technologies;
- clearly defined metrics for outcomes measurement.

These principles are common to a variety of delivery system models and are readily transparent in traditional managed care and physician-led care delivery models, as well as in cooperative healthcare models and newly designed **accountable care organizations (ACOs)**.

The use of timely data (both clinical and self-reported) and analyses conducted through the use of predictive modeling methods is critical to the appropriate identification of individuals and population cohorts who could benefit from population health management services. Timely data ensure that individuals have not progressed in their conditions beyond the scope of the services to be delivered, a key consideration in elderly populations served by fee-for-service Medicare. Predictive modeling applications ensure the appropriate identification of individuals and population cohorts for intervention.

Enhanced care coordination and coaching support services are key components to effectively teach patients or their caregivers to manage their conditions and to navigate the healthcare system. Models of care coordination may range from a physician group providing care coordination services to its patients to an external care management or health advocacy organization offering these services. There is evidence that programs aimed at improving coordination of care for the chronically ill have resulted in positive health outcomes, such as a reduction in hospital readmissions among patients who are provided assistance with care transition between settings. Care coordination has also proved beneficial in assisting patients in managing their own conditions.[10] Population health management has played a vital role in successfully managing transitions from acute care to home for many patients. Working with hospitals, providers, and ancillary care organizations, population health management can reduce avoidable morbidity associated with transitions across different sites and levels of care by leveraging its experience and employing the most advanced technology.

Widespread adoption and integration of health information technology is another key strategy for improving population health management. This technology, paired with skilled and coordinated interdisciplinary healthcare teams and activated patients and families, provides access to the data and supports improvements in outcomes. Systematic improvements in management of information are crucial to improving the quality of healthcare for patients with chronic disease and decreasing costs of their care. Specifically, tools available to individuals for health support in the home are proliferating. These devices, including biometric monitors and diagnostic devices, can populate data fields in providers' and care managers' electronic health records. Further, electronic medical records and personal health records hold great promise for enhancing care coordination, eliminating waste and duplication, and providing individuals with greater resources for improving their own health.

Population health management leaders continue the process of defining guidelines and best practices for evaluating program outcomes. Just as a single care delivery model is not appropriate for all settings or populations, policy makers must recognize that no single measure or method of value assessment is appropriate to all programs. Examining specific program components, strategies, and goals is essential to ensuring the appropriate evaluation of outcomes for all metrics.

CONCLUSIONS

Significant new opportunities for the population health management industry are likely to develop through ongoing federal activities to enact healthcare reform legislation. Congressional leaders and the Obama administration have strongly emphasized the importance of physician-led care models, sought to improve access to care coordination and coaching support programs to targeted beneficiaries, and promoted the expanded role of prevention and wellness services as well as widespread adoption of health information technologies to collect, share, and analyze health-related data. Many of the approaches designed to test and implement these models present new opportunities for population health management.

Proponents of a "medical home" or other physician-led care models underscore the benefits of a designated primary care physician or healthcare "team leader." In addition, many providers recognize the benefits of practice transformation, workflow enhancement, capacity-expanding health information technologies, and expanded provider partnerships to better meet the ever-diversifying needs of various patient populations. This recognition has led to innovative collaborations among healthcare providers who recognize that while physicians must lead these efforts, they can benefit from additional staff and capabilities, both within their practice walls and beyond, to provide health support to patients. Healthcare delivery system reform debates have centered on these practice model changes and collaborative delivery approaches. Expanded pilot programs and payment mechanisms are likely to provide new opportunities for population health management to offer services and resources to physicians implementing these models.

Transitions of care for vulnerable populations have been another key focus of healthcare reform debates. Healthcare reform advocates have recognized the importance of managing transitions between acute care settings and the home for vulnerable populations, especially in Medicare. Population health management providers that have incorporated strategies, such as use of advanced technologies and collaboration with hospitals, providers, and ancillary care organizations, have demonstrated the ability to eliminate avoidable morbidity associated with transitions across different sites and levels of care. Healthcare reform efforts will undoubtedly provide opportunities to test these programs in Medicare populations with the likelihood of expansion in the coming years.

President Obama and congressional reform advocates have also recognized the importance of expanded wellness and health prevention programs in supporting healthy behaviors, identifying at-risk individuals, and assisting in the mitigation of risk factors to avoid the later development of chronic disease. Various healthcare reform proposals have included expanded coverage of preventive services and wellness activities in public programs such as Medicare and Medicaid that will provide expanded opportunities for population health management.

Federal government efforts in recent years have focused on the expansion and use of health information technologies, including electronic medical records (EMRs). Clearly, EMRs and personal health records hold great promise for enhancing care coordination, eliminating waste and duplication, and providing individuals with greater resources for improving their health than ever before. Healthcare reform's goal of improved quality and more cost-efficient care makes the expanded adoption and use of HIT resources more significant and timely. Population health management strategies have greatly expanded service delivery and improved outcomes through the utilization of varied HIT applications.

Finally, a key opportunity for population health management is seen in the potential creation, through healthcare reform legislation, of a Center for Medicare and Medicaid Innovation within the Centers for Medicare and Medicaid Services (CMS). The Innovation Center would be tasked to research, develop, test, and expand innovative payment and delivery arrangements to improve quality and reduce the cost of care provided to beneficiaries. Successful models tested by the Innovation Center would be expanded nationally. Population health management advocates can encourage the development and testing of key strategies successfully deployed in numerous private and public sector populations. The Innovation Center would also likely benefit from a range of previous experiences in Medicare pilot and demonstration programs employing wellness, disease management, and population health strategies.

STUDY AND DISCUSSION QUESTIONS

1. What factors have influenced the need for a population health focus?
2. Who are the key players for federal policy making and what role do they play?
3. Why was the Medicare Payment Advisory Commission created and what role does the Commission play?
4. What is the CBO? What is its role? What has been its assessment of population health?
5. What role does health information technology play in population health?
6. How does Medicare shape the commercial side of population health?
7. Describe and discuss the key design principles of population health for Medicare.
8. Is care coordination important to population health? If so, why?
9. What are some of the key concepts and proposals shaping the population health strategy debate?

SUGGESTED READINGS AND WEB SITES

READINGS

Baicker K, Cutler D, Song Z. Workplace wellness programs can generate savings. *Health Aff.* 2010;29(2):304–311.

Congress of the United States, Congressional Budget Office. *Budget Options.* Washington, DC: Congressional Budget Office; 2008. *Health Care;* vol I. Pub. No. 3185. http://www.cbo.gov/ftpdocs/99xx/doc9925/12-18-HealthOptions.pdf. Accessed February 5, 2010.

Congress of the United States, Congressional Budget Office. *Key Issues in Analyzing Major Health Insurance Proposals.* Washington, DC: Congressional Budget Office; 2008. Pub. No. 3102. http://www.cbo.gov/ftpdocs/99xx/doc9924/12-18-KeyIssues.pdf. Accessed February 5, 2010.

Fisher ES, McClellan MB, Bertko J, et al. Fostering accountable health care: moving forward in Medicare. *Health Aff (Millwood).* 2009;28(2):w219–w231.

WEB SITES

Agency for Healthcare Research and Quality: http://www.ahrq.gov
Centers for Medicare and Medicaid Services: http://www.cms.hhs.gov
The Commonwealth Fund: http://www.commonwealthfund.org.

Congressional Budget Office: http://www.cbo.gov

DMAA: The Care Continuum Alliance: http://www.dmaa.org

   Advocacy: http://www.dmaa.org/advocacy_about.asp

   Case Studies Registry: http://www.dmaa.org/Quality/phi_QICSR.asp

   Population Health: http://www.dmaa.org/phi_definition.asp

Health Affairs: http://www.healthaffairs.org

Health Information Technology: http://www.healthit.hhs.gov

Institute of Medicine: http://www.iom.edu

The Kaiser Family Foundation: http://www.kff.org

Medicare Overview: http://www.medicare.gov/choices/Overview.asp

MedPac: http://www.medpac.gov

New England Journal of Medicine: http://www.nejm.org

Partnership to Fight Chronic Disease: http://www.fightchronicdisease.org

U.S. House of Representatives: http://www.house.gov

   Committee on Education and Labor: http://www.edlabor.house.gov

   Committee on Energy and Commerce: http://www.energycommerce.house.gov

   Committee on Ways and Means: http://waysandmeans.house.gov

U.S. Senate: http://www.senate.gov

   Committee on Finance: http://www.finance.senate.gov

   Committee on Health, Education, Labor and Pensions: http://help.senate.gov

REFERENCES

1. Jaffe S. Health policy brief: key issues in health reform. *Health Aff.* August 20, 2009.
2. Medicare Payment Advisory Commission. Report to the Congress: Improving Incentives in the Medicare Program. June 2009.
3. Congressional Budget Office. Frequently asked questions. Congressional Budget Office Web site. http://www.cbo.gov/aboutcbo/faqs.shtml. Accessed February 5, 2010.
4. O'Grady MJ, Capretta JC. *Health-Care Cost Projections for Diabetes and other Chronic Diseases: The Current Context and Potential Enhancements.* Washington, DC: Partnership to Fight Chronic Disease; 2009.
5. Rula E, Pope J, Hoffman JC. *Potential Medicare Savings Through Prevention & Health Risk Reduction: A Report from the Center for Health Research.* Franklin, TX: Healthways Center for Health Research; 2009.
6. Hillestad R, Bigelow J, Bower A, et al. Can electronic medical record systems transform health care? potential health benefits, savings, and costs. *Health Aff.* 2005;24(5):1103–1117.
7. Institute of Medicine. *Crossing the Quality Chasm: A New Health System for the 21st Century.* Washington, DC: National Academies Press; 2001.
8. Carmona RH. Evaluating care coordination among Medicare beneficiaries. *JAMA.* 2009; 301(24):2547–2548.
9. Oestreich G, Rogers D. Engaging providers in achieving chronic care improvement in a Medicaid population. Paper presented at: 10th Annual Meeting of DMAA: The Care Continuum Alliance; November 2008; Hollywood, FL.
10. Wennberg D, Doyle M. *From Hospital to Home: A New Approach for Reducing Readmissions and Easing Transitions in Care for the Medicare Population.* Boston, MA: Health Dialog; 2009.

<table>
<tr><td>Chapter
13</td><td># ETHICAL DIMENSIONS OF POPULATION HEALTH</td></tr>
</table>

ETHICAL DIMENSIONS OF POPULATION HEALTH

FRANCIS BARCHI, MS, MBE

Executive Summary

Decision making based on shared public values is the hallmark of ethical population health

Decision making at a population health level often involves setting priorities and distributing limited resources in order to improve health outcomes. Such decisions reflect underlying values about what is important to a society, the extent to which that society should promote the health of its members, and the obligations of individuals to their own health and the health of others. Ethical dilemmas arise when values such as individual autonomy, fairness, justice, and beneficence compete for primacy and require trade-offs. Distinct moral traditions shape how these values are weighted in public opinion and bear on the character of health policy and healthcare delivery. Inherent tensions between the best interests of individuals and the population as a whole must be addressed through fair and reasonable processes that examine the inherent values in an action and recognize that stakeholders may assign different meanings to them. Ethics, with its emphasis on deliberative, value-based reasoning, can illuminate common ground, identify new bases for agreement, and contribute to policies that have social consensus and support.

Learning Objectives

1. Appreciate the role of ethics in advancing population health.
2. Identify some of the key moral traditions and theories that underlie population health ethics.
3. Distinguish between population-based health ethics and medical ethics.
4. Recognize the ethical dimensions of priority setting, resource allocation, and access.
5. Become familiar with the analytical skills that enhance ethical reasoning in population health.

Key Words

autonomy	nonmaleficence
beneficence	prima facie principles
equity	resource allocation
ethics	utilitarianism
justice	

INTRODUCTION

Population health focuses on groups of people, with particular concern for the distribution of health outcomes within and between groups, the social determinants of those outcomes and distributions, and the policies and practices that can influence them.[1] Because its unit of analysis is a group, population health is less concerned with the health of any one individual or subgroup than it is with the health of a defined group as a whole. As a result, most issues in population health are characterized by inherent tensions between the needs of the population and the needs of the individual and between an individual's rights and his or her obligations to the group. Because the resources available to meet the totality of health needs across populations are limited, choices must be made in their distribution among and within groups, introducing concerns about **equity** and fairness.[2] In the face of these tensions, setting priorities requires moral choices driven by the beliefs and standards of what one defines as good, bad, right, and wrong.

Ethics is a term used to describe systems of moral principles or values that guide decision making and conduct. An ethical *system* can reflect a set of values held by an individual or values shared by members of a professional, cultural, or social group. Not all ethical systems are the same, nor do they reflect the same values. Ethics can be reinforced by social expectations of behavior, codes of conduct, or laws and regulations. Most individuals determine what constitutes right behavior based on implied or codified rules from several sources, including those reflected in the social expectations of their reference groups, codes of conduct relating to their professions, and the laws and regulations of their governments.

Put more simply, ethics reflect the values that we feel are important to who we are and how we choose to live.[3] As such, ethics can provide a framework for making decisions that are in keeping with those values, particularly in situations where there is no obvious answer regarding what is right or wrong. Ethical reasoning invites us to look beyond an action to the values it reflects, not only from our vantage point but from that of others whom the action affects. Ethics can serve as a framework for decision making that identifies those values of greatest importance to society, illuminates issues from multiple vantage points, and enables a process of consensus building that generates health policies and practices based on shared public values.[4]

THE ROLE OF ETHICS IN POPULATION HEALTH

There are several forms of ethics that relate to population health. *Professional* ethics involves systems of principles and practice guidelines regarding the conduct of persons engaged in health policy and population health practice and research. Those working directly in the health sciences are guided by codes of ethics relating to their particular fields, for example, the AMA *Code of Medical Ethics*,[5] the American Nurses Association *Code of Ethics for Nurses*,[6] the American Pharmacists Association *Code of Ethics for Pharmacists*,[7] the Public Health Leadership Society *Principles of the Ethical Practice of Public Health*,[8] and the Society for Public Health Education *Code of Ethics for the Health Education Profession*.[9] Population health also engages many professions not principally focused on health, including law, environmental science, transportation, education, and social work, each of which rely on their own code of ethics to guide professional conduct. Some codes of ethics are reinforced by certification processes that link adherence to professional licensure.

Applied ethics is the process of identifying values and using them to guide decision making. Values common to the health field include respect for persons, the promotion of good, the prevention of harm, and social justice.[10] These values often compete with each other and ethical dilemmas arise when it is not clear which of these values has primacy. Compulsory screening and vaccination programs against certain diseases, for example, may be the best way to monitor and control their spread in the population, but individual members of that population may feel that such programs limit their freedom of choice or infringe on their privacy. Worse yet, a small subset may receive significant side effects from the screening or immunization.

DISTINCTION BETWEEN ETHICS IN POPULATION HEALTH AND MEDICAL ETHICS

In contrast to normal healthcare practice, which places emphasis on what is best for the individual patient, a system of ethics focused on populations is grounded in concepts of the common good and the collective actions necessary to achieve what is determined to be best for the population as a whole. As such, it introduces obligations for healthcare providers that are distinct from those encountered in individual patient care. At the population level, the emphasis shifts from concerns about individual rights to issues of equity and fairness and from the protection of the individual to prevention of harm to others. It requires health professionals to promote the public good, or at least the collective good of the patient population, as a first goal—rather than individual well-being. At the same time, they must balance these efforts against their obligation to avoid harm to individuals where possible or impose limits on their individual freedoms.[11]

Medical ethics focuses on the morality of individual behaviors, ascribing values to the conduct of individual practitioners, patients, and research subjects. Ethics at the population level, by contrast, focuses on the obligations of societies to their members and to each other, as well as the duties of individual members to their societies or groups. Ethics that focus on health at the population level naturally extend over space and time, taking a global interest in the distribution of health outcomes across populations and the impact of events in one generation on the health outcomes of subsequent generations.[12]

MORAL TRADITIONS AND THEORIES

Like medical ethics, ethical reasoning in population health is not guided by any single moral tradition or underlying theory. Rather, several traditions, among them deontology, **utilitarianism**, principal-based reasoning, casuistry, and more recently, communitarianism, create a framework for ethical problem solving and for weighing the primacy of competing moral obligations at the individual and group level.

Deontology, based largely on the work of 18th-century German philosopher Immanuel Kant, is a normative theory, which holds that some actions are intrinsically right or wrong regardless of their effects.[13] Individuals have unconditional worth based on their capacity to be the authors of their own moral destinies. As such, they should never be used simply as a means to an end, regardless of the value or purpose of that end. As moral agents, individuals are obligated to conform to a set of *right* actions—do not lie, do not kill, etc.—without weighing the consequences of those actions on others. In contrast, utilitarianism, a philosophical movement most commonly associated with Jeremy Bentham and John Stuart Mill, establishes the moral worth of an action by virtue of its consequences.[14] Morally right actions are those that produce the most good for the most people. For the utilitarian, *good* is synonymous with *happiness* and *utility*; one person's utility does not have any greater value than anyone else's. The consequences of any action must be gauged according to its benefit to others as well as to oneself.

Principlism, or principle-based reasoning, establishes a framework for moral reasoning based on four principles—**autonomy, beneficence, nonmaleficence**, and **justice**—which serve as the underlying values in contemporary biomedical and biobehavioral ethics.[10] Autonomy, from the Greek *autos* (self) and *nomos* (rule, governance, or law), recognizes that human beings have the right to determine what happens to their persons. This right obligates us to show respect for persons by refraining from actions that would limit their self-determination, by enabling them to act autonomously, and by protecting those with diminished capacity by virtue of age, mental or physical abilities, or life situation. Applied in a clinical setting, this principle requires that healthcare providers ensure that patients have the right to choose, as well as the right to accept or decline information or treatment.

The principle of beneficence carries with it the obligation to act in the interests of others and to contribute to others' welfare; such actions can take the form of outright benefit, as well as those efforts that balance benefits and drawbacks to produce the best overall result. Nonmaleficence, or "do no harm," admonishes us to refrain from any action that could harm another and to avoid imposing risks of harm.

Justice, as a formal principle, requires that equals should be treated as equals. In healthcare settings, justice raises issues of fair and equitable treatment and access to treatment; applied in biomedical research settings, justice requires that the benefits of the research should accrue to those who bear the burden of participation. These are not **prima facie principles** and may compete with each other in any given situation. For example, while nonmaleficence on its own would proscribe causing a person pain, beneficence would obligate a physician to give a patient a painful injection if it would protect that person from disease.

Distinct from principle- or rule-based reasoning, casuistry provides a framework for decision making in the medical arena that relies on paradigmatic cases to guide right action in cases of similar moral context.[15] In this framework, a person faced with an ethical dilemma must weigh the facts of the situation against similar situations in which the morally right action was clear and from which maxims of right and wrong behaviors are derived. Casuistry, which forms the basis for case-based law and applied ethics, uses these maxims as the basis for moral judgment.

Communitarianism arose in the late 1980s in reaction to the growing emphasis on individual rights and freedoms, countering that ethical decision making must take into account the social dimension of human existence, as well as individual autonomy.[16] The movement emphasizes the need to balance rights and responsibilities; individuals have a duty to their society to ensure its moral order and society and, in turn, must respect an individual's rights to self-determination. Communitarianism has been suggested by some authors to be of particular relevance to public health interventions, which must balance the rights and well-being of populations or subpopulations against the rights and well-being of individuals or groups of individuals.[17]

ETHICS IN POPULATION HEALTH PRACTICE

The biomedical model of healthcare practice carries with it a bias toward the individual, emphasizing the obligations of health providers to individual patients and the rights of patients to accept or refuse care. Estimations of "good" medicine are based on the aggregated health outcomes of individuals. By contrast, a population health focus is group centered. Principles of beneficence and utility, with their emphasis on achieving the best outcomes for the many, carry more weight than the autonomy-based rights of individual members.

In the doctor–patient relationship, it is generally the patient who seeks care, most often because of illness. Public health professionals and others concerned with population health are often the initiators of health interventions, targeting populations to reduce risks of future harm or to prevent the spread of disease. This raises interesting ethical challenges because it introduces the notion that interventions to protect the group may require the participation of individuals, even when it is not in their perceived best interests or may ask them to accept a risk with no assurance of personal benefit. Water fluoridation programs, disease registries and reporting, compulsory vaccination programs, and contact tracing for sexually transmitted diseases, for example, place concerns for group health and protection over preservation of individual choice.

ETHICS IN POPULATION HEALTH RESEARCH

Ethical guidelines governing research involving human subjects are grounded in the principles of respect for persons, beneficence, and justice, as recommended by the 1979 report of the National Commission for the Protection of Human Subjects of Biomedical and Behavioral Research (The Belmont Report).[18] Codified in the U.S. Code of Federal Regulations (45 CFR §46), known as the Common Rule, these guidelines define research as "a systematic investigation, including research development, testing and evaluation, designed to develop or contribute to generalizable knowledge" (§46.102(d)).[19] Research in population health that involves human subjects falls within the jurisdiction of this code. Human subjects' protections ensure that (1) individuals have the right to make an informed choice about whether or not they participate in research, (2) research protocols balance the potential for benefit and harm to individual research subjects, and (3) research subjects, who bear the burden of risk in research, have an opportunity to participate in its benefits. In domestic as well as international settings, health professionals who conduct research must also resolve ethical dilemmas arising from differences in cultural norms, attitudes, rules and regulations, and access to resources.

Not all population health investigations involve human subjects, such as research involving nonhuman biological processes; environmental research on air quality, water safety, and sanitation studies; or safety research involving aspects of the built environment. Some types of systematic data collection relating to population health, for example, are not considered research. Not generally considered to be research, population-based surveillance systems managed by state and local health authorities, such as the CDC's National Notifiable Diseases Surveillance System,[20] are used to monitor the prevalence and distribution in the population of certain diseases (such as tuberculosis, syphilis, and AIDS) and sentinel surveillance efforts, which draw their data from samples of physicians. This is because their purpose is not to generate new knowledge about the nature of a disease,[21] but rather to inform appropriate public health responses and allocation of resources. Evaluation studies designed to test the efficacy of public health interventions, measure efficiency, and determine cost-effectiveness are also not considered research, provided that their intent is to improve existing programs rather than test the efficacy of a new program. Similarly, data collection that is done to guide public health responses during emergencies is not treated as research.

ALLOCATION OF RESOURCES AND ACCESS

At the heart of issues dealing with the allocation of resources to promote population health and access are concerns about fairness, human rights, and individual responsibility. Population health recognizes the fundamental role that social, political, and economic forces play in determining the prevalence and distribution of health outcomes. These same forces also shape the distribution of health resources within the population and the extent to which individuals or specific groups of individuals can access them.[22]

Three moral arguments help us analyze the ethical dimensions of access to healthcare resources. A human rights approach posits that societies have a moral obligation to provide for the basic needs of their members; because health is a basic need (and, in this argument, a basic human right), societies are obligated to ensure access to health care.[23] Others call on the common good as justification for access; because the health of a society depends on the health of its members, it is in society's interest to promote collective health through access for all.[24] A third moral argument centers on the individual; society should provide its members with access to health resources because healthy individuals are the essential building blocks of a productive society.[25] Current debates over health care in the United States focus on ensuring that all Americans have access to health insurance. These debates mask larger issues of access, namely the kinds and quality of health services that are available, how these services are distributed, and the extent to which such factors as proximity of healthcare facilities to one's community and the availability of services suitable to the language or cultural needs of particular groups enable or restrict access.

Although the allocation of health resources is often driven by economic and political realities, it rests on value assumptions that involve moral choices. Most people would agree that **resource allocation** should be cost-effective, but what exactly does this mean? Cost-effectiveness analyses (CEAs), studies that examine health interventions for their efficiency in producing health, may appear to be objective calculations. Their findings, however, depend on the selection of costs and benefits attributed to the intervention, the period of time over which they are measured, and how they are quantified.[26] If two interventions work equally well at restoring health to an employee workforce, but one requires substantially more days of recuperation, should the costs or savings to employers for missed or saved days of work be included in the analysis? Is the gain of an additional year of life for an elderly person valued the same as an additional year of life gained for a child or a person in his or her productive years? How does one estimate the extent or cost of a disability to quality of life, given evidence that chronically ill and disabled persons are likely to place a higher value on their quality of life than persons without the condition would if asked to imagine living under similar conditions?[27] Which should be worth more: saving a life or adding years to one? How much should one discount health benefits to future generations over benefits to the current one? Even when a consensus exists on what should be included in a cost-effectiveness analysis, many argue that a purely utilitarian approach, which calls for the distribution of resources to maximize benefits for as many as possible, is unjust.[28]

Were decisions about health resource allocations based simply on cost-effectiveness, the distribution of those resources among and within different groups would not be a consideration; it would make no difference who received the benefit as long as the gains were the same.[29] However, calls for justice and equity may require the distribution of benefits and costs to particular groups or individuals within a population in the name of fairness. But what is fair and how is it determined? Some health scholars find that Rawls's theory of justice, although proposed in the context of constitutional rights and obligations, also has validity as a principle for health resource allocation; it holds that justice embodies those principles that free and rational persons would accept from an initial position of equality.[28,30] What would we agree is fair if we all had the same starting position? Different points of view see fairness in distributions according to equal shares, need, effort, contribution, merit, or free market exchanges; each of these viewpoints reflects values about what is due or owed to persons. These underlying values must be examined and harmonized if there is to be broad social consensus behind our health policies on resource allocation.

ETHICAL REFLECTION AND DECISION MAKING IN POPULATION HEALTH

Because choices in population health policies and practice are embedded with underlying values and the trade-offs one is willing to make among them, it stands to reason that rational actors, each faced with the same decision, will not always agree on what constitutes the morally right action. Ethics can serve as an analytical framework for decision making, finding new bases for agreement among stakeholders, stimulating discussion about ways to reconcile differences, and giving legitimacy to the decision-making process. Policy and resource allocation decisions at a population level inevitably face challenges from groups and individuals who feel that their rights and needs are being ignored in favor of other, more "popular" claims. Decisions resulting from a deliberative process in

---

BOX 13-1   AN ANALYTICAL FRAMEWORK FOR ETHICAL DECISION MAKING

The APHA Model Curriculum in Ethics and Public Health has identified six strategies to use in analyzing the ethical dimensions of a given situation:

1. Identify the ethical problem(s) germane to the decision.
2. Assess the factual information available and determine what is relevant to the ethical question.
3. Identify the stakeholders in the decision and consider the benefits or harms that will accrue to them.
4. Identify the values at stake in the decision.
5. Identify the available options.
6. Consider the process for making the decision and the values (such as legitimacy, due process, etc.) that pertain to that process.[31]

which competing interests have been considered and stakeholder voices heard are more likely to be seen as the products of "fair play." Policies and practices thus derived take on salience as social goods that should be supported by all members of society, even while they may continue to be seen as individually burdensome.

CONCLUSIONS

Decision making to improve health outcomes at the population level requires priority setting in health practice, research, education, and policy. Choices must be made as to what treatments to utilize, whom to treat, how to determine the cost-effectiveness of those interventions, which research agendas to pursue, and what training will be needed to prepare a future health workforce. Public policies that drive these decisions must also address the allocation of limited resources, the role of government in promoting health, and the laws and regulations that will advance population health objectives. Embedded in these actions are choices about what values are important to us as a society, the extent to which we are willing to second our interests to those of the group, and the expectations we have of society to provide for our well-being. Differences in our belief systems about rights and obligations, fairness, equity, and deservedness will constrain policy and programmatic efforts to build a healthy society unless common ground can be found. Ethics provides a framework for considering the underlying values of human actions and can be harnessed to identify shared values, craft policies that reflect them, and pursue a population health agenda supported by social consensus.

STUDY AND DISCUSSION QUESTIONS

1. What key moral traditions and ethical frameworks form the basis for resolving ethical dilemmas that arise in population health?
2. In what ways do population health ethics differ from medical ethics? In what ways are they similar?
3. How might concepts of justice help us analyze the ethics of resource allocation and access to health services in the population? What interpretation of justice do you think is most appropriate to use in health policy and priority setting, and why?

SUGGESTED READINGS AND WEB SITES

READINGS

Coughlin SS, Soskolne CL, Goodman KW. *Case Studies in Public Health Ethics.* Washington, DC: American Public Health Association; 1997.

Gostin LO, ed. *Public Health Law and Ethics: A Reader.* Berkeley, CA: University of California Press; 2002.

Jennings B, Kahn J, Mastroianni A, Parker LS, eds. *Ethics and Public Health: Model Curriculum.* Washington, DC: Association of Schools of Public Health; 2003. http://www.asph.org/document.cfm?page=782. Accessed August 27, 2009.

Powers M, Faden R. *Social Justice: The Moral Foundations of Public Health and Health Policy.* New York, NY: Oxford University Press; 2006.

Public Health Leadership Society. *Principles of the Ethical Practice of Public Health,* Version 2.2. New Orleans, LA: Public Health Leadership Society; 2002. http://www.apha.org/NR/rdonlyres/1CED3CEA-287E-4185-9CBD-BD405FC60856/0/ethicsbrochure.pdf. Accessed September 16, 2009.

World Health Organization. Social determinants of health. World Health Organization Web site. http://www.who.int/social_determinants/en/. Accessed August 27, 2009.

WEB SITES

Gostin LO. *Public Health Law and Ethics: A Reader* [companion Web site]: http://www.publichealthlaw.net/reader

REFERENCES

1. Kindig D, Stoddart G. What is population health? *Am J Public Health.* 2003;93(3):380–383.
2. Starfield B. Pathways of influence on equity in health. *Soc Sci Med.* 2007;64(7):1355–1362.
3. Daniels N. *Just Health Care.* Cambridge, UK: Cambridge University Press; 1985.
4. Kingdon J. What ethics can contribute to health policy. In: Danis M, Clancy C, Churchill LR, eds. *Ethical Dimensions of Health Policy.* New York, NY: Oxford University Press; 2005:51–64.
5. American Medical Association. Code of Medical Ethics. American Medical Association Web site. http://www.ama-assn.org/ama/pub/physician-resources/medical-ethics/code-medical-ethics.shtml. Accessed September 16, 2009.
6. American Nurses Association. Code of Ethics for Nurses. American Nurses Association Web site. http://www.nursingworld.org/MainMenuCategories/EthicsStandards/CodeofEthicsforNurses.aspx. Accessed September 16, 2009.
7. American Pharmacists Association. Code of Ethics for Pharmacists. American Pharmacists Association Web site. http://www.pharmacist.com/AM/Template.cfm?Section=Code_of_Ethics_for_Pharmacists&Template=/CM/HTMLDisplay.cfm&ContentID=5420. Accessed December 8, 2009.
8. Public Health Leadership Society. *Principles of the Ethical Practice of Public Health,* Version 2.2. New Orleans, LA: Public Health Leadership Society; 2002. http://www.apha.org/NR/rdonlyres/1CED3CEA-287E-4185-9CBD-BD405FC60856/0/ethicsbrochure.pdf. Accessed September 16, 2009.
9. Society for Public Health Education. Ethics. Society for Public Health Education Web site. http://www.sophe.org/ethics.cfm. Accessed September 16, 2009.
10. Beauchamp TL, Childress JF. *Principles of Biomedical Ethics.* 4th ed. New York, NY: Oxford University Press; 1994.
11. Dawson A, Verweij M. Introduction: ethics, prevention, and public health. In: Dawson A, Verweij M, eds. *Ethics, Prevention, and Public Health.* New York, NY: Oxford University Press; 2007:1–12.
12. Wikler D, Brock DW. Population-level bioethics: mapping a new agenda. In: Dawson A, Verweij M, eds. *Ethics, Prevention, and Public Health.* New York, NY: Oxford University Press; 2007: 78–94.

13. Alexander L, Moore M. Deontological ethics. In: Zalta EN, ed. The Stanford Encyclopedia of Philosophy (Fall 2008 edition). Available at: http://plato.stanford.edu/archives/fall2008/entries/ethics-deontological/. Accessed August 27, 2009.

14. Driver J. The history of utilitarianism. In Zalta EN, ed. The Stanford Encyclopedia of Philosophy (Summer 2009 edition). http://plato.stanford.edu/archives/sum2009/entries/utilitarianism-history/. Accessed August 27, 2009.

15. Jonsen AR, Toulmin SE. *The Abuse of Casuistry: A History of Moral Reasoning.* Berkeley, CA: University of California Press; 1988.

16. The Communitarian Network. http://www.gwu.edu/~icps/Home.html. Accessed September 2, 2009.

17. Forster JL. A communitarian ethical model for public health interventions: an alternative to individual behavior change strategies. *J Public Health Policy.* 1982;3(2):150–163.

18. National Commission for the Protection of Human Subjects of Biomedical and Behavioral Research. *The Belmont Report: Ethical Principles and Guidelines for the Protection of Human Subjects of Research,* 1979. Office of Human Subjects Research Web site. http://ohsr.od.nih.gov/guidelines/belmont.html. Accessed September 2, 2009.

19. US Department of Health and Human Services. Protection of human subjects. 45 CFR §46; 2005. www.hhs.gov/ohrp/humansubjects/guidance/45cfr46.htm. Revised January 15, 2009. Accessed September 2, 2009.

20. Centers for Disease Control and Prevention. National Notifiable Diseases Surveillance System. http://www.cdc.gov/ncphi/disss/nndss/nndsshis.htm. Accessed September 2, 2009.

21. Garland M, Stull J. Public health and health system reform: access, priority setting, and allocation of resources. In: Jennings B, Kahn J, Mastroianni A, Parker LS, eds. *Ethics and Public Health: Model Curriculum.* Washington, DC: Association of Schools of Public Health; 2003. http://www.asph.org/UserFiles/Module9.pdf. Accessed August 1, 2009.

22. Thomas J. Introduction to Modules 3 and 4: research ethics in public health. In: Jennings B, Kahn J, Mastroianni A, Parker LS, eds. *Ethics and Public Health: Model Curriculum.* Washington, DC: Association of Schools of Public Health; 2003. http://www.asph.org/UserFiles/IntroToMods3n4.pdf. Accessed August 1, 2009.

23. Mann JM. Medicine and public health, ethics and human rights. *Hastings Cent Rep.* May-June 1997;27(3):6–13.

24. President's Commission for the Study of Ethical Problems in Medicine and Biomedical and Behavioral Research. *Securing Access to Health Care: The Ethical Implications of Differences in the Availability of Health Services.* Vol 1. Washington, DC: Government Printing Office; 1983.

25. Churchill LR. *Self-Interest and Universal Health Care: Why Well-Insured Americans Should Support Coverage for Everyone.* Cambridge, MA: Harvard University Press; 1994.

26. Brock DW, Wikler D. Ethical issues in resource allocation, research, and new product development. In: Jamieson DT, Breman JG, Measham AR, et al., eds. *Disease Control Priorities in Developing Countries,* 2nd ed. Washington, DC: The International Bank for Reconstruction and Development/The World Bank; 2006.

27. Menzel P, Dolan P, Richardson J, et al. The role of adaptation to disability and disease in health state valuation: a preliminary normative analysis. *Soc Sci Med.* 2002;55(12):2149–2158.

28. Rawls J. *A Theory of Justice.* Cambridge, MA: Belknap Press of Harvard University Press; 1971.

29. Emanuel EJ. Patient v. population: resolving the ethical dilemmas posed by treating patients as members of populations. In: Danis M, Clancy C, Churchill LR, eds. *Ethical Dimensions of Health Policy.* New York, NY: Oxford University Press; 2005:227–245.

30. Daniels N, Kennedy BP, Kawachi I. Justice, health, and health policy. In: Danis M, Clancy C, Churchill LR, eds. *Ethical Dimensions of Health Policy.* New York, NY: Oxford University Press; 2005:19–47.

31. Jennings B, Kahn J, Mastroianni A, Parker LS, eds. *Ethics and Public Health: Model Curriculum.* Washington, DC: Association of Schools of Public Health; 2003. http://www.asph.org/document.cfm?page=782.

Chapter 14

POPULATION HEALTH IN ACTION: SUCCESSFUL MODELS

PAUL WALLACE, MD

Executive Summary

Success = Improved Population Health

For the disciplines of quality and safety, public health, health policy, and chronic care management to evolve into the collaborative field of population health and be trusted as a resource for policy and innovation, the combined effort must improve the health of the population. Patients with chronic medical conditions consume the majority of the United States's healthcare resources while quality, service, and cost outcomes lag behind what is desired by patients, payers, and many care providers. The efforts to improve care for patients with chronic medical conditions are instructive in how population health practices emerge and build on models of change. Improving care for chronic conditions has centered on two dominant models: disease management (DM) and coordinated primary care. Disease management services are delivered directly to patients to guide their care and create behavior change, while coordinated redesign of primary care clinical practices aims to improve chronic care management by directly involving clinicians.

Durable models of population health need to provide broad access to care across the whole population while reliably improving critical health outcomes over time. Successful models also need to be acceptable to clinicians and to the funders of healthcare services. The achievements of both DM and practice redesign are mixed. Success varies by both type of funder and type of clinical need addressed. While both policy makers' and payers' decision criteria to allocate resources may differ, they can be evidence-based, drawing different conclusions because of decision-making rules and perspective of the need for change. Development of policy for a full population encompasses a broad spectrum of requirements. Similar to chronic care, policy approaches may leverage more than one model to meet the needs of both the purchaser and provider environments.

Learning Objectives

1. Identify key characteristics of a successful population health model.
2. Compare and contrast disease management and practice redesign as models for improving chronic condition care.
3. Characterize the differences in decision making about chronic care services between private and public healthcare financing.
4. Project how the chronic care experience to date may form a foundation for future evolution of population models.

Key Words

chronic care management

Chronic Care Model

commercial health plan

disease management (DM)

employers

fee-for-service

practice redesign (PR)

publicly financed health care

INTRODUCTION

The goal for population health is bold and is built upon the four domains of quality and safety, public health, health policy, and **chronic care management**. In positioning this collective effort so that the future *health* system can dependably benefit, much can be learned from examining existing change models that have been tested and have helped form a spectrum of collaborative actions. For population health management to be a validated approach, it must improve the health status of the population served. It must help successfully transition appropriate cohorts of people from existing providers and processes to those that more reliably achieve necessary health outcomes. Further, the care provided must be affordable to patients and acceptable to professionals accountable for care delivery. This is not an easy task. However, much has been learned over the last two decades, particularly from the **disease management (DM)** industry. Some of these efforts have demonstrated improvements in caring for chronic conditions. These examples offer guidance to the processes, challenges, and success factors required for population health management to consistently deliver meaningful outcomes.

WHY FOCUS ON CHRONIC MEDICAL CONDITIONS?

Meeting the full needs of patients with chronic health conditions remains a major goal for forming effective health policy and reforming healthcare services and their delivery. Patients with chronic medical conditions consume the majority of U.S. healthcare resources, yet quality, service, and cost outcomes lag behind what is required to meet clinical and administrative goals for American population health.

CARE AS USUAL

The "care as usual," or the status quo, standard traditional approach is the target for change. Not as much a formal model as a default position, care as usual fails to deliver evidence-based interventions approximately half of the time when an opportunity exists.[1] Care as usual is fraught with concerns about the quality and safety of services delivered in our healthcare system and it has led us to where we are today—a system that focuses more on "sick care" than "health care." The present structure of office practice does not provide the necessary time, incentives, or support systems, such as patient registries, required for primary care providers to successfully and proactively manage the care of their entire patient population.[2] This is the incumbent model associated with lagging U.S. performance on indices of population health in comparison to other similarly developed countries.[3] As long as care as usual remains the dominant model for healthcare delivery in the United States, the results it produces will remain unchanged and unacceptable.

Many innovations have been promoted to improve historically deficient "usual" chronic condition care. Over time, two basic change implementation models have emerged: (1) expanded *direct patient engagement* through newly created services, such as freestanding and health plan–associated disease management resources, and (2) *reorganization of the practice design and roles of primary care practices*, most prominently packaged as the **Chronic Care Model**, which occurs in large integrated delivery systems. In this chapter, the first approach will be categorized as disease management (DM) and the second method will be referred to as **practice redesign (PR)**.

DISEASE MANAGEMENT AND PRACTICE REDESIGN

DM and PR coexist within a continuum of population care interventions.[4] Both aim to minimize disease and maximize health among patients with conditions such as diabetes, asthma, and heart disease. Both act by changing practice approaches and the processes that drive performance. However, although these approaches have generally been cast as competing, if not mutually exclusive, DM and PR are ideally complementary. Fortunately, both DM and PR have been evaluated comprehensively and concurrently for more than a decade in diverse practice and payment environments. Consequently, the accumulating experience obtained from these two approaches is increasingly valid and extensive. It is producing a complex and highly relevant body of knowledge to support future operational improvement and policy development for overall population care.

GAUGING SUCCESS—ASSESSMENT FRAMEWORK

To gain broad policy support, a successful population care model must achieve a passing grade on two key tests:

access: Is the model replicable and feasible for population-wide dissemination?
outcomes: Does the model improve the critical health outcomes of quality, service, and cost for individual patients and the population served?

A sustainable approach for the whole population also must meet the professional requirements of clinicians and deliver adequate value to satisfy whoever is paying the bills for these services. For the whole U.S. population to be included, the approach needs to include **employers**, individual citizens who pay for commercial insurance, and the federal and state governments that fund Medicare and Medicaid.

While no practice model can currently deliver results to match the expectations for all payer and care delivery settings, both DM and PR, as model paradigms, have persisted since 1997 and continue to grow and evolve. Examples of productive implementation of these models, combined with the appreciation of what has not succeeded, form the foundation for continued improvements and guide necessary collaboration in pursuit of population health.

In the following sections, the overall successes and challenges accrued by disease management and clinical practice redesign "in action" will be described and some specific examples highlighted.

While not included in this chapter, it should be mentioned that efforts in risk reduction through the use of health assessments have been another successful methodology in improving population health. This activity has been implemented by large employers and has contributed to their ability to reduce their healthcare expenditure and "bend the curve." (See the Future of Population Health section at the end of this book.)

DISEASE MANAGEMENT: A MODEL FOR POPULATION CARE

Disease management services have become a core part of almost every U.S. **commercial health plan**, either by internal development or by contracting with an independent DM company. The number and types of conditions addressed have increased substantially over time, from an initial focus on a handful of solitary conditions such as diabetes, asthma, and heart disease, to more recent capacity for dozens of unique conditions in addition to an increasing set of capabilities directed at patients with multiple comorbidities.[5]

ACCESS AND SPREAD

While each implementation of DM is unique, to some extent, the range of included technical and professional services has continued to expand to include remote patient engagement via telephone and Internet, personalized coaching, use of predictive utilization models, and incorporation of financial incentives for increasing patient participation. Another evolving trend is the use of remote patient monitoring technologies to extend patient engagement and DM company access to patient-associated clinical information.[6]

While an indirect measure of clinical success at best, the revenue of freestanding disease management companies has risen since 1997 to approximately $2 billion annually (2009–2010).[7] As the DM model continues to evolve, several DM companies have been in sustained operations for more than 10 years and continued growth of the DM industry is projected into the future.

In surveys of the major U.S. employers, who pay for the majority of health care for Americans younger than 65 years, most respondents identify DM as a core element in their internal strategies for purchasing health benefits for their employees and families. Many also anticipate expanding this commitment in scope of conditions covered and actual investment going forward.[5] Therefore, DM is a major market and policy solution for the majority of the population younger than 65 years old who are served by commercial insurance plans, which are financed individually or through employers.

Impact on Care Outcomes   While the DM model has been successful in establishing broad access to care management services among the commercially insured, the impact of DM on health outcomes has been scrutinized widely and remains controversial.[4,8–10] Debate persists about how results are best measured and, as improvement is defined, whether DM can legitimately claim the full magnitude of observed effects or the existence of any beneficial effect at all.

There is general agreement that DM has consistently improved adherence to evidence-based guidelines for common chronic conditions such as diabetes, heart failure, ischemic heart disease, and asthma. DM programs also reliably produce positive changes in intermediate measures of disease control, such as blood sugar control in diabetes and meeting cholesterol control targets for diabetes and heart disease. For a select set of conditions, most notably heart failure, DM has consistently led to reduced hospital admissions and improvement in patient satisfaction and quality of life.[8] Practicing physician acceptance of DM has been more variable and often negative, at least according to anecdotal accounts.[11]

Finally, while commercial payers have continued to pursue and purchase growing amounts of DM services, methods to gauge financial return on DM investments and overall financial impact of DM have been subject to extensive critique by consultants and researchers, as well as DM industry advocates, and remain highly controversial.[8,12,13] Nonetheless, as a model for improving chronic condition care, DM has spread substantially and continues to grow in both scope and magnitude of populations served among the commercially insured population. While it has generally high acceptance in the marketplace among health plans and employers, the impact on outcomes, particularly cost, remains controversial.

DISEASE MANAGEMENT AND MEDICARE

Access and Spread   In contrast to the common use of DM services by commercial health plans, DM is not a benefit routinely covered for **fee-for-service** (FFS) Medicare beneficiaries. However, the 22% of Medicare beneficiaries enrolled in a private Medicare-managed care plan through the Medicare Advantage program[14] may have elements of DM and PR included in their care.

Under the FFS Medicare program, since 1999, CMS has sponsored a series of seven DM demonstration projects involving 35 specific interventions.[15] While a full summary of the demonstrations is beyond the scope of this chapter, approximately 300,000 Medicare recipients have received some DM-related services through these demonstrations.

Impact on Care Outcomes Measures of clinical quality processes and intermediate outcomes, such as glucose testing and control for patients with diabetes, have generally shown significant improvements within the CMS DM demos.[15] Patient satisfaction has been variable. However, in the more recent demonstrations, active promotion and improved communication to beneficiaries have increased participation and DM was valued as a benefit by the involved patients.[16,17]

Each CMS DM demonstration intervention has been required to remain budget neutral and generally expected to achieve targeted aims within relatively short time frames of one to three years of operations. That is, as policy, programs have been required to deliver quantifiable utilization and financial savings equal or greater to their overall implementation costs. In analyses done by external evaluators, only 3 of 20 programs that have reached these evaluation end points have met this cost goal, while an additional 4 of 15 other interventions in progress in 2009 were deemed to have the potential to eventually achieve budget neutrality.[15]

Two examples of DM demos are discussed in the following section to demonstrate the success and challenges in reaching financial targets.

DM for Dual Eligibles (2005–2009 [ongoing]) was designed for Florida-based beneficiaries receiving both Medicare and Medicaid benefits. This program originally broadly targeted 30,000 dually eligible patients, but after two years and interim analyses, the care model was redesigned to focus on care coordination for 20,000 patients with heart failure alone or in combination with CAD or diabetes. The interventions included telephonic care management by registered nurses (RNs) supplemented by in-home visits. The program achieved budget neutrality (program costs equal to or less than the achieved reduction in claims costs), and further outcome analysis is under way.[15]

Medicare Health Support (MHS) Phase I (2006–2008) was designed to provide DM services through contracted, private DM companies and health plans for patients with the comorbid conditions of heart failure and diabetes, predicted to be at the highest risk for intensified health services or hospitalization in the immediate future. When the program was launched, the end point for financial success and consideration for program expansion was a net 5% reduction in overall costs, inclusive of the fees for the MHS services. This cost target was later changed to budget neutrality.

MHS was designed as a randomized trial with a control population selected in parallel to the intervention group. Eight organizations initially enrolled patients in Phase I of MHS, and at the outset, each had the opportunity to engage approximately 20,000 patients. For each site, a control population of an additional 10,000 was selected. During the course of the MHS demo, two organizations dropped out before the demo concluded, leaving several thousand patients without management. The remaining sites were later given further access to several thousand additional patients to manage. Before the program was terminated in

2008, more than 200,000 Medicare beneficiaries received care through MHS. Failure to achieve budget neutrality caused the program to be terminated and the potential for a second phase to be cancelled. In the final evaluation, MHS program fees had increased Medicare costs 5–11% for the enrolled populations, while the resulting reduction in overall claims within the 18-month period of operation was insufficient to balance the incurred costs.

The MHS participating organizations did achieve participation rates of 74–95% with refusal rates of 0.3–13%. However, only two of the MHS organizations met the MHS satisfaction standard, measured by the survey item, "beneficiaries were helped by their health care team to cope with their chronic conditions." Finally, in interviews with randomly selected community physicians, there was a shared impression that the MHS interventions could benefit the targeted patients.

The mixed overall and frequently negative financial results of the FFS Medicare DM demonstrations have been a disappointment to both CMS and the participating organizations, especially those involved in the MHS demonstration. Debate continues about how to better meet the needs of the older, and often complex, Medicare beneficiary, with anticipation of additional but restructured chronic care demonstrations to commence in the future. Important policy concerns to be addressed in future demonstrations include how to identify, mobilize, and coordinate services for the most ill and complex Medicare beneficiaries and determine the appropriate time frame for anticipating and measuring cost impacts of similar interventions.[15–17]

DISEASE MANAGEMENT AND MEDICAID

Access and Spread   Because Medicaid programs vary substantially among states, a diverse range of approaches have been applied to Medicaid beneficiaries with chronic health conditions. Beyond near universal constraints on program financing, the challenge of delivering chronic condition care in the Medicaid program is often confounded by low patient income, high social risks among beneficiaries, and common use of month-to-month program enrollment eligibility requirements that may compromise efforts to develop longitudinal care continuity. An additional challenge for this population is the relatively high prevalence of mental health and substance abuse–related diagnoses, both in isolation and in association with other chronic medical illnesses.[18]

Despite these challenges, states have been both persistent and creative in developing DM and related chronic care programs and in testing their impact and success. CMS has also encouraged the testing and use of DM in Medicaid programs[19] and, as of 2004, at least 30 states had implemented DM programs for their beneficiaries.

In reviewing DM contracting by state Medicaid agencies, the most commonly covered conditions were diabetes, asthma, heart failure, and chronic obstructive pulmonary disease. Many other conditions received attention, including HIV/AIDS, obesity, and tobacco use.[20] Several areas of care management that have been identified as having particular value in Medicaid include high-risk pregnancy, high-risk asthmatic children, and high-risk and high-cost members with multiple comorbid chronic conditions.[21]

> ## BOX 14-1 EXAMPLES OF DM IMPLEMENTATION IN MEDICAID
>
> ### Florida
> The first DM programs implemented were in 1998 for diabetes, asthma, HIV/AIDS, and hemophilia. From 2001 to 2005, Florida contracted with pharmaceutical vendors for DM services in lieu of supplemental rebates included in a preferred drug program. Those contracts were terminated because of the inability to resolve conflict about the program's financial impact.[22]
>
> ### Washington
> Initially, contracted DM services included asthma, diabetes, heart disease, and renal disease/dialysis. While these programs did generally improve service access and reduce hospital utilization in asthma and renal disease, cost targets were not achieved. Washington has subsequently transitioned to targeting high-risk beneficiaries with multiple conditions for more intensive care and case management.[23]

Not surprisingly, no single dominant DM approach has emerged in Medicaid, and states have continued to experiment with investment in DM by internally building programs, contracting with DM vendors and employing combinations of both.

AN ALTERNATIVE MODEL: CLINICAL PRACTICE REDESIGN

Poor coordination with the participants' primary care physician practice has been a frequent criticism of the DM model, regardless of payer. Consequently, there have been substantial efforts to create an alternative to DM through internal redesign of clinical practices to better equip and position them to directly meet the needs of patients and populations with chronic conditions. Prominent examples of practice redesign include the Chronic Care Model, proposed in 1998 by Wagner and colleagues,[24] the efforts of integrated delivery systems over the last two decades, and efforts within the clinical safety net and community-based care networks.

THE CHRONIC CARE MODEL

Access and Spread The Chronic Care Model (CCM) foresees improved health outcomes as the product of increasingly effective interactions between patients and their primary care clinicians. Key design features include development of an interdisciplinary practice team led by the primary care clinician and improved patient engagement and education about their health care and options. Policy and operational support for this core clinician–patient interaction is achieved through refining the design of overall care delivery and physician payment, improving primary and specialty care interaction, and building health IT capabilities to record and track care and communicate well with patients, placing emphasis on patient self-care, and expanding linkages to community health resources.[24-26]

An additional key contribution associated with the CCM is its strategy for spread through practice collaboratives. Transformation of practices requires a substantial commitment of time, leadership, and resources. Consequently, small practices, the predominant medical care providers in the United States, have been challenged in both initiating this change and securing the added resources and capabilities required to maintain it. However, substantial success in sustainable spread of the model has been achieved through multipractice collaboratives and ongoing consultative support. More than 1,500 practices have been directly involved in CCM-linked collaboratives. Of practices that transition to the CCM, three-quarters sustain the changes made for at least a year; a similar proportion further extend the clinical scope in their practice and/or geographic reach to other sites.[27,28]

A few examples illustrate some of the efforts initiated to spread the CCM.

The Health Disparities Collaborative sponsored by the Bureau of Primary Health Care in the U.S. Department of Health and Human Services has collaborated with the Cambridge, MA–based Institute for Healthcare Improvement to work with more than 800 community health centers to adopt practices modeled after the CCM, including the systematic tracking and reporting of population-based and individual patient care.[29]

The Improving Chronic Illness Care (ICIC) organization formed by the originators of the CCM has helped deliver the Breakthrough Series to practices and academic medical centers. This effort is a 6- to 15-month learning system that joins teams from practices and hospitals to evolve new practices and team-based systems in focused topic areas such as diabetes care.[30]

Both of these examples illustrate that for innovations to truly improve population health, they must be extended to multiple practices so that most, if not all, of the population served can benefit. The systematic spread achieved through these collaboratives demonstrates how a conceptual model like CCM can be translated into widely distributed care improvement.

Impact of the CCM on Care Outcomes   In randomized trials of CCM practice change, improvement in at least some process and outcome measures has been consistently achieved. Further, qualitative studies of practices adopting the CCM have documented improvements in clinical process and outcome plus some reductions in hospital utilization and cardiovascular risk within reconfigured practices. Clinical processes, such as laboratory testing, generally improve within a year or two of implementation, and intermediate outcomes, such as blood sugar and cholesterol control, may take at least two years.[4,31] The impact of cost on CCM remains to be fully realized. One report, now several years old, identified cost savings from CCM-driven improvements in care for patients with diabetes.[32]

PRACTICE REDESIGN AND INTEGRATED DELIVERY SYSTEMS

The CCM has been closely linked to evolution of care delivery design within larger integrated delivery systems such as Kaiser Permanente, Group Health Cooperative, Geisinger Health System, and the Veterans Health Administration.

Kaiser Permanente (KP) offers an example of the effectiveness of practice redesign in achieving integrated care and improved quality of care delivery. Kaiser Permanente is a multiregion integrated care delivery organization that serves more than eight million members, including approximately one million patients with coverage through Medicare Advantage (Medicare managed care). KP consists of the Kaiser Family Foundation health insurance plan, based on prepaid and globally capitated care services, in mutually exclusive partnership with the self-governing and independent Permanente Medical Groups (PMG). The PMGs are multispecialty practices employing salaried physicians. KP has run internally developed programs for improving chronic condition care since the early 1990s. The design of programs aligns closely with the elements of the CCM.[33] Formal evaluation of programs in the Northern California region of KP, which focused on the care of patients with diabetes, heart disease, and asthma, demonstrated substantial quality improvement and reductions in apparent cost trends for the population of managed patients, but were unable to show net cost savings for the programs evaluated.[34]

PR IN THE SAFETY NET AND MEDICAID

Access and Spread   The CCM has also guided regional practice improvement programs in several states, including North Carolina and Minnesota. As noted previously, the transition from traditional primary care to the CCM is resource-intensive and challenging. Many state Medicaid programs have elected to address deficiencies in chronic condition care through purchase or internal development of DM programs, which require less disruption of existing models of care delivery and lower overall investment. However, among the Medicaid chronic care improvement efforts with the most impact are those that have employed significant redesign of practices and their supporting environment.

Redesigning environment resources in addition to the practice environment affords increased opportunities for success. Community Care of North Carolina (CCNC), formed in 1991 by the state through its Medicaid program, has established a statewide series of local nonprofit networks of primary care practices, hospitals, community resources, and local payers. These state resources provide each enrollee with a robust medical home that offers acute, chronic, and preventive services. Infrastructure investments include extensive case management resources, guidelines, measurement support, and a commitment to continuous quality improvement at all levels of the organization. Structured external evaluations have documented substantial cost savings, compared to prior programs, and improved quality and utilization for patients with diabetes and asthma.[35]

CONCLUSIONS

The cumulative experience of addressing the care of patients with chronic health conditions has drawn from many disciplines and perspectives. While two dominant models have emerged, neither alone has fully met the challenge of providing consistent, widely available, affordable, high-quality care in all payer settings. DM has wide application among commercial insurance, but lacks appeal to practicing clinicians and **publicly financed health care** programs, especially Medicare. The CCM and similar approaches to practice redesign have met a number of challenges in terms of spread and impact on healthcare costs. However, disease management and efforts at practice redesign, together, are transforming expectations for the care of patients with a broad spectrum of chronic health conditions.

The temptation is to ask, "What is the 'best' model for chronic condition care?" and expect a clear, cross-cutting answer. This is likely the wrong question. The more productive population health questions are: "What have we learned from a vast and diverse experience of more than 10 years? And how is that knowledge best leveraged into effective future policy and practice going forward to improve the health of the population overall?" DM and PR address a common set of patients and challenges, but have not been rigorously compared to each another, and likely never will be.

Can the commercial insurance and health plan emphasis on DM be reconciled with the mixed results from research and CMS Medicare demonstrations plus provider reluctance to embrace DM or practice redesign on a large scale?

Commercial insurers, along with many employers who provide the majority of their funding, have concluded that clinical "practice as usual" has clearly been proven insufficient for the future, if not the present. In other words, from their perspective, there is a powerful and extensive evidence base that care, as usually provided, will not meet their common business needs. Consequently, there is an urgent requirement to do something different now for their beneficiaries, and DM is the most readily accessible option with credibly demonstrated impact.

In contrast, because of Medicare's statutory constraints, CMS needs to demonstrate unequivocal improvement before whole scale change in its established programs can be undertaken.

A similar need to firmly prove superiority of a change before wholesale adoption also prevails in the provider and academic perspectives. In other words, the absence of sufficient evidence of benefit is a barrier to change.

Ironically, both are defensibly evidence-based approaches. The insurer and employer are acting on evidence they find compelling and evidence of the insufficiency for the given model, care as usual. They see the potential positive impact of DM as a way to avoid repeating the projected ongoing failure of continuing the status quo. In direct contrast, CMS and providers are constrained from taking new action by the absence of definitive evidence proving the likely success for the proposed changes.

Medicaid, with its diversity of program design, financing, and governance, offers the most complex picture of all, providing multiple examples of adaptation to local needs through a variety of approaches. The success of CCNC is both an advertisement for purposeful and cost-effective design and an argument to practitioners and providers about the potential for the emerging medical home concept.

Where both the DM and PR efforts have an additional common policy impact is in forming broadly based opportunities for ongoing learning or serving as complex learning organizations. Neither endeavor has been static over time. Both models have evolved in terms of services provided and in demonstrating the effectiveness of those services. DM, which began with management of a few isolated medical conditions, has evolved sophisticated predictive modeling and care protocols to target the most complex patients and focus resources to areas of high clinical and business opportunity. DM has also evolved into a component of population health management, which encompasses more robust prevention and health promotion capabilities as part of workplace "total health" programs. As an industry, DM has worked to evolve evaluation and measurement standards to guide value determination. The CCM and related approaches have also evolved in both content and approaches for widespread adoption by practicing clinicians. Even more immediately important, the accrued experience with practice redesign now serves as much of the basis for the emerging patient-centered medical home demonstrations and approaches to better manage care transitions and end-of-life issues.

Building policy for an entire population will likely provide a portfolio of approaches, and the experience of DM with different payers helps to frame the boundaries and provide direction for needed services. DM is likely a good fit for many aspects of chronic care management for commercially insured populations, especially interventions requiring broad reach at a relatively low price. Therefore, DM can provide the framework for the development of health promotion programs. As previously noted, the recent growth and transition within DM companies has been through conceptual and service delivery expansion to support wellness and prevention-based services. These programs provide value-generating services for major portions of an employer's insured population, which is quite different than DM historically focused more narrowly on a sick minority of the population. The core methodology of DM is also expanding to further embrace techniques promoting behavior change, a critical intervention for population health improvement.

DM did not do well with the moderately and severely ill Medicare beneficiaries. Focusing on practice redesign and intensive case management by clinicians who know the patient well and establish an ongoing relationship over time may offer the best care for the complex elderly patient, especially in terms of coordination after hospitalizations and end-of-life care.

What DM and practice redesign approaches most clearly have in common is that they both reflect evolution, albeit down somewhat dissimilar paths, from the most common care model in use today for confronting the population's health needs—care as usual. Consequently, the gains of DM and practice redesign, despite the barriers they had to overcome, offer guidance for what can be done to further advance population health beyond the status quo.

STUDY AND DISCUSSION QUESTIONS

1. What are the strengths and weaknesses of disease management and practice redesign as models for improving chronic condition care? To what extent do they share common goals and where do they diverge?
2. How do the current decision-making and business needs of private vs. public payers differ? In what ways are they the same?
3. Are disease management and practice redesign competitive or complementary models? Why?
4. How has DM transitioned to support health and wellness activities?
5. How has spread of practice redesign been supported?

SUGGESTED READINGS AND WEB SITES

READINGS

Chronic Condition Care

Coleman K, Mattke S, Perrault PJ, Wagner EH. Untangling practice redesign from disease management: how do we best care for the chronically ill? *Annu. Rev. Public Health.* 2009;30:385–408.

Schoen C, Osborn R, How SK, Doty MM, Peugh J. In chronic condition: experiences of patients with complex health care needs, in eight countries, 2008. *Health Aff.* 2009;28(1):w1–w16. Published November 13, 2008.

Disease Management

Matheson D, Wilkins A, Psacharopoulos D. *Realizing the promise of disease management: payer trends and opportunities in the United States.* The Boston Consulting Group Web site. http://www.bcg.com/documents/file14744.pdf. Published February 2006. Accessed September 19, 2009.

Mattke S, Seid M, Ma S. Evidence for the effect of disease management: is $1 billion a year a good investment? *Am J Manag Care.* 2007;13(12):670–676.

Practice Redesign and the Chronic Care Model

Bodenheimer T, Wagner EH, Grumbach K. Improving primary care for patients with chronic illness. *JAMA.* 2002;288(14):1775–1779.

Bodenheimer T, Wagner EH, Grumbach K. Improving primary care for patients with chronic illness: the chronic care model, Part 2. *JAMA.* 2002;288(15):1909–1914.

Institute for Healthcare Improvement. *The Breakthrough Series: IHI's Collaborative Model for Achieving Breakthrough Improvement.* Boston, MA: Institute for Healthcare Improvement; 2003. http://www.ihi.org/IHI/Results/WhitePapers/TheBreakthroughSeriesIHIs CollaborativeModelforAchieving%20BreakthroughImprovement.htm. Accessed September 19, 2009.

Population Care in Publicly Funded Programs

Bott DM, Kapp MC, Johnson LB, Magno LM. Disease management for chronically ill beneficiaries in traditional Medicare. *Health Aff.* 2009;28(1):86–98.

California Health Care Foundation. Disease Management in Medicaid. 2004 [chart pack]. California Health Care Foundation Web site. http://www.chcf.org/documents/policy/DiseaseManagementInMedicaid2004.pdf. Accessed September 19, 2009.

Rosenbaum S, Markus A, Sheer J, Harty ME. Negotiating the new health system at ten: Medicaid managed care and the use of disease management purchasing. Hamilton, NJ: Center for Health Care Strategies Inc; May 2008. http://www.chcs.org/usr_doc/Negotiating_the_New_Health_System_at_Ten.pdf. Accessed September 19, 2009.

WEB SITES

Center for Health Care Strategies, Inc.: http://www.chcs.org/

Centers for Medicare and Medicaid Services: http://www.cms.hhs.gov/

Community Care of North Carolina: http://www.communitycarenc.com/

DMAA: The Care Continuum Alliance (formerly the Disease Management Association of America): http://www.dmaa.org/

Improving Chronic Illness Care: http://www.improvingchroniccare.org/

The Kaiser Permanente Care Management Institute: http://www.kpcmi.org/

National Business Group on Health: http://www.businessgrouphealth.org/

Partnership to Fight Chronic Disease: http://www.fightchronicdisease.org/

REFERENCES

1. McGlynn EA, Asch SM, Adams J, et al. The quality of health care delivered to adults in the United States. *N Engl J Med.* 2003;348(26): 2635–2645.

2. Yarnall SH, Pollak KI, Ostbye T, Krause KM, Michener JL. Primary care: is there enough time for prevention? *Am J Public Health.* 2003;93(4): 635–641.

3. Schoen C, Osborn R, How SK, Doty MM, Peugh J. In chronic condition: experiences of patients with complex health care needs, in eight countries, 2008. *Health Aff.* 2009;28(1):w1–w16. Published November 13, 2008.

4. Coleman K, Mattke S, Perrault PJ, Wagner EH. Untangling practice redesign from disease management: how do we best care for the chronically ill? *Annu. Rev. Public Health.* 2009;30:385–408.

5. Matheson D, Wilkins A, Psacharopoulos D. *Realizing the promise of disease management: payer trends and opportunities in the United States.* The Boston Consulting Group Web site. http://www.bcg.com/documents/file14744.pdf. Published February 2006. Accessed September 19, 2009.

6. Monegain B, ed. Remote patient monitoring improves outcomes for chronically ill, study shows. Healthcare IT News Web site. http://www.healthcareitnews.com/news/remote-patient-monitoring-improves-outcomes-chronically-ill-study-shows. Published March 24, 2009. Accessed September 19, 2009.

7. Health Industries Research Companies. Leading disease management organizations. http://hirc.com/files/public/Update_Dis_Mgmt_su08_0.pdf. Published Summer 2008. Accessed September 19, 2009.

8. Mattke S, Seid M, Ma S. Evidence for the effect of disease management: is $1 billion a year a good investment? *Am J Manag Care.* 2007;13(12): 670–676.

9. Sidorov J, Shull R, Tomcavage J, Girolami S, Lawton N, Harris R. Does diabetes disease management save money and improve outcomes? A report of simultaneous short-term savings and quality improvement associated with a health maintenance organization–sponsored disease management program among patients fulfilling health employer data and information set criteria. *Diabetes Care.* 2002;25(4):684–689.

10. Villagra VG, Ahmed T. Effectiveness of a disease management program for patients with diabetes. *Health Aff.* 2004;23(4):255–266.

11. Geyman JP. Disease management: panacea, another false hope, or something in between? *Ann Fam Med.* 2007;5(3):257–260.

12. Meyer J, Smith BM; Health Management Associates. *Chronic Disease Management: Evidence of Predictable Savings.* http://www.healthmanagement.com/files/chronic%20disease%20savings%20report%20November%20final.pdf. Published November 2008. Accessed September 19, 2009.

13. Linden A, Adams JL, Roberts N. An assessment of the total population approach for evaluating disease management program effectiveness. *Dis Manag.* 2003;6(2):93–102.

14. The Kaiser Family Foundation. Medicare Fact Sheet. http://www.kff.org/medicare/upload/2052-12.pdf. Published April 2009. Accessed September 19, 2009.

15. Bott DM, Kapp MC, Johnson LB, Magno LM. Disease management for chronically ill beneficiaries in traditional Medicare. *Health Aff.* 2009; 28(1):86–98.

16. Foote SM. Next steps: how can Medicare accelerate the pace of improving chronic care? *Health Aff.* 2009;28(1):99–102.

17. McCall N, Cromwell J, Urato C, Rabiner D. *Evaluation of Phase I of the Medicare Health Support Pilot Program under Traditional Fee-for-Service Medicare: 18-Month Interim Analysis.* http://www.cms.hhs.gov/reports/downloads/MHS_Second_Report_to_Congress_October_2008.pdf. Published October 2008. Accessed September 19, 2009.

18. California Health Care Foundation. Disease Management in Medicaid. 2004 [chart pack]. California Health Care Foundation Web site. http://www.chcf.org/documents/policy/Disease ManagementInMedicaid2004.pdf. Accessed September 19, 2009.

19. Smith DG. CMS Letter to State Medicaid Director [letter]. http://www.cms.hhs.gov/smdl/downloads/smd022504.pdf. Published February 25, 2004. Accessed September 19, 2009.

20. Rosenbaum S, Markus A, Sheer J, Harty ME. Negotiating the new health system at ten: Medicaid managed care and the use of disease management purchasing. Hamilton, NJ: Center for Health Care Strategies Inc; May 2008. http://www.chcs.org/usr_doc/Negotiating_the_New_Health_System_at_Ten.pdf. Accessed September 19, 2009.

21. Bella M, Goldsmith S, Somers S. Medicaid best buys: promising reform strategies for governors. Center for Health Care Strategies. http://www.chcs.org/publications3960/publications_show.htm?doc_id=434341. Published December 2006. Accessed on September 19, 2009.

22. White C, Fisher C, Mendelson D, Schulman KA; Health Strategies Consultancy LLC, Duke University. *State Medicaid Disease Management: Lessons Learned from Florida.* http://www.avalerehealth.net/research/docs/Duke_DM-Florida.pdf. Published March 2005. Accessed September 19, 2009.

23. Washington state Medicaid: an evolution in care delivery [case study]. Center for Health Care Strategies, Inc. http://www.chcs.org/publications3960/publications_show.htm?doc_id=759948. Published December 2008. Accessed September 19, 2009.

24. Wagner EH, Austin BT, Von Korff M. Organizing care for patients with chronic illness. *Milbank Q.* 1996;74(4):511–544.

25. Bodenheimer T, Wagner EH, Grumbach K. Improving primary care for patients with chronic illness. *JAMA.* 2002:288(14):1775–1779.

26. Bodenheimer T, Wagner EH, Grumbach K. Improving primary care for patients with chronic illness: the chronic care model, Part 2. *JAMA.* 2002;288(15):1909–1914.

27. Cretin S, Shortell SM, Keeler EB. An evaluation of collaborative interventions to improve chronic illness care: framework and study design. *Eval Rev.* 2004;28(1):28–51.

28. Pearson ML, Wu S, Schaefer J, et al. Assessing the implementation of the chronic care model in

quality improvement collaboratives. *Health Serv Res.* 2005;40(4):978–996.

29. Landon BE, Hicks LS, O'Malley AJ, et al. Improving the management of chronic disease at community health centers. *N Engl J Med.* 2007; 356(9):921–934.

30. Institute for Healthcare Improvement. *The Breakthrough Series: IHI's Collaborative Model for Achieving Breakthrough Improvement.* Boston, MA: Institute for Healthcare Improvement; 2003. http://www.ihi.org/IHI/Results/WhitePapers/ TheBreakthroughSeriesIHIsCollaborativeModel forAchieving%20BreakthroughImprovement. htm. Accessed September 19, 2009.

31. Coleman K, Austin BT, Brach C, Wagner EH. Evidence on the Chronic Care Model in the new millennium. *Health Aff.* 2009;28(1):75–85.

32. Wagner EH, Sandhu N, Newton KM, McCulloch DK, Ramsey SD, Grothaus LC. Effect of improved glycemic control on health care costs and utilization. *JAMA.* 2001;285(2):182–189.

33. Wallace PJ. Physician involvement in disease management as part of the CCM. *Health Care Financ Rev.* 2005;27(1):19–31.

34. Fireman B, Bartlett J, Selby J. Can disease management reduce health care costs by improving quality? *Health Aff (Millwood).* 2004;23(6): 63–75.

35. The Kaiser Family Foundation. Community care of North Carolina: putting health reform ideas into practice in Medicaid. Kaiser Commission on Medicaid and the Uninsured. http://www.kff. org/medicaid/7899.cfm. Published May 2009. Accessed September 19, 2009.

RESEARCH AND DEVELOPMENT IN POPULATION HEALTH

Chapter 15

R. DIXON THAYER, RAYMOND J. FABIUS, MD, AND SHARON FRAZEE, PhD

Executive Summary

Measurements are essential to track the health of people, worksites, and communities

Research and development in population health is a challenging but potentially rewarding experience. Fortunately, those that enter the field today can learn from the early efforts of population health pioneers. Seminal works by Dee Edington[1] and John Wennberg[2] have provided an understanding of the natural trend toward illness over time and the impact of variations in care. Yet there is much more work to be done before standardized, effective programs keep the healthy well, successfully minimize health risks, reduce the spread of acute illness, mitigate the burden of illness from chronic disease, and sufficiently comfort those with catastrophic and terminal conditions. Using the best experimental research techniques for research and development, with rigorous measurement of outcomes, we can be confident that the next generation of population health programming will markedly improve on what has been accomplished thus far.

Learning Objectives

1. Appreciate the different views of population health from the multiple constituencies in health care.
2. Be familiar with key elements and tasks associated with effective research processes and development tasks.
3. Analyze the various approaches to research and measurement in population health.
4. Mitigate the challenges of population health research.
5. Discuss the five segments of population health.

Key Words

acute illness

bias

body mass index (BMI)

catastrophic illness

chronic disease

double blind confirmation

effectiveness

efficiency

functional status

health coach

Health Risk Assessment (HRA)

predictive modeling

primary research

proof of concept

regression to the mean

scientific method

secondary research

severity adjustment

spectrum of illness

systematic process optimization (SPO)

trend analysis

INTRODUCTION

The vision of population health is healthy people, healthy worksites, and healthy communities. If the health status of a population is to be improved, then objectives for health and measurement of progress toward these objectives must be identified. The understanding and measurement of population health is supported by work done in the public health arena and the regulatory space of occupational health.[3] Organizations, such as the Centers for Disease Control and Prevention (CDC) and the American College of Occupational and Environmental Medicine, have developed community and workplace health metrics in response to legislative and regulatory mandates. Measures of progress toward improvements in population health should include various clinical indicators including process and outcome measures, assessment of patient and provider satisfaction with health care, functional status and quality of life, economic and healthcare utilization indicators, and impact on known population health disparities.

Process measures may be used to assess the delivery pathway of population health services. These measures might include: percentage of **Health Risk Assessments (HRA)** completed by a population compared to performance benchmarks or the rate of screening colonoscopies for those members of the population older than age 50 years. Clinical process indicators may also reflect the pathway of disease, injuries, and population risk factors. For example, one can track the average number of risk factors within a particular population over time. Measures of patient or provider satisfaction can focus on the consumer's or clinician's perception and assessment of value of a service or the impact of the intervention.

Outcome measures are quantifiable expressions of the desirable effects of an intervention that are to be achieved by a certain time. For example, Healthy People is a national initiative to advance a comprehensive health promotion and disease prevention agenda, which includes 467 population-based objectives.[4] While most population health improvement programs are not as ambitious in terms of measurement and improvement, they do need to focus on specific outcomes they are attempting to achieve. Accurate assessment of outcomes requires both numerator and denominator data to allow measurement of baseline health status and improvements over time. Outcome measures might include healthcare costs, percentage of participants who achieve normal blood pressure, or percentage of overweight individuals who reduce their **body mass index (BMI)**. Ideally, outcome data from one population should be comparable to other populations to facilitate benchmarking and to allow data to be aggregated at various levels. This requires agreement on the outcomes to be measured and possibly the technology to support transparency. Measurement should be longitudinal and comparable instruments should be applied across measurement periods to support **trend analysis**. The frequency at which each measure is collected should be determined by the interval over which meaningful change can be expected and linked to long-term, intermediate, and near-term objectives for health programs. While counting health events such as illnesses and injuries is a common activity in both medical and public health practice, the systematic use of health data to improve population health requires measuring lifestyle and behavioral risk factors as well as the burden of chronic diseases in populations.[5]

This isn't easy! Efforts to quantify the impact of interventions on the health status of populations have led to both an increased realization of this challenge as well as a growing awareness of opportunities for improvement. The old adage that you cannot improve what you do not measure definitely applies to population health improvement programs. However, as described in a previous chapter, population health measurement efforts are often inconsistently applied. This has hampered the ability of researchers to produce outcomes that can be generalized to the larger population by providing outcomes that are universally accepted by employers and other payers as to the impact of population health improvement programs. The importance of producing research that creates evidence of impact or "proof of concept" is of extreme importance.

This chapter will provide an overview of measurement techniques, challenges to research, and the viewpoints of different constituencies in health care, as well as research approaches applicable across the **spectrum of illness**. In addition, this chapter will describe development techniques and the challenges of establishing effective population health management programs.

EFFECTIVE POPULATION HEALTH RESEARCH

Research can be described as any systematic investigation to establish facts. It is carried out to increase understanding of fundamental drivers and responses to drivers of behavior: that is, to isolate *cause and effect*.[6] In population health, research is usually focused on understanding how different actions affect behavior change, and how those changes influence population health and wellness. There are two basic kinds of research:

Primary research involves the collection and analysis of original source data, which is collected specifically for the research study.

Secondary research involves the analysis of existing data and prior research information for possible new uses or conclusions.[7]

The **scientific method** provides a framework for conducting research. The steps of the method include (1) identifying a topic, (2) generating a hypothesis, (3) defining a data collection and analysis strategy, (4) gathering data, (5) testing the hypothesis, and (6) making decisions based on the results. Whether applied to primary or secondary research, the scientific method provides structure for a research project.

Additional research in the area of population health is greatly needed. The upward trend of healthcare costs in the United States challenges the competitive nature of American business.[8] Establishing evidence-based solutions that improve the **effectiveness** and **efficiency** of care delivery will help advance healthcare delivery for everyone.

While there are a number of possible approaches to population health research, studies typically utilize one of four research designs: **double blind confirmation**, trend analysis, comparative effectiveness, or **predictive modeling**. Double blind confirmation is the quintessential research approach to establishing a causal link between intervention and outcome based on severity matched, double blind study methodology. In this approach, members of a population, referred to as a cohort, are matched by their relative level of illness and separated into experiment and control groups. A new treatment or service is provided to the experiment group while the control group receives usual care. After a sufficient period of time, determined by the research team, progress of the experiment and control groups is compared. After controlling for external factors, differences can be attributed to the new intervention. Cohort matched double blind experiment and control studies remain the hallmark of population health; however, these studies are expensive and often impractical. The pharmaceutical industry has traditionally applied this methodology to demonstrate the effectiveness of new medications when compared to placebo or, less frequently, to proven drug alternatives. In the pharmaceutical context, the results can support efficacy, superiority to present recommended treatment, or equal potency to standard therapy; the latter example refers to so-called "me too" drugs that provide no distinct advantages over current therapies.

Trend analysis is a study design that is more common, less expensive, and often a more practical approach. This design allows study of the same cohort of a population throughout a new treatment or service in order to determine whether the new intervention had an impact. The approach is sometimes referred to as a "Time 1 versus Time 2" study. Because this is not a double blind, illness burden matched design, researchers are less able to establish causality, but associations can be drawn. This method allows the comparison of a population cohort at two different points in time, generally before and after an intervention. An example might be the assessment of an obese population before and after participating in a weight management program. When using this method, researchers have to consider the impact of **regression to the mean**. Generally speaking, populations of patients who are dealing with significant illness will improve over time without treatment. This challenges researchers to prove that the *intervention* produced a greater impact than would have been observed after the normal healing process.

Comparative effectiveness and predictive modeling are two additional research designs that can be applied to population health. Comparative effectiveness studies compare two or more different treatment approaches. For example, researchers have compared balloon angiography to arterial stenting against by-pass. This quasi-experimental model attempts to utilize a practical setting and, at the same time, approximate the precision and validity of cohort matched experimental and control methods. This is generally accomplished by comparing the impact of a population health program on a group of people who participated to a severity-adjusted cohort who did not participate. As the size of the comparative groups increases, the need for **severity adjustment** decreases. Smaller comparative studies of control and experimental groups require this adjustment because the burden of illness may be significantly different between groups, thus influencing the outcome. This is particularly true when there is a known selection **bias** between the two groups. To mitigate bias, comparisons can be made between local organizations—one where a new intervention is piloted and the other where a traditional approach is taken.

Predictive modeling is an approach that uses existing data to predict future behavior or consequences. This concept may best be illustrated through asking three primary questions: "How are we doing? How can we make this better? What if?"[9] The "*what if*" question can help formulate and pretest hypotheses about improvement. Data analysis is used both to generate mathematical estimates of current state (how we are doing) and to run possible alternate scenarios (what if). Findings from such modeling exercises allow researchers to anticipate consequences of an intervention on a population. Altering the trend predicted is an important goal of population health research and development.

Development can be described as a systematic process to transform research into actions. These actions can take many forms, including programs, procedures, and protocol design–redesign; products and services innovation; and behavior change program design. There are many different development approaches from which to choose. Two primary categories of development processes to consider are new concept development and **systematic process optimization (SPO)**. The former is often applied to the exploration and development of new products and services while SPO has been used to reduce the number defects (suboptimization) in an existing process. New concept development processes consist of five primary steps. The first is to *search* for unmet needs. The second is to *explore* alternative possible solutions (to the unmet need). The third is to *develop* the best solution. Fourth is to *apply* and assess the developed solution in the marketplace. The fifth (and final) step is to then *maximize* the impact and penetration of this new product or service in the marketplace. This process can be summarized as the "SEDAM Process."

Existing process improvement can be achieved via point-in-time research; however, continuous improvement via continuous process tracking and measurement will ensure organic culture of improvement. Systematic process optimization utilizes statistical measurement of current processes and procedures and looks for opportunities to improve them within the current program. This method has been shown to be very effective in reducing defects and error rates in repeatable process steps. Six Sigma, Lean, and TPS (Toyota Production Systems) have become well-documented approaches to simultaneous improvement of both effectiveness and efficiency. These processes can be categorized as Systematic Process Optimization (SPO) tools. All of these industry-based approaches have been successfully applied to health care.[10,11]

Development process programs have also demonstrated the power of creating common frameworks for continuous improvement that translate into three keys to success for effective population health program development. By engaging the entire community in a consistent process and by using these techniques, one can garner three results:

issue ownership (by all core constituents): Research must be compelling, accessible, and relevant to each participant in order to develop true ownership.

champions for change (by key respected and trusted figures in the specific population, as well as the population at large): This point is best illustrated by the adage *what gets measured gets done or improved*. It is important to be clear about who are the respected champions and cheerleaders for a population's health in a specific community. It is equally important to be clear on how the champions will measure success. Research must be made clear, compelling, accessible, and relevant to each key champion.

convergence of constituencies: Aligned measurement approaches (across the five constituencies) are key to driving convergent behaviors by each. How each constituent defines success determines how it will be measured, and how success is measured will drive the systems, processes, and behaviors within each constituency. If key definitions and measures are aligned at the outset, then measurement and relevant reporting will improve success by driving convergence (as opposed to random divergence).

STATE OF THE ART OF POPULATION HEALTH MEASUREMENT

Systematic measurement of improvement in the health status of populations is a key component of research and development. **Proof of concept** refers to demonstrating the impact of a program or product; measures may include effectiveness, efficiency, or both. Efficiency studies are increasingly in demand as global healthcare inflation continues to outpace general inflation. These efforts explore ways to deliver improvements less expensively, such as using technology or substituting less costly clinical resources (e.g., nurse practitioners for physicians). Examples of the types of outcomes studied include the impact of a program on reducing the frequency or cost of hospitalization, the impact on absence from work, cost and frequency of diagnostic services, and the change in use of cost-effective pharmaceuticals or shifts to generic drugs. These types of efficiency studies often analyze utilization data, such as health and disability claims, laboratory data, or pharmacy information.

In contrast to the economic focus of efficiency studies, effectiveness studies seek to determine better ways to improve care outcomes. These studies often rely on the aggregation of data extracted from medical records and frequently include laboratory and pharmacy data. One could argue that there is a sensitive balance between efficiency and effectiveness. While these two system measures would ideally be aligned—that is, maximizing efficiency would be associated with greater effectiveness—systems that attempt to see too many patients per hour will fail to produce the desired results.

Assessment of the value of population health efforts includes return on investment (ROI) studies, as well as capture of less tangible impacts. Increasingly, the comprehensive assessment of population health programs includes the satisfaction of key constituents, including patients, caregivers, providers, and purchasers. Measuring perceived value from multiple perspectives is crucial to the development of lasting, successful programs. **Functional status** trumps survival rates from the perspective of most patients and purchasers of care. The ties between health and productivity cannot be denied. Capturing parameters, such as absenteeism and disability, can augment the research and development of population health products and services.[12]

THE VIEW FROM THE FIVE CONSTITUENCIES OF HEALTH CARE

When embarking on the research and development of population health initiatives, it is important to understand the perspectives of the key constituents of healthcare delivery. From the *patient's* perspective, ease of access to programs and services that can produce tangible benefits with minimal inconvenience and expense is of interest. Ideally, these programs can be delivered or facilitated by trusted, caring clinicians and improve patient self-care and feelings of self-efficacy. *Providers* are most concerned with applying evidence-based guidelines and producing clinical outcome improvements. They rely on clinical measures, such as biometrics (e.g., weight, blood pressure, lab values) and patient self-report. *Payers,* such as health plans, pursue studies utilizing claims data to demonstrate efficiency gains. *Purchasers*, especially employers, increasingly demand evidence of improved functional status and reduced absenteeism, presenteeism, and disability. *Suppliers,* such as the pharmaceutical and durable medical equipment industries, apply population health research to demonstrate the value of their drugs and devices.

CLASSES OF MEASURES

One of the simplest ways to categorize measures is based on the work of Donabedian, who described a framework of structure, process, and outcomes.[13] (See Chapter 5.) Without much difficulty, one can tie structural and process components to better results. These are called structural and process indicators of improved outcomes. It is often the case that structural and process indicators are in fact easier to measure than are patient outcomes. For example, because we know that patients who are cared for by a primary care provider in a trusted relationship over an extended time have better outcomes, it is reasonable to study the effectiveness of programs that drive more members of a population into medical homes. Additionally, research has shown that improved engagement and retention rates of disease management programs can be used as an upstream process indicator for improved outcomes.[14,15] Another example would be to study the results of a program that improved the rate of colonoscopies, knowing that this will lead to improved outcomes.

TECHNIQUES OF MEASUREMENT

Generally speaking, research and development in population health draw from a measurement toolkit. One of the easiest tools to deploy is a satisfaction survey. Valuable information can be gained by assessing the perceived value of a program or service from the perspective of as many constituents as possible, while always starting with the patient. They can be questioned on many levels, from specific improvement in control of a disease process to a self-assessment of general well-being. They can report on improved convenience or functional status. More recently, with the use of health risk appraisals and health and productivity tools, self-assessment and self-reporting are becoming fundamental components of population health research and development. The future may rely increasingly on personal health records (PHRs), which may be tied electronically to electronic health records (EHRs). Surveys requesting patients' evaluations of care providers are also being utilized. For example, patients are being asked to comment on the performance of their doctors or delivery systems. Providers are also being asked to evaluate their patients' compliance with and adherence to treatment plans.

When focusing on efficiency studies, the use of claims data is foundational. If the purpose of a population health research study is to reduce medical expenditure or demonstrate a reduced need for intensive medical services, the data warehouse of claims-based information is a key data source. Health plans and health informatics organizations are expert at evaluating the impact of programs and services based on hospitalization rates, total hospital days, and the use of emergency room resources and specialty services. Health plan claims data can also demonstrate the use of recommended services by a population, such as screenings and preventive services, or such analyses may reveal overuse of questionable treatments. In fact, claims-based studies can even measure the impact of health services that are misused, such as knee surgery for arthritic patients. Pharmacy benefit management organizations can use their claims information to illuminate the impact of medication use and adherence. Linking claims, lab, and pharmacy data can produce elegant measurement of the burden of illness on populations. This becomes particularly important when studying the differential impact of programs and services between populations that are not severity-matched control and experimental groupings.

Medical records, whether electronic or paper-based, are a rich source of data that can be used to assess the need for new population-based programs and services. In both cases, inter-reviewer reliability is very important, especially when data are being extracted from patient records. Aggregate data from electronic medical records offer great promise for improved accuracy and real-time results.

Tangible clinical results of population-based research and development can be obtained through biometrics, such as urine and blood tests. These results can demonstrate wellness, as indicated by a low cholesterol level; indicate a risk, such as a high blood pressure reading; or indicate control of a chronic illness, such as an Hgb A1C test for diabetics.

Disability reports track the incidence, cause, and cost of short-term and long-term cases. This can give an employer a measure of the most compromised cohort of their employee population. From a research and development standpoint, this population is particularly attractive because of the potential for significant improvement in functional status and return to work. It must be mentioned that there are other factors that influence disability, such as job satisfaction and recent job performance. Job dissatisfaction and poor performance are measures of occupation or career wellness. Robust return to work efforts that include a broad spectrum of modified work options are more likely to return employees with moderate illness back to work sooner, reducing the perceived magnitude of the catastrophic or disabled sector. This emphasizes the multifactorial nature of population health research and development.

CHALLENGES TO SUCCESSFUL RESEARCH

Bias is a form of systematic error in research; it is a formidable challenge. There is concern about selection bias in participant cohorts, clinical and administrative bias by those who provide the intervention, and even publication bias because journals are much more eager to accept manuscripts that demonstrate effectiveness. As discussed previously, double blind cohort matched experimental models offer the best defense against much of this bias. Importantly, reputable journals are publishing reports of efforts in population health that did not have a great impact. Publication of negative, as well as positive, findings contributes to the evidence base for population health and supports continued research and development toward more effective interventions.

Time can be a significant challenge to effective research as well. Demonstration of the true effectiveness of population-based programs often requires several years. Many programs have claimed success in changing people's behavior to stop smoking or lose weight. The test of true success requires tracking these participants over an extended time to record the long-term maintenance of this change. Some disease state complications also require years to develop; therefore, adequate time is necessary to demonstrate their effectiveness in disease prevention.[16]

Confounding influences are difficult to eliminate in population health studies. A health prevention or disease management program is markedly affected by an individual's community or residence, media influences, the treating healthcare providers involved, economic status, gender, language spoken, and cultural beliefs. It is nearly impossible to eliminate these influences, although a greater sample size in both the experimental and the control group may allow researchers to measure and statistically control their effects.

As discussed earlier, unrecognized or uneven illness severity and regression to the mean are key challenges to conducting credible research and evaluating pilot projects. Using severity adjustment techniques and tracking experimental and control groups over time are the best ways to deal with these issues.

ESTABLISHING GOALS

When conducting research in population health or developing programs, it is important to establish clear goals. This can best be accomplished by establishing baseline measures and determining what may be changed under ideal circumstances. It is then important to engage in a crosswalk from that baseline to these "stretch" or ideal goals. By doing this, one can develop a pilot program to test whether the intervention steps were successful in achieving the goals.

Goals can be based on government or nationally respected efforts such as Healthy People 2020, the National Quality Forum, or the National Committee for Quality Assurance's HEDIS measures. Establishing quantitative benchmarks is an effective approach to goal setting. These benchmarks establish the base result against which improvement will be measured objectively. Benchmarks are derived from three primary sources; history (by measuring participants' personal best), aspirational (what program designers hope to accomplish), or assigned (e.g., according to an established goal such as those contained in Healthy People 2020), or another cohort (others such as a control or best practice).

THE FIVE SEGMENTS OF POPULATION HEALTH STATUS

Research and development in population health can cover the spectrum from wellness to **catastrophic illness**. The best population health efforts attempt to impact the health status of all segments of a patient–consumer community. Such programs try to keep the well free of disease while reducing the illness burden of others.

Increasingly, wellness is broadly viewed. There are many domains of wellness, including physical, emotional, spiritual, intellectual, environmental, and social wellness. Increasingly, research and development in the domain of workforce health and productivity provides measures for the multiple dimensions of wellness.

Beyond wellness research and development, population health researchers have also studied the at-risk population and efforts that have been exerted to mitigate health risks. The premise underlying such studies is that certain risks can be reduced or eliminated before the onset of disease, especially **chronic disease**, and that risk mitigation can markedly improve the long-term health status of populations. To accomplish risk reduction, great efforts in the population health industry have been dedicated to the development and refinement of health risk appraisals and biometric screening. **Health coaches** and care managers have specialized in assisting cohorts of patients to reduce identified risks, such as high cholesterol, obesity, drinking and driving, sedentary lifestyle, and smoking. Research has demonstrated that patients carrying multiple risks have higher medical expenditures and reduced work performance. The mitigation of health risks can result in lower healthcare costs and improved functionality.

The next segment of population health status is **acute illness**. This is usually defined as sickness that is short-lived and typically resolves without complications. Examples include ear infections, sore throats, flu, intestinal infections, and acute low back pain. While acute illnesses receive less attention in population health research than chronic or life-threatening health issues, they can have a significant impact on the health of a population, as evidenced by the preparation that countries, states, counties, and local employers and institutions undertake to prepare for and prevent pandemic flu.

Efforts to reduce the illness burden of the chronically ill segment have been characterized as disease management (DM). Common chronic illnesses that have been targeted for research and development of population health programs include diabetes, coronary heart disease, asthma, emphysema, congestive heart failure, and depression. Research has demonstrated that a large percentage of people enrolled in disease management programs are living with multiple diseases and conditions. Programs dedicated to helping patients with complex and rare conditions, such as hemophilia and renal failure, are promising and they provide an important service to patients and their families as they navigate the complex American healthcare system.[17] These programs have included referrals to local, regional, or national centers of excellence.

Lastly, population health research and development efforts have included programs to ease the burden of illness among the most fragile cohort, those with catastrophic illness. Included in this group are persons with end-stage cancer, stroke and trauma victims, children with genetic complexes, and others requiring continuous nursing assistance. From an economic standpoint, health plans, insurers, and employers have often defined these population segments by the economic costs associated with their care. Catastrophic population segments are those whose healthcare costs exceed $25,000–50,000 in a year. They normally comprise only 1–2% of a covered population. There are individualized case management programs that have demonstrated good return on investment (ROI) for interventions with catastrophically ill cohorts.

CONCLUSIONS

Research and development within population health integrates clinical medicine, health informatics, and creative innovation. The research process utilizes a variety of techniques of measurement to demonstrate impact, including satisfaction surveys, self-reported health appraisals and functional status, claims databases, and clinical records. When researchers use well-respected research approaches, such as double blind or comparative effectiveness methods, it is not difficult to produce proof of concept results. Understanding potential biases and the normal trends of illness within populations can reduce the misinterpretation of outcomes. Increasingly precise and sophisticated biometric analysis can both compare the past to the present and validate improvement in future performance against the predicted performance. Such techniques can shorten the window of time required to reach statistical significance and move a project into mainstream production faster.

Pilot efforts can bridge research and development. Those that demonstrate improvements in the effectiveness or efficiency of existing or new population health products or services are worthy of further development and, in some cases, large-scale application in the marketplace. When designing and producing new products and services, great care must be taken throughout the process to appreciate the viewpoint of all constituents.

STUDY AND DISCUSSION QUESTIONS

1. Is it more valuable to assess the effectiveness or the efficiency of population health programs?
2. Compare and contrast the different views of the five constituencies of healthcare delivery. Why is this important to know when conducting research or development in population health?
3. What are the key elements and tasks of the research process and development programs?
4. How can you mitigate the challenges of population health research?
5. What are the five segments of population health? Why is this important to know when conducting research or development in population health?

SUGGESTED READINGS AND WEB SITES

READINGS

Edington DW. *Zero Trends: Health as a Serious Economic Strategy.* Ann Arbor, MI: University of Michigan Health Management Research Center; 2009.

Kane RL, ed. *Understanding Health Care Outcomes Research.* 2nd ed. Sudbury, MA: Jones and Bartlett Publishers; 2006.

Kessler RC, Stang PE, eds. *Health & Work Productivity: Making the Business Case for Quality Health Care.* Chicago, IL: University of Chicago Press; 2006.

Leutzinger J, Sullivan S, Chapman L, eds. *Platinum Book: Practical Applications of the Health & Productivity Management Model.* Omaha, NE: Institute for Health and Productivity Management (IHPM); 2004.

Lynch WD, Gardner HH. *Aligning Incentives, Information, and Choice: How to Optimize Health and Human Capital Performance.* Cheyenne, WY: Health as Human Capital Foundation; 2008:49–50.

Solberg LI, Mosser G, McDonald S. The three faces of performance measurement: improvement, accountability, and research. *Jt Comm J Qual Improv.* 1997;23(3): 135–147.

WEB SITES

Employer Measures of Productivity, Absence and Quality (EMPAQ): http://www.empaq.org
Health Enhancement Research Organization (HERO): http://www.the-hero.org/
Institute for Health and Productivity Management: http://www.ihpm.org

REFERENCES

1. Edington DW. *Zero Trends: Health as a Serious Economic Strategy.* Ann Arbor, MI: University of Michigan Health Management Research Center; 2009.

2. Wennberg JE, Fisher ES, Sharp SM, et al. *The Care of Patients with Severe Chronic Illness.* Lebanon, NH: The Center for the Evaluative Clinical Sciences, Dartmouth Medical School; 2006. http://www.dartmouthatlas.org/. Accessed June 11, 2009.

3. Szreter S. The population health approach in historical perspective. *Am J Public Health.* 2003;93(3):421–431.

4. US Department of Health and Human Services. *Healthy People 2010.* 2nd ed. With Understanding and Improving Health and Objectives for Improving Health. 2 vols. Washington, DC: US Government Printing Office; 2000. http://www.health.gov/healthypeople/document. Accessed July 5, 2009.

5. Yen L, Schultz AB, Schnueringer E, Edington DW. Financial costs due to excess health risks among active employees of a utility company. *J Occup Environ Med.* 2006;48(9):896–905.

6. Davenport TH, Harris JG. *Competing on Analytics: The New Science of Winning.* Boston: Harvard Business School Press; 2007.

7. Lentz CA, ed. *The Delphi Primer: Doing Real-World or Academic Research Using a Mixed-Method Approach.* Las Vegas, NV: The Lentz Leadership Institute; 2006. *The Refractive Thinker*; vol 2.

8. Shortliffe EH, Cimino JJ. *Biomedical Informatics: Computer Applications in Health Care and Biomedicine.* New York, NY: Springer; 2006.

9. Towers Perrin. *2008 Health Care Cost Survey.* New York, NY: Towers Perrin; 2008. http://www.towersperrin.com/tp/getwebcachedoc?webc=HRS/USA/2008/200801/hccs_2008.pdf. Accessed November 24, 2009.

10. Lloyd DH II, Holsenback JE. The use of Six Sigma in health care operations: application and opportunity. *Acad Health Care Manage J.* 2006;2: 41–50.

11. Lean in Healthcare. In: *Lean Administration: Case Studies in Leadership and Improvement.* New York, NY: Productivity Press; 2007:90–105.

12. Change Agent Work Group. *Employer Health Asset Management: A Roadmap for Improving the Health of Your Employees and Your Organization.* Minneapolis, MN: Change Agent Work Group; 2009. http://www.aon.com/attachments/improving_health.pdf. Accessed November 24, 2009.

13. Donabedian A. *The Definition of Quality and Approaches to its Assessment.* Ann Arbor, MI: Health Administration Press; 1980.

14. Frazee SG, Kirkpatrick P, Fabius R, Chimera J. Leveraging the trusted clinician: documenting disease management program enrollment. *Dis Manag.* 2007;10(1):16–29.

15. Frazee SG, Sherman B, Fabius R, et al. Leveraging the trusted clinician: increasing retention in disease

management through integrated program delivery. *Popul Health Manag.* 2008;11(5):247–254.

16. Knight K, Badamgarav E, Henning JM. A systematic review of diabetes disease management programs. *Am Journal Manag Care.* 2005;11(4): 242–250.

17. Rula E, Hobgood A, Hamlet KS, Zeng H, Montijo MF. Maximizing care management savings through advanced total population targeting. *Outcomes Insights Health Manag.* 2009; 1(2). http://medicarehealthsupport.com/success/library.aspx?id=188.

Chapter 16

POPULATION HEALTH EDUCATION

BROOKE SALZMAN, MD, JAMES D. PLUMB, MD, MPH, AND RICHARD WENDER, MD

Executive Summary

Teach what we practice

Flaws in education for health professions both reflect and contribute to the failures in our current healthcare delivery system. The Institute of Medicine (IOM), in its report *Health Professions Education: A Bridge to Quality* (HPE), has provided compelling evidence that our current approach to educating health professionals falls woefully short of preparing individuals to address the central needs of a healthcare workforce in a transformed delivery system.[1] In 2004, the Healthy People Curriculum Task Force emphasized that "an essential element of any effort to change a health care system must be the education of future clinicians who will practice new approaches in new contexts."[2] Failure to fundamentally alter health professions education will constitute a profound obstacle to realizing actual transformation of healthcare delivery and improving the health of our population.

Education for clinicians traditionally focuses on the medical conditions acutely affecting individuals and fails to incorporate principles of population health and prevention that are necessary to achieve a greater impact on our nation's health. Similar to healthcare reform, health education reform requires fundamental redesign. Education for health professionals needs to expand beyond the traditional biomedical focus and integrate new skills and approaches that support the health of populations. In doing so, education reform will play a key role in "transforming the nation's health care delivery system from one that historically has focused on care for acute illness—at the expense of chronic condition management, coordination of care across settings, and disease prevention—to one that values patient-centered care, quality improvement, and resource conservation."[3]

Learning Objectives

1. Explain the vital role of educating health professionals and preparing the health profession workforce to both create and reflect transformed models of care that address current problems in our healthcare delivery system.
2. Identify essential knowledge and skills required by health professionals in a transformed healthcare delivery system.
3. Discuss key concepts and methods of population health to frame education reform for health professions.

Key Words

core competencies   interdisciplinary teams

INTRODUCTION

The need for healthcare reform in the United States is a moral imperative. For every healthcare worker, promoting health for all is an absolute social responsibility. Yet despite the good intentions and best efforts of clinicians from all disciplines, healthcare administrators, and other stakeholders, the U.S. healthcare system is disjointed, inefficient, and ineffective in promoting the health of populations and in providing full value for the resources invested.[4]

The United States devotes enormous resources to medical care—well over 50% more per person than any other nation—yet it ranks 29th in the world in life expectancy and 36th in infant mortality.[5] In addition, deep disparities in health outcomes and access to care exist in the United States. One example was presented by former Surgeon General David Satcher, who estimated that the "black–white mortality gap" results in more than 80,000 excess preventable deaths each year among African Americans.[6] Furthermore, the Institute of Medicine (IOM) estimates as many as 24,000 people die each year in the United States because they lack health insurance.[7]

While the need for healthcare reform remains uncontested, debate regarding the scope and specific elements of reform continues. In general, healthcare reform efforts address two major aspects of healthcare delivery: reform our healthcare insurance system, with the goal of broadening coverage, and transform our healthcare delivery. The call for healthcare delivery reform is derived from the recognition that our current approaches to providing care fail to ensure safety and quality, and contribute to health disparities and excessive costs of care. Most proposals for healthcare delivery reform call for realigning payment incentives to promote quality, leveraging skill sets of healthcare professionals, relying on evidence-based systems of care, and ensuring that care is provided by **interdisciplinary teams** of prepared professionals. However, the IOM, in its *Health Professions Education: A Bridge to*

Quality, has provided compelling evidence that our current approach to educating health professionals falls woefully short of preparing individuals to address the central needs of a healthcare workforce in a transformed delivery system.[1] Failure to fundamentally alter health professions education will constitute a profound obstacle to realizing actual transformation of healthcare delivery and improving the health of our population.

Flaws in health professions education both reflect and contribute to the failures in our delivery system. In 2004, the Healthy People Curriculum Task Force emphasized that "an essential element of any effort to change a health care system must be the education of future clinicians who will practice new approaches in new contexts."[2] Education for clinicians traditionally centers on the medical condition(s) acutely affecting individuals and fails to incorporate principles of population health and prevention that are necessary to achieve a larger impact on our nation's health. Similar to healthcare reform, health education reform requires fundamental redesign. Education for health professionals needs to expand beyond the traditional biomedical focus and integrate new skills and approaches that support the health of populations. In doing so, education reform will play a key role in "transforming the nation's health care delivery system from one that historically has focused on care for acute illness—at the expense of chronic condition management, coordination of care across settings, and disease prevention—to one that values patient-centered care, quality improvement, and resource conservation."[3]

This chapter will describe some of the major shortcomings in the current education of health professionals and suggest how education may be redesigned utilizing a population health approach to both create and reflect positive changes in the larger healthcare system, as well as to better prepare and support health professionals to provide care and leadership in new healthcare delivery models.

THE NEED FOR HEALTH PROFESSIONAL EDUCATION REFORM

The inadequacy of health professional education to adapt to a changing healthcare environment and to address evolving societal needs and expectations has been well established.[1,4,8–16] Multiple reports have described deficiencies in the preparation of future health professionals to deal with major contemporary realities that include suboptimal and inconsistent healthcare quality and safety, unsustainable rising healthcare costs, rapidly expanding science and technology, increasing public accountability, escalating burden of chronic disease, and widening disparities in health and health care.[16] The IOM reported in 2001 that "clinical education [for health professionals] simply has not kept pace with or been responsive enough to shifting patient demographics and desires, changing health system expectations, evolving practice requirements and staffing arrangements, new information, a focus on improving quality, or new technologies."[8]

Several leading organizations have identified key sets of knowledge and skills that need to be integrated into education curricula in order to better prepare the health professional workforce, as well as enable transformation of the healthcare delivery system. For instance, the IOM, in *Health Professions Education: A Bridge to Quality*, proposes a core set of competencies that all health clinicians should possess, regardless of their discipline, to meet the needs of the 21st-century healthcare system. This set of **core competencies** includes the ability to provide patient-centered care, work in interdisciplinary teams, employ evidence-based practice, apply quality improvement, and utilize informatics.[1] The report describes in detail the rationale supporting each selected competency, as well as the current lack of knowledge and skills in these key domains, summarized in Table 16-1.

Table 16-1 Proposed Set of Core Competencies and Examples of Their Deficiencies in Health Professions Education

Provide patient-centered care

Definition	Examples of deficiencies
Identify, respect, and care about patients' differences, values, preferences, and expressed needs; relieve pain and suffering; coordinate continuous care; listen to, clearly inform, communicate with, and educate patients; share decision making and management; and continuously advocate disease prevention, wellness, and promotion of healthy lifestyles, including a focus on population health[1]	• Dominance of the biomedical model of practice whereby patients are viewed in terms of signs and symptoms[17] • Belief in physician-only decision making[18] • Training in communication for pharmacists can be irregular and not well developed[19] • Limited training in pain assessment and management[20] • Inconsistent training for nurses about end-of-life care[21] • Limited training in cross-cultural communication[22]

Work in interdisciplinary teams

Cooperate, collaborate, communicate, and integrate care in teams to ensure that the care of populations and communities is continuous and reliable[1]	• Social isolation of health professionals and isolated decision making[23] • Separate schedules prevent interprofessional curriculum design[24] • Fewer than 15% of U.S. nursing and medical schools had any interdisciplinary programs[25] • Attitudes among students may present a barrier to interprofessional teamwork[23]

Employ evidence-based practice

Integrate best research with clinical expertise and patient values for optimum care, and participate in learning and research activities to the extent feasible[1]	• More than 25% of medical school graduates from schools teaching skills related to evidence-based medicine feel unprepared to interpret clinical data, research, literature reviews, and critiques[1] • Limited diffusion of evidence-based practice into nursing curriculum[26]

Apply quality improvement

Identify errors and hazards in care; understand and implement basic safety design principles, such as standardization and simplification; continually understand and measure quality of care in terms of structure, process, and outcomes in relation to patient populations and community needs; design and test interventions to change processes and systems of care, with the objective of improving quality[1]

- Little available information on the extent to which students are educated about error reduction, process measurement and redesign, and monitoring of patient data[27–29]
- Limited education for nurses on quality improvement strategies in clinical areas[30]

Utilize informatics

Communicate, manage knowledge, mitigate error, and support decision making using information technology to study the care delivered to populations and communities[1]

- Fewer than one-third of nursing schools addressed informatics[31]

With the IOM report, the Association of American Medical Colleges (AAMC), Accreditation Council for Graduate Medical Education (ACGME), National League for Nursing (NLN), and the Federation of Associations of Schools of the Health Professions (FASHP) have revealed their position on the need for health professions education reform. Recognizing this need, the AAMC set forth learning objectives, as part of the Medical School Objectives Project (MSOP), to assist medical schools in developing curricula to better align educational content and goals with "evolving societal needs, practice patterns, and scientific developments."[9] The MSOP is an ongoing process of examining the state of clinical education at U.S. medical schools and specifying necessary reforms. Several reports have come out of the MSOP that propose education reform relating to key aspects of healthcare delivery, including increasing knowledge and skills related to improving quality and safety of care, population health, medical informatics, communication and coordination of care, and interdisciplinary teamwork.[9–13]

In addition, the ACGME, in its Outcome Project, has generated six general competencies designed to better prepare physicians to practice medicine in the changing healthcare delivery system. The competencies outline skills considered essential for all practicing physicians, including patient care, medical knowledge, professionalism, systems-based practice, practice-based learning and improvement, and interpersonal and communication skills.[14] Specifically, competency in practice-based learning and improvement requires that residents "systematically analyze practice using quality improvement methods, and implement changes with the goal of practice improvement."[14] Competency in systems-based practice entails that residents "demonstrate an awareness of and responsiveness to the larger context and system of health care" and work in interdisciplinary teams, incorporate considerations of cost awareness, advocate for quality patient care, and participate in identifying system errors and implementing solutions.[14]

Leading organizations from multiple health professions, not only those addressing medical education, are also calling for innovations in education to create and shape the future of healthcare delivery. For example, the National League for Nursing (NLN), in its position statement on transforming nursing education (2005), recognizes the need to better prepare nurses to meet the healthcare needs of the public.[32] The NLN recommends that education programs be redesigned to address significant changes arising from healthcare reform and embrace principles of accountability and evidence-based practice. In addition, the Federation of Associations of Schools of the Health Professions (FASHP), which is a forum for representatives from organizations of health professions education, asserts the vital role education plays in preparing health professionals and the need to reshape and invest in health professions education in order to provide high-quality, team-based, and patient-centered care.[33]

Similar to the health professions education associations, other key organizations have also weighed in on the discussion about education reform. The Medicare Payment Advisory Commission (MedPAC), an independent congressional agency established to advise the U.S. Congress on issues affecting the Medicare program, has also expressed concern that, "health professionals are not gaining certain skills they need to provide the kinds of care that will best serve the public's needs."[3] MedPAC contracted with RAND researchers to evaluate the content of curricula for medical graduates in internal medicine, and found that curricula fell far short of instruction recommended by the IOM and others. In particular, the study identified a lack of formal instruction and experience in interdisciplinary teamwork, cost awareness in clinical decision making, comprehensive health information technology, and patient care in ambulatory (versus inpatient) settings.[34]

Another key organization focused on safe, quality healthcare delivery is the Institute for Healthcare Improvement (IHI). The IHI recommends that new health system designs be developed to simultaneously accomplish three critical objectives, or what is called the "Triple Aim," including: (1) improving the health of the population, (2) enhancing the patient's experience of care (including quality, access, and reliability), and (3) reducing, or at least controlling, the per capita cost of care.[4] However, the IHI affirms that achieving such objectives requires new approaches to the education of health professionals. As a result, the IHI identified eight knowledge domains that incorporate the teaching of quality improvement into health professions education curricula as essential core content for all health professionals. Such domains focus on understanding the organization of healthcare systems, the processes involved in healthcare delivery, and the utilization of outcomes measurement to allow increased accountability, collaboration, and quality improvement.[4]

Finally, the IOM report, *Who Will Keep the Public Healthy: Educating Public Health Professionals for the 21st Century*, emphasizes the central role of health professionals from diverse disciplines in contributing to the health of the public, as well as the critical need to strengthen public health education for all health professionals in order to improve health on a population level.[15] The report offers a framework and recommendations for advancing public health education and integrating eight vital new areas, including informatics, genomics, communication, cultural competence, community-based participatory research, policy and law, global health, and ethics.[15]

Ultimately, consensus exists among leading organizations in health care and health professions education about the imperative to fundamentally alter the education of health professionals in order to adapt to changing standards of patient care and to ensure the delivery of safe, high-quality health care. Such organizations acknowledge that failure to adequately prepare the health profession workforce will impede our ability to transform healthcare delivery and improve health on a population level. Although a variety of knowledge and skills have been identified by different organizations as core content areas to incorporate into health professions education, there is general agreement that new approaches to education must impart competence to deliver patient-centered care (including effective communication and cultural competence), perform practice-based quality improvement, work in interdisciplinary teams, navigate growing bodies of information and new technology to employ evidence-based practices, utilize information technology in clinical practice, demonstrate cost awareness, and apply population-based approaches to improve health on a population level.

THE NEED FOR A POPULATION HEALTH APPROACH TO HEALTH PROFESSIONS EDUCATION

Despite the well-documented need to fundamentally change the education of health professionals and multiple efforts by leading organizations to revise and expand curricula to address pressing societal needs and demands, widespread transformation of education continues to be slow to materialize. The NLN position statement proposes that "more must be done than merely updating or rearranging content" of the curricula.[32] Clearly, there is limited room to incorporate all the aforementioned content into already overcrowded curricula. Most leading organizations in health professions education agree that just as healthcare delivery reform requires a systems-based approach to improve the health status of populations on a larger scale, health professions education reform requires a systems-based approach to produce clinicians who can make meaningful and lasting contributions to the delivery of health care and to the emerging field of population health.

A systems approach to improving health education requires consideration of fundamental features of educational systems, including but not limited to the composition of the population of learners, characteristics of the learning environment, organizational structures, and sources of support (institutional and financial). Although defining major competencies and learning objectives are essential aspects of curriculum redesign, a pedagogical shift is required in order to truly reform the current provision of health professional education and provide an understanding of the treatment of populations of patients, not only individuals.

A useful and dynamic framework for formulating a new approach to health professions education that has broad national support utilizes the concepts and methods of population health.[35] A population health perspective is essential for reshaping the way in which health and health care are understood and approached, and more pointedly, the way in which the education of health professionals can be redesigned. The AAMC Population Health Perspective Panel defines a population health perspective as one that "encompasses the ability to assess the health needs of a specific population; implement and evaluate interventions to improve the health of that population; and provide care for individual patients in the context of culture, health status, and health needs of the populations of which that patient is a member."[10] Major concepts and methods employed in a population-based approach to health, such as measurement, system change, and accountability, provide a structure for organizing and integrating key approaches into education.[36]

A fundamental principle of population health involves developing an understanding of the determinants of health and health disparities that includes, but importantly goes beyond, the provision of individual medical care.[37,38] This broader view enables health professions students to consider influences on health that exist both inside and outside the healthcare system and to link the medical care provided to individuals to larger contexts of family, community, and society. By doing so, population health represents a vital strategy for integrating clinical care with community and public health. Although the call for building bridges between medical care and public health is hardly new, the urgent need for healthcare delivery reform has created the opportunity for the two fields to come together, with a population-based approach facilitating their synergy.[36,39]

In 1997, the New York Academy of Medicine published a monograph named *Medicine and Public Health: The Power of Collaboration.*[40] In this publication, the authors called for medicine and public health to reevaluate their relationship and better coordinate their efforts because both sectors are concerned about the direction of the health system, both are under economic and performance pressure, and neither can accomplish its mission alone. The Academy presented multiple examples of improving health on both an individual and population level that result from the collaboration of medical care and public health. Such examples include improving health care by coordinating services for individuals, improving access to care by establishing frameworks to provide care for the uninsured and underinsured, improving the quality and cost-effectiveness of care by applying a population health perspective to medical practice, using clinical practice to identify and address community health problems, strengthening health promotion and health protection by mobilizing community campaigns, and shaping the future direction of the health system by collaborating about policy, training, and research.[40]

To facilitate an alliance between medical care and public health, health professionals need to understand and value their role as public health professionals.[41,42] The IOM report, *Training Physicians for Public Health Careers* (2007), states that, "effective public health actions rely upon a well-trained public health workforce," which is "composed of individuals from many disciplines, including physicians, nurses, environmental health specialists, epidemiologists, and health educators, among others."[41] To advance health on a population level, public health education and training needs to be embedded into the education of health professionals. Moreover, education reform utilizing a population-based approach aimed at overcoming the deficiencies and disparities in our current healthcare system may produce health professionals that become "agents of change, committed to designing a system of care that is equitable, cost-effective, prevention-oriented, universal, and thus moral."[43]

ESTABLISHING A FRAMEWORK IN POPULATION HEALTH EDUCATION

EXAMPLES OF DEVELOPED FRAMEWORKS IN POPULATION HEALTH AND STRATEGIES FOR IMPLEMENTATION

The AAMC Population Health Perspective Panel, as part of the Medical School Objectives Project, developed education objectives related to population health and strategies on how to design and implement population health education.[10] The panel formulated a foundation of knowledge, skills, and attitudes involved in a population health curriculum (Table 16-2).

Table 16-2   Population Health Perspective Panel's Population Health Curriculum: Knowledge, Skills, Attitudes

Knowledge	Skills	Attitudes
Evidence-based medicine	Mechanisms to gather information from diverse sources	Cultural responsiveness
Social and behavioral determinants of health, at an individual and population level	Use of nonquantitative descriptors	Constructive attitudes and ability to work with other disciplines
Ethics	Measuring performance in populations	Influence of doctors on the health system
Distribution of resources	Patient satisfaction	Field experience with economically disadvantaged populations
Barriers to access	Functional status	
Distributive justice	Costs and cost-effectiveness	Identification and collaboration with external organizations
Use of scarce resources for individuals vs. populations	Clinical outcome measurement	
	Performance scorecards	
Organization and financing of U.S. health care	Severity adjustment approaches	
The principles, practice, and financing of preventive care	Skills to cause change (leadership skills, advocacy, change strategies, communication)	
Cost-analytic approaches and information in prioritizing the use of resources	Use of test characteristics in routine decisions of day-to-day practice	
Describe population demographics	Application of quality improvement methods to improve the systems and individual care	

Source: Association of American Medical Colleges. *Report II—Contemporary Issues in Medicine: Medical Informatics and Population Health.* Washington, DC: Association of American Medical Colleges; 1998.

The panel also identified three education principles to guide effective implementation of a population health curriculum, including: teach students the practical fundamentals of the core disciplines that underpin the effective application of population health, give students experiences in studying real populations (because the subject matter is best taught through examples and experiences rather than courses), and integrate teaching and learning into all parts of medical curriculum rather than relying solely on a stand-alone population health course.[10]

Additionally, the panel recommended strategies to facilitate the widespread development of a curriculum to teach population health:

1. Develop an explicit list of mechanisms by which population health objectives are to be met by each school and conduct periodic evaluations to track their success.
2. Identify faculty to serve as teachers and mentors; support their development.
3. Form liaisons with others to help, such as the American Board of Preventive Medicine and Association for Prevention Teaching and Research.
4. Ensure that the Liaison Committee on Medical Education (LCME) requires that schools show evidence that they have developed objectives, designed and delivered a curriculum, and tested students for these competencies.
5. Ensure that national board examinations test population health competencies.[10]

Of interest, the panel also identified three important barriers to change that must be addressed in order to advance the teaching of population health, which include the lack of "ownership" of population health by any one department in the medical school organization, the absence of dedicated funding to support new initiatives in teaching population health, and the misconception within the academic community that population health is simply a response to concerns expressed by the managed care industry.[10] To confront such obstacles, the panel underscores the need for accountability among leading national organizations, including the AAMC, to clearly articulate the priority of ensuring instruction and support of a population health curriculum.

Building on the work and recommendations of the Population Health Perspective Panel, a collaborative effort of the AAMC and the Centers for Disease Control and Prevention (CDC) to improve population health/public health education for medical students and residents established Regional Medicine-Public Health Education Centers (RMPHECs) and Regional Medicine-Public Health Education Centers-Graduate Medical Education (RMPHEC-GMEs).[44] RMPHEC and RMPHEC-GME sites were required to partner with at least one state or local public health agency to help integrate population health/public health content into their curricula. Grantees developed their own education approaches and materials that were consistent with their institutions' curricular structures and themes. The April 2008 edition of *Academic Medicine,* which had a theme of population health education, profiled 6 of the 16 schools that participated in the RMPHEC program, describing the different strategies employed at their schools to integrate population health across their curricula.[45–52]

In 2004, the Healthy People Curriculum Task Force, convened by the Association of Prevention Teaching and Research (APTR) introduced the Clinical Prevention and Population Health Curriculum Framework with the intent of increasing health promotion and disease prevention content in health professions education.[2,53] The task force included representatives from eight health professional education associations on behalf of allopathic medicine (AAMC), dentistry (American Dental Education Association), nursing (American Association of Colleges of Nursing), nurse practitioners (National Organization of Nurse Practitioner Faculties), osteopathic medicine (American Association of Colleges of Osteopathic Medicine), pharmacy (American Association of Colleges of Pharmacy), allied health, and physician assistants (Association of Physician Assistant Programs). The updated framework (released in 2009) consists of four components, including evidence-based practice, clinical preventive services and health promotion, health systems and health policy, and population health and community aspects of practice.[53] The full Curriculum Framework is comprised of 19 different domains organized under the four components (see Table 16-3). In addition, a variety of methods are recommended for teaching the materials and integrating them into existing curricula, such as the use of service learning and problem-based learning, as well as innovative approaches to interdisciplinary education.

Table 16-3   The Clinical Prevention and Population Health Curriculum Framework

Evidence-based practice	Problem description—descriptive epidemiology Etiology, benefits, and harms—evaluating health research Evidence-based recommendations Implementation and evaluation
Clinical prevention services and health promotion	Screening Counseling for behavioral change Immunization Preventive medication Other preventive interventions
Health systems	Organization of clinical and public health systems Health services financing Health workforce Health policy process
Population health and community aspects of practice	Communicating and sharing health information with the public Environmental health Occupational health Global health issues Cultural dimensions of practice Community services

Data from: Association for Prevention Teaching and Research. *Clinical Prevention and Population Health Curriculum Framework*. Washington, DC: Association for Prevention Teaching and Research; 2009. http://www.atpm.org/about/pdfs/Revised_CPPH_Framework_2009.pdf. Accessed October 1, 2009.

Community–Campus Partnerships for Health (CCPH) has long championed the idea that community-based education and organized service-learning activities are essential in preparing health professionals to effectively understand and practice in a new healthcare system.[54] In an effort to equip health professions educators with the necessary knowledge and skills to expand prevention and population health curricula and promote Healthy People 2010 Objectives in partnership with the community, the CCPH developed a guide titled *Advancing the Healthy People 2010 Objectives Through Community-Based Education: A Curriculum Planning Guide.*[54] The stated goals of this guide are to:

- demonstrate effective community-oriented curriculum strategies to facilitate the achievement of the Healthy People 2010 objectives by future health professionals in partnership with their communities;
- demonstrate effective community-oriented curriculum strategies to equip future health professionals with competencies in health promotion and disease prevention;
- facilitate awareness about health disparities and solutions for addressing them through community-oriented curriculum strategies;
- facilitate awareness about community–campus partnerships as a tool for curriculum reform and improving community health; and
- contribute to a national effort to improve student education and the overall health of communities.

The CCPH guide emphasizes the central value of incorporating the perspectives of community partners and students into the development of the curriculum. Of note, the guide was designed not only for health professional faculty (from a wide variety of disciplines), but also for community leaders interested in establishing partnerships with leaders of health professional schools. It is anticipated that the partnerships that have been driving the efforts to include health promotion and prevention will continue their efforts into the next decade through the next iteration, Healthy People 2020.

While the guide is intended to provide faculty with the information to design coursework directly linked to the Healthy People Objectives, it can also be used to assist faculty in other curriculum reform efforts and community activities; provide leaders in the community–campus partnership movement with the tools to build and sustain their partnership efforts; provide direction to students and residents on strategies for improving community service activities; equip community leaders and students with insight into the curriculum planning process and the important role each plays in student education and improving community health; equip faculty with new directions for evaluation and assessment of community-based courses and activities; and foster possible collaboration and sharing of resources with other leaders in the field around health, health disparities, and the Healthy People Objectives.[54] Linking community-based education and service-learning activities with endeavors to address the healthcare needs of communities can successfully convey fundamentals of population health while improving health outcomes.

CHALLENGES AND BARRIERS TO HEALTH PROFESSIONS EDUCATION REFORM AND IMPLEMENTING CURRICULA IN POPULATION HEALTH

COMPOSITION OF THE POPULATION OF LEARNERS

Increasing Diversity   Attention to the composition of the future healthcare workforce, as well as the geographic and specialty distribution of future healthcare professionals, is essential to efforts to eliminate health disparities, improve access and quality of care, adapt to changing demographics, and address recognized professional shortages. Making changes in education without substantially altering the composition and distribution of learners will most likely perpetuate current problems and fail to meet future demands.

Diversity in the healthcare workforce is associated with better access and quality of care for disadvantaged populations, greater patient choice and satisfaction, and better education experiences for students.[22,55,56] Of note, minority physicians are more likely to provide care for poor and underserved communities.[57] However, the composition of students enrolled in U.S. medical schools is remarkable for its lack of racial and ethnic diversity. For instance, in the 2007–2008 academic year, African Americans accounted for 12.3% of the U.S. population, but just 6.3% of allopathic and 3.5% of osteopathic medical school matriculants.[58] Similarly, Hispanics accounted for 15.1% of the U.S. population, but just 7.9% of allopathic and 3.6% of osteopathic medical school matriculants.[58] Steps to ensure a more diverse pool of physicians and other health professionals are pivotal for reducing health disparities and building a workforce that is attuned to the increasingly diverse population being served.

In addition to the lack of diversity in regards to race and ethnicity, medical students have limited diversity when it comes to economic and geographic background. In 2005, 55% of students came from families in the top quintile of family income, and only about 5% came from families in the lowest quintile.[59] Nevertheless, at least 85% of medical students report substantial debt at graduation. The median total debt of medical school graduates in 2006 was reported at $160,000.[60] And, while geographic diversity is considered important for maintaining access to care across the United States, medical students tend to come disproportionately from urban areas.[61,62] Innovative methods to attract students from more diverse economic, ethnic, and geographic backgrounds, such as developing loan forgiveness policies, will be required to create a more diverse health professional workforce.

Increasing the Supply of Primary Care Providers   Countries with primary care providers as the foundation of the healthcare system achieve better health outcomes at lower cost. Projections anticipate a growing shortage of primary care providers,[57] the supply of which many already believe to be insufficient. The National Resident Matching Program (NRMP) results document a disturbing decline in the number of medical students choosing primary care specialties, such as family medicine, over the past decade and an overall preference for subspecialties.[63] Student perceptions of the demands, rewards, and prestige of primary care specialties, as well as the influence of medical school faculty and curriculum, continue to impact career choice.[64] In the face of heavy debt upon exiting medical school, graduates are hard pressed to choose the less lucrative primary care specialties. Loan forgiveness to those who elect primary care careers may reverse the trend and entice a greater number of medical school graduates to enter primary care specialties. Clearly, education institutions must play a vital role in increasing the number of health professionals choosing a career in primary care.

CHARACTERISTICS OF THE LEARNING ENVIRONMENT

Education in Transformed Models of Care   The Medicare Payment Advisory Commission's report on medical education in the United States aptly recognized that "residents and other health care professionals will best learn the skills needed to provide high-quality, efficient care when medical education occurs in settings where such care is actually performed."[3] Essentially, health professions education needs to occur in settings implementing innovative approaches to health care in order to teach students the necessary knowledge and skills to effectively function in transformed systems. Investments in health professions education must reward healthcare institutions and practices applying systems improvement and population health approaches to enhance learning opportunities.

The IOM committee on HPE emphasized the need to support existing exemplary practice organizations, including academic health centers that are already delivering care utilizing innovative, population-based approaches. Such leading organizations should be provided the resources necessary to serve as training models for other organizations and to test different methods for improving outcomes in clinical education.

For instance, the medical home is a model of care delivery described by the American Academy of Pediatrics (AAP), American College of Physicians (ACP), American Osteopathic Association (AOA), and the American Academy of Family Physicians (AAFP) that holds great promise for improving the health of populations. The National Committee for Quality Assurance (NCQA) has partnered with leading organizations and other stakeholders to support the Physician Practice Connections program, where practices can be recognized as medical homes if they meet specified criteria. The medical home relies upon the provision of care that is accessible, continuous, comprehensive, coordinated, and culturally sensitive. Education and training of health professionals in such models of care may effectively impart desired knowledge, skills, and values.

The Academic Chronic Care Collaborative (ACCC), an initiative of the Association of American Medical Colleges' Institute for Improving Clinical Care and the Robert Wood Johnson Foundation's Improving Chronic Illness Care program, represents another example of combining healthcare delivery reform with educational endeavors. The ACCC aims to improve the care of patients with chronic illness and to educate healthcare teams providing care by facilitating the implementation of the Chronic Care Model in 22 different academic settings.[65] The Chronic Care Model involves creating prepared, proactive clinical teams with informed, activated patients by using clinical information systems, decision support, delivery system design, and self-management support, all of which are integrated into the community and healthcare system.[66]

Education Utilizing Informatics   Despite the fact that utilizing advanced information systems has been identified as a core competency for medical professionals and for the delivery of population health services, many healthcare organizations are not equipped with such systems. Even institutions that have invested in information technology and provide related education and training are commonly not integrating the technology into the delivery of care. Therefore, additional support will be required to widely implement information technology in healthcare organizations, universities, and delivery systems, as well as retool current practices not only to improve clinical care, but also to provide opportunities for students to develop related knowledge and skills.

Education in Community-Based Settings and Practices   Although the vast majority of health care in the United States occurs in community-based outpatient practices, graduate medical programs are largely based in inpatient, acute care teaching hospitals and offer very limited experiences in community-based medicine.[34] In addition, medical school curricula often place major emphasis on the delivery of tertiary services in the inpatient setting to individual patients.[67] Efforts to reform health professions education must consider "how the clinical setting of education prepares graduates to practice in modern health care settings."[67] Enhancing training and skills in nonhospital settings, including skilled nursing, rehabilitation, assisted living, and other outpatient and community-based practices, is crucial for understanding population health and affecting important health outcomes, as well as reducing healthcare spending. However, financing mechanisms for clinical education are largely based on hospital inpatient care and significantly limit incentives to provide education in outpatient settings.[3] In addition, students generally rate the quality of instruction in ambulatory settings lower than inpatient settings. Therefore, providing clinical education in outpatient, community-based settings will entail addressing graduate medical education (GME) funding policies that may be "out of synchrony with the public good"[67] and developing high-quality training experiences in outpatient settings.

Education and Interdisciplinary Teams   The division of health professions into silos poses an obstacle to achieving the higher levels of cooperation and coordination required to improve the quality, safety, effectiveness, and efficiency of healthcare delivery to populations. In practice, there is a general lack of understanding among health professions about what each profession does, the level of training and education required in each profession, and the existing or potential competencies of each profession.[1] The "silo culture" of health professionals in practice is both created and reinforced by education settings that train health professionals in isolation. Although the ability to work in interdisciplinary teams has been identified as a core competency for all health professionals, they are generally not educated together nor trained in team-based skills that would enhance their ability to work as part of interdisciplinary teams. Changes in education must contain specific aims and strategies to break down the "silos" of individual disciplines, as well as develop and reward collaborative efforts in interdisciplinary education.

Interdisciplinary health professions education has yet to become the norm, despite the fact that there are many examples of successful efforts to provide education in working in teams and in developing team-related skills.[68] Obstacles to implementing interdisciplinary education usually involve lack of funding and competition for scarce resources among disciplines that can inhibit collaboration. Accrediting bodies, which drive the educational agenda, often fail to set standards on core competencies and measurable outcomes pertaining to interdisciplinary education or collaborative performance.[68]

ORGANIZATION STRUCTURES AND SOURCES OF SUPPORT

Oversight of Health Professions Education　　Although the need for education reform is clear, several barriers have prevented the education system from changing. In particular, the IOM identified the lack of coordinated oversight *across* the continuum of education and *between* oversight processes, including accreditation, licensing, and certification within and among the various health professions.[1] Oversight systems hold one key to bringing about real change. A concerted effort to enhance communication and collaboration between disciplines can provide a critical lever in competency development and education reform, yielding improvements in population health delivery. In an effort to address oversight challenges in health professions education, the IOM recommended that leading organizations develop an interdisciplinary effort focused on developing a common language in order to achieve consensus across the health professions on a core set of competencies that impact the delivery of population health programming that includes patient-centered care, interdisciplinary teams, evidence-based practice, quality improvement, and informatics. A shared set of competencies should be integrated into the health professions' oversight processes in order to align incentives and provide a catalyst for change. Further, those responsible for developing high-stakes tests and evaluations (i.e., admission, licensure, and certification) should make certain that their assessments support these shared competencies.

Financing System of Health Professions Education　　The financing of health professions education has been identified as a key impediment to education reform, which is integrally linked to the overall healthcare financing system. The IOM committee strongly encourages Medicare and other payers to support changes and innovations in practice that will enhance patient care outcomes and provide productive training experiences for health professionals in population health. Others have called upon public and private entities to

> ## BOX 16-1   CHALLENGES TO HEALTH PROFESSIONS EDUCATION REFORM
>
> Health professions education reform faces many challenges:
> * lack of funding to review curriculum and teaching methods and to acquire the resources required to make needed changes
> * too much emphasis on research and patient care in many academic settings, with little reward for teaching
> * lack of faculty and faculty development to ensure that faculty will be available at training sites and able to effectively teach students new competencies
> * fragmented responsibilities for undergraduate and graduate education and no coordinated oversight across the continuum of education
> * no integration across oversight processes, including accreditation, licensing, and certification
> * lack of an evidence base assessing the impact of changes in teaching methods or curriculum
> * a shortage of visionary leaders
> * silo structures and long-standing disciplinary boundaries among and across the professions
> * unsupportive culture and norms in health professions education
> * overly crowded curricula and competing demands
> * insufficient channels for sharing information and best practices[1]

provide the funding necessary to support the evaluation and research addressing education strategies and outcomes, as well as dissemination of successful innovations and approaches to population health.[16]

Changing the Culture of Organizations   The key goals of professional education are to transmit knowledge, impart skills, and inculcate the values of the profession.[69] Most students acquire their professional identities and norms of behavior from observing how respected role models interact with patients, staff, and others, in the healthcare environment rather than in the classroom.[16] A variety of factors and historical trends, however, shape the attitudes and behavior of faculty, which are ultimately passed on to students. The current culture of medicine has been characterized by the subordination of teaching to research, the intensifying pressure to increase clinical productivity, and the narrowing focus of medical education on biologic matters.[69] As Inui writes:

> And how are we faring as medical educators in preparing future physicians for professional roles in our complicated world? I would conclude that the "formative arc" of education today is strong on the acquisition of technical knowledge and weak-to-negative on the acquisition of values and moral formation. While preparing

successfully to pass tests of knowledge, our students measurably move from being open-minded and curious to test-driven and minimalistic, from open-hearted and idealistic to self-centered and well-defended, and from altruistic to cynical. In the course of their educational experience with us, they also move from taking notes and focusing on the explicit curriculum (what we say) to learning most from what we do. Here, then, is the greatest challenge of educating for professionalism. If we wish to change our students' preparation for their careers, we ourselves will need to change.[70]

In a complicated healthcare system, the values of health professionals and educators are becoming increasingly difficult for learners to discern. The call to reform healthcare delivery and health professions education is an opportunity to imbue professional values and the virtues of population health into our healthcare and education systems. Reframing education through the lens of population health to emphasize the social, economic, and political aspects of healthcare delivery is an essential step in transforming professional values. Support for the development of professionalism requires that institutions support appropriate "role model" faculty by giving them the time, opportunity, and professional development to learn, embrace, and impart intended virtues.

RECOMMENDATIONS

Despite existing innovative models, numerous updates to curricula, and proposals for reform, much work needs to be done to achieve the goal of a health profession workforce that can effectively deliver health care in the 21st century and implement the tenets of population health. Recommendations to facilitate this process for all schools teaching health professionals must include the following elements:

1. Introduce education experiences that involve learners from more than one discipline. These experiences need to be led or taught by teams of interprofessional faculty. Rigorous evaluation of interdisciplinary education efforts must be supported and should include qualitative and quantitative elements.
2. Introduce curricula explicitly examining the roles, contributions, and skills of different health professionals. As an essential competency, effective participation in interdisciplinary teams should be rigorously assessed. Knowledge and skills pertaining to interdisciplinary teamwork should be included in formative examinations.
3. Students must participate in a community experience that addresses the needs of a traditionally underserved population. These experiences must be designed and conducted in partnership with people who live in the community and work or live in the domicile that is the focus of the education experience.
4. Develop a population health steering group to formulate population health objectives and ensure that those objectives are routinely monitored and achieved.

5. Education research focusing on outcomes of population health curricula must be supported. Evidence that we can produce better-equipped and more effective health professionals is desperately needed.

The product of these updates will be a healthcare workforce adequately prepared with the knowledge and skills to provide population-based care.

CONCLUSIONS

Flaws in health professions education both reflect and contribute to the failures in our current healthcare delivery system. Education for clinicians traditionally focuses on the medical conditions acutely affecting individuals and fails to incorporate principles of population health and prevention that are necessary to achieve a larger impact on our nation's health. Similar to healthcare reform, health education reform requires fundamental redesign. Education for health professionals needs to expand beyond the traditional biomedical focus and integrate new skills and approaches that address the health of populations. A population health perspective is essential for reshaping the way in which health and health care is understood and approached, and more pointedly, the way in which the education of health professionals can be redesigned. Multiple challenges and barriers to education reform exist, but the imperative to improve our healthcare delivery system and adequately prepare the healthcare workforce to successfully participate in the provision of care creates an unprecedented opportunity to overcome these obstacles.

STUDY AND DISCUSSION QUESTIONS

1. What inadequacies exist in the education of current health professionals to address societal needs and expectations?
2. What are the core competencies outlined in the IOM report, *Health Professions Education: A Bridge to Quality*, that all health clinicians should possess, regardless of their discipline, to meet the needs of the 21st-century healthcare system?
3. Who should be engaged in redesigning health professions education to address the critical need to improve health at the population level?

SUGGESTED READINGS AND WEB SITES

READINGS

Association of American Medical Colleges. *Report II—Contemporary Issues in Medicine: Medical Informatics and Population Health.* Washington DC: Association of American Medical Colleges; 1998.

Cohen JJ. Chairman's summary of the conference. In: Hager M, ed. *Revisiting the Medical School Educational Mission at a Time of Expansion.* Charleston, SC: Josiah Macy, Jr. Foundation; 2008.

Institute of Medicine. *Health Professions Education: A Bridge to Quality.* Washington, DC: National Academies Press; 2003.

Maeshiro R. Responding to the challenge: population health education for physicians. *Acad Med.* 2008;83(4):319–320.

Royeen CB, Jensen GM, Harvan RA. *Leadership in Interprofessional Health Education and Practice.* Boston, MA: Jones and Bartlett Publishers; 2009.

WEB SITES

Association for Prevention Teaching and Research: http://www.atpm.org

Community–Campus Partnerships for Health: http://depts.washington.edu/ccph/guide-healthypeople.html

Institute for Healthcare Improvement; The Triple Aim: http://www.ihi.org/IHI/Programs/StrategicInitiatives/TripleAim.htm

Medicare Payment Advisory Commission: http://www.medpac.gov

National League for Nursing: http://www.nln.org

REFERENCES

1. Institute of Medicine. *Health Professions Education: A Bridge to Quality.* Washington, DC: National Academies Press; 2003.

2. Allan J, Barwick TA, Cashman S, et al. Clinical prevention and population health: curriculum framework for health professions. *Am J Prev Med.* 2004;27(5):471–476.

3. Medicare Payment Advisory Commission (MedPAC). *Report to the Congress: Improving Incentives in the Medicare Program.* Washington, DC: Medicare Payment Advisory Commission; 2009. http://www.medpac.gov/documents/Jun09_Entire Report.pdf. Accessed December 3, 2009.

4. Institute for Healthcare Improvement. The Triple Aim. Institute for Healthcare Improvement Web site. http://www.ihi.org/IHI/Programs/Strategic Initiatives/TripleAim.htm. Accessed December 3, 2009.

5. World Health Organization. *World Health Statistics 2009.* Geneva, Switzerland: WHO Press; 2009. http://www.who.int/whosis/whostat/2009/en/index.html. Accessed December 3, 2009.

6. Satcher D, Fryer GE Jr, McCann J, Troutman A, Woolf SH, Rust G. What if we were equal? A comparison of the black–white mortality gap in 1960 and 2000. *Health Aff.* 2005;24(2):459–464.

7. Institute of Medicine. *Coverage Matters: Insurance and Health Care.* Washington, DC: National Academies Press; 2001.

8. Institute of Medicine. *Crossing the Quality Chasm: A New Health System for the 21st Century.* Washington, DC: National Academies Press; 2001.

9. Association of American Medical Colleges. *Report I—Learning Objectives for Medical Student Education: Guidelines for Medical Schools.* Washington, DC: Association of American Medical Colleges; 1998.

10. Association of American Medical Colleges. *Report II—Contemporary Issues in Medicine: Medical Informatics and Population Health.* Washington, DC: Association of American Medical Colleges; 1998.

11. Association of American Medical Colleges. *Report V—Contemporary Issues in Medicine:*

Quality of Care. Washington, DC: Association of American Medical Colleges; 2001.

12. Association of American Medical Colleges. *The Medical Home: Position Statement.* Washington, DC: Association of American Medical Colleges; 2008.

13. Association of American Medical Colleges. *Principles for U.S. Health Care Reform: A Guide for Policy Makers.* Washington, DC: Association of American Medical Colleges; 2008.

14. Accreditation Council for Graduate Medical Education. Outcome Project. Accreditation Council for Graduate Medical Education Web site. www.acgme.org/outcome. Accessed December 3, 2009.

15. Institute of Medicine. *Who Will Keep the Public Healthy? Educating Public Health Professionals for the 21st Century.* Washington, DC: National Academies Press; 2003.

16. Cohen JJ. Chairman's summary of the conference. In: Hager M, ed. *Revisiting the Medical School Educational Mission at a Time of Expansion.* Charleston, SC: Josiah Macy, Jr. Foundation; 2008.

17. Mead N, Bower P. Patient-centeredness: a conceptual framework and review of the empirical literature. *Soc Sci Med.* 2000;51(7):1087–1110.

18. Beisecker AE, Murden RA, Moore WP, Graham D, Nelmig L. Attitudes of medical students and primary care physicians regarding input of older and younger patients in medical decisions. *Med Care.* 1996;34(2):126–137.

19. Beardsley RS. Communication skills development in colleges of pharmacy. *Am J Pharm Educ.* 2001;65(4):307–314.

20. Institute of Medicine. *Improving Palliative Care for Cancer.* Washington, DC: National Academies Press; 2001.

21. American Association of Colleges of Nursing. Peaceful death: recommended competencies and curricular guidelines for end-of-life nursing care. American Association of Colleges of Nursing Web site. www.aacn.nche.edu/publications/deathfin.htm. Published 2004. Accessed October 1, 2009.

22. Smedley BD, Stith AY, Nelson AR, ed. *Unequal Treatment: Confronting Racial and Ethnic Disparities in Health Care.* Washington, DC: National Academies Press; 2003.

23. Hall P, Weaver L. Interdisciplinary education and teamwork: a long and winding road. *Med Educ.* 2001;35(9):867–875.

24. Holmes DE, Osterweis M, ed. *Catalysts in Interdisciplinary Education: Innovation by Academic Health Centers.* Washington, DC: Association of Academic Health Centers; 1999.

25. Larson EL. New rules for the game: interdisciplinary education for health professionals. *Nurs Outlook.* 1995;43(4):180–185.

26. French P. The development of evidence-based nursing. *J Adv Med.* 1999;29(1):72–78.

27. Headrick LA, Knapp M, Neuhauser D, et al. Working from upstream to improve health care: the IHI interdisciplinary professional education collaborative. *Jt Comm J Qual Improv.* 1996;22(3):149–164.

28. Henley E. A quality improvement curriculum for medical students. *Jt Comm J Qual Improv.* 2002;28(1):42–48.

29. Mosher SA, Colton D. Quality improvement in the curriculum: a survey of AUPHA programs. *J Health Adm Educ.* 2001;19(2):203–220.

30. Buerhaus PI, Norman L. It's time to require theory and methods of quality improvement in basic and graduate nursing education. *Nurs Outlook.* 2001;49(2):67–69.

31. Carty B, Rosenfeld P. From computer technology to information technology: findings from a national study of nursing education. *Comput Nurs.* 1998;16(5):259–265.

32. National League for Nursing. Position statement: transforming nursing education. National League for Nursing Web site. http://www.nln.org/aboutnln/PositionStatements/transforming05 2005.pdf. Published May 9, 2005. Accessed October 1, 2009.

33. Federation of Associations of Schools of the Health Professions (FASHP). Statement on health professions education in health reform. Federation of Associations of Schools of the Health Professions Web site. http://www.asph.org/UserFiles/FASHPStatementOnHealthReform.pdf.

34. Cordasco KM, Horta M, Lurie N, Bird CE, Wynn BO. *How Are Residency Programs Preparing Our 21st Century Internists? A Review of Internal Medicine Residency Programs' Teaching on Selected Topics.*

Santa Monica, CA: RAND Corporation; 2009. www.rand.org/pubs/working_papers/WR686. Doc. No. WR-686-MEDPAC.

35. Kingdig DA, Asada Y, Booske B. A population health framework for setting national and state health goals. *JAMA*. 2008;299(17):2081–2083.

36. Fielding JE, Teutsch SM. Integrating clinical care and community health: delivering health. *JAMA*. 2009;302(3):317–319.

37. Young TK. *Population Health: Concepts and Methods*. 2nd ed. New York, NY: Oxford University Press; 2005.

38. Kingdig D, Stoddart G. What is population health? *Am J Public Health*. 2003;93(3):380–383.

39. Lurie N, Fremont A. Building bridges between medical care and public health. *JAMA*. 2009; 302(1):84–86.

40. The New York Academy of Medicine. Public Health/Center for the Advancement of Collaborative Strategies in Health. The New York Academy of Medicine Web site. http://www. nyam.org/initiatives/ph-pub.shtml. Accessed December 3, 2009.

41. Institute of Medicine. *Training Physicians for Public Health Careers*. Washington, DC: National Academies Press; 2007.

42. Shortell SM, Swartzberg J. The physician as public health professional in the 21st century. *JAMA*. 2008;300(24):2916–2918.

43. Federman DD. *Healing and Heeling* [presentation]. Jordan J. Cohen Lecture at the AAMC annual meeting November 5, 2007. http://www. aamc.org/meetings/annual/2007/highlights/ cohen_federman.pdf. Accessed December 3, 2009.

44. Maeshiro R. Responding to the challenge: population health education for physicians. *Acad Med*. 2008;83(4):319–320.

45. Finkelstein JA, McMahon GT, Peters A, Cadigan R, Biddinger P, Simon SR. Teaching population health as a basic science at Harvard Medical School. *Acad Med*. 2008;83(4):332–337.

46. Chamberlain LJ, Wang NE, Ho ET, Banchoff AW, Braddock CH 3rd, Gesundheit N. Integrating collaborative population health projects into a medical student curriculum at Stanford. *Acad Med*. 2008;83(4):338–344.

47. Kerkering KW, Novick LF. An enhancement strategy for integration of population health into medical school education: employing the framework developed by the Healthy People Curriculum Task Force. *Acad Med*. 2008;83(4):345–351.

48. Koo D, Thacker SB. The education of physicians: a CDC perspective. *Acad Med*. 2008;83(4): 399–407.

49. Johnson I, Donovan D, Parboosingh J. Steps to improve the teaching of public health to undergraduate medical students in Canada. *Acad Med*. 2008;83(4):414–418.

50. Michener JL, Yaggy S, Lyn M, et al. Improving the health of the community: Duke's experience with community engagement. *Acad Med*. 2008; 83(4):408–413.

51. Ornt DB, Aron DC, King NB, et al. Population medicine in a curricular revision at Case Western Reserve. *Acad Med*. 2008;83(4):327–331.

52. Riegelman RK, Garr DR. Evidence-based public health education as preparation for medical school. *Acad Med*. 2008;83(4):321–326.

53. Association for Prevention Teaching and Research. *Clinical Prevention and Population Health Curriculum Framework*. Washington, DC: Association for Prevention Teaching and Research; 2009. http://www.atpm.org/about/ pdfs/Revised_CPPH_Framework_2009.pdf. Accessed October 1, 2009.

54. Community–Campus Partnerships for Health. Advancing the Healthy People 2010 objectives through community-based education: a curriculum planning guide. University of Washington Web site. http://depts.washington.edu/ccph/ guide-healthypeople.html. Accessed September 16, 2009.

55. Institute of Medicine. *In the Nation's Compelling Interest: Ensuring Diversity in the Health-Care Workforce*. Washington, DC: National Academies Press; 2004.

56. Cohen JJ, Gabriel BA, Terrell C. The case for diversity in the health care workforce. *Health Aff*. 2002;21(5):90–102.

57. Dill MJ, Salsberg ES; for Center for Workforce Studies. *The Complexities of Physician Supply and Demand: Projections Through 2025*. Washington, DC: Association of American Medical Colleges; 2008.

58. Association of American Medical Colleges. *Diversity in Medical Education: Facts & Figures 2008*. Washington, DC: Association of American Medical Colleges; 2008.

59. Association of American Medical Colleges. Diversity of U.S. medical students by parental income. *Analysis in Brief.* 2008;8(1):1–2.

60. Association of American Medical Colleges. *Medical School Tuition and Young Physician Indebtedness: An Update to the 2004 Report.* Washington, DC: Association of American Medical Colleges; 2007.

61. Fordyce MA, Chen FM, Doescher MP, Hart LG. *2005 Physician Supply and Distribution in Rural Areas of the United States.* Seattle, WA: University of Washington Rural Health Research Center; 2007. Report 116.

62. Rabinowitz HK, Diamond JJ, Markham FW, Hazelwood CE. A program to increase the number of family physicians in rural and underserved areas: impact after 22 years. *JAMA.* 1999;281(3):255–260.

63. McGaha AL, Schmittling GT, DeVilbiss AD, Pugno PA. Entry of US medical school graduates into family medicine residencies: 2008–2009 and 3-year summary. *Fam Med.* 2009;41(8):555–566.

64. Pugno PA, McGaha AL, Schmittling GT, De Vilbiss AD, Ostergaard DJ. Results of the 2009 National Resident Matching Program: family medicine. *Fam Med.* 2009;41(8):567–577.

65. Association of American Medical Colleges. Practice change. Improving Chronic Illness Care Web site. http://www.improvingchroniccare.org/index.php?p=ACCC&s=41, Accessed December 7, 2009.

66. Improving Chronic Illness Care. The Chronic Care Model. Improving Chronic Illness Care Web site. http://www.improvingchroniccare.org/index.php?p=The_Chronic_Care_Model&s=2. Accessed December 7, 2009.

67. Newton WP, DuBard CA. Shaping the future of academic health centers: the potential contributions of departments of family medicine. *Ann Fam Med.* 2006;4(Suppl 1):S2-S11.

68. Royeen CB, Jensen GM, Harvan RA. *Leadership in Interprofessional Health Education and Practice.* Boston, MA: Jones and Bartlett Publishers; 2009.

69. Cooke M, Irby DM, Sullivan W, Ludmerer KM. American medical education 100 years after the Flexner report. *N Engl J Med.* 2006;355(13): 1339–1344.

70. Inui TS. *A Flag in the Wind: Educating for Professionalism in Medicine.* Washington, DC: Association of American Medical Colleges; 2003.

THE POLITICAL LANDSCAPE IN RELATION TO THE HEALTH AND WEALTH OF NATIONS

ALAN LYLES, ScD, MPH, RPh

Executive Summary

The nation's wealth—a predictor of the population's health

The health of a population is not an immutable fact, but a consequence of multiple economic, political, and cultural influences. Political processes and the structures of government form the model used to view policies to promote population health. The health of a population has a strong but imperfect relationship to national wealth, and to the proportion of the resources devoted directly to health services. The reciprocal is also true. The wealth of a nation is a by-product of its citizens' health status. Even with metrics to measure and compare the health of the same population at different times or of different populations at the same time, the observed differences may be a consequence of multiple, complex, and even earlier life experiences. The observed health of populations is influenced by many factors, only some of which are a consequence of policies. Even the policies differ by domain, such as agriculture, education, tax, immigration, and economic policies. The international economic crises that began in 2008 raise questions about the utility of narrowly focused measures of growth, particularly gross domestic product (GDP) or even **gross national income (GNI),** and have prompted proposals for broader measures that would also assess well-being, social costs, and, particularly, sustainability. The U.S. Constitution creates dual sovereignty between states and the federal government. Interest group politics influence the agenda, substance, and outcomes for population health policies. Although there has been an expansion in U.S. federal powers related to the health of the population, through preemption and legislation, many authorities remain at the state level. It may be efficient to have a central authority that would oversee the health of the population, but the existing diversity of state and sometimes even local areas having responsibilities provides a natural laboratory for experimentation and innovation.

Learning Objectives

1. Describe the relationship between national wealth and population health and how it has evolved.
2. Illuminate the U.S. constitutional structures that influence population health policy.
3. Discuss the public and private sectors' interests in population health.
4. Explain the Preston Curve and its implications.
5. Describe the Public Choice Model as it applies to individual and special interest group political activity and voter behavior.

Key Words

disability adjusted life years (DALYs)

expected years of life

gross domestic product (GDP) per capita

gross national income (GNI)

lobbying

Millennium Development Goals (MDGs)

preemption

Preston Curve

Preventive Paradox

Public Choice Model

purchasing power parity (PPP)

Quality-Adjusted Life Years (QALYs)

years lived with disability (YLD)

INTRODUCTION

More than 30 years ago, the International Conference on Primary Health Care expressed the urgent need for all nations to protect and promote the health of their citizens. Named for the location of the conference, the 1978 Alma-Ata Declaration proclaimed: "[H]ealth is a fundamental human right ... whose realization requires the action of many other social and economic sectors in addition to the health sector ... [but] Governments have a responsibility for the health of their people which can be fulfilled only by the provision of adequate health and social measures."[1] Political processes and the structures of government form the model that must be used to view policies to promote population health. The health of a population has a strong but imperfect relationship to national wealth and to the proportion of the society's resources devoted directly to health services.[2]

In the ensuing years, nations have continued to wrestle with the distribution of resources to enable health and the role of government in population health. For example, is access to health care a right of citizenship, a privilege of economic circumstances or a negotiation among the public and private sectors and individuals? For the United States, a nation founded on individual liberties, what is the government's responsibility for the health of the population? For policies developed in the private sector, are resources used for health-care costs or investments? The answers to these questions determine and reflect the political landscape in which population health policies and innovations occur.

In the 20th century, the United States's experiences with conscription (a crude but useful proxy for assessing the health of a population) revealed alarming health deficiencies among men of age for military service. In World War I, roughly 15% of the approximately 3.8 million men who underwent a military draft physical were deemed unfit for military service, and almost half of the 2.7 million who did serve had physical impairments.[3] A January 1944 draft proposal to President Roosevelt to improve access to medical care noted that "[W]e are reaping today in wartime the consequences of our past neglect. Between 40 and 50% of those called in the military draft have been rejected on grounds of health."[4] This realization highlights the imperative for nations to invest in the health of their citizens rather than mitigate costs.

When engaging in discussion about the political landscape, one may perceive that it is based on narrow self-interest and favoritism, with decisions determined by power rather than merit. While politics does concern authority relationships between individuals and governments and within levels of governments, it is more appropriate to understand it as the legitimate processes and structures to manage and resolve competing interests where public life and government intersect. Politics reflect the composite of decisions about the appropriate roles of the individual; the private sector and government reflect national values, the accidents of history, and legal and constitutional structures. Different nations approach the same issues with quite different expectations or constraints on the actions of their government. Consequently, the political landscape sets the context for decisions about the generation and retention of wealth, direct and indirect public services that influence health and the rights and responsibilities of individuals, and the private sector and levels of government. Differences in the inherent relative susceptibility of populations to disease, the level and distribution of wealth, and access to health services result in widely divergent levels of comparative health status and viable policies to improve it.

Constitutional provisions, legislation, case law, and, in the private sector, negotiations determine who receives which health services, as well as who pays for them and how. Internationally, approaches to health services' organization, financing, and delivery vary from mainly market-based to substantial central government roles. The particular forms and their outcomes are a result of history, political structures and processes, values, and wealth. Because no nation has found a comprehensive solution, comparative studies provide an opportunity to identify best practices.

Averages obscure subgroup distinctions, such as disparities in access, utilization, and outcomes by gender, age, race, or ethnicity. Even with metrics to measure and compare the health of the same population at different times or different populations at the same time, the observed differences may be a consequence of multiple, complex, and even previous life experiences. Empiric research has established links between experiences across the life span: some protective and some that increase health risks. Annual cross-sectional survey data can easily miss these associations. The Life Course Health Development model emphasizes the temporal connections among policies, access, and longer-term health status.[5] That is, the health of an individual and of a population is more than the consequences of health policies.

Financial crises and business cycles also influence aggregate population health. M. Harvey Brenner received the American Public Health Association's Award for Excellence in 1996 for his lifetime of applied research into the lagged relationship(s) between economic downturns, unemployment, and adverse consequences for health, including increased rates of suicide and mental disorders.[6]

Population health, however, is influenced by more factors than medical services alone and can vary widely within subgroups. The observed health of populations is influenced by many factors, only some of which are a consequence of policies. The direction and specifics of these policies are shaped through the political process and its leverage points for representing specific stakeholders. Leonhardt explained stakeholder reactions to a proposed tax on more complete (and more costly) health insurance plans, even though the tax might lower overall healthcare costs: "By opposing the tax, the AFL–CIO [American Federation of Labor and Congress of Industrial Organizations, a leading federation of labor unions] is simply doing its job. It is defending the interests of its members who have such plans—just as business groups are defending the interests of its members. That is what special interests do: look out for their own constituents, even at the expense of the national interest."[7] While it might seem that special interests are a relic of the past or represent the seedy underside of politics, they are the expression of pluralism in political life. The pursuit of a future population health system, which has everyone's interests in mind, will require organized interest groups also. Effective advocacy of community-wide rather than narrow interests can only influence policies and budgetary priorities through the political process. Quixotic alternatives exist, but they are unlikely to achieve intended population health results.

MEASURING AND COMPARING POPULATION HEALTH AND WEALTH

HEALTH

Assessing a population requires sound metrics to determine the level of health and its trends and to evaluate those against policy aims. Different metrics seek to measure different aspects of the health of populations. Natural units, such as years of life, are often used for summary statistics of health. However, unadjusted expected values, such as life expectancy at birth, represent the net result on health of numerous and often dissimilar factors, such as diet, sanitation, environment, access to primary health care, age pyramid, and the distribution of the population into socioeconomic strata. This issue is multifactorial—the same outcome can result from changes in different combinations of these factors.

An encyclopedia of measures of health exists, but one of the more commonly used indicators is the expectation for additional years of life beginning at a specific age. Each measure provides insight into the experience prior to the age referenced in the measure. In this way, the expectation of life at birth and the expectation of life at one year of age concern related but different contributing factors. Similarly, the infant mortality rate (IMR) is a summary indicator of prenatal care, nutrition, environment, and related factors, while the maternal mortality rate is a crude comparator of the health system and of the general economic well-being among women.

Average life expectancy at birth in the United States has increased 18 years from 1930 to 2006 (Table 17-1). However, at every period for which data are reported, females had greater expected longevity than males, as did Caucasians over other ethnic groups. Disparities also exist among other races and ethnicities, age groups, and locations.[8]

Measurement of **expected years of life** does not capture the variability within subgroups of the population. Additional measures that go beyond absolute years of life lived are useful in policy planning and evaluation, particularly in the evaluation of the health impact of technologies and policies. **Quality-Adjusted Life Years (QALYs)**, a measure commonly used in cost utility analysis or cost-effectiveness analyses, discount the years of life lived at less than full health. **Disability adjusted life years (DALYs)**, or **years lived with disability (YLD)**, quantify the gap between potential years of healthy life compared to years lived with

Table 17-1 Life Expectancy at Birth in the United States, Overall, and by Gender and Race: 1930–2006

Factor	2006*	1996**	1986**	1976**	1966**	1935**	1930**
Both genders: All races	77.7	76.1	74.7	72.9	70.2	61.7	59.7
Female	80.2	79.1	78.2	76.8	73.9	63.9	61.6
Male	75.1	73.1	71.2	69.1	66.7	59.9	58.1
Both genders: White	78.2	76.8	75.4	73.6	71.1	62.9	61.4
Female: White	75.7	79.7	78.8	77.5	74.8	65.0	63.5
Male: White	80.6	73.9	71.9	69.9	67.5	61.0	59.7
Both genders: Black	73.2	70.2	69.1	67.2	64.2	53.1	48.1
Female: Black	76.5	74.2	73.4	71.6	67.6	55.2	49.2
Male: Black	69.7	66.1	64.8	62.9	60.9	51.1	47.3

*Xu J, Kochanek KD, Tejada-Vera B. Deaths: preliminary data for 2007. *National Vital Statistics Reports.* 2009;58(1):27–28. http://www.cdc.gov/nchs/data/nvsr58/nvsr58_01.pdf. Accessed April 7, 2010.

**Arias E. United States life tables, 2001. *National Vital Statistics Reports.* 2004;52(14):33–34. http://www.cdc.gov/nchs/data/nvsr/nvsr52/nvsr52_14.pdf. Accessed April 7, 2010.

less than full health and years of life lost to premature mortality. These measures provide insight into the magnitude of disease and disability within a population.

As a nation's income increases, it typically undergoes an epidemiologic transition. Acute infectious disease is more typical of the leading illnesses in low-income nations while chronic illness and the consequences of lifestyle are more critical contributors to the burden of illness for high- and medium-income nations.[9] Consequently, burden of illness determinations for populations are more useful if the epidemiologic profile includes details beyond the aggregate measures discussed so far and include, for example, the leading specific conditions and their incidence and prevalence by the appropriate demographic categories.

The United Nations Millennium Declaration in 2000 set **Millennium Development Goals (MDGs)**, including health, that would "free our fellow men, women and children from the abject and dehumanizing conditions of extreme poverty."[10] Disability adjusted life years (DALYs) are one measure of progress on health goals that potentially provide a planning and evaluation metric to align the activities of those who participate in international development and humanitarian assistance. Nations, nongovernment organizations (NGOs), and faith-based organizations (FBOs) perform important roles in the politically charged environment of international development. Table 17-2 includes several MDGs and relevant health targets.[11]

WEALTH

Health insurance is a critical factor in the effective demand for health services. Recent research indicates that lack of health insurance among people ages 17 to 64 years may be responsible for as many as 45,000 excess deaths per year.[12] Just 3 of the 30 nation members of the Organization for Economic Co-operation and Development (OECD) lack universal or near-universal health insurance: the United States, Turkey, and Mexico.[13] In reviewing these three countries, it is clear that the general economic level of a nation is not the determining factor for the provision of health insurance for its citizens. Instead, the

Table 17-2   Selected Population Health-Relevant Millennium Development Goals (MDGs)

MDG	Descriptor
MDG 4, Target 5	Reduce by two thirds, between 1990 and 2015, the under-five mortality rate
MDG 5, Target 6	Reduce by three quarters, between 1990 and 2015, the maternal mortality ratio
MDG 6	Combat HIV/AIDS, malaria, and other diseases
MDG 6, Target 7	Have halted by 2015 and begun to reverse the spread of HIV/AIDS
MDG 6, Target 8	Have halted by 2015 and begun to reverse the incidence of malaria and other major diseases

United Nations General Assembly. 55/2 United Nations Millennium Declaration. September 18, 2000.

proportion of a nation's population with health insurance coverage reflects cumulative societal decisions regarding the relative authorities and responsibilities between the public and private sectors, and with the individual members of a society.

International comparisons reveal similarities and differences in economic and health status between countries that require a taxonomy if the comparisons are to be meaningful. Two conventional measures are used to compare wealth across nations: (1) **gross domestic product (GDP) per capita**—a measure of productivity that can be influenced by the relative value of different currencies, but is generally available for all nations; and (2) GDP adjusted for **purchasing power parity (PPP)**, which establishes a comparable monetary scale across currencies. Unlike measures for health, there have been relatively few alternatives to quantifying the wealth of a nation, until recently.

The World Bank's lending policies reference gross national income (GNI). The income divisions that comprise GNI also prove useful in grouping nations for population health and health system performance comparisons. In 2008, the GNI income groups were: low-income countries (LIC) at ≤ $975 per capita; lower-middle-income countries at $976–3,855; upper-middle-income countries at $3,856–11,905; and high-income countries at ≥ $11,906.[14]

The international economic crisis that began in 2008 raises questions about the utility of narrowly focused measures of growth, particularly GDP or even GNI, because tracking such measures was not able to predict the economic failures. G20 is the group of finance ministers and Central Bank governors from eight prominent industrialized nations, 11 emerging markets, and the European Union. At the September 2009 G20 Conference, French President Nicolas Sarkozy presented the Report by the Commission on the Measurement of Economic Performance and Social Progress, which was authored by Nobel Prize–winning economists Joseph Stiglitz and Amartya Sen, as well as the Coordinator of the Commission, Jean-Paul Fitoussi.[15] The report concluded that productivity alone is insufficient to assess the wealth of a nation and that GDP ignores too much of the collateral impacts on individuals and nations. It proposed broader measures that would assess well-being, social costs, and, particularly, sustainability.

HEALTH AND DISPARITIES

A comparison of the relative, absolute, and mix of individual, public, and private sectors' expenditures on health demonstrates stark contrasts between the United States and selected other nations with developed economies (Table 17-3). Although the United States is seventh in life expectancy at birth among this group, it devotes a substantially greater percentage of its GDP to health expenditures. Government expenditures as a percentage of all health expenditures are the lowest for the United States, but health expenditures as a percentage of all government expenditures are highest for the United States (19.3%). That is, for comparable, yet lower, life expectancy at birth, the United States pays the highest percentage of its productivity on health expenditures. Government health expenditures are the lowest percentage of national

Table 17-3   National Health Accounts: Life Expectancy at Birth and Health Expenditure Shares, 2006

	USA	France	Finland	Germany	Canada	UK	Spain
Life expectancy at birth, years (2006)	78.0	80.7	79.4	79.8	80.6	79.2	80.8
Health expenditures as a percentage of GDP	15.3	11.0	8.2	10.6	10.0	8.2	8.4
Government expenditures as a percentage of health expenditures	45.8	79.7	76.0	76.9	70.4	87.3	71.2
Private expenditures as a percentage of health expenditures	54.2	20.3	24.0	23.1	29.6	12.7	28.8
Government health expenditure as a percentage of all government expenditures	19.3	16.7	12.7	17.9	17.8	16.3	15.5

Data from: World Health Organization Statistical Information System (WHOSIS). Life tables for WHO member states. World Health Organization Web site. http://apps.who.int/whosis/database/life_tables/life_tables.cfm. World Health Organization. National health accounts. World Health Organization Web site. http://www.who.int/whosis/whostat/EN_WHS09_Table7.pdf. Accessed October 5, 2009.

health expenditures at the highest percentage of total government expenditures. Private expenditures are a substantially greater percentage of all health expenditures. U.S. private expenditures as a percentage of total health expenditures are 83% more than that of Canada and 426% of the share that this represents for the UK (which is the lowest).

State and federal programs since the mid-1960s have been increasing as total national health expenditures from private sources have been decreasing (Table 17-4). In 1966, when Medicare and Medicaid programs became operational (they were passed in 1965), 70% of national health expenditures were paid from private sources. By 2006, this percentage

Table 17-4   U.S. National Health Expenditures and Sources of Funds, 1966–2006

	2006	1996	1986	1976	1966
Total ($USD B)	2,113	1,069	0.471	0.152	0.046
Per capita ($USD)	7,062	3,937	1,932	687	230
Private (%)	54	54	59	58	70
Public (%)	46	46	41	41	30
Federal (%)	33	33	28	28	16
State and local (%)	13	13	13	13	14

Data from: Centers for Medicare & Medicaid Services, Office of the Actuary. National Health Statistics Group. Historical. US Department of Health & Human Services Web site. http://www.cms.gov/nationalhealthexpenddata/02_nationalhealthaccountshistorical.asp?.

had decreased to 54%. The change in composition is mainly attributable to increases in the share covered by the federal government.

National health expenditures do not, by themselves, produce health. A comparison of the United States and United Kingdom between 1970 and 2001 revealed that U.S. health expenditures consumed 9.5% of the U.S. gross domestic product (GDP) in 1970, compared to 5.6% in the UK, and 13.9% of U.S. GDP by 2001, which was 6.3 percentage points higher than the UK. Despite spending a smaller share of its GDP on health, the UK's all-cause mortality during 1974 through 2000 was lower in England and Wales than in the United States.[16]

The relationship between national wealth and life expectancy showed a similar but improved nonlinear pattern in the 1960s compared with the 1930s. Just 16% of the estimated 12.2 years improvement in life expectancy at birth during that period could be explained by changes in average national income; clearly multiple factors are at work.[17] The curvilinear relationship (the **Preston Curve**) still held when data from 196 countries were compared for 1975 and 2005.[18] (See Figure 17-1.) Increasing average wealth does not explain much of the increase in average life expectancy; it has a stronger association at the lowest income levels with decreasing marginal returns at higher incomes.

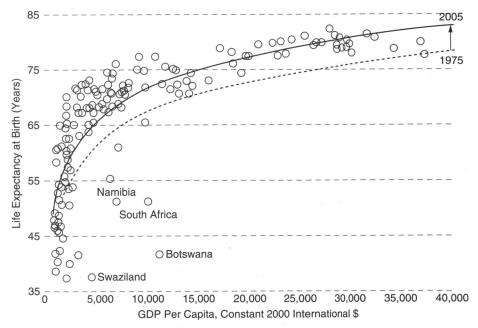

Note: Outlying countries are indicated by name.

Figure 17-1 GDP Per Capita and Life Expectancy at Birth in 169 Countries, 1975 and 2005
Source: World Health Organization. *The World Health Report 2008: Primary Health Care Now More Than Ever.* Geneva, Switzerland: WHO Press; 2008.

The aggregate mean life expectancy at birth (Table 17-1) in the United States has been increasing over the period displayed (1930–2006), yet differences persist by gender and by race: Caucasian women consistently had the greatest mean life expectancy at birth and African American males had the lowest.

It is possible, however, that differences by levels of national wealth might be attenuated by the diffusion of medical advances from the most to the least wealthy countries. Conversely, increases in health may come first, resulting in healthier students and more productive workers who also live longer, which in turn raises the average wealth of a nation.[19] An area of active interest is whether the unequal distribution and not just the average income within a nation is associated with differential life expectancy. The instruments to assess this are blunt and the findings to date are either inconsistent or inconclusive.

FEDERALISM, POLITICS, AND POPULATION HEALTH

The U.S. Constitution created a republic: "a government which derives all of its powers directly or indirectly from the great body of the people; and is administered by persons holding their office during pleasure, for a limited period, or during good behavior."[20] The delegates wrote the Constitution to ensure that it protects individual liberties and balances federal authority with necessity, while retaining state powers as much as feasible. The Constitution also implements a coherent set of political values: representative democracy; individual liberty in which the rights of minorities are respected by the majority; rule of law; separation of powers among the legislative, executive, and judicial branches; federalism; judicial independence and civilian control of the military. Collectively these represent the national identity of that time. The authorities and limitations on the government powers they created stretch across the centuries to influence current health policy initiatives.

A brief historical review is required to place the U.S. model for federalism in context, specifically the division of authorities between states and the national government. It begins with independent former colonies operating as a confederation during and immediately following the American Revolution. As such, each state ceded only the most modest authorities to the central government, which prevented the federal government from functioning effectively. The national government lacked a common currency, trade was impeded by taxes levied on commerce between states, and treaties were signed between individual states and foreign powers—to the disadvantage of those relatively less powerful individual states.

It did not work. The Constitutional Congress that met in the summer of 1787 to draft a written constitution had to overcome these deficiencies, but was not able to impose a central government upon the states. Authority began with and resided in the independent states. The final form of the new government and the specific partitioning of authorities between the states and the central government depended upon each state's voluntary relinquishing of some authorities to the federal government. It was uncertain whether a balance acceptable to all could be achieved, and whether such efforts could lead to a constitution that would be ratified and accepted by the newly independent states.

Through compromise and an elaborate system of checks and balances on power within the new federal government and between that government and each of the states, a workable, though fragile, Constitution was created. Since the Constitution replaced the Articles of Confederation in 1789, the size and scope of the federal government's role in health care has grown through legislation and case law—slowly at first but much more in the 20th century.

In response to concerns that the powerful British government that had been defeated in the Revolution must not now be replaced by a powerful domestic central government, a set of 10 amendments was offered and ratified two years after the Constitution itself. Between the Constitution and its amendments, there are enumerated powers for the federal government and denied[21] and implied powers for the state governments. The enumerated powers of the federal government mainly remedy the shortcomings of the Articles of Confederation. Because state constitutions at that time predated the U.S. Constitution, the primacy clause in the U.S. Constitution asserted the limited form of federalism that was being created: "This Constitution, and the Laws of the United States which shall be made in Pursuance thereof; and all Treaties made, or which shall be made, under the Authority of the United States, shall be the supreme Law of the Land; and the Judges in every State shall be bound thereby, any Thing in the Constitution or Laws of any State to the Contrary notwithstanding."[22]

However, according to the 10th Amendment, "The powers not delegated to the United States by the Constitution, nor prohibited by it to the States, are reserved to the States respectively, or to the people."[23] Police powers, as the term was understood in the 18th century, were retained by the state: notably, health, education, law enforcement, and welfare. Writing to encourage states to ratify the Constitution, Alexander Hamilton specifically noted that "the proposed constitution ... leaves in their [state government's] possession certain exclusive, and very important, portions of the sovereign power."[24]

There are, however, circumstances where federal law preempts state law: (1) under *express preemption*, federal law restricts specific state regulatory actions, though a "savings clause" may remove some state actions from the prohibition;[25] (2) *field preemption* applies when federal law regulates a matter to such an extent that there is no opportunity for state law to be introduced without conflicting with it—for example, employee benefit plans; and (3) *conflict preemption* occurs when state and federal law actually conflict or when the state law impedes achieving the intent of the federal law. Where the state law concerns the health or safety of the public, the U.S. Supreme Court has a strong presumption against preemption unless achieving the explicit intent of Congress requires that preemption.[25]

Interpretations of two other provisions in the Constitution have, over time, supported expanded federal authorities: the Commerce Clause,[26] which provides the federal government with the authority to regulate interstate commerce, and the Necessary and Proper Clause,[27] which is quite elastic—giving the federal government the power to make laws that may be required to implement or achieve the other powers that it has been given. The expansion is not a full transfer of authority from states to the federal government regarding population health law. Consequently, indirect means are used to influence healthcare quality, safety, and access where direct federal authority is lacking.

INTEREST GROUPS: THE FIRST AMENDMENT, PLURALISM, AND POLITICAL CAMPAIGN FINANCING

James Madison, an influential delegate to the Constitutional Convention of 1787 and a key contributing author to the document, warned against "the mischiefs of factions"[28] (as political parties were then called). He cautioned that conflicts between rival parties lead to the neglect of the public good. Nonetheless, Madison also asserted that "among the numerous advantages promised by a well constructed Union, none deserves to be more accurately developed, than its tendency to break and control the violence of faction." Despite this optimism, political parties developed in the early years of the nation and have continued to evolve. Persons with similar interests also form associations that directly and indirectly seek to advance their interests through government actions. Between the associations and the elected members of political parties, there is a third group that works to influence government's decisions: lobbyists. The flow of money was deemed to be sufficiently large and regular that Congress passed the Federal Regulation of Lobbying Act (FRLA) in 1946,[29] which required registration and financial disclosure. The FRLA was amended and subsequently repealed by the Lobbying Disclosure Act of 1995,[30] though regulation of **lobbying** activities, particularly financial activities, continues to trail the evolution of these activities and to be less than effective in achieving their intended results.

The political values of pluralism, respect for the rights of minorities within the majority rule, and effective checks on power require certain freedoms. The first amendment to the Constitution declares these rights: "Congress shall make no law ... abridging the freedom of speech, or of the press; or the right of the people peaceably to assemble, and to petition the Government for a redress of grievances."[31] Organizing into political parties to develop policies that express the political philosophy and interests of its members follows from this.

The organization, financing, and delivery of health services partially represent a response to incentives, but interest groups influence these incentives through the political process. As explained by the **Public Choice Model**,[32] the costs and gains from political activity to influence legislation and regulation do not fall equally on everyone. The costs of political activity tend to be high for individuals because of the relatively low frequency of events of potential interest or relevance to them and the low probability of an individual's position prevailing when such issues arise. Additionally, the time and opportunity cost of staying informed are relatively high for individuals versus an interest group or other organized stakeholders because of the many issues that arise versus the few issues that would be relevant for them. According to the Public Choice Model, general voters are rationally uninformed and politically inactive, based on their expected individual gains versus the costs of their political activity. By contrast, other stakeholders have more enduring interests and are more often potentially affected by government policies and regulations in their focused area of interest. Interest groups organize to influence the distributed impacts of government policies that would influence these stakeholders. For them, it is rational to commit the resources to remain engaged in attempting to influence the probability of a preferred outcome. The result can be to the advantage of the interest group, even at the expense of the greater good.

"Through a combination of focused contributions to reelection campaigns, well-connected lobbyists, nurtured relationships with committee chairpeople and selected staff members, and intimate knowledge of leverage points in key processes, special interest groups routinely stall or torpedo policy changes, even when there is broad consensus that action is needed."[33]

The **Preventive Paradox** is a population health corollary to the Public Choice Model. Changes in population health measures are influenced less by intervening with high-risk individuals than by even modest changes in exposure to risk factors by the population as a whole. This Preventive Paradox, that "a preventive measure that brings much benefit to the population offers little to each participating individual,"[34] suggests that effective long-term preventive changes will require some public role. Fluoridation, for example, applied this lesson to control the incidence of dental caries in populations; however, it was the focus of intense political opposition.[35]

Major interest groups in health care include the American Medical Association, America's Health Insurance Plans, the National Alliance on Mental Illness, and the National Business Group on Health, to name a few. These include healthcare providers, insurers, employers, patient advocacy groups, and more. The amounts and methods of payment for lobbying and donations for political campaigns have the potential to exert undue influence on legislation.[36] During the period of 1998 to 2009, five of the top spending lobbying clients were from the health sector and spent a combined $820,509,780 (Table 17-5). To counter the risks that such sums may pose, the Bipartisan Campaign Reform Act of 2002 (the McCain-Feingold Act)[37] established categories and limits for monies that could be raised beyond those amounts specified under campaign finance law.

PUBLIC–PRIVATE SECTOR ARRANGEMENTS IN HEALTH CARE

The development of means to detect disease at an earlier stage stimulated screening of healthy individuals, changing the traditional, sole reliance on medical services after a person became ill. As the number of these tests grew, health departments began offering

Table 17-5   Lobbying Payments 1998–2009, Center for Responsive Politics

Rank	Lobbying client	Amount ($)
2	American Medical Association	212,602,500
4	AARP	169,752,064
5	American Hospital Association	168,880,431
6	Pharmaceutical Research & Manufacturers of America	161,638,400
13	Blue Cross/Blue Shield	128,818,703
Total		841,692,098

Data from: Center for Responsive Politics. Top spenders. Center for Responsive Politics Web site. http://www.opensecrets.org/lobby/top.php?indexType=s. Accessed December 7, 2009.

the screenings and then, in an efficiency reorganization, initiated *multiphasic* screenings, at which multiple screenings would occur at one encounter. As these services were implemented, there was resistance from physicians, whose position was "that [the] multiphasic screening concept placed a government agency between them and their patients ... that primary responsibility for disease prevention rested with them and not the health department. They insisted that the individual not go first to the health center for tests and then to the doctor: the order must be reversed."[38] In its opposition both to public health clinics' performance of multiphasic screenings[3] and to inclusion of national health insurance in the Social Security Act of 1935[39] and subsequent incarnations of health care reform, the American Medical Association has shown a consistent interest in maintaining strict physician autonomy in the practice of medicine.

The division of healthcare authorities between state and federal government and the vibrant role that voluntary associations play in American life has resulted in a variety of mechanisms to influence healthcare delivery, insurance, medical quality, and health practitioners' credentialing.

The Joint Commission is a private, not-for-profit organization that reviews and accredits healthcare entities. The Medicare and Medicaid programs require participating entities to continuously meet eligibility requirements, though they do not directly assess or certify such standards. Instead, the entities can meet deemed status either by a state agency survey or through accreditation by The Joint Commission.

Accreditation of schools of medicine, a requirement for participation in Department of Education programs and funding, is performed by the Liaison Committee on Medical Education (LCME), a joint private entity comprised of the American Medical Association and the Association of American Medical Colleges.

The National Association of Insurance Commissioners (NAIC) offers a similar model. Each state has authority over regulation of insurance within the state; however, national or multistate employers have a strong interest in consistent laws and regulations in each of the states in which they have employees. State insurance commissioners meet through the NAIC and draft Model Acts, which are then acted upon within each state. In this way, state authority is maintained but coherence is improved.

Establishing national goals for the health of the nation is not under the authority of the federal government. However, in 1979 the U.S. Surgeon General issued the first of the decennial Healthy People reports. The reports provide a snapshot on the health of Americans, including both baseline and quantitative goals for improvement over the following decade. Healthy People 2010 consisted of 28 focus areas and 467 measurable objectives; the intent was to align autonomous entities toward jointly developed goals and track achievements. These focus areas and objectives were collaboratively developed by hundreds of private organizations, state and federal agencies, and individuals—not dictated by the federal government. To sharpen the focus, 10 conditions carrying the highest priority for improvement were identified as Leading Health Indicators (LHIs). This process was repeated for Healthy People 2020.

Similarly, the National Strategy for Suicide Prevention (NSSP) provides a framework of goals and objectives to improve efforts at suicide prevention, but it is the responsibility and decision of each state as to whether and how it will modify, adopt, and implement its own plan based on the NSSP. These public–private sector arrangements in health care strive to set standards for health (Healthy People), reductions of harm (National Strategy for Suicide Prevention), quality in facilities (The Joint Commission) and medical education (Liaison Committee on Medical Education), and consistency in health insurance regulation. These particular structures are necessary as a consequence of U.S. federal structure, evolving policies, legislation, and case law. Consequently, they are not all working to achieve population health goals (the National Association of Insurance Commissioners), but their work does influence population health goals.

CONCLUSIONS

The health of a population is not an immutable fact, but a consequence of multiple economic, political, and cultural influences. The curvilinear relationship between wealth and expected length of life at birth holds for data from the 1930s as it does today. It implies that the largest gains can be achieved at the low end of GDP per capita with decreasing marginal results at high income levels. Over time, however, this Preston Curve has shifted upward. Modeling the relationship for observed versus expected changes in life expectancy at birth for different nations yields the surprising result that most of the observed increase in life expectancy is caused by factors other than income *per se*.

Policies to influence the organization, financing, and delivery of health care are strongly influenced by each nation's history, culture, political values, structures, and processes. The political process and structures of government in the United States are inefficient. This inefficiency is by design and continues in order to protect core values, such as checks and balances on government authorities, pluralism, individual freedom, and the rights of states. The organization of stakeholders into special interest groups gives voice to these values, yet it can result in perverse results or inaction when change or innovations are introduced. Over time, the political landscape is an evolving rather than fixed map. Opportunities and constraints, interests, and capacities change, but the path for public expression provides enduring boundaries and processes for resolving the competing and conflicting interests of the nation's population.

STUDY AND DISCUSSION QUESTIONS

1. What are the relative merits of alternative measures for measuring the health of a population?
2. What is the relationship between the health and wealth of a population? Is increased wealth always associated with increased health? Explain why or why not.
3. When might measures other than economic productivity be appropriate?

4. What is the relationship between the political process and access to health services in the United States? How might policies other than those directly concerning health care influence the health of a population?

5. There are differences between countries in population health, but why are there differences in the health of subgroups within countries?

SUGGESTED READINGS AND WEB SITES

READINGS

Acs ZJ, Lyles A, ed. *Obesity, Business and Public Policy.* Cheltenham, UK: Edward Elgar Publishing; 2007.

Blumenthal D, Morone JA. *The Heart of Power: Health and Politics in the Oval Office.* Berkeley, CA: University of California Press; 2009.

Fisher ES, Bynum JP, Skinner JS. Slowing the growth of health care costs—lessons from regional variation. *N Engl J Med.* 2009;360(9):849–852.

Patel K, Rushefsky ME. *Health Care in America: Separate and Unequal.* New York, NY: M. E. Sharpe; 2008.

Redman E. *The Dance of Legislation.* Seattle, WA: University of Washington Press; 2001.

Starr P. *The Social Transformation of American Medicine.* New York, NY: Basic Books; 1982.

WEB SITES

Center for Responsive Politics: http://www.opensecrets.org/index.php

Centers for Disease Control and Prevention
    Health, United States (updated annually): http://www.cdc.gov/nchs/hus.htm
    Healthy Communities Program: http://www.cdc.gov/healthycommunitiesprogram/
    Morbidity and Mortality Weekly Report: http://www.cdc.gov/mmwr/

The Commonwealth Fund: http://www.commonwealthfund.org

Healthy People 2010: http://www.healthypeople.gov/

The Joint Commission: http://www.jointcommission.org

Kaiser Family Foundation
    Kaiser Daily Health Policy Report: http://www.kaiserhealthnews.org/Daily-Report.aspx
    The Kaiser Family Foundation: http://www.kff.org
    (The Kaiser Family Foundation is not associated with Kaiser Permanente or Kaiser Industries.)

World Health Organization: http://www.who.int/en/

REFERENCES

1. Declaration of Alma-Ata International Conference on Primary Health Care, Alma-Ata, USSR, September 6–12, 1978. *Dev.* 2004;47(2):159–161.

2. World Health Organization. *World Health Statistics 2009.* Geneva: World Health Organization; 2009. http://www.who.int/whosis/whostat/

EN_WHS09_Full.pdf. Accessed October 5, 2009.

3. Reiser SJ. The emergence of the concept of screening for disease. *Milbank Mem Fund Q Health Soc.*1978;56(4):403-425.

4. Handler M. Memo to Judge Rosenman, January 28, 1944. In: Blumenthal D, Morone JA. *The Heart of Power: Health and Politics in the Oval Office.* Berkeley, CA: University of California Press; 2009.

5. Halfon N, Hochstein M. Life course health development: an integrated framework for developing health, policy, and research. *Milbank Q.* 2002;80(3):433–479.

6. Amick B III, Levine S, Tarlov AR, Walsh DC, eds. *Society and Health.* New York, NY: Oxford University Press; 1995.

7. Leonhardt D. "Cadillac tax" offers opportunities. *New York Times.* September 30, 2009:B1.

8. Patel K, Rushefsky ME. *Health Care in America: Separate and Unequal.* New York, NY: M. E. Sharpe; 2008.

9. Omran AR. The epidemiologic transition: a theory of the epidemiology of population change. *Milbank Q.* 2005;83(4):731–757.

10. United Nations General Assembly. 55/2 United Nations Millennium Declaration. September 18, 2000.

11. World Health Organization. *Health and the Millennium Development Goals.* Geneva, Switzerland: WHO Press; 2005.

12. Wilper AP, Woolhandler S, Lasser KE, McCormick D, Bor DH, Himmelstein DU. Health insurance and mortality in US adults. *Am J Public Health.* 2009;99:2289–2295.

13. Organization for Economic Cooperation and Development. *Health at a Glance 2007: OECD Indicators.* Paris, France: Organization for Economic Cooperation and Development; 2007:96.

14. The World Bank. A short history. The World Bank Web site. http://go.worldbank.org/U9BK7IA1J0. Accessed October 5, 2009.

15. Stiglitz JE, Sen A, Fitoussi JP. *Report by the Commission on the Measurement of Economic Performance and Social Progress.* http://media.ft.com/cms/f3b4c24a-a141-11de-a88d-00144feabdc0.pdf. Accessed October 5, 2009.

16. Pritchard C, Galvin K. A comparison of British and US mortality outcomes. *Nursing Times.* 2006; 102(48):33–34.

17. Preston SH. The changing relation between mortality and level of economic development. *Popul Stud.* 1975;29(2):231–248.

18. World Health Organization. *The World Health Report 2008: Primary Health Care Now More Than Ever.* Geneva, Switzerland: WHO Press; 2008.

19. Bloom DE, Canning D. Commentary: the Preston Curve 30 years on: still sparking fires. *Int J Epidemiol.* 2007;36(3):498–499.

20. Madison J. The Federalist no. 39: Madison. In: Hamilton A, Madison J, Jay J. *The Federalist Papers.* New York, NY: Bantam Books; 2003.

21. U.S. Const. art. 1, §10

22. U.S. Const. art. 6, cl. 2.

23. U.S. Const. amend. 10.

24. Hamilton A. The Federalist no. 9: Hamilton. In: Hamilton A, Madison J, Jay J. *The Federalist Papers.* New York, NY: Bantam Books; 2003.

25. Mermin SE, Graff SK. A legal primer for the obesity prevention movement. *Am J Public Health.* 2009;99(10):1799–1805.

26. U.S. Const. art. 1, §8, cl. 3.

27. U.S. Const. art. 1, §8, cl. 18.

28. Madison J. The Federalist no. 10: Madison. In: Hamilton A, Madison J, Jay J. *The Federalist Papers.* New York, NY: Bantam Books; 2003.

29. Federal Regulation of Lobbying Act, 2 USC §261.

30. Lobbying Disclosure Act of 1995, Pub L No. 104-165, 109 Stat 691.

31. U.S. Const. amend 1.

32. Jensen GA, Morrisey MA. Employer-sponsored health insurance and mandated benefit laws. *Milbank Q.* 1999;77(4):425–459.

33. Watkins MD, Bazerman MH. Predictable surprises: the disasters you should have seen coming. *Harv Bus Rev.* 2003;81(3):72–80.

34. Rose G. Strategy of prevention: lessons from cardiovascular disease. *Br Med J.* 1981;282(6279): 1847–1851.

35. Gamson WA. The fluoridation dialogue: is it an ideological conflict? *Public Opinion Q.* 1961;25: 526–537.

36. Lyles A. Politics, public policy, and national healthcare reform: Medicare and the Medicare

Modernization Act of 2003. In Navarro RP. *Managed Care Pharmacy Practice.* 2nd ed. Sudbury, MA: Jones & Bartlett Publishers; 2009.

37. Bipartisan Campaign Reform Act of 2002, Pub L No. 107–155.

38. Smillie WG. "Multiphasic" screening tests. *J Am Med Assoc.* 1951;145(16):1254–1256.

39. Starr P. *The Social Transformation of American Medicine.* New York, NY: Basic Books; 1982.

THE FUTURE OF POPULATION HEALTH: MOVING UPSTREAM

DEE W. EDINGTON, PhD,
AND ALYSSA B. SCHULTZ, PhD

Executive Summary

Health—much more than absence of disease

The medical establishment has been focused on sick care during the past several decades, which has proven to be unsustainable, especially in terms of cost. Population health calls for a shift to an "epidemic of wellness." The true measures of population health are not rates of disease or even prevalence of risk factors; instead, they are the vitality, wellness, and high performance of its people.

Corporations will continue to be the major stakeholders in defining the value of healthy and high-performing employees. The most successful organizations will be those that create a culture of wellness and move totally upstream by creating population- and individual-level interventions focused on things such as resilience, positive psychology, social networks, and self-leader training. Future research must elucidate the vague connection between "culture" and health. In order to achieve true population health, the same emphasis needs to be placed on promoting wellness and treating illness. The success of this initiative will require collaboration from all of the stakeholders, including governments, communities, employers, care providers, and individuals.

Learning Objectives

1. Describe the natural flow of populations in terms of health risks, disease, and costs.
2. Explain the challenges of early efforts aimed at health promotion and behavior change.
3. Explain why we need to move "upstream" to create a culture of wellness rather than an expanded system of sick care.

313

4. Explain the strategy of "keeping the healthy people healthy."
5. Identify the types of interventions that might be used in the future of population health management.

Key Words

culture of health
wellness

INTRODUCTION

Population health clearly has developed as an important framework upon which to build strategies for the health of individuals, families, companies, communities, states, and nations. It also has developed into an important field of scholarly activity. The growth has occurred since the mid-1990s, although the roots of population health extend back several decades. While population health is related to public health, the latter is focused more on a government's responsibility in protecting the health of its constituents and includes disease surveillance and communicable disease control.[1] A bibliometric analysis of the term "population health" indicates that this area of research is growing rapidly.[2]

In the 2009 national dialogue about healthcare reform, access to affordable health care and how to pay for it still ruled the debates. But, for the first time in American history, population health, health promotion, positive health status, and **wellness** began to emerge as important components of any long-term solution. American leaders (in politics and other areas) have finally observed that after people become sick or high risk, it is frequently too late to reverse the downward spiral of illness. We also have learned that health is a complex system and that the "medical reductionism" solution, such as single disease management, is not going to solve our population health concerns.

Still, corporations worldwide are often footing the cost of sickness, either directly or indirectly, through taxes and lost productivity. That is why innovative population health management solutions are most often initiated by employers. Health policies are too important to be left solely to medical or public health officials, especially based on the results we have seen over the past several decades. Business leaders, given their experience defining business strategies, may be better trained to engage the whole population and impact the total value of health.

In order to discuss the future of population health, we must first examine its history over a few relatively arbitrary timelines to develop a perspective of where it is headed. Table FPH-1 summarizes the outcome measures used in health management over this time period.

The medical establishment has always been focused on disease, so health has been defined as the absence of disease. True wellness is achieved when individuals have a high

Table FPH-1   The Progression of Population Outcome Measures over Time

Time period	Population health outcome measures	
Prior to 1970	Mortality rates	
	General	Avoidable deaths
	Infant mortality	Maternal mortality
	Infectious disease rates	
1970–2000	Same as previous, plus:	
	Incidence of disease	Environment hazards
	Injury, violence, and crime	Prevalence of risk factors
	Quality and availability of medical care	
	Adverse event measures	NCQA and HEDIS measures
	Preventive services compliance	Risk–cost relationships
	Disease management process measures	Return on investment
2000–2010	Same as previous, plus:	
	Total value of outcomes	
	Healthcare costs	Pharmacy costs
	Productivity costs	
	Absenteeism	Presenteeism
	Job effectiveness	Recruitment
	Turnover	Morale
	Socioeconomic measures	Functional status
	Cost-effectiveness on interventions	
2010–2015	Same as previous, plus:	
	Outcomes versus do-nothing strategies	Health consumerism
	High deductible health plans	Early communities focus
	Begin to think of health as a system (zero trends)	
2015 and beyond	Same as previous, plus:	
	Quality of life	Quality of work
	Positive psychology	
	Resilience	Optimism
	Precursors of wellness rather than precursors of disease	
	Quality of each person's environment	
	Effective resource management	Social support
	Culture of health in home, community, and workplace	

level of health, vitality, resilience, and performance. As other chapters in this book have stated, population health has to move away from "sick care" to integrate health and wellness into the culture. This movement will require a focus on the social and community determinants of health.

While primary medical care and health promotion have focused on the health of individuals and prevention of disease, they placed little emphasis on social, cultural, or community determinants of health.[3] Public health has focused appropriately on prevention and the health of populations, but little on the health of individuals; nor has it accomplished equity or universal access to care in the United States. Health promotion has yet another set of priorities, mostly targeted at individuals.

The lessons learned from the previous chapters in this text, our own work at the University of Michigan, and the growth of population health management throughout the corporate sectors have demonstrated that population health has come of age as a new way to think about health in the United States and the world. Every country has the same issues: how to maintain the health, vitality, and high performance levels of its population.

A BRIEF HISTORY OF POPULATION HEALTH

THE PAST: PRIOR TO 1960

Following an era of public health interventions to greatly minimize infectious diseases related to poor sanitation, unsafe drinking water, infested areas, and so on, the medical professions dominated the nation's healthcare emphasis. In the late 1940s and early 1950s, companies added health insurance for their workers and insurance companies accepted the role of the third-party payer for health care as provided by the medical community.[4] American affluence, driven by the success of the American business community, drove the creation of the American way of life—abundance, much of the time to excess. These three developments left no one in charge of the health of the population and, while life expectancy improved, so did the prevalence of chronic diseases.

During these years, health was and continues to be mistaken for health care in the general public and in health policies. The focus was on waiting for sickness and then taking care of the sick. Medicine, hospitals, and insurance companies were left in charge. Unfortunately, their business model was to provide health care only when individuals got sick; thus, a culture of entitlement was created, supported by employers who were paying for health care. Fifty years later, employers were to regret this decision.

In this time period, affluence led to increases in life expectancy, which was the barometer of healthcare progress compared to the rest of the world that was trying to catch up with the economic strength of America. The tools utilized to drive our success were remnants of the public health success earlier in the century, as well as research on cardiovascular disease and cancer. A major development in this area was an early beginning of population health: a delineation of population risk factors for cardiovascular disease, which later would lead to an understanding of the environment health risks associated with exposure to secondhand smoke.

THE PAST: STATUS OF POPULATION HEALTH: 1960–2000

The findings from the Framingham Heart Study[5] and other longitudinal studies uncovered risk factors that were the precursors to cardiovascular disease. Within a few years, corporations realized that the loss of an at-risk executive would be a major economic loss for the company. Given that realization and the intuition that the risks could be modified, early efforts at risk factor reduction were initiated.

In 1980, the Centers for Disease Control and Prevention introduced a computerized form of the Health Risk Appraisal (HRA). This was an important tool used early in population health efforts. It was one that any person could, in a matter of 15 minutes, use to become more aware of his or her individual health risks and learn about the consequences of those health risks or behaviors. Thus began the early growth of risks and behavioral interventions, albeit limited to those individuals with high risks as identified by the results from the Health Risk Appraisals.

The early Health Risk Appraisals were developed to calculate health ages, including actual age, appraised age, and achievable age; determine chances of dying and morbidity; identify precursors to disease; and guide health education materials. Along with the HRA came a host of health enhancement and disease management companies. These companies focused on behavior changes, driven to a great extent by the transtheoretical model created by Prochaska[6] (see Chapter 2). In addition to risk reduction, a major role was developed for primary prevention, guided by the Guideline for Preventive Services developed by the CDC and the National Business Group on Health.[7]

While some organizations felt that health promotion efforts were "the right thing to do," without much concern for the savings, others became very interested in the return on investment (ROI) of their health promotion efforts. When comparing the cost of programs to the avoided costs of health events, ROI research showed some promise in a few cases, but evidence of widespread success was still lacking.[8–11] Much of this confusion was caused by a lack of understanding of the impact of the individual as a complex system driving high risk and disease and the resulting cost increases in terms of health care and productivity.

THE PAST: EMERGENCE OF POPULATION HEALTH: 2000–2010

Behavior change and risk reduction strategies had modest success as the cost of medical care escalated. Not only did few individuals participate in these programs, but if someone did make a change, it was only a short period of time until recidivism occurred. Thus, we observed a continuing march toward increasing numbers of Americans who were obese and not physically active as well as increases in the number of individuals with metabolic diseases. The work with private and public sector companies and organizations produced at least six important lessons during the first decade of the 21st century:

1. The paraphrased words of Einstein were finally heard: "The level of thinking that got us into these unsatisfactory results is not the level of thinking that will get us out of this situation."
2. One cannot solve a problem by waiting for defects and then attempt to fix the defects; one has to fix the systems that lead to the defects.
3. Population health management needs a framework or systems approach rather than the isolated programs that attempt to fix defects one risk or disease at a time.
4. One cannot put a changed person back into an unchanged environment and expect the change to be sustained.
5. Only the actions that are rewarded are the actions that are sustained.
6. Successful population health management systems require continuous improvement through quality assurance metrics.

These lessons propelled population health to the top of the strategies for achieving and maintaining high health status and established it as a leading partner in healthcare cost containment and improved performance of individuals.

FUTURE TRENDS IN POPULATION HEALTH MANAGEMENT

Kindig[12] as well as Meiris and Nash[13] are in relative agreement for an operating definition of population health that focuses on the distribution of health outcomes within a population as well as the determinants that affect this distribution. As they suggest, population health consists of interventions in wellness, risk reduction, acute illness reduction, chronic care management, catastrophic case management, quality and safety, public health, and health policy. The primary discussion presently is whether population health is a term to be applied to a field of study of health determinants or as a concept of health.[12] The result of this discussion will greatly influence the future of population health as a field of study or resign it to being considered just another health strategy.

During the latter half of the first decade of the 21st century, there were a few early adopting organizations that modified their health strategies from waiting for high risk or sickness to begin to examining the systems that lead to high risk or sickness, increases in healthcare costs, and decreases in performance of the workforce. This latter point was another major turning point when companies realized the total value of health in economic terms.

THE FUTURE: NEAR- TO MID-TERM: 2010–2014

Corporations will continue to be the major stakeholders in defining the value of healthy and high-performing employees. During this period, corporate and community leaders will finally make the assessment that initiating care when sickness or high risks become apparent is an unsustainable strategy. Employers will convince insurance companies to address the health status issues that lead to sickness. When insurance companies shift their focus from illness to wellness, they will then be able to partner with purchasers of health benefits sharing aligned incentives. Communities will realize the health and economic advantage of healthy and high-performing populations.

In addition to fixing the systems that lead to poor health status, companies will ask their benefit directors to begin to find benefits for all covered lives, including spouses and other dependents, and including all costs (e.g., medical, drugs, absence, disability, and worker compensation). This movement will support the transition toward population health. They will invest in corporate programs that have something for everyone in their total population and begin the move from solely focusing on individual interventions to include an expanded focus on interventions at the population level. These population-level interventions will focus on environment and culture issues. Thus, companies and communities will realize that they have the ability to integrate the community resources to align with the objectives of a community **culture of health**.

NATURAL FLOW OF A POPULATION AMONG HEALTH RISK CATEGORIES

The information in Figure FPH-1 provides a graphic example of what happens to any given population over time. Individuals move among low risk, medium risk, and high risk. This example demonstrates the flow of individuals moving among the three risk

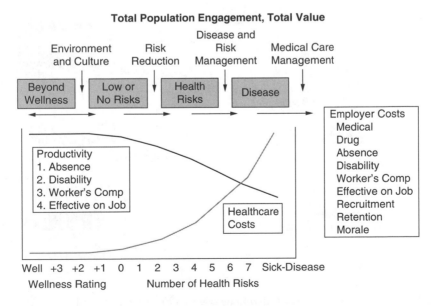

Figure FPH-1   Near- to Mid-Term Future Strategies for Managing Population Health

categories over a three-year period. In the absence of any health management efforts, the population naturally flows toward higher risk. The percentage of people in the low-risk category is reduced while more people are in the high-risk category. This also can be referred to as the "do-nothing strategy:" Wait for people to move to high risk or disease and then try to treat them.

A population health management approach offers an opportunity to address all levels of risk in the population, including the low-risk individuals who have previously been ignored by general medicine, public health, and health promotion. The majority of the population is low risk and helping them stay that way is the easiest way (mathematically, this is the only way) to stem the natural flow of individuals toward higher levels of risk and disease.

NATURAL DISTRIBUTION OF HEALTHCARE COSTS

Another example of natural flow is costs over time, shown in Figure FPH-2. When a disease or serious medical problem is discovered (e.g., a heart attack occurs), there is a large spike in healthcare costs. However, well before that event occurred, costs were significantly elevated for this group of individuals. Population health can address three different

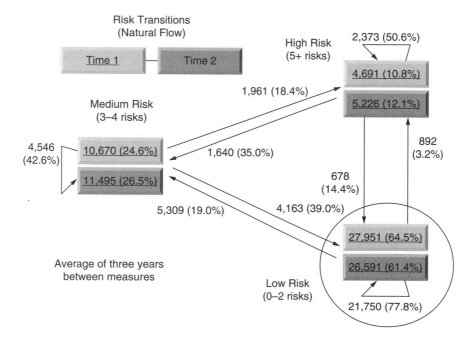

Figure FPH-2   Natural Flow of Individuals over a Three-Year Period
Modified from Edington DW. Emerging research: a view from one research center. *AJHP.* 2001;15(5):341–349.

stratifications of this natural flow, as demonstrated in Figure FPH-2. Sickness management occurs during the event. Surgeries, hospitalizations, and other intensive uses of resources fall into this category. Disease management strategies are initiated after a disease event or identification. An example is helping individuals adhere to the correct medication protocol for diabetes. What has been mostly ignored until now is true wellness management, which occurs upstream from sickness management and medical events. Wellness strategies help healthy people stay healthy. Strategies such as preventive services fall into this category. But there is much more that should be done to help healthy people stay healthy. A true culture of health would be one that includes wellness management through sickness management and follow-up support. The best economic strategy is obviously the wellness management philosophy, which could eliminate much of the sickness and disease management required today.

INFORMATION TECHNOLOGY

Developing technology will also play a role in population health management in the future. Health information technology (HIT) has been advancing for the past 25 years. In 2004, the U.S. Department of Health and Human Services designated the first decade of this century as the "decade of health information technology."[14] This dovetails with the increase in consumer health informatics (CHI).[15] Advances in technology and availability to more and more individuals have changed the traditional patient–provider roles from a paternalistic design[16] to a more participatory model using shared decision making and healthcare consumerism. In the latter model, individuals are encouraged to be self-leaders who take charge of their own health.[17]

CULTURE OF HEALTH

In addition to the internal environment within the workplace, managers will realize that community and home environments are also part of the social determinants of health. Communities will give attention to health as an economic outcome and health as a driver of economic policy. Companies will show an increased interest in impacting public policy. In the same way that companies evaluate the tax climate in a particular community before deciding to build a manufacturing plant there, they will examine the culture of health in a community because that is the population pool from which they will draw their future employees.

Evaluation of the success of programs will move away from attempting to measure the success of individual single-risk or disease programs and ROI calculations to population interventions and trend analyses of outcomes versus the do-nothing or natural flow trends.

One of the reasons that wellness or health promotion programs did not work as effectively as promised is that they lacked an overall framework to build the program as a serious health, business, or economic strategy. The following five-pillar framework is suggested as a model for building a culture of health inside organizations and corporations.

Fundamental Pillars of Health Management   Using the corporate setting as an example, a culture of health can be thought of as consisting of two major elements: environment support and culture. Tom Golaszewski, a professor of health sciences at the State University of New York in Brockport, defines health culture in terms of environment support as a sum of the services that are made available to all employees.[18] Judd Allen, president of the Human Resources Institute, LLC, a research, publishing, and consulting firm that focuses on the creation of supportive cultural environments, defines culture as the sum total of social influences on attitudes and behavior, including shared values, norms, peer support, touch points, and climate within the organization.[18] The first of five fundamental pillars needed to create a supportive culture is a vision from senior leadership. Specifying the vision of a healthy, high-performing workplace and connecting the vision to the objectives of the organization are absolutely critical to a supportive culture.

Senior leadership then turns the implementation over to operations leadership, who have the task of creating environment support and a health-promoting culture that will allow the vision to come alive. This pillar requires an integration of all the internal resources (e.g., food services, personnel managers, wellness centers, training programs, absence and disability managers, and others), as well as requiring integration of all the external partners who supply resources to the organization (e.g., health plans, benefit consultants, pharmaceutical benefits managers, primary care physicians, behavioral health, and EAP providers).

The previous two pillars are the secret to success: implant a serious business vision, coupled with environment support and culture of health strategies, in front of a behavior change strategy. The sum of these two pillars is the first measure of success: engagement level of the company. Without high company engagement any program is doomed to fail.

The third pillar is communication of the vision, environment, and culture rationale to the employees with the intention of developing employees as self-leaders. Self-leaders are defined as those who understand their barriers and resources and use them to devise their own positive solutions.[19] Each employee must be given the opportunity to engage in activities, allowing them to develop and maintain healthy and high-performing behaviors and lifestyles. The available health plan and on-site resources must include programs to meet the needs of all employees: lifestyle management programs; health risk reductions; care coordination; care management; disease management; and behavioral health, including employee assistance programs (EAP).

The fourth pillar is rewarding positive actions. It is well known that only that which is rewarded is sustained. The third and fourth pillars are the second measure of success: engagement level of the employees. As with the first engagement metric, without a high employee engagement level, the program is doomed to fail.

The final pillar is a quality assessment program. The metrics should be in place to measure progress toward the vision, effectiveness of the supportive environment and culture, and the success in developing self-leaders to reduce risks and maintain healthy behaviors; metrics also confirm that positive actions are being rewarded. In addition, the quality assessment program has to be constructed to measure the agreed-upon economic metrics, and finally, to meet the necessary and sufficient criteria to demonstrate that the positive results are an outcome of the health management program.

THE FUTURE: LONGER TERM, 2015 AND BEYOND

The further the world moves away from focusing on the precursors to disease and toward an upstream focus on the precursors to wellness and well-being, the more important population health management will become. It is clear that health, wellness, and well-being are the result of complex systems. Within these complex systems are the individual, genetic, environment, and workplace determinants of health and all higher levels of population organization, plus all the possible interactions.

Population health seeks to address many of the underlying factors in the health of people: equity, social determinants, community participation, universal access to care, social issues, and prevention.[3] As always, measurement of any policy, strategy, or intervention is crucial to determining whether success has been achieved. The Population Health Intervention Research Initiative of Canada (PHIRIC) defines population health intervention research as "the use of scientific methods to produce knowledge about policy and program interventions that operate within or outside of the health sector and have the potential to impact health at the population level."[20] Their survey (EQ-5D) has been used in several studies to measure the health status of general population samples in various countries.[21–26] However, this simple instrument relies on the traditional measures of sickness (e.g., mobility, self-care, usual activities, pain–discomfort, and anxiety–depression),[27,28] which do not necessarily measure wellness or vitality as we should be thinking about it. As research moves forward in population health, true wellness will need to be assessed, not simply identified as the absence of disease.

Resilience, positive psychology, social networks, and self-leader training will all become important and standard population- and individual-level interventions within the overall environment and cultural interventions. The impact of social networking technologies and other self-learning and communications will be fully developed. It will be important to further divest population health from the medical model and define health as much more than just wellness and the absence of disease and risk factors contributing to it.

PRECURSORS TO BEYOND WELLNESS (TOTALLY UPSTREAM)

Some researchers have begun to explore the precursors to wellness, although it will take time before something so complex can be understood completely. For example, it has long been thought that cultural qualities influence health. But what are these vague qualities, and how exactly do they exert their influence?[29,30] Culture can have a positive impact in some situations and a negative impact in others.[31]

A review of the literature[32] on the relationship between culture and health found that the appearance of the word "culture" in the titles of papers published in top epidemiology journals has increased more than fourfold since the 1980s. However, the pathway of the cultural influence in these studies is often labeled as generic or unknown and problems with measuring culture are often cited. It still appears as if this line of research is focused on precursors to disease and barriers to equal health care, rather than exploring how culture can positively impact well-being.[33] In order to achieve true population health, the same emphasis needs to be placed on promoting wellness as is currently placed on treating illness.

CONCLUSIONS

It will take an unprecedented cooperative and synergistic effort for companies, communities, and countries to be successful in shifting from a focus on sickness care to a population health approach, in which wellness care and disease prevention are equally considered. It is clear that there are a host of potential players in this endeavor. Each has its own self-serving objectives. There are ten simple concepts that can be applied to population health management in the future if it is to be successful.[34]

1. The current healthcare system has proven that the "wait for sickness" or "wait for high risks" strategies are unsustainable.
2. We need to change the definition of health from "absence of disease" to "high-level vitality, energy, resilience, and so on" and approach health as a combination of sickness and wellness strategies.
3. The economic case for health management indicates that the critical strategy is to "help the low-risk people stay low risk" or "help the healthy people stay healthy." In the future the economic case will be to move beyond low risk.
4. The first step is "don't get worse." Let's create winners.
5. Effective healthcare strategies must target the total population in order to capture the total value of health to individuals, communities, and nations.
6. Health, business, and policy leaders need to "create the vision, create the culture, market, execute, measure, and make it sustainable."
7. Leaders need to engage "partners, not vendors." This includes health plans, benefit consultants, primary care physicians, pharmaceutical and health enhancement companies, health systems, and communities.
8. An effective overall strategy begins with a clear vision from the leadership that is consistent with national objectives, followed by engagement of all of the internal partners in creating a culture aligned with the healthy and productive vision.
9. Communities need to get "full engagement of the leadership and of the total population" in order to bend the trend lines and get to world-leading trends in each of the outcome measures.

10. "Clear vision from the leadership" translates to adopting the Five Fundamental Pillars of Health Management to build a culture of health and to grow into a healthy and productive nation.

Successful implementation of these concepts will propel our nation upstream and lead us toward improved population health.

STUDY AND DISCUSSION QUESTIONS

1. Discuss why the past strategies of public health and behavior change have become unsustainable.
2. Identify what it means to develop a culture of health and an "epidemic of wellness" as an integral strategy for the future of population health.
3. Who are the major stakeholders in population health, and what role does each play?

SUGGESTED READINGS AND WEB SITES

READINGS

Allen J. *Wellness Leadership: Creating Supportive Environments for Healthier and More Productive Employees.* Burlington, VT: Healthyculture; 2008.

Blanchard K, Fowler S. *Woodring. Empowerment: Achieving Peak Performance through Self-Leadership.* Boca Raton, FL: Successories; 2007.

Blanchard K, Fowler S, Hawkins L. *Self Leadership and the One Minute Manager.* New York, NY: HarperCollins Publishers; 2005.

Edington DW. *Zero Trends: Health as a Serious Economic Strategy.* Ann Arbor, MI: Health Management Research Center; 2009.

Golaszewski T, Allen J, Edington D. The role of the environment in health management programs. *Am J Health Promotion.* 2008;22(4):1–10.

Rearick D. *Good Health Is Good Business: An Implementation Guide for Corporate Wellness.* Atlanta, GA: Strategic Benefit Solutions; 2007.

WEB SITES

Canadian Institutes of Health Research, Institute of Population and Public Health (IPPH): http://www.cihr-irsc.gc.ca/e/13777.html

Centers for Disease Control and Prevention, Communities Putting Prevention to Work: http://www.cdc.gov/nccdphp/recovery/

University of Michigan, Health Management Research Center: http://www.hmrc.umich.edu

REFERENCES

1. Last LM. *A Dictionary of Epidemiology*. 4th ed. New York, NY: Oxford University Press; 2001.
2. Tricco AC, Runnels V, Sampson M, Bouchard L. Shifts in the use of population health, health promotion, and public health: a bibliometric analysis. *Can J Public Health*. 2008;99(6):466–471.
3. Neuwelt P, Matheson D, Arroll B, et al. Putting population health into practice through primary health care. *N Z Med J*. 2009;122(1290):98–104.
4. Blumenthal D. Employer-sponsored health insurance in the United States—origins and implications. *NEJM*. 2006;355(1):82–88.
5. Dawber TR, Meadors GF, Moore FE Jr. Epidemiological approaches to heart disease: the Framingham Study. *Am J Public Health*. 1951; 41(3):279–286.
6. Prochaska JO, DiClemente CC. Transtheoretical therapy: toward a more integrative model of change. *Psychotherapy: Theory, Research and Practice*. 1982;19(3):276–288.
7. National Business Group on Health. Prevention makes good business sense. National Business Group on Health Web site. http://www.businessgrouphealth.org/preventive/index.cfm. Accessed December 2009.
8. Chapman L. Meta-evaluation of worksite health promotion economic return patterns. *The Art of Health Promotion Newsletter*. 2003;6(6):1–23.
9. Fielding JE. Health promotion and disease prevention at the worksite. *Ann Rev Public Health*. 1984;5:237–265.
10. Fielding JE. Worksite health promotion programs in the United States: progress, lessons and challenges. *Health Promot Int*. 1990;5(1):75–84.
11. Pelletier KR. A review and analysis of the clinical- and cost-effectiveness studies of comprehensive health promotion and disease management programs at the worksite: 1998–2000 update. *Am J Health Promot*. 2001;16(2):107–116.
12. Kindig D, Stoddart G. What is population health? *Am J Public Health*. 2003;93(3):380–383.
13. Meiris DC, Nash DB. More than just a name. *Popul Health Manag*. 2008;11(4):181.
14. Thompson TG, Brailer DJ. *The Decade of Health Information Technology: Delivering Consumer-Centric and Information-Rich Health Care. A Strategic Framework*. Washington, DC: US Department of Health and Human Services; 2004.
15. McDaniel A, Stratton R. Consumer health informatics: the nature of caring in the 21st century. In: Weaver C, Delaney CW, Weber P, Carr R, eds. *Nursing and Informatics for the 21st Century: An International Look at Practice, Trends, and the Future*. Chicago, IL: Healthcare Information Management and Systems Society; 2006.
16. Houston TK, Ehrenberger HE. The potential of consumer health informatics. *Semin Oncol Nurs*. 2001;17(1):41–47.
17. McDaniel AM, Schutte DL, Keller LO. Consumer health informatics: from genomics to population health. *Nurs Outlook*. 2008;56(5):216–223.
18. Golaszewski T, Allen J, Edington D. The role of the environment in health management programs. *Am J Health Promotion*. 2008;22(4):1–10.
19. Blanchard K, Fowler S, Hawkins L. *Self Leadership and the One Minute Manager*. New York, NY: HarperCollins Publishers; 2005.
20. Institute of Population and Public Health, Canadian Institutes of Health Research. Population Health Intervention Research Initiative for Canada ("PHIRIC") Workshop Report. Banff, Alberta: Canadian Institutes of Health Research; 2006. http://www.cihr-irsc.gc.ca/e/33515.html. Accessed September 2009.
21. Kind P, Dolan P, Gudex C, Williams A. Variations in population health status: results from a United Kingdom national questionnaire survey. *BMJ*. 1998;316(7133):736–741.
22. Badia X, Schiaffino A, Alonso J, Herdman M. Using the EuroQol 5-D in the Catalan general population: feasibility and construct validity. *Qual Life Res*. 1998;7(4):311–322.
23. Bharmal M, Thomas J III. Comparing the EQ-5D and the SF-6D descriptive systems to assess their ceiling effects in the US general population. *Value Health*. 2006;9(4):262–271.
24. Hinz A, Klaiberg A, Brahler E, Konig HH. The Quality of Life Questionnaire EQ-5D: modelling and norm values for the general population. *Psychother Psychosom Med Psychol*. 2006; 56(2):42–48.

25. Johnson JA, Coons SJ. Comparison of the EQ-5D and SF-12 in an adult US sample. *Qual Life Res.* 1998;7(2):155–166.

26. Johnson JA, Pickard AS. Comparison of the EQ-5D and SF-12 health surveys in a general population survey in Alberta, Canada. *Med Care.* 2000;38(1):115–121.

27. EuroQol—a new facility for the measurement of health-related quality of life. *Health Policy.* 1990; 16(3):199–208.

28. Brooks R. EuroQol: the current state of play. *Health Policy.* 1996;37(1):53–72.

29. Dressler WW. Taking culture seriously in health research. *Int J Epidemiol.* 2006;35(2):258–259.

30. Janes CR. 'Culture,' cultural explanations and causality. *Int J Epidemiol.* 2006;35(2):261–263.

31. Eckersley R. Is modern Western culture a health hazard? *Int J Epidemiol.* 2006;35:252–258.

32. Hruschka DJ. Culture as an explanation in population health. *Ann Human Biol.* 2009; 36(3):235–247.

33. Kohrt B, Hadley C, Hruschka D. Culture and epidemiology special issue: towards an integrated study of culture and population health. *Ann Human Biol.* 2009;36(3):229–234.

34. Edington DW. *Zero Trends: Health as a Serious Economic Strategy.* Ann Arbor, MI: Health Management Research Center; 2009:174–175.

CASE STUDIES

SECTION I: PROVIDING POPULATION HEALTH

BEHAVIOR CHANGE

The following case study illustrates the types of treatments an individual can receive within programs designed for and delivered to at-risk populations. Multiplying these types of experiences by the percentage of a community that participates would demonstrate the impacts that such programs can have on enhancing the health of populations.

Emily is a 45-year-old woman, married, and a member of the "sandwich generation." She has the responsibility of caring simultaneously for her three school-aged children and her elderly parents. When Emily's company administered its first Health Risk Assessment (HRA) to employees, she was identified as experiencing high levels of stress and encouraged to seek counseling for stress management. She was referred to a health coach, to whom she admitted she felt "stretched to the limit," exhausted, and discouraged. Cutting back on her hours at work wasn't an option because her family relied on her entire income.

Emily and her coach decided to connect every two weeks by phone. During the first few weeks, Emily followed through with her stress management plan. She took a 20-minute walk every morning and got a minimum of seven hours of sleep at night. With the assistance of her coach, she arranged for transportation and food delivery for her parents, and asked her sister to help with their parents' housework and laundry.

At their six-week call, however, Emily reported a new stressor: Her mother had been hospitalized. Her mother had undergone surgery a few days before and was scheduled to be released later that day.

Health Coach: It sounds like your mother is having a good recovery.... That's good news.... How have you been doing with your stress management during this period?

Emily: It's gone down the tubes. Before that, I was doing well: walking in the morning, getting seven hours of sleep at night, and getting the help we talked about from the agency and my sister.

Health Coach: What parts of your stress management plan have you been having trouble keeping up lately?

Emily: All of it. There aren't enough hours in the day for exercise and sleep, and everyone's schedules have been disrupted with the hospitalization. The agency is still delivering meals. I guess that helps.

Health Coach: What did it feel like when you were able to follow your stress management plan?

Emily: It felt pretty good. I felt less stressed and exhausted.... I was able to think more clearly.... I guess the biggest change was the feeling of being more in control.

Health Coach: So you were already noticing a lot of the benefits of managing stress. Do you think your family noticed those things?

Emily: My husband would probably say that I was more pleasant to be around.

Health Coach: Excellent.

Emily: But now I'm back to where I started.

Health Coach: Not really. You had a 3- or 4-week period when you were successfully managing stress. That was a new experience for you. You've shown yourself—and me—that you can do it. If you've done it once, you can do it again.

Emily: It's hard to imagine taking time for myself right now.

Health Coach: One of the challenges of stress management is keeping it up when you're especially stressed and need it the most! What could you do differently next time to stay on track when there's an upheaval or things get especially stressful?

Emily: I guess I could get even more help. The hospital talked about getting a visiting nurse for my mother after she's discharged. I don't know if that's something you can help arrange. Also, I think it would help if my kids and husband nagged me about exercise and getting to bed at a reasonable hour.

Health Coach: So it would be helpful if your family showed their support and kept reminding you that taking care of yourself is a priority. Have you told them that you're working on your stress management?

Emily: They know I'm talking to you, but they don't know why. Maybe I should tell them what I'm trying to accomplish here.

The coach agrees to help Emily arrange for a visiting nurse for her mother, and the two role-play how Emily will ask family members for support around stress management. Emily agrees to restart her stress management routine in the next few days, and they arrange for a check-in call in one week.

Discussion Questions

1. When Emily agrees to restart her stress management routine in the next few days, what stage is she in?
2. Is there anything you would have done differently during this session?
3. What processes of change did the health coach use?
4. Were they stage-appropriate?
5. Are there any other TTM stage-matched processes of change that the coach could have used?

RISK MANAGEMENT AND LAW

You are a risk manager at an academic medical center. One of your duties is to implement a new "apology" program at your institution. As you develop the guidelines and meet with appropriate stakeholders, a major error occurs in the surgical suite requiring notification to The Joint Commission, the state patient safety authority, and to the governing body. You decide to call in-house legal counsel to discuss how to proceed. What steps might you suggest to make appropriate disclosures and reduce potential risk to the institution?

SECTION II: THE BUSINESS OF HEALTH

EMPLOYEE HEALTH

Situation Analysis   Between 2003 and 2005, a leading national health services management company helped a national employer (The Company), which had more than 5,000 employees, develop an integrated population health improvement program. The Company recognized that employees who have health risks and chronic health conditions tend to have relatively high medical and disability expenditures and significant health-related productivity loss. To lower costs and increase profitability, the organization implemented a comprehensive integrated health and productivity improvement strategy. Following a two-year program and data analysis, findings from the program were published. This case study highlights that, when properly implemented, integrated population health management programs can produce significant clinical and economic outcomes for employers.

Program Components   The Company's population health enhancement program began with an HRA distributed to all employees enrolled in a self-insured health plan. To encourage participation, employees received a $15 gift certificate. Based on risks identified from their HRAs, employees could earn an additional $300 credit off their health insurance premium for the following year, depending on their participation in health improvement initiatives. Employees were also encouraged to participate in the on-site biometric screening where they could have their blood pressure, cholesterol, height, and weight checked by a nurse. A total of 2,098 employees—about 60% of those eligible—completed the HRA.

The primary health improvement initiatives were health coaching and disease management programs available to qualifying employees. For example, a person who had a fasting glucose level higher than 110 was eligible for the pre-diabetes program. Employees received coaching in person or online from a personal coach who was a registered nurse, dietician, or exercise physiologist. They also received a personalized 6- to 12-month action plan.

The model also took great care to align incentives and engage physicians and patients with feedback and support to meet prevention and treatment evidence-based medicine guidelines to ensure consistency of care.

Key Findings   At the completion of the initial program, findings were measured against a group of 534 associates who had completed an HRA and participated in the health improvement programs and two external reference groups of employees who were not employed by The Company and, therefore, did not receive the health improvement programming.

In a comparison of participants, employer cohorts participating in health enhancement programs showed a significant reduction in health risks. Relative to a matched comparison group, the proportion of low-risk employees at the end of the program was 8.2 percentage points higher, the proportion of medium-risk employees was 7.1 percentage points lower, and the proportion of high-risk employees was 1.1 percentage points lower ($p < 0.001$).

Most significant findings included a reduction in the proportion of employees with high cholesterol, an improvement in diet, a reduction in heavy drinking, management of high blood pressure, improved stress management, increased exercise, fewer smokers, and a drop in obesity rates. Of equal importance, the majority of employees who improved risk levels maintained gains the following year.

This study highlights that integrated population health enhancement positively impacts employees' health status by reducing identified risks over time. Other studies have demonstrated that reducing health risks improves productivity while reducing medical costs and disability, thus supporting the view that "good health is good business."[1]

Available in Loeppke R, Nicholson S, Taitel M, Sweeney M, Haufle V, Kessler RC. The impact of an integrated population health enhancement and disease management program on employee health risk, health conditions, and productivity. *Popul Health Manage.* 2008;11(6):287–296.

DECISION SUPPORT

Predictive Modeling   In any year and on many measures, a relatively small proportion of members in a health plan is responsible for a large proportion of the utilization and cost. This is true even among members with the same chronic condition. Table A-1 provides some statistics for members with diabetes in one health plan.

Table A-1 Health Plan Members with Diabetes

	Year 1 2001	Year 2 2002	Year 3 2003
Adult members with diabetes	22,797	24,186	25,199
Total number of inpatient stays (all causes)	4,858	5,085	5,257
Total number of associated inpatient days	22,131	23,484	24,408
Percentage of these members with ≥ 1 stay	14%	14%	14%
5% of these members accounted for:			
What percentage of all stays among diabetics?	57%	57%	56%
What percentage of all days among diabetics?	67%	72%	72%

In each year, 5% of the members accounted for nearly 60% of all hospital stays and approximately 70% of all hospital days. But *which* members are in that 5%? Are they the same members? Can we know far enough in advance to intervene? Can feasible interventions prevent poor health outcomes and unnecessary costs?

Hospital days for members in one year are not a very good predictor of hospital days in the next year. Among members with diabetes who were hospitalized for at least one day in either 2003 or 2004, the correlation between the total inpatient days in each year was only 0.14. Can we do better than simply targeting the high utilizers in one year for increased attention in the following year? A simple predictive model based on age, sex, prior inpatient utilization, and chronic disease status was developed using 2001–2002 data (adults, continuously enrolled both years):

$$DAYS_{2000} = C1*AGE_{2001} + C2*SEX + C3*INP_{2001} + C4*DAYS_{2001} \\ + C5*CAD + C6*CP + C7*DEP + C8*HF$$

In this model, $DAYS_{2002}$ is the number of inpatient days in 2002, AGE_{2001} is member's age in 2001, SEX is member's sex, INP_{2001} is the number of inpatient stays in 2001, $DAYS_{2001}$ is the number of inpatient days in 2001, CAD is the presence of coronary artery disease, CP is the presence of chronic pain, DEP is the presence of depression, and HF is the presence of heart failure. The most important predictors were the presence of chronic pain (CP) and heart failure (HF) and the number of inpatient stays (INP_{2001}). This model, developed using 2001–2002 data, was then used to predict 2003 utilization with 2002 data. This simple model correctly identified more than one-quarter of the top 5% of inpatient day users in 2003 (vs. one-fifth using a simple threshold approach). Table A-2 compares the sensitivity and specificity of the threshold model and the simple regression model.

Current commercially available predictive models can do *much* better, depending on what is being predicted.

Table A-2   **Sensitivity and Specificity of the Threshold and Simple Regression Models to Predict Top 5% of Inpatient Day Users among Members with Diabetes**

	Threshold Model					Simple Regression Model			
		Actual						Actual		
		Yes	No					Yes	No	
Predicted	Yes	158	616	774	Predicted	Yes	200	574	774
	No	616	14,090	14,706		No	574	14,132	14,706
		774	14,706	15,480			774	14,706	15,480

Sensitivity	0.204		Sensitivity	0.258
Specificity	0.958		Specificity	0.961

SECTION III: MAKING POLICY TO ADVANCE POPULATION HEALTH

ETHICS AND POPULATION HEALTH

The Oregon Experiment in Health Services Prioritization   In 1989, the Oregon legislature passed the Oregon Basic Health Services Act, a legislative experiment in health services prioritization and resource allocation designed to expand coverage and access to health care for Oregon citizens. It did so by extending Medicaid coverage to all citizens whose annual income fell below 100% of the federal poverty line and by creating a Medicaid insurance pool for "medically uninsurables," persons who did not qualify for Medicaid and who were ineligible for private health insurance because of preexisting conditions. The act also mandated that all employers provide their employees with health benefits that were at least equal to or greater than those offered under Medicaid. A unique and controversial feature of the new program was that the state would limit benefits, rather than eligibility, to control costs. All those individuals eligible to participate in Medicaid were entitled to the same benefits; the legislature would make biennial adjustments to what services it could afford to include in the benefit package, given its available resources. Decision making was based on determining how far down a list of prioritized conditions and their treatments (C/T pairs) the state could afford to go and still cover 100% of those who were eligible for the benefit. Priorities reflected public input on what Oregonians valued most about health and health care; clinician data on health services to describe medical conditions and appropriate treatments; objective measures of relative costs, benefits, and importance of healthcare services; and the final rankings of C/T pairs by commissioners appointed to lead the prioritization process.[2] After an initial prioritization list was accepted by the legislature, a waiver from Medicaid to deviate from the national policy was secured, and state appropriations were authorized. The Oregon Basic Health Services Program was launched in 1993.

A number of ethical values are at stake in the program.[3] First are issues of equity. What is an adequate standard of care, and are appeals to justice met by a system that, in effect, creates two tiers of health care—one for the poor and one for those who can afford to pay for more services or are covered by employment insurance plans? Are the inequities of the status quo perpetuated, and should the poor have basic rights to equal access? Should the social value of the program be compared to the program we already have, compared to some "ideal" system, or be judged as a first step along the way to a single system of health services prioritization for all? A second area of ethical concern focused on how costs and benefits are quantified. An initial effort using a cost/utility analysis failed to assess "value," resulting in very inexpensive but highly effective treatments for minor health conditions ranking higher in priority than expensive but moderately effective treatments for very serious conditions. Is it fair, the debate runs, to exclude certain forms of care that are of intrinsic and essential importance to the few on grounds that it consumes resources that could be used to benefit the many? Lastly, there are issues of procedural justice. If a process of priority setting is inclusive and fair, is it acceptable that the resultant system may not be in the best interests of particular groups or individuals?

The Oregon Basic Health Services Program has benefited more than 1.5 million people, almost one-third of the state's residents. Ethical issues that arose at the program's inception continue to fuel dissent about the program's social value and foreshadow the nature of debate that will characterize future healthcare reform.

REFERENCES

1. Loeppke R, Nicholson S, Taitel M, Sweeney M, Haufle V, Kessler RC. The impact of an integrated population health enhancement and disease management program on employee health risk, health conditions, and productivity. *Popul Health Manage.* 2008;11(6):287–296.

2. DiPrete B, Coffman D. *A Brief History of Health Services Prioritization in Oregon.* 2007. http://www.oregon.gov/OHPPR/HSC/docs/PrioritizationHistory.pdf. Accessed September 10, 2009.

3. Dougherty CJ. Setting health care priorities: Oregon's next steps. *Hastings Cent Rep.* 1991;21(3):S1–10.

GLOSSARY

absenteeism—employee is absent from work; typified when an employee is not at work for a wide range of issues, including chronic or acute illness, injury, health risks, short- or long-term disability, poor morale, or outside obligations (e.g., child care or parent care). [7]

accountable care organization (ACO)—refers to a network or organization that assumes responsibility for coordinating the continued care of post–acute care patient referrals. The patient-centered medical home will ideally become the accountable care organization in the future. [4, 8, 12]

accounts receivable—patient accounts on which money is owed for care provided; an invoice or insurance claim generated by the provider when the account has not been written off by the provider or fully paid by the patient or a third party. [9]

acute illness—clinically speaking, an acute illness is one that has severe symptoms of relatively short duration; may be self-limiting or respond well to treatment, or may result in death or permanent disability. [15]

alert fatigue—user insensitivity to pop-up alerts and reminders in electronic health records (EHRs) when there are too many "trivial" alerts, such as minor drug–drug or drug–food interactions; users develop the habit of clicking through trivial alerts without carefully considering each one, which can result in missing an important alert. [9]

American Recovery and Reinvestment Act (ARRA)—(2009) passed by Congress on February 13, 2009, to stimulate the economy by creating new jobs and saving existing ones, spurring economic activity, investing in long-term economic growth, and fostering accountability and transparency in governmental spending. This act also enacted expansions to the Health

Insurance Portability and Accountability Act (HIPAA) and includes the provisions of the Health Information Technology for Economic and Clinical Health (HITECH) Act. [6]

apology laws—prevent admissibility of comments made by healthcare providers in a court of law when expressing an apology or sympathy when an unanticipated medical outcome is experienced. [6]

autonomy—the act of self-governing. [13]

B

beneficence—obligation to act in the interests of others and to contribute to others' welfare. [13]

bias—systematic error in research; deviation from the "true" finding based on the strategy used to select study participants and administer the intervention. [15]

body mass index (BMI)—indicator of body fat; used as an indicator for assessment of a population's rate of overweight and obesity. The calculation is based on a person's height and weight. [15]

breach notification rules—the requirement to notify individuals of breaches of their protected health information established by the Health Information Technology for Economic and Clinical Health (HITECH) Act, which promulgated a federal standard for breach notifications in the healthcare setting. [6]

C

care management—refers to programs that apply systems, science, financial incentives, and information to improve medical care and assist patients to self-manage their conditions more effectively. [4]

carve-outs—health benefits services that are not provided by the same company that provides the company's basic health coverage. [3]

case management—a hands-on approach to managing care that includes collaborative and coordinated patient care that is reimbursable by a third party and focuses on linking clients with needed services. [4]

case mix—refers to the various types of health insurance coverage that patients in healthcare facilities or outpatient practices may have; includes privately insured patients, those covered by Medicare or Medicaid, self-pay clients, and unreimbursed care. [4]

catastrophic illness—fragile population characterized by extreme illness requiring extensive medical treatment creating an economic burden generally exceeding $25,000–50,000 in a year. [15]

chronic care management—coordination of care focused on reducing fragmentation and unnecessary use of resources, preventing avoidable conditions (complications), and promoting independence and self-care to improve the quality of care and self-management, clinical information systems, evidence-based clinical decision support, redesigned healthcare delivery, clinical and community systems, and policies. [PHM, 1, 4, 8, 14]

Chronic Care Model—care delivery prototype that summarizes the basic elements for improving care for patients with chronic conditions in health systems at the community, organization, practice, and patient levels. [14]

chronic condition—illness or disease that is expected to persist for more than one year; may require long-term medical care and lead to functional limitations or disability. [4, 8]

chronic disease—disease that is expected to persist for more than one year; may require long-term medical care and may lead to functional limitations or disability. [4, 15]

claims data—datasets, created for third-party payers, that contain data from health insurance claims. Claims data are structured, by definition, because billing standards dictate the data content, format, and code sets (terminology systems) for claims. [9]

clinical decision support—providing clinicians or patients with clinical knowledge and patient-related information, intelligently filtered and presented at appropriate times, to enhance patient care. Often implemented as context-specific pop-up alerts or reminders in electronic health records (EHRs), e-prescribing, computerized provider order entry systems, or convenient links to reference materials appropriate to the clinical situation. [9]

commercial health plan—health insurance that is paid for by a nongovernment entity, including the client, client's employer, union, or the client and employer sharing the cost. There is also one kind of commercial insurance that the government does pay for: coverage for its own civilian employees. [14]

communication objectives—information sharing for the purposes of educating, motivating, and engaging consumers to manage, maintain, and improve their health status. [11]

communication outcome measures—measure of communication effectiveness based on health outcomes, such as increased compliance, declining disease prevalence, or reduction in costs. [11]

comparative effectiveness research (CER)—generation and synthesis of evidence that compares the benefits and harms of alternative methods to prevent, diagnose, treat, and monitor a clinical condition or improve the delivery of care. [9, 10]

computable data—an alternative term for structured data; it can be used by computer algorithms for clinical decision support, in contrast to information stored in an unstructured form such as free-text narrative. [9]

computerized physician order entry (CPOE)—computer-based systems for ordering medications; they share the common features of automating the medication ordering process. [9, 12]

consumer-driven health care—the broad term for health benefit plan designs that require employees to spend more of their own money in the form of a deductible or coinsurance before the plan pays benefits. Because consumers must pay a significant portion of the cost of their care, the hope is that they will become more engaged in care decisions and make healthcare purchasing choices in a more informed fashion. Another goal of such programs is that the influence consumers exert on payers and providers will lead to increasing transparency throughout the medical delivery system. CDHC plans are often linked to various forms of medical savings accounts. More narrowly defined, a consumer-driven health plan is a high-deductible health plan that has deducible and coverage levels that comply with the Internal Revenue Service's requirements and, so, allows the individual to establish a tax-advantaged Health Savings Account. [3]

continuity—the individual experience with health care. There are three types of continuity: informational, management, and relationship. [4]

controlled vocabulary—a set of terms or codes for expressing information within a certain domain of interest, including industry-standard systems such as SNOMED-CT and "local" code sets that may be adopted for use within a provider organization. [9]

core competencies—fundamental knowledge, ability, or expertise in a specific subject area or skill set. [16]

cost-effectiveness—the cost of a program or intervention associated with a given level of effectiveness. [10]

cultural change—a shift in values and beliefs that represent the character of an organization. [8]

culture—pattern of shared basic assumptions—invented, discovered, or developed by a given group as it learns to cope with its problems of external adaptation and internal integration—that has worked well enough to be considered valid and, therefore, to be taught to new members as the correct way to perceive, think, and feel in relation to those problems. [5]

culture of health—an environment that fosters all aspects of preventive health including primary, secondary, and tertiary efforts; promotes healthy lifestyles; utilizes evidence-based diagnostic tools; and mobilizes medical services to manage illness. [FPH]

D

data warehouse—a repository of electronically stored data, either within an organization or across organizations, designed to facilitate reporting and analysis. Typically integrates data from multiple transaction systems with defined processes for periodic updates and data validation. [9]

diagnosis codes—data about a patient's diagnoses or clinical conditions, expressed in a particular coding system, such as ICD-9 or ICD-10, that are commonly used for healthcare claims. [9]

diagnosis-related groups (DRGs)—a set of approximately 500 categories used to classify hospital stays, based primarily on the patient's diagnoses and surgical procedures developed and used mainly for prospective payment. Several variants of DRGs take different approaches to accounting for severity of illness. [9]

direct costs—the medical expenditures associated with treatment of a disease or illness. [4]

disability adjusted life years (DALYs)—The sum of years of potential life lost due to premature mortality and the years of productive life lost due to disability. [17]

discrete field—a data element that stores a specific concept or piece of information. One aspect of structured data. (The other aspect is a controlled vocabulary or code set for expressing the information.) [9]

discretionary spending—budget authority that is provided and controlled by appropriation acts and the outlays that result from that budget authority. [12]

disease management (DM)—a system of targeted, coordinated, population-based healthcare interventions and communications for specific conditions in which patient self-care efforts are significant; it seeks to reverse the skyrocketing incidence and prevalence of serious, costly, chronic illness through improving patient outcomes with quality and cost-effective care that includes the patient-centered medical home. [1, 8, 14]

disease registry—an electronic system that aggregates information about all of an organization's patients who have a particular disease or condition for surveillance and tracking at the population level. Enables proactive identification of patients who may be overdue for screening, periodic testing, or follow-up care but have not scheduled an appointment. Typically supports patient outreach via phone calls, e-mail, and so on, and allows documentation of patient interactions. (Also called a patient registry.) [9]

double blind confirmation—research approach that establishes a causal link between intervention and outcome by matching participants based on the severity of their illness and designating an experimental group (receives intervention) and a control group (received normal care). [15]

E

effectiveness—whether an intervention works in routine clinical care. [10, 15]

efficacy—whether an intervention can work under ideal conditions. [10]

efficiency—measure of cost of care or resource utilization associated with a specified level of care quality. [10, 15]

electronic health record (EHR)—an electronic record of health-related information on an individual that conforms to nationally recognized interoperability standards and can be created, managed, and consulted by authorized clinicians and staff across more than one healthcare organization. An electronic medical record (EMR) is defined similarly, but within a single healthcare organization. [9]

Employee Retirement Income Security Act (ERISA)—(1974) federal law that sets minimum standards for health and retirement plans sponsored by employers. It provides protections available to plan participants and their families. [6]

employers—legal entity that controls and directs a worker under an express or implied contract of employment and pays (or is obligated to pay) him or her salary or wages in compensation. Health benefits are a common form of additional compensation from employers to workers. [14]

equity—justice; freedom from bias. [13]

ethics—moral principles or values that guide decision making and conduct. [13]

expected years of life—length of time an average person is expected to live. [17]

F

fee-for-service—a payment mechanism by which a provider is paid for each individual service rendered to a patient. [12, 14]

fully insured—contract, typically between an employer and another organization, to assume financial responsibility for the enrollees' (employees') medical claims and for all incurred administrative costs. [3]

functional status—capacity to engage in daily activities. [15]

G

genomic profile—a set of genetic markers present in a given patient. Specific genomic and molecular (proteomic) markers or combinations of markers may indicate a patient's risk of developing certain diseases or how a patient will respond to certain drugs. The number of markers that are clinically useful is rapidly expanding, providing greater opportunities to tailor prevention and treatment to an individual patient, often called "personalized medicine." [9]

gross domestic product (GDP) per capita—the monetary value of all of a nation's goods and services produced within a nation's borders and a particular period of time, such as a year; serves as the official measure of the U.S. economy. [17]

gross national income (GNI)—The sum of value added by all resident producers plus any product taxes (less subsidies) not included in the valuation of output plus net receipts of primary income (compensation of employees and property income) from abroad. (Formerly gross national product.) [17]

H

health—a state of complete physical, mental, and social well-being and not merely the absence of disease or infirmity. (Definition provided by the WHO.) [7]

health advocate—independent professionals who have an understanding of the medical care delivery system and benefits environment. Health advocates may have a narrow focus, such as helping those with a specific illness or condition, or a broad focus providing general assistance to individuals facing any health or health benefits issue. Health advocates may work in a variety of settings and business structures, from individuals who provide assistance to individuals for a fee, to staff working with nonprofit and charitable organizations, to those working with for-profit advocacy and assistance companies. [3]

health coach—Individuals who function as "advisor, motivator, and mentor" in the delivery of health coaching. Health coaching is the practice of health education and health promotion, within an interactive and individualized context, to enhance the well-being of individuals and to facilitate the setting and achievement of their own health and healthcare-related goals. The objective of health coaching is to empower individuals to actively and optimally manage their health, risk factors, and medical conditions in the short and long term in accordance with their own preferences, based on accurate evidence-based information. [15]

health determinants—the wide variety of interacting proximate and distal influences on the health of individuals and populations, including, but not limited to, political contexts, policies, distribution of power and wealth, physical and social environments, health systems and services, and genetic, biological, and historico-cultural characteristics. [1]

health disparities—differences in the incidence, prevalence, mortality, and burden of diseases, as well as other adverse health conditions or outcomes that exist among specific population groups and have been well documented in subpopulations based on socioeconomic status, education, age, race and ethnicity, geography, disability, sexual orientation, or special needs. [1]

health information exchange—system to facilitate electronic access to patient-level health information across organizations within a region, community, or healthcare system. Allows clinical information to be shared among disparate healthcare information systems while maintaining the meaning of the information being exchanged, using nationally recognized standards (for messaging and for encoding content). [9]

health information technology (HIT)—the use of a variety of electronic means for managing information about the health and medical care of patients. [12]

Health Information Technology for Economic and Clinical Health (HITECH) Act— A component of the American Recovery and Reinvestment Act (ARRA), which aims to advance the use of health information technology (HIT) to allow a nationwide electronic exchange for use of health information to improve quality and coordination of care, to encourage use of health IT by doctors and hospitals to exchange patient information, to provide resources to improve quality and coordination, and to strengthen laws to secure patient information. [6]

Health Insurance Portability and Accountability Act (HIPAA)—(1996) provides protection of personal health information at the federal level. [6]

Health Level 7 (HL7)—a set of messaging standards widely used for exchanging data such as orders, results, and patient registration information among disparate healthcare information systems. Newer HL7 standards address clinical document architecture and a reference information model for health care. The term refers to the seventh, or highest, layer of an international standard for open systems integration, the layer where "content" is transmitted. Also refers to the international organization that maintains the HL7 standards. [9]

health literacy—the degree to which individuals have the capacity to obtain, process, and understand basic health information and services needed to make appropriate health decisions. [11]

health policy—a field of study and practice in which the priorities and values underlying health resource allocation are determined and supported by government policy makers. [PHM]

health promotion—the process of enabling people to increase control over their health and its determinants, and thereby improve their health. [1]

health-related productivity—the dimension of productivity impacted by health. [7]

Health Risk Assessment/Appraisal (HRA)—a tool used to evaluate health and identify potential risks. [7, 15, FPH]

health services research—The multidisciplinary field of scientific investigation that studies how social factors, financing systems, organizational structures and processes, health technologies, and personal behaviors affect access to health care, the quality and cost of health care, and ultimately our health and well-being. Its research domains are individuals, families, organizations, institutions, communities, and populations. [9]

healthy life expectancy—a term that indicates one's span of healthy life. It is based on the life expectancy minus one's current age. The result indicates the number of years of health life that one can reasonably expect to live if free of disease and disabilities. [10]

Healthy People 2020—a comprehensive set of disease prevention and health promotion objectives developed to improve the health of all people in the United States during the first decade of the 21st century. (http://www.healthypeople.gov/) [1]

I

indirect costs—the costs associated with treatment of a chronic condition, including disability costs, lost earnings, and premature mortality due to the condition. [4]

inferential gap—a twofold gap in health care; the non-application of relevant existing evidence in the care of individual patients and the lack of evidence germane to a particular clinical situation. [9]

integrated healthcare delivery system—a managed care system (in the United States) that includes a hospital organization that provides acute patient care, a multispecialty medical care delivery system, the capability of contracting for any other needed services, and a payer. [8]

interdisciplinary teams—a group of individuals from different disciplines who contribute their knowledge, skill set, and experience and work closely to optimize care for patients. Often used to describe collaboration among medical specialties. This term can be used interchangeably with *interprofessional*, but is used to describe the collaboration among students from different disciplines in education throughout this book. [16]

J

justice—equality of treatment; equal shares for all. [13]

L

lobbying—the act of attempting to influence political decisions through various forms of advocacy directed at policy makers on behalf of another person, organization, or group for your or your organization's benefit. [17]

M

mandatory spending—budget authority provided and controlled by laws other than appropriation acts and the outlays that result from that budget authority. [12]

meaningful use—a set of criteria promulgated by the U.S. government to reflect not just adoption of EHRs and other health IT, but the constructive use of these systems in patient care. These criteria are the basis for incentive payments to healthcare providers, with the policy goal of promoting transformation of healthcare organizations and processes to take full advantage of information technology. [9]

medical home—a term coined by Grumbach and Bodenheimer (2002) to refer to a comprehensive and coordinated model of health care that is provided by a consistent group of providers and that offers a full spectrum of care from acute and episodic to long-term care. [4]

medical model—a model for managing chronic care, particularly in those at risk for hospitalization, that focuses on assisted self-management. Medicare is the usual payer for these services. [4]

Medicare Advantage—a comprehensive plan for Medicare beneficiaries, which is privately run by a health insurance organization with extra benefits and lower copayments than traditional Medicare. [6]

Millennium Development Goals (MDGs)—a set of aims to improve human well-being by reducing poverty, hunger, child and maternal mortality; ensuring education for all; controlling and managing diseases; tackling gender disparity; ensuring sustainable development; and pursuing global partnerships. [17]

models of care—a general term that refers to the evolving healthcare systems for the purpose of improving the provision of health care to all persons, particularly those with chronic disease. [4]

multiple behavior changes—the interrelationships among health behaviors and interventions designed to promote change in more than one health behavior at a time. Evidence suggests that the potential for multiple-behavior interventions have a greater impact on the population's health than single-behavior interventions. [2]

N

National Priorities Partnership—the National Priorities Partnership, convened by the National Quality Forum, has a vision for world-class, affordable health care and transforming the U.S. healthcare system. The 28 organizations in the Partnership, all committed to improving health care, have collaboratively developed National Priority Goals targeted at proven ways to eliminate harm, waste, and disparities in care. [PHM, 1]

national provider identifier (NPI)—a system of unique identifiers for all individual and institutional healthcare providers in the United States, mandated by administrative simplification provisions of HIPAA, the Health Insurance Portability and Accountability Act of 1996. [9]

Nationwide Health Information Network (NHIN)—a collection of standards, protocols, legal agreements, specifications, and services that enables the secure exchange of health information over the Internet. [9]

negligence—failure to exercise the care that a reasonably prudent person would exercise in like circumstances. [6]

nonmaleficence—"do no harm"; refrain from any action that could harm another and avoid imposing risks of harm. [13]

Nurse Licensure Compact—licensure recognized by state law that permits nurses licensed in states where the Compact has been adopted to practice in other states that have also adopted the Compact. [6]

O

Office of the National Coordinator for Health Information Technology (ONC)—an office within the U.S. Department of Health and Human Services, charged with coordination of nationwide efforts to implement and use advanced health information technology (IT) and promotion of the electronic exchange of health information. Coordinates policy and standards relating to health IT. [9]

ontology—a terminology system that provides names for concepts within a certain domain and defines relationships among the concepts. Used loosely for any controlled vocabulary. [9]

outcome—evaluation of how a system is performing. [5]

P

palliative care—a term often confused with or used synonymously with hospice care. Palliative care is a broader concept that encompasses care of persons with advancing and terminal conditions, not only at the end of life, but also in the months preceding death, in order to control pain and other adverse effects and improve quality near the end of one's life. [4]

patient accounting—a transaction system designed to accumulate charges for healthcare services provided to a patient (as during a hospital stay) to create invoices and, typically, claims for third-party payers. Also manages patient accounts receivable. [9]

patient self-management—the management of chronic illness taught to patients, including diet, exercise, self-monitoring, and medication compliance, involving teaching skills, building confidence, self-assessment, and referrals. [1]

Patient-Centered Medical Home—a concept that integrates patients as active participants in their own health and well-being. Patients are cared for by a physician who leads the medical team that coordinates all aspects of preventive, acute, and chronic needs of patients using the best available evidence and appropriate technology. These relationships offer patients comfort, convenience, and optimal health throughout their lifetimes. [1, 4]

personal health record (PHR)—an electronic record of health-related information on an individual that conforms to nationally recognized interoperability standards and that can be drawn from multiple sources while being managed, shared, and controlled by the individual. [9]

pharmacovigilance—detection, assessment, understanding, and prevention of adverse long-term and short-term effects of medications, biological products, herbal preparations, and other medicines. Involves collecting, monitoring, assessing, and interpreting data from healthcare providers and patients, plus developing methods for "signal" detection in large databases assembled from multiple sources. [9]

pharmacy benefit manager (PBM)—a company that manages prescription drug benefits for self-insured clients. These companies negotiate with pharmaceutical companies for discounted rates and manage a delivery network that usually includes both retail pharmacies and mail order suppliers. Because of their discount relationships, they will typically create a preferred list of drugs in various categories called a formulary. PBMs may return rebates to their clients based on the overall discounts they have negotiated with drug companies. Most PBMs also offer drug utilization review programs, and some also offer disease management programs. [3]

point-of-care systems—transaction systems, such as electronic health records (EHRs), used in the care of individual patients, in real time, in the environment where care is provided. Such systems provide the opportunity to embed clinical decision support tools into the care process. [9]

population health—a cohesive, integrated, and comprehensive approach to health care considering the distribution of health outcomes within a population, the health determinants that influence distribution of care, and the policies and intervention that impact and are impacted by the determinants. [PHM, 1]

population health management—the process of addressing population health needs and controlling problems at a population level. [PHM]

practice management system—an administrative transaction system designed for physician practices that typically provides several patient financial applications: patient registration, appointment scheduling, billing (including insurance claims), and patient accounts receivable management (collections). [9]

practice redesign—quality improvement efforts aimed at redesigning the organization and delivery of primary care and better supporting patient self-management. [14]

predictive modeling—a research approach that uses existing data to predict future behavior or consequences. [10, 15]

preemption—a doctrine that indicates federal law takes precedence over state law. [17]

preferred provider organization (PPO)—a health benefit program that features access to a network of contracted physicians referred to as preferred providers. PPO plan designs differ from HMO plans by offering coverage for out-of-network care. However, these plans are designed to encourage use of participating network providers by offering better benefits and lower costs to members who stay in-network for services. [3]

presenteeism—employee is present for work, but not optimally productive because of health conditions or health risks; health-related productivity loss while at work, including time not on task (e.g., at work, but not working), decreased quality of work, increased injury rates, decreased quantity of work, negative impact on work teams, employee turnover, and replacement costs. [7]

Preston Curve—the concept that increased wealth leads to increased health. [17]

prevention—interlocking and mutually supportive strategies and interventions aimed at the deterrence, early detection, and minimization or cessation of disease and injury at a population level. [1, 7, 8]

Preventive Paradox—a measure that brings much benefit to the population, but offers little to each participating individual. [17]

prima facie principles—valid rules of action that should generally be adhered to, but that may be overridden by another moral principle in cases of moral conflict. [13]

primary research—collection and analysis of "source" data or data collected for the purpose of the study. [15]

procedure codes—data about services provided or procedures performed for a patient, expressed in a particular coding system, such as ICD-9, ICD-10, CPT-4, or HCPCS, which are commonly used for healthcare claims. [9]

process—measure of whether a system is functioning as planned. [5]

processes of change—experiential and behavioral activities that people use to progress through the stages of change. [2]

productivity—a measure relating a quantity or quality of output to the inputs required to produce it. [7]

proof of concept—evidence that establishes that an idea, invention, process, or business model is feasible. [15]

prospective payment—the practice of paying a healthcare provider a fixed amount, determined in advance, for caring for a particular patient, as during a hospital admission. The amount typically depends on the type of care provided or the condition treated, as described by a diagnosis-related group (DRG) or a similar categorical system. Payment rates may be adjusted for individual cases, called outliers, which involve unusually long stays or high costs. [9]

Public Choice Model—describes that the costs and gains from political activity that influence legislation and regulation do not fall equally on everyone. [17]

public health—the science of protecting and improving the health of communities through education. [PHM]

publicly financed health care—health insurance and care services that are provided or paid for by government. In the United States, programs included are Medicare, Medicaid, and Children's Health Insurance Program (CHIP). [14]

purchasing power parity (PPP)—a comparable monetary scale across currencies. [17]

Q

quality—the degree to which health services for individuals and populations increase the likelihood of desired health outcomes that are consistent with current professional knowledge. [PHM, 5]

Quality-Adjusted Life Years (QALYs)—a year of life lived in less than perfect health as compared to a year of life in perfect health. [10, 17]

R

regional health information organizations (RHIO)—a multistakeholder organization formed to provide services related to health information technology (IT) within a community or region, typically including the operation of a health information exchange. May also offer advice or consulting services related to IT adoption and information exchange. May be designated as a Regional Extension Center for health IT, under a program administered by the Office of the National Coordinator for Health Information Technology. [9]

registry—operational system used by provider organizations for active management of a defined patient population. [9]

regression to the mean—statistical phenomenon that causes natural variation to appear as a real change. [15]

relational coordination—coordination of work through relationships of shared goals, shared knowledge, and mutual respect. [5]

resource allocation—the process of dividing and distributing available resources to satisfy needs and desires. [13]

return on investment (ROI)—size of a return relative to an investment. [10]

risk adjustment—statistical methods used to account for patient factors that cause some patients to be at greater risk of certain outcomes. [9]

risk management—the approach to developing and implementing safe and effective patient care practices, preserving financial resources, and maintaining safe working environments. [6]

S

safety—freedom from accidental injury. [PHM, 5]

scientific method—a framework for conducting research that includes identifying a topic, generating a hypothesis, defining a data collection and analysis strategy, gathering data, testing the hypothesis, and making decisions based on the results. [15]

screening—presumptive identification of unrecognized disease or health risks by the application of tests or other procedures that can be applied rapidly. [1]

secondary research—research strategy that involves analysis of existing data and prior research to determine new methods for using the information and drawing conclusions. [15]

self-care agency—a concept that represents the personality traits and personal capabilities (e.g., knowledge, skills, energy, judgment, and decision making) needed to perform self-care activities. [4]

self-insured—a financial structure in which an employer pays medical claims directly as opposed to buying health insurance to cover these expenses. Most companies in the United States with more than 1,000 clients are self-insured and more than half of all American workers get their health benefits from companies that are self-insured. These companies have determined that it is less expensive to simply pay their medical claims than to pay the premiums associated with buying health insurance. They may purchase stop-loss insurance to protect themselves from excess medical costs, but are otherwise at risk for the costs of providing medical care to their employees. Being self-insured also offers employers greater flexibility to design their own benefit plans. They typically hire an administrator, who may be a health plan or a third-party administrator (TPA), to provide access to discounted, contracted provider networks and process the medical bills their employees incur. [3]

self-management—can be a process or outcome; having the skills and abilities to practice specific behaviors that reduce the physical and emotional impact of illness, either alone or in collaboration with the interdisciplinary health team. [4]

severity adjustment—identifying and accounting for the effect of a patient's condition on clinical processes and outcomes. [15]

social model—a term that typically refers to Medicaid waiver programs that provide a range of services, such as information on referrals, screening, assessment, care planning, and authorization for other Medicaid-covered services. [4]

spectrum of illness—the progression of clinical and pathophysiologic features of an illness over time. [15]

stages of change—a categorization of population segments based on where individuals are in the process of change. [2]

step-edit—a change made during the process of step therapy that aims to reduce the average cost for treating a given condition (e.g., hypertension or heartburn), requiring beneficiaries to use an equally effective, lower-cost drug prior to coverage of a higher-cost, second-line drug. [3]

stratification—the act or process of dividing or arranging items into classes, groups, or strata. [11]

structure—measure of an organization and its physical attributes as they relate to performance. [5]

structured data—data stored in discrete fields (separate data element for each distinct concept) using a controlled vocabulary or standard code set. (Also called computable data.) [9]

systematic process optimization (SPO)—a strategy used to reduce the number of defects in an existing process. [15]

T

tax-exempt status—a special designation under federal law provided to many hospitals and other charitable organizations to enable the organization to avoid the payment of federal income tax in return for provision of charitable services. [6]

teamwork—a group of individuals, usually from different disciplines, who work together to drive and participate in improvement. [5]

third-party administrator (TPA)—an organization that provides claims processing services to self-insured companies. In the marketplace, TPAs compete with health plans and several health plans own TPAs. The TPA will usually affiliate with a network administrator to provide its clients with access to discounted contracts with hospitals, physicians, and other providers, although some large TPAs may negotiate their own contracted rates directly. [3]

third-party payer—an insurance plan or government program that pays all or part of the cost for healthcare services provided to a patient. Depending on the terms of the insurance policy, the patient may be responsible for a portion of the cost of certain services, called a copayment, and the third-party payer may assume responsibility only after the patient has paid a certain amount, called a deductible. Third parties often negotiate prospective rates, fee schedules, or discounts with providers, so that the total paid by the third party plus the patient's responsibility is less than the provider's usual charges. [9]

tort system—a collective reference to the process of bringing an action, defending it, and the deliberations of the trier of fact under state or federal law. [Torts, under the law, are defined as private or civil wrongs or injuries that are independent of contract rights. Usually, a tort is a violation of a duty owed by one to another.] [6]

transaction systems—systems that support granular business or clinical processes, typically involving one patient at a time, including point-of-care systems. A transaction system provides specific views into the data, which are optimized for the functions the system supports, such as patient registration, appointment scheduling, or visit documentation. Contrast with disease registries and data warehouses, which aggregate data for multiple patients and provide flexible, population-level views. [9]

Transtheoretical Model of Behavior Change (TTM)—a framework for using stages to integrate processes and principles of change across major theories of intervention. [2]

trend analysis—a study design that allows study of the same cohort of a population throughout a new treatment or service in order to determine whether the new intervention had an impact. [15]

Triple Aim—initiative of the Institute for Healthcare Improvement (IHI) that provides a framework for accountability by focusing on improving population health, per capita cost, and the care experience. [10]

U

utilitarianism—the belief that value is determined by utility; the greatest good for the greatest number. [13]

V

value—worth, utility, or importance in comparison with something else. [10]

value-based benefit design—designing the health insurance benefit with a focus on improving overall value to the employee and employer rather than merely reducing medical and/or pharmacy costs alone. The value-based benefit design emphasis is increasingly on the full value of improving health by reducing health risks and promoting the quality of evidence-based medicine (EBM) care for those with health conditions through such approaches as waiving copays for fulfillment and adherence to EBM medications, which translates into lower total costs (reducing health-related productivity losses as well as medical/pharmacy costs). [7]

W

wellness—the quality or state of well-being. [7, FPH]

Y

years lived with disability (YLD)—the number of years that a person lives with disease. [17]

INDEX

A

AAMC. see Association of American Medical Colleges (AAMC)

absenteeism
   chronic conditions and, 126
   costs of, 122, 125–126

Academic Chronic Care Collaborative (ACCC), 284–285

access
   to CCM services, 248–249
   to disease management care, 244–245, 247
   in gauging successful care models, 243–244
   to health care, 55–57, 128–129
   in measures of quality/safety, 95, 97, 99
   to Medicaid and PR, 250
   to resources, 235–236

accountability measures. see also measurement in population health
   measuring care experience, 191, 193
   measuring per capita cost, 193–194
   measuring population health, 189–191, 192
   measuring value/efficiency, 194
   Triple Aim framework, 188–189

accountable care organization (ACO)
   community-based prevention and, 147–148
   palliative care and, 81
   policy making and, 223

accounts receivable, 159

accreditation
   education reform and, 286
   medical school, 308
   professional licensure and, 110–111

URAC Health Web Site, 206

Accreditation Council for Graduate Medical Education (ACGME), 275

ACO. see accountable care organization (ACO)

action stage, in TTM, 27

acute illness
   chronic conditions vs., 144–145
   research and development, 267

administrative systems, 159–160

administrators, health plan, 51–52

Advancing the Healthy People 2010 Objectives Through Community-Based Education: A Curriculum Planning Guide, 282

advocacy. see also health advocacy/assistance programs
   patient, 109–110
   provider, 110–113

aging population
   chronic disease and, 65, 71, 79–80
   communication and, 204–205
   Geriatric Care Management model, 79

alert fatigue, EHRs and, 158

Alma-Ata Declaration, 296

American Medical Association, 307, 308

American Medical Group Association (AMGA), 170

American Recovery and Reinvestment Act (ARRA)
   features of, 108
   incentives for meaningful EHR use, 174
   protecting health information, 113

American Society for Healthcare Risk Management (ASHRM), 108